A CONVENIENT PARALLEL DIMENSION

HOW GHOSTBUSTERS
SLIMED US FOREVER

James
Greene, Jr.

LYONS
PRESS

Essex, Connecticut

An imprint of Globe Pequot, the trade division of
The Rowman & Littlefield Publishing Group, Inc.
4501 Forbes Blvd., Ste. 200
Lanham, MD 20706
www.rowman.com

Distributed by NATIONAL BOOK NETWORK

British Library Cataloguing in Publication Information available

Library of Congress Cataloging-in-Publication Data available

ISBN 978-1-4930-4824-3 (hardcover: alk. paper)
ISBN 978-1-4930-4825-0 (electronic)

♾™ The paper used in this publication meets the minimum requirements of
American National Standard for Information Sciences—Permanence of Paper for
Printed Library Materials, ANSI/NISO Z39.48-1992.

*This book is dedicated to my wife Amy,
my daughter Lola, and my son Jason.
I could not have done this without
your love, support, and laughter.*

Contents

Introduction:
Why Are You Came?

This is a story about people, art, commerce, comedy, evolution, "Hollywood," and America. It is the story of the *Ghostbusters* film franchise.

I was born in 1979 and raised in a town with only one movie theater. The majority of films that affected me during my youth I saw on television or videocassette. Ian MacKaye from Fugazi once said that a great song can always survive a bad recording, and I think you can apply the same logic to movie presentation. *Star Wars*, *Planet of the Apes*, *Amadeus*—they all resonated even though they only existed for me on a small, smudged piece of glass.

Then there was *Ghostbusters*. This outré and imaginative fantasy was in a class by itself. The comedy was refreshingly weird, the concept so fertile. I was an instant fan. When I saw the first ad for *Ghostbusters II* in 1989, I was elated. I leapt into the air like I'd won the lottery. Like any true ghosthead, I also became obsessed with the creative figures behind *Ghostbusters*. Who were they? What made them tick? Why was it taking them so long to make *Ghostbusters III*?

Other books about *Ghostbusters* have been published throughout the years, but even the official accounts omit a wealth of details pertaining to the films, their internationally renowned players, and the brand's place in our cultural history. This volume aims to fill in the gaps and facilitate a better understanding of everything surrounding these movies.

I considered myself pretty well-versed in *Ghostbusters* and its lore when I started work on this book in 2019. Three years of newspaper articles, magazine features, websites, scripts, books, production reports, call sheets, emails, and firsthand interviews proved I didn't know as much as I thought. I was happy to be so humbled. While we're on the subject, interviews conducted by myself specifically for this volume are denoted by use of the present tense.

In the early stage of this book, there was a conversation with *Ghostbusters* majority rights holders Sony Pictures Entertainment about making my work officially licensed. The caveat was that my manuscript would be subject to their approval. In the interest of objectivity, I declined. I'm trying to tell the full story.

This one's for all the ghostheads, young and old. Enjoy!

—James Greene, Jr.
Deep in the Heart, 2022

RUBBER SOULS

When Ivan Reitman was four years old, his most cherished possession was a slide projector that displayed images of various Disney characters. It would not become a family heirloom. Reitman was forced to abandon his projector that year when he and his parents fled their homeland of Czechoslovakia. It was 1951; a coup d'état four years earlier had given control of the nation to Communist Klement Gottwald. Distress clouded the citizenry's hearts as Gottwald's regime stamped out democracy via scores of arrests and imprisonments. As Holocaust survivors, Ivan's parents, Clara and Ladislav Reitman, would take no chances. Ladislav gave up ownership of a successful vinegar factory so he, Clara, and Ivan could escape an oppression that ultimately lasted forty years. The Reitmans began their journey by spending twenty-four hours under the floorboards of a Vienna-bound tugboat until the vessel passed government inspection.

To keep him calm and quiet aboard the boat, Clara and Ladislav fed their son sleeping pills. They made it to Vienna unscathed, and that's where Ivan enjoyed the taste of his very first banana. It was a small reward for what Ladislav knew was a difficult ordeal. "We were five days on that boat," the elder Reitman said. "It was very hard on [Ivan]. This affects a child."[1]

The family's immigration continued across the Atlantic and ultimately placed them in Toronto, where the brood expanded to include twin girls, Agi and Susan. A dry cleaning business and then a car wash helped them flourish in their new homeland. For the aspiring filmmaker living inside young Ivan, the vast cultural melting pot of

Ontario's capital proved the perfect milieu.[2] He grew into a gaunt, dark-haired young man with a wide grin who matriculated at Ontario's McMaster University. There, during his junior year in 1967, Ivan served as vice president of the school's Film Board. He took the position very seriously; the malfeasance of exiting board leaders upset him so much that he led a charge to reconfigure the entire organization. After moving up to Film Board president, Reitman decided McMaster needed a short motion picture that could serve as the university's cinematic cornerstone. The result was *Orientation*, a comical story he directed about a freshman adjusting to life on campus.

Dan Goldberg, vice president under Reitman, cowrote and starred in *Orientation*, wherein his bespectacled and bewildered character is the subject of heavy peer ridicule until, of course, he starts making his own films. His popularity is further boosted after he sleeps with his first coed. *Orientation* is a parody taking aim at all aspects of the campus experience, including the film club (at one point, the director of a film within the film instructs a performer to "be an elf" because "that's how you get places in acting"). Reitman poured his life into *Orientation*, working on it all day every day for three months straight. In the end, the film cost under $2,000 to make.

Reitman asserted that *Orientation* was only meant to lightly rib collegiate life. Others saw it as a steamroller crushing all that higher education held dear. In a decade's time, many would call *Orientation* the infant to *Animal House*'s rampaging beer-soaked adult. "[*Orientation*] was a nod to a freshman audience's similar experience of alienation," film historian Stephen Broomer observed, "inviting them to share in the hero's bored annoyance at things artistic and academic, and his sheer disbelief at the insanity of the university."[3]

Reaction was so favorable to *Orientation* that 20th Century Fox of Canada picked it up to play ahead of the 1969 Mia Farrow drama *John and Mary* (the short also ran for seven weeks in Ontario with *Beyond the Valley of the Dolls*). Theatrical rentals of *Orientation* earned $15,000, making Reitman's debut "featurette" Canada's most successful student film in history. Journalist Clyde Gilmour remarked that "an amateur moviemaker has perhaps one chance in 10,000 of doing a student film that is not only acceptable for commercial distribution but also runs for two months and wins audience applause at one of Toronto's major [theaters]. But young Ivan Reitman has done it, and he's only starting."[4] Reitman enjoyed visiting cinemas during *Orientation*'s general release and watching audience reaction. "That was the beginning of my addiction in terms of this work," he said.

"To sit in the back of that theatre with people really appreciating it. You know, the film got applause. That was the rush. That was what gave me the idea that maybe there was a living to be made in this line of work."[5]

For all of *Orientation*'s success, McMaster University never embraced it. The administration refused to cover any costs related to reediting or reformatting the film for public consumption. School bigwigs "sat through [a screening] completely stone-faced," Reitman said. He believed McMaster officials were put off by *Orientation*'s slightly risqué nature.[6] The university clearly wasn't prepared for what Reitman become embroiled in next.

John Hofsess was the founder of McMaster's Film Board; he was also a persistent thorn in the school's side thanks to a rampant social idealism that many perceived as outright flimflam.[7] Hofsess had ambitions to direct "a film of beautiful ideas" that would simultaneously tear away at modern society's sexual taboos and puritan mindset. He decided he could best accomplish this by creating a loose adaptation of the famously erotic 1888 publication *My Secret Life*.[8] The identity of *My Secret Life*'s author is debated to this day—the figure is credited only as Walter[9]—but the eleven-volume book is sexually frank even by current standards.[10]

Goldberg and Reitman agreed to produce Hofsess's effort, titled *The Columbus of Sex*, and supplied him with $3,000. The movie premiered on August 8, 1969, treating an audience of several hundred to a pastiche of straight and gay sexual pantomimes intercut with a narrator reading selections from *My Secret Life*.[11] *Variety* dispatched a reviewer who wrote that *The Columbus of Sex* "clearly aims at producing a meditative mood" and "displays the human body with an austere reverence that will probably disorient the usual skinflick customer."[12]

Reitman was of similar mind. He felt *The Columbus of Sex* was too "incomprehensible" to be provocative. At least one person in the theater that night disagreed. Gary Kellem, a public school teacher who attended the film with coworker and McMaster graduate Rein Ende, was offended by what unfolded before his eyes. Ende, a former police officer, encouraged Kellem to escalate his concerns. The pair contacted local authorities before that evening's scheduled second screening. The vice squad arrived on campus and viewed *The Columbus of Sex* for twenty minutes before deciding the film was violating obscenity laws. The dual projectors used to screen the avant-garde film were switched off, the audience was ordered to vacate, and Reitman, Goldberg, and Hofsess were arrested.[13]

On May 19, 1970, the filmmakers found themselves standing trial in Canada's first-ever film-related obscenity case. Hofsess remained true to his loony image when he bounded through a legal loophole to escape prosecution, successfully arguing that it was never proven in the pretrial that he was the same John Hofsess who directed *The Columbus of Sex*. After seven days, Judge Theodore McCombs ruled that the film did not benefit viewers in any way: "If there is any artistic merit in the technique used in the film, it is completely overshadowed by the obscene content." Reitman and Goldberg were found guilty, and each were handed a suspended sentence along with a year of probation and $300 in fines. The defendants could have swapped the last penalty for a two-month prison sentence; they declined.[14]

The copy of *The Columbus of Sex* screened the previous August was seized by Hamilton police and was destroyed.[15] The film received a second chance of sorts when schlock producer Jack Harris caught wind of the legal flap and decided to buy the movie in an attempt to profit from the controversy. Harris had the negative recut with brand-new footage, creating a far seedier entity. The film was rated X and retitled *My Secret Life* for an April 1971 opening in New York City. The *New York Times* panned the film and its popularity languished well below the erotica it was grouped with, like *I Am Curious (Yellow)* (the original *Columbus of Sex* is now considered a lost film).[16] The brouhaha surrounding *The Columbus of Sex* got financiers interested in Reitman's next project, 1970's *Foxy Lady*, but the director was so shell-shocked by the entire ordeal that he considered giving up film completely and opening his own Montreal-based sandwich shop.[17]

Career change may have remained on Reitman's mind during post-production of *Foxy Lady*. While editing the romantic comedy, he became convinced this story about "the richest girl in the world" and her paramour was a complete turkey.[18] "I realized I had to do something else quickly or my very short-lived career as a filmmaker would be over," he said. That "something else" became the 1973 smirking horror lark *Cannibal Girls*,[19] starring his friends and *Foxy Lady* bit players Andrea Martin and Eugene Levy (another McMaster student and veteran of its Film Board).[20] *Cannibal Girls* focuses on Martin and Levy as a young couple who run afoul of a bloodthirsty cult when their car breaks down in a rural area.[21] The film attempts to blend the natural irreverence of its two leads with typical grind house gore. The results are uneven, but it offers trace elements of what Reitman would later ride to unprecedented Hollywood glory.

A penniless Reitman and his girlfriend, Geneviève Deloir, took *Cannibal Girls* to the Cannes Film Festival that year. Thanks to fierce promotion and basic curiosity, the movie packed in the crowds, prompting American International Pictures to buy *Cannibal Girls* for $50,000.[22] This behind-the-scenes success was followed by Reitman's first large-scale hit—though it occurred away from the cinema. Magician Doug Henning was a friend and fellow McMaster graduate who had convinced Reitman a few years earlier to help him produce a stage show of fantastical illusions.[23] The resulting act, *Spellbound*, opened in Toronto during Christmas of 1973 before heading to Broadway as *The Magic Show* in 1974.[24] Henning's wildly popular tricks garnered a Tony nomination in that first season, putting the sprightly magic-maker on the American map.[25]

While in New York with *The Magic Show*, Reitman became obsessed with the idea of producing something for the theatrical arm of *National Lampoon* magazine.[26] *National Lampoon* was the biting, hilarious, often tasteless voice of the counterculture and now the brand seemed poised to take over live comedy thanks to the success of *Lemmings*, a play satirizing the Woodstock music festival. Reitman was desperate to work with the likes of John Belushi, Chevy Chase, and Christopher Guest, all of whom starred in *Lemmings*.[27] He phoned *Lampoon* head Matty Simmons every week, begging for a shot. Eventually, Simmons relented and offered Reitman a spot producing their next show.[28] Getting the job was one thing, being accepted was something else entirely. When Reitman arrived for the first day of rehearsals for what would become *The National Lampoon Show*, he discovered the wagons were tightly circled.

Two of the actors were having a dispute, and Reitman started to interject as a mediator. "Suddenly everything stopped," he remembered, "and these six formidable comedic geniuses slowly turned to me like I'd made a bad smell in the room. They just looked at me for what seemed like the longest, most soul-chilling moment." Eventually, one of the actors sauntered over to Reitman and slowly began putting the producer's winter clothes back on his body. "So why don't you come on by some other time?" he said as he shoved the befuddled Reitman out the door. That actor was Bill Murray. It was the beginning of a beautiful relationship.[29]

Bill Murray grew up the fifth of nine children, always fighting for food or attention in his suburban Illinois home. The cramped, rowdy atmosphere helped mold a sharp insouciance that became the essential component of his personality and persona. Emotions surely calcified for Murray at seventeen when he was forced to wrestle with the diabetes-related death of his father, Edward Joseph II. By the time Bill Murray reached adulthood, he was the type of person who'd crack jokes about terrorism while visiting the airport. He did exactly that on September 21, 1970—his twentieth birthday—prompting a swift arrest at O'Hare International.

Murray was trying to board a flight to Denver so he could continue his studies as a medical student at Regis University when he couldn't produce the proper identification to qualify for the airline's under twenty-one discount. "That's too bad," he remarked to another passenger. "I wanted to get on 'cause I got two bombs in my suitcase." Vice detectives were already on the lookout for Murray, not because he possessed any explosives but due to a tip they received that suggested he was carrying ten pounds of marijuana in his luggage. Indeed he was; Murray was dealing pot to supplement his meager student income. The flippant remark touched off a baggage search, which led to a possession charge and a night in jail. "William Murray" of "1930 Elmwood Dr," as the *Chicago Tribune* identified him, was released the following morning on probation. "'Bomb' Comment Misfires" read the *Tribune*'s news brief covering the incident.[30]

The dealer lifestyle was soon abandoned, along with any serious intent Murray had to enter the medical field. "It turned out you had to study a lot," he said. "That's terrible."[31] Bill decided to commit himself to comedy instead. This kid with the unkempt style and permanently drowsy visage rose through the ranks at Chicago's improv and sketch collective Second City, where his older brother Brian Doyle was already a fixture.[32] Brian left Chicago in 1973 to work on *The National Lampoon Radio Hour* in New York at the behest of Second City's most potent alum, John Belushi.[33] That same year, Bill was ready for the theater's coveted main stage.[34] It didn't take long for the *Tribune* to rave about the vapid lounge singer he liked to portray ("fantastically banal," they marveled).[35] Another creation of Murray's that garnered acclaim was the Honker, a muttering dweeb who fell somewhere between charming pervert and Quasimodo.[36]

In 1974, Bill Murray was poached for the *Radio Hour*. Belushi knew this upstart's deft talent, particularly for ad-libbing, would be a vital asset.[37] But what about his temper? People were already murmuring behind the scenes about Murray's violent antagonism and utter disregard for his contemporaries' feelings. Belushi lectured his new hire about anger management. The irony was not lost on Murray. "John said, 'Now, Bill, we understand that, you know, you're a little aggressive and that you've got some violent tendencies and stuff like that,'" Murray recalled. "'You're kinda wild and you can't control yourself. We want you to be real serious.' I just stared at him like, 'Who the hell are you talking to?' I'd known John at this point for about five years. This was a guy who went down the stairs on his head just for fun, but he was acting very serious and very professional because he was supposedly in charge of the whole thing . . . and the job turned out to be a zoo, of course."[38]

The National Lampoon Radio Hour was stacked with a vibrant array of diverse creatives, many of whom were just as rambunctious, destructive, and difficult as Belushi and Murray—Richard Belzer, Christopher Guest, Michael O'Donoghue, Chevy Chase, and Harry Shearer, to name a few.[39] On the sweeter end of the spectrum were Gilda Radner, who wrapped oddness in an irresistible warmth, and Harold Ramis, a genial wit with thin glasses and outrageously thick hair. Ramis was another Second City disciple but his pedigree also included more urbane work, such as freelance writing for the *Chicago Daily News* and editorial work for *Playboy*'s joke section.[40] The latter gig afforded Ramis an extensive catalog of gags he could recall instantaneously thanks to his photographic memory (friends dubbed him "Dr. Jokes").[41] Bill Murray had met Ramis several years earlier when Brian invited him home for dinner. Fresh out of high school, Bill was greatly impressed by Ramis. "Harold was like a mythical creature," he said, "He even had his own apartment! He was in a very different category from the rest of us when I first met him."[42]

Murray caught up to Ramis by early 1975. That's when the pair shared billing alongside Belushi, Radner, and Brian Doyle in *The National Lampoon Show*, which made it to Manhattan's New Palladium theater despite the rocky start with its fledgling producer, Ivan Reitman. The *New York Times* singled out Murray's solo spot as one of the show's highlights: "[It's a] manic little number about urban living . . . leaping into paroxysms of ecstasy to express love of such mundane things as neighborhood delicatessens. The juxtaposition of the ordinary with extreme emotionalism makes this a devilish satire."[43]

The National Lampoon Show wasn't as popular as *Lemmings*, but that didn't dampen Reitman's enthusiasm about the exceptional talents before him. His contract for the show included a clause that gave him the exclusive right to direct and produce a feature-length film based on the *Lampoon* if he could also convince a studio to finance it.[44] Before leaping to the big screen, however, most of the actors Reitman was admiring took a detour into television to break down the medium's staid barriers and change Saturday nights forever.

"We wanted to redefine comedy the way the Beatles redefined what being a pop star was. That required not pandering, and it also required removing neediness, the need to please. It was like, we're only going to please those people who are like us. The presumption was there were a lot of people like us. And that turned out to be so."

That's how producer Lorne Michaels summarized the mission statement of *Saturday Night Live* decades after its inception, and there is probably no more succinct picture of this television program's founding sensibility and initial impact.[45] NBC handed Michaels a ninety-minute void in their weekend schedule and he filled it with talent from *National Lampoon*, including Gilda Radner, John Belushi, Chevy Chase, and Michael O'Donoghue. *Saturday Night* (as it was first known) established a precedent with its very first cold open on October 11, 1975. The sketch featured a nonnative English speaker learning "rudimentary" phrases such as "I would like to feed your fingertips to the wolverines" and "Let's boil the wolverines." The piece is absent any preamble, and we only know it is over when a stagehand enters to say so.

Brian Doyle-Murray, Bill Murray, and Christopher Guest weren't involved in *Saturday Night*'s October Revolution because they had been drafted for a similarly named variety show on a competing network. ABC's *Saturday Night Live with Howard Cosell* was a shameless vanity project for loquacious sportscaster Cosell that debuted a few weeks before NBC's *Saturday Night*. Although it did employ contemporary sketch actors—whom Cosell adored and were dubbed the Ready for Prime Time Players—overall the ABC entry clung to the hoary showbiz traditions Lorne Michaels and his company hoped to dismantle. Cosell was a fearless wizard of commentary during athletic events, but he stiffened to oak as an emcee. High-profile guests like Evel Knievel and Frank Sinatra were no help.[46] Reviewers eviscerated *Saturday Night Live with Howard Cosell*, the public wasn't interested, and the whole thing was off the air by February.[47]

NBC's *Saturday Night* had only aired six episodes when the *New York Times* hailed it as "the most creative and encouraging thing to happen in American TV comedy since [1950s hit] 'Your Show of Shows.'"[48] From its inception, *Saturday Night* made self-effacing reference to Cosell's program by dubbing its cast the Not Ready for Prime Time Players.[49] Among those players was twenty-three-year-old Dan Aykroyd.[50] The boyishly handsome Aykroyd was an Ottawa Catholic who briefly considered entering the priesthood.[51] Law enforcement held greater interest, and he studied criminal psychology and deviant sociology at Carlton University (Aykroyd also spent most of the '70s getting around on a dead stock police motorcycle).[52] The performing bug hit Aykroyd after his friend Val Bromfield convinced him to help her create comedy shorts for Ottawa's community television channel. Bromfield also landed Aykroyd a spot on the 1970 CBC variety show *The Hart and Lorne Terrific Hour*, cocreated by and costarring Lorne Michaels.[53]

Aykroyd excelled at creating intense, jargon-spewing oddities that commanded immediate attention. John Belushi tried recruiting him for *The National Lampoon Radio Hour*, but the comic was doing just fine working in Canadian television and running his own bar. "I had rockets going everywhere," Aykroyd explained. "I was making more money than the prime minister, . . . I was living a beautiful life up there. There was no way I wanted to go to the States."[54]

That changed when *Saturday Night* came calling. Aykroyd stood out on the show in roles as a frenetic huckster for the Bass-O-Matic (a blender specifically designed for liquefying fish) and as the grizzled founder of Mel's Char Palace. He was also a gifted impressionist whose take on Richard Nixon was especially savory. Aykroyd did such an expert job amplifying the disgraced president's awkward, inhuman idiosyncrasies that some wondered if he spent time shadowing Nixon in the White House. Despite this, *Saturday Night*'s breakout star was Chevy Chase, a stately figure whose humor was so achingly dry that even his pratfalls felt deadpan.

In season two, *Saturday Night* added not only the *Live* tag that Howard Cosell's show orphaned but also one of that program's comedians: Bill Murray. Though NBC's vanguard was an outlet better tailored for Murray's oddball sensibilities, he struggled to find his footing. A fear he might be fired from the hippest show on television inspired Murray to pitch a monologue in which he begs for audience support. On March 19, 1977, he tried to hide his nerves behind a smile as he looked into the camera and put it bluntly: "I don't think

I'm making it on the show. I'm a funny guy, but I haven't been so funny on the show. My friends say, 'How come they're giving you all those parts that aren't funny?' Well . . . it's not the material. It's me."

Murray won the audience over with his genial plea for compassion, one that also dipped into the morbid. "That reminds me of something funny—my father died when I was seventeen. That's not what was funny. *He* was funny." Fourth wall breaking was nothing new in comedy or on *Saturday Night*. Murray, however, found the perfect way to buck the convention-bucking of the show, directly violating Lorne's "remove the neediness from comedy" doctrine by literally asking for laughs. In Murray's hands, the request is measured and seems utterly reasonable. It's not the desperation of a sad clown. It's a likable guy owning up to his recent shortcomings.

This character, a Bill Murray not living up to all his earthly potential, is one the mischievous actor would play again and again throughout his career.

The summer before *Saturday Night*'s debut, Ivan Reitman offered Harold Ramis $2,500 to write a treatment for a *National Lampoon* film that Reitman could then shop around to studios. Ramis had a great idea: a story based on his college experiences that he'd been considering since his days at *Playboy*. The resulting draft, *Freshman Year*, didn't light any fires. Ramis and Reitman believed the problem lay in the script's warmhearted tone. Two other *Lampoon* vets, magazine cofounder Doug Kenney and writer Chris Miller, were hired to give the story more bite.[55] Ramis grew especially close to Kenney, who believed *Freshman Year* could and should be an "edgy, adult Disney [film]." "[Doug] understood," Ramis said, "that if you make [a movie] look like Disney and feel like Disney, and then inject a much edgier message, you have a way of reaching people without threatening them."[56]

Reitman was busying himself producing horror films at this point, a lucrative practice for the aspiring comedy director that started a year earlier with his college friend David Cronenberg's debut outing *Shivers* (alternately titled *The Parasite Murders*, *They Came from Within*, or *Frissons*). After that came 1976's *Death Weekend*, aka *The House by the Lake*, the tagline for which was "It began with rape. It ended with a massacre!"[57] *Variety* doled out praise for Reitman in its *Death Weekend* review, noting that the producer "knows how to get on the screen a senseless violence pic that in acting, script and technical departments looks and feels as if it came out of a Hollywood film factory."[58] Reitman also worked on 1977's *Rabid*, the mouth-in-the-armpit shocker also directed by Cronenberg and starring adult film actress Marilyn Chambers. These films were all distributed by Canada's notorious soft-core company Cinépix and helped define the sub-subgenre of Canucksploitation. Many viewed Cinéplex's output as nothing more than tax shelter productions with little to no artistic merit.[59] Reitman didn't seem to mind, save for one entry—when he coproduced the 1977 Nazi sex torture sequel *Ilsa, the Tigress of Siberia* with Roger Corman, their work was credited to the fictitious Julian Parnell.[60]

In December 1976, the trades reported that Universal Studios had struck a deal with *National Lampoon* for a film based on the Ramis, Kenney, and Miller version of *Freshman Year*, now titled *Animal House*.[61] Set in the early '60s, this raunchy collegiate farce aimed to be the antidote to the tender nostalgia of 1973's *American Graffiti*, the George Lucas smash about young adults that also takes place right before the Kennedy assassination. Ramis noted that college kids during that period had "nothing to do with all their energy except throw it out there, because there were no issues floating around."[62] If *American Graffiti* presents the last chapter of America's innocence, *Animal House* would offer the last chapter of America's willful ignorance.

Ramis had broken into television by this point. After contributing material to several one-off specials starring guerrilla comedy troupe TVTV (who would pose as journalists to crash high-profile events), Ramis accepted a position as head writer for *SCTV*, this era's other groundbreaking sketch-based series. *SCTV* was a Canadian production that funneled the irreverence of the Second City theater into living rooms across the Great White North beginning in the fall of 1976.[63] The show set itself apart from *Saturday Night Live* by insisting that it was its own broadcast station serving a fictional backwater called Melonville. In addition to writing, Ramis appeared on-screen as either himself or exasperated station manager Moe Green. Green's flop sweat mirrored Ramis's own performance anxiety.

"Harold didn't consider himself a performer," said Joe Flaherty, a fellow *SCTV* writer and actor. "He didn't like performing at the time. He lacked confidence, and so he had his mind made up that he wasn't performing. . . . He always felt that he was a writer rather than a performer."[64]

SCTV's narrative conceit coupled with its existence outside the pressure cooker of American entertainment allowed its creators to explore stranger themes and deeper character studies. The show was often dismissed as too weird or cerebral; in the early days, cast members like John Candy, Andrea Martin, and Eugene Levy didn't believe anyone was watching. They all recognized the value of what they were being afforded, though. When *Saturday Night Live* offered Harold Ramis a position during that program's second season, he turned them down.

"'SNL' was completely fueled by cocaine," Ramis explained. "The show was being written literally overnight. I didn't want to stay up all night writing. And the show had a veneer of New York sophistication—very snide and superior. I thought, *It's just not me*."[65]

As the ball began to roll on *Animal House*, Ivan Reitman received what he called "one of the great heartbreaks" of his life. The other people involved with *Animal House* didn't want him directing the film. "They didn't think I was experienced enough," he said. Reitman was relegated to a production credit, while *The Kentucky Fried Movie*'s John Landis was tapped as director.[66]

Reitman's chagrin was not softened when *Animal House* exploded onto screens in July 1978. Roger Ebert spoke for the nation in his *Chicago Sun-Times* review: "The movie is vulgar, raunchy, ribald, and occasionally scatological. It is also the funniest comedy since Mel Brooks made *The Producers*."[67] *Animal House* spent eight weeks as the most popular film in America, leaving a seismic imprint on our culture and bringing a new fame to almost everyone involved— especially John Belushi, whose riotous turn as Bluto catapulted him into legend.[68]

Reitman was not given a victory lap in the wake of *Animal House*'s monolithic success. "I contributed to the story and the script. I was on the set every single day," he'd later complain. "I was in on all the casting. I helped cut the picture. And when it came out, there was the sense that I had nothing creatively to do with it, that I was just a guy that stood to make a lot of money from it. . . . Suddenly I realized that, especially in Hollywood, the role of the producer is not a happy one."[69]

Animal House made Reitman a millionaire, but that didn't satisfy his yearning to direct a big-screen comedy.[70] He'd get his chance with *Meatballs*, a summer camp romp written by Dan Goldberg, Lenny Blum (yet another McMaster graduate), and Goldberg's friend Janis Allen. *Meatballs* was sold to Paramount prior to the release of *Animal House*, and the writing team knocked out the script in a month.[71] Reitman wasn't very satisfied with that first draft, so once again he turned to Harold Ramis. "[Harold] was buying furniture for a new apartment and he needed $1,700. . . . I said to him, 'I will pay for your new furniture. I'll give you $1,700 if you do a polish of this draft.' He said yes, and did some really nice work on it."[72]

There was another reason to get Ramis involved with *Meatballs*—it prompted Bill Murray to take the starring role of mischief-maker Tripper Harrison. Murray had turned *Meatballs* down when Reitman first pitched it to him, but his reverence for Ramis made him flip.[73] Not that anchoring his first feature film was enough to convince Murray to rearrange his plans for that summer. While Reitman prepped for *Meatballs*, its mercurial star spent his first extended break from *Saturday Night Live* traveling with a Washington State minor-league baseball team called the Grays Harbor Loggers.

Loggers owner Van Schley became friendly with Murray a few years earlier after the pair met via TVTV. Schley thought it would be fun to hire this unpredictable goofball to coach first base for a while (Lorne Michaels dispatched a camera crew to capture the hijinks for a future *Saturday Night* episode themed around cast members' vacation activities). Murray, who also pinch-hit in a game against the Walla Walla Padres, had a blast while Reitman and Goldberg pulled their hair out. The filmmakers were sending copies of the *Meatballs* script to assorted baseball fields and hearing nothing back.[74]

Reitman insisted he never had anyone else in mind for Tripper, but rumors spread among the *Meatballs* cast that Dan Aykroyd would be their star. "That's what we all believed," said actor Russ Banham. "We would talk about it. 'Can you believe we're in a movie with Dan Aykroyd?' Everybody knew who Dan Aykroyd was. . . . We show up for the movie and there's Bill Murray. And we were like, [deflated] 'Oh. It's the new guy from *SNL*. Okay.'"[75]

Murray didn't actually arrive at the Ontario set until two days into filming, and he was underwhelmed as well. Reitman said the actor, whose only previous film credit was a cameo in Paul Mazursky's *Next Stop, Greenwich Village*, dramatically heaved the *Meatballs* script into the garbage after ostensibly reading it on set for the first time.[76] Other anecdotes find Murray being more direct, telling the Reitman, "This is crap!" while pointing to several pages inscribed with "S.O.T." (shorthand for "same old thing"). Murray rewrote the majority of his lines that first night in his car; what he couldn't get to, he'd ad-lib.[77] Reitman did his best to assuage his finicky lead, telling Murray that if *Meatballs* turned out lousy, he would prevent it from being released in the United States.[78]

Meatballs ended up being good enough to screen below the border come June 1979. In fact, it became an unexpected hit. The $26 million the film earned in its first four weeks was enough to qualify it as Canada's most lucrative homegrown property.[79] Moviegoers responded to the risible antics that pad a sweet story about a lonely adolescent played by Chris Makepeace who discovers a surrogate father in his counselor Murray. "Amazing vitality and elan" are the words *Variety* used to describe Murray as Tripper. "Without ever demeaning himself or the film, Murray has a flip, cool style that transfers astonishingly well from videotape to film."[80] In a retrospective a few years later, *New Yorker* critic Pauline Kael said she believed Murray acquits himself so well in *Meatballs* because in the scenes with Makepeace he "[contrives] to look above the kid's head, off screen—anywhere but at that moist, adoring face."[81] This conveys a truth about the difficulty adults often have with raw emotions that flow so freely through the young.

Meatballs reaches its climax when Murray delivers a manic pep talk to the entire camp about a pending athletic competition the kids assume they'll lose. Tripper's diatribe, nearly a religious testimonial, is centered on the mantra "It just doesn't matter!" which he chants repeatedly while hurling himself around the room. It's a sequence that almost tears the fabric of the film's reality. You can see background actors trying to stifle grins the moment Murray strides into the scene, serious as a heart attack, adorned in a maroon bowling shirt and matching fez. His volume and theatrical gesticulations increase and genuine laughter ripples through the crowd. Putting Murray in front of a live audience was a savvy move in the sense that it gave him a safety net, a spot where he would be more in his element, and the end result lends *Meatballs* another satisfying hunk of plausibility.

"It just doesn't matter" is also a great rejoinder to the impassioned rant John Belushi delivers toward the end of *Animal House*, in which he bellows that "nothing is over until we decide it is!" One could accept Murray's speech as a parody of Belushi's, which itself is already a send-up of the "Give 'em hell" monologue that serves as the cornerstone for so many dramatic action films. Both monologues appear to reflect the basic tenet of each performer: Belushi's psychotic devotion, Murray's liberation through disengagement.

There were no Oscar nominations for *Meatballs*, but the film took home a handful of statuettes at Canada's inaugural Genie Awards, held in March 1980. Murray's romantic foil Kate Lynch won Best Actress, while the screenwriters nabbed Best Original Screenplay. Murray himself was nominated for Best Foreign Actor, and he actually attended the ceremony. He lost to George C. Scott, who was nominated for *The Changeling*.[82]

Dan Aykroyd's graduation to the silver screen wasn't exactly smooth. His film debut came when Val Bromfield's director brother Rex cast him as the lead in the 1977 romantic comedy *Love at First Sight*. The story of a vision-impaired barber and the woman who loves him against her father's wishes, *Love at First Sight* quickly vanished after earning scathing reviews that summer (the *Ottawa Citizen* condemned the movie as "insensitive" and "downright embarrassing").[83] Aykroyd's next movie can only be considered such on a technicality. *Mr. Mike's Mondo Video*, a sketch collection assembled by *Saturday Night's* morbid prince Michael O'Donoghue, began life as a TV special for NBC. The network balked when confronted with the finished product, deeming *Mondo Video* too off-color to broadcast (one bit involves Japanese women bathing in dolphin blood; another shows Nazi oven mitts). O'Donoghue wanted his special to be seen, so he brokered a deal to give it a theatrical run in September 1979. *Mondo Video* angered some ticket-buying audiences to the point of physical violence.[84]

After wunderkind director Steven Spielberg cast John Belushi as a pilot in his World War II satire *1941*, Belushi insisted Aykroyd would be the perfect ground sergeant. Spielberg agreed, adding Aykroyd to a sprawling cast that included Christopher Lee, Toshirō Mufine, Robert Stack, Nancy Allen, and Tim Matheson.[85] Most were thrilled to be working with Spielberg on the heels of masterworks like *Jaws* and *Close Encounters of the Third Kind*. Excitement dissipated when it became obvious during production that the director was in over his head trying to stage his first comedy.[86] Still, there was great faith in Spielberg's magic touch, which is why Universal Pictures and Columbia Pictures partnered to spend nearly $35 million on *1941*.[87] This price tag was considered egregious even at the dawn of Hollywood's megabuck era (to wit: when the budget for the *Star Wars* sequel *The Empire Strikes Back* hit $30 million, financiers panicked and immediately canceled the loans they'd given the filmmakers).[88] For movies released in 1979, only *Star Trek: The Motion Picture* beat *1941* with a rumored final cost of $50 million.[89]

All the money in the world may not have saved *1941*, which hit movie screens on December 14, 1979. The film was so bad, critics were in awe. "I've seldom seen a comedy more ineptly timed," marveled Vincent Canby in his *New York Times* review.[90] The *Washington Post*'s Gary Arnold dubbed *1941* "an appalling waste" that's "pointless at best and occasionally hateful."[91] Some write-ups hailed Aykroyd and Belushi as saving graces, but the comics couldn't avoid absorbing *1941*'s failure—their images were largest on most promotional materials. The pair hoped that *1941* (which actually turned a profit, just not a "Spielberg" profit) wouldn't doom their own increasingly expensive film they were in the midst of shooting. That film was *The Blues Brothers*, the story of a Chicago singing duo that grew out of Aykroyd and Belushi's genuine adoration for American roots music.

The Blues Brothers act started on *Saturday Night Live*, and the actors displayed a keen business sense when they lobbied the program to hire their alter egos as musical guests. This circumnavigated a legal mandate that all characters appearing in *Saturday Night* sketches automatically became NBC's intellectual property. And so the Blues Brothers were free to record their own LP, *Briefcase Full of Blues*, which they released to widespread popularity in November 1978. Less than a year later, they began shooting their film for Universal with John Landis at the helm.[92]

The starting budget of $5 million for *The Blues Brothers* rapidly escalated into double digits to accommodate the outrageous automotive stunts Landis insisted on cramming into the musical comedy.[93] Skeptics nicknamed the production *1942* as costs continued to balloon, eventually resting near $30 million. *The Blues Brothers* didn't face the same critical drubbing as *1941* when Universal rolled it out in June 1980, but the movie also failed to become a cultural watershed à la *Animal House*. Viewers seemed perplexed by the emotionless vessels chaperoning this revue–cum–demolition derby. "[The Blues Brothers] are so dour and limited that they constrain the full range of [Aykroyd and Belushi's] personalities," observed writer John Rockwell, though he ultimately surmised that the "tension between concept and potential is in itself interesting."[94]

The Blues Brothers was John Belushi's sixth feature in just three years. The cinematic future looked bright for *Animal House*'s hottest commodity, and his position on *Saturday Night* rotated to the back burner. It came as no surprise when news broke three months into filming *Blues Brothers* that Belushi wouldn't be returning to *SNL* for the show's fifth season. Dan Aykroyd dropped a bombshell, though, announcing at the same time that he was also through with *Saturday Night*. Anger coursed through the show's dedicated staff. Aykroyd had given the impression he'd be back for another season, and his resignation came just a week before the start of rehearsals. Years later, Aykroyd claimed he exited *SNL* because he believed "we'd really explored [the sketch] form fully." Insiders, however, felt Belushi had cajoled him away from *SNL* with talk of conquering Hollywood together. Bill Murray was particularly incensed; with Aykroyd's departure, he felt marooned at sea.[95]

Even if Aykroyd had returned to *Saturday Night Live*, it wouldn't have prevented Lorne Michaels from burning out. The producer decided he needed a year off following the fifth-season finale in May 1980. When NBC made it clear the show would go on without him, the cast and writers quit en masse, bringing an end to *Saturday Night*'s classic period.

Like Ivan Reitman, Harold Ramis felt a dissatisfaction with the *Animal House* experience, vexed by the attention given to director John Landis. *Animal House* had started, after all, with Ramis's original treatment *Freshman Year*, and he had cowritten the shooting script. Moving forward, Ramis sought to create a property from which he couldn't be divorced. He and Doug Kenney soon had the ears of Warner Bros. subsidiary Orion Pictures, who (like so many other studios) wanted any piece of *Animal House* they could get. A Nazi comedy, a Buddhist monk adventure, and a Western were all rejected by Orion before Kenney offered the winning idea (one that originated with Brian Doyle-Murray): *Caddyshack*, a comedy set on a golf course.[96]

Ramis cowrote *Caddyshack* with Kenney and Doyle-Murray, and he was given the director's chair. That was thrilling, but Ramis's inexperience and insecurities threatened to get the best of him as shooting kicked off toward the end of 1979. He calmed his nerves on set by quietly chanting to himself, "It's not my money."[97] The movie's troupe of wacky stars, including Chevy Chase, Rodney Dangerfield, and Ted Knight, were sure to make something out of the script. However, just to be safe, the filmmakers added Bill Murray.

Murray's popularity was heating up; once he signed on, trade headlines changed from "'Caddyshack' For Orion" to "Bill Murray's Orion Pic."[98] A character hadn't been written for Murray when he agreed to get involved, but no one was really concerned about that.[99] Of some worry, however, was Murray's character off-screen. The actor had just finished the Hunter S. Thompson biopic *Where the Buffalo Roam*, and friends noticed he was having trouble shaking his titular role as the muttering counterculture crank (Murray's transformation proved for naught; *Buffalo* was jeered during its 1980 run for turning its underground hero into a clown).[100] Thompson's clenched paranoia eventually gave way to the goofy affectations of Murray's dweeb creation, the Honker. The Honker had already appeared on *Saturday Night* and in *Mr. Mike's Mondo Video*. For *Caddyshack*, this character was reborn as groundskeeper Carl Spackler.

Ramis likened *Caddyshack* to "a $7 million [film school] scholarship," admitting that he had to view it through this filter to soften the blow of the movie's early failure.[101] As the years passed, *Caddyshack*'s playful and often crude meandering through golf's social constructs would attract legions of fans who repeated its non sequiturs incessantly. In the immediate wake of its July 25, 1980, release, however, the world was lukewarm toward this *Animal House* on the links. Business was okay, while phrases like "marginally amusing"[102] and "immediately forgettable"[103] dotted the reviews. There were harsher words, but Doug Kenney knew *Caddyshack* wouldn't be a hit before a single appraisal was printed. Earlier in the month he had seen the disaster parody *Airplane!* by Jim Abrahams and the Zucker brothers. *Airplane!* was the unflinching, ironclad spoof that *Caddyshack* was not. Depression washed over Kenney as he realized Abrahams and Zucker had dethroned *National Lampoon* as America's court jesters.[104] Verily, *Airplane!* became the runaway comedy hit of the summer that kicked off a new forefront of parody.

A dejected Kenney retreated to Hawaii following *Caddyshack*'s release. Friends prayed the tropical escape would rejuvenate him as he struggled to stay clean and sober in the wake of this perceived failure. It didn't. In late August, Kenney's body was discovered at the bottom of a rocky cliff. To this day, no one's certain if it was an accident or suicide. Harold Ramis considered Kenney to be family, but that didn't stop him from quipping that Doug probably "fell [while] looking for a place to jump."[105]

Bill Murray was vacationing in Bali when Doug Kenney died. He was still wearing a wet suit when he arrived in Newton, Connecticut, for his friend's funeral service.[106]

Doug Kenney died and took *National Lampoon* with him. The brand never again enjoyed the lofty triumphs that flowed throughout the 1970s. Most of the figures the *Lampoon* ushered in, however, still had their own heights to reach.

Ivan Reitman must have felt flush with success when Paramount Pictures offered him a three-picture deal in the wake of *Meatballs*. Unfortunately, the company reneged almost immediately. Paramount CEO Michael Eisner had led the cheer for Reitman, but studio chair Barry Diller didn't share his enthusiasm. In response, Reitman's agent Michael Ovitz moved all his client's future projects to Columbia Pictures.

The first of these endeavors was a military comedy that began life as a vehicle for stoner comedy team Cheech & Chong.[107] The duo liked the script by Len Blum, Dan Goldberg, and Harold Ramis, but they irked Reitman by wanting too much creative control. Ovitz later took credit for suggesting Bill Murray as a star in place of Cheech & Chong, though Reitman has said the idea originated with Goldberg. Murray was contracted, and *Cheech & Chong Join the Army* became *Stripes*.[108] Harold Ramis was cast as a sidekick to Murray's roustabout, even though his screen test was, in Reitman's words, "awful." Again Ramis was used as bait to make sure Murray actually followed through on the film. It worked.

"The fact that he put Harold in it was kind of a cheap shot," Murray joked. "Because if I said no, I said no to Harold, too. His screen debut. I mean, Ivan could have laid a baby on the railroad tracks, too."[109] As with *Meatballs*, Murray's actual level of commitment to *Stripes* remained a mystery to his collaborators before filming. Frank Price, Columbia's chairman and president at that time, says the studio had another actor on retainer in case Murray failed to show up to the first week of shooting in Kentucky. Price doesn't recall the identity of Murray's understudy, but he'll never forget other industry titans expressing disbelief that Columbia would invest in a lead actor with such an unpredictable nature. "Barry Diller said I was destroying the business and overpaying Bill with his $1 million salary," he says today with a laugh.[110]

Stripes was another movie that was rewritten on set. Reitman, Ramis, Goldberg, and Murray spent their nights and weekends during the 1980–1981 shoot discussing scenes and deciding exactly what would work. This approach, coupled with comments to the press from Bill Murray that "a script is just something you [use] to sell [the studio] on making a movie," gave rise to theories that *Stripes* and other films from this creative unit were largely improvised. Reitman shot down those rumors, saying "there was no time" for improvising once the cameras were rolling. "I hate movies that just go on indefinitely, where people are making things up as they go along. You can feel it—it has no core, no direction."[111]

The authority figure Murray and Ramis bump against in *Stripes* is the grizzled, seen-it-all Sergeant Hulka, played by Warren Oates. Oates was a veteran of new American classics such as *The Wild Bunch* and *Two-Lane Blacktop* who could be just as ornery as the characters he portrayed. Regardless, Bill Murray wasn't rattled working with Oates. "Bill does not get intimidated," said Goldberg. "You cannot intimidate Bill. Even before he became a star, that whole group—Belushi, Bill—they were all so confident, even when they were broke. . . . They knew they were superstars even when they were nothing. They just had this confidence, and they really understood what comedy should do."[112]

Stripes was released in June 1981 during a crowded stretch that included *Superman II, Raiders of the Lost Ark, For Your Eyes Only*, and *The Great Muppet Caper*. The film had no problem finding its footing, however. By season's end, *Stripes* had earned $75 million and the crown as Columbia's most successful summer movie ever.[113] "You can't take your eyes off Murray," Pauline Kael wrote of the film, "because even when he's in an Army barracks he's never completely in the situation—he's slightly withdrawn, watching everyone else. . . . [He's] like a bomb ticking, and he keeps erupting with smart ass remarks. . . . It's a rare comic who acts superior to the people around him and is still funny."[114]

No one was laughing during the press tour for *Stripes* when Murray threw a tantrum at the Ritz-Carlton in Boston. The actor lost his cool after being photographed near a large buffet spread that included smoked salmon and fancy wine. "People are going to think I'm a fat pig!" the actor screamed. "I didn't order this stuff. I don't even eat any of it. They'll publish the picture and people will think I did." The photographer had left the room before Murray's complaints began, but she was still in the hotel parking lot. Murray picked up a plate from the table, leaned out the seventh-story window, and threw it in her general direction. "I've never done [a promotional tour] before," Murray remarked afterward. "This is harder than making the movie. Maybe I'll just go back to writing and then I won't have to worry about some jerk taking stupid pictures."[115]

While filming *Stripes*, Ivan Reitman started working on another magazine-to-film adaptation. The publishers of *Heavy Metal* hired him to produce an animated feature based on their bible of semi-erotic fantasy and sci-fi stories.[116] Reitman was intrigued by the possibilities of "cartoons for adults";[117] he also believed animation as a commercial art form was in one of its nadirs. "There hasn't been a decent animated feature since Walt Disney died," he told the *Globe and Mail* during *Heavy Metal's* production. Reitman simultaneously bragged that this project "will be the best animated feature in the history of movies."[118]

Reitman would eat those words when Columbia Pictures released *Heavy Metal* in August 1981. The film did not reestablish the genre or attain a best of anything status. Truth be told, it was barely completed. Originally slated for late fall, Reitman decided *Heavy Metal* had to come out at the end of summer, immediately canceling three to four months of work for the animators.[119]

The big comedy Columbia Pictures was banking on for Christmas 1981 was *Neighbors* starring Dan Aykroyd and John Belushi. It was based on Thomas Berger's *Neighbors*, a novel of bleak satire and suburban discomfort that mines humor from its protagonist's misery. Academy Award–winning director John Avildsen expressed interest shortly after Columbia acquired the rights. He was hired and imagined *Neighbors* as a vehicle for Rodney Dangerfield. The studio pushed Aykroyd instead, who at that time was practically a guaranteed package deal with Belushi.

Clever source material, an acclaimed director, a hot comedy team— *Neighbors* glowed with potential. That potential ran aground almost immediately. First, Aykroyd and Belushi decided to play against type, with the former taking the obnoxious cretin role and the latter as the put-upon straight man. Then the stars clashed with Avildsen over how to make the material funny. Their lobbying for a new director fell on deaf ears; Columbia was too entranced by Avildsen's Oscar.[120] Belushi's rage was immeasurable. He told several people during the production of *Neighbors* that he literally wanted to kill Avildsen, even remarking to *SNL* writer Jim Downey how inexpensive it would be to line up a professional hit.[121]

John Avildsen wasn't murdered, and *Neighbors* was released as scheduled. The film turns out an enormously weird satire with deeply humorous flashes but, as Frank Price put it, "the cake didn't rise." *Neighbors* wasn't the victory any of the parties involved needed (at least not until it landed on videocassette and cable television markets some time later, earning the studio a respectable profit).[122] Although this was the second dud in a row for John Belushi—a foray into romantic comedy called *Continental Divide* was met with tepid reviews a few months earlier—he remained a hero to the nation's youth. With Aykroyd, he was part of a comedy team with perceived longevity; the *Boston Globe* declared they were "the Me Generation's Laurel and Hardy" in a 1982 profile.[123] Unfortunately, the incredible stress of making *Neighbors* had pushed Belushi back into serious drug use.[124]

Substances tightened their hold on the increasingly wayward comic. Winter thawed and Belushi hadn't made any future movie commitments. On Thursday, March 4, 1982, Bernie Brillstein, manager to both Aykroyd and Belushi, met with Belushi in Los Angeles and implored his client to get back on track. There were four immediate script options on the table. Brillstein wanted Belushi to commit to them all to keep him working and because he was certain that any one of them could be a huge success. Brillstein's loose multipicture offer included *National Lampoon's Joy of Sex*, French director Louis Malle's *Moon Over Miami*, and the wine comedy *Noble Rot*. The fourth spot was reserved for one of several scripts being penned by Aykroyd, including the Cold War farce *Spies Like Us*, a Canadian-based endeavor called *Never Say Mountie*, and the supernatural adventure *Ghost Smashers*—which Aykroyd was writing that week in New York. Belushi was vague about work, changing the subject to the $1,500 he wanted for a new guitar. He obtained the cash and left.[125]

When Aykroyd arrived at his office that morning to work on *Ghost Smashers*, he found a "very slurred" message from Belushi on his answering machine. "He was fucked up, and he was hurting," Aykroyd said. "I'd never heard him that bad before. I thought, *I'm going to finish this paragraph and then I'm going to get on a plane and get the fuck out there*. And I didn't. I tracked him down that afternoon on the phone instead. He sounded sad and defeated. I said to him, 'John, c'mon man, you gotta come home. I'm writing something great for us here that's gonna solve everything. But you've gotta come back.' And he said okay. He said he was coming back on the red-eye, so I didn't go."[126]

The following day, Belushi was found dead from a drug overdose at the Chateau Marmont.[127] Aykroyd was shattered. Following the burial, he retreated to a mews house in London and sank into alcoholism.[128] Aykroyd considered leaving Hollywood. "My first impulse after [John] died was to split—to quit the business, pack up, jump on my Harley, and just disappear. I honestly thought it through. I'd liquidate, reorganize, give myself a new orientation and name."[129] Bruce Smechter, Baton Rouge welder, was one rebirth Aykroyd mapped out.[130]

Aykroyd pulled himself together after six months and threw himself into work. This included a starring role in a prostitution comedy based on Bruce Jay Friedman's short story *Detroit Abe* as well as continuing the scripts for *Spies Like Us*, *Never Say Mountie*, and *Ghost Smashers*. *Ghost Smashers*, a story about a trio of paranormal exterminators, was a concept to which Aykroyd was especially committed, in part because he had personal history with the occult. His great-grandfather Samuel Aykroyd regularly held séances, and many family members had their own individual experiences with the unearthly.[131] Aykroyd himself once saw "ectoplasmic tubes of light" in "shimmering patterns of iridescent green" that shook him to his core.[132]

Two of the lead parts in *Ghost Smashers* were always meant for Aykroyd and Belushi; Aykroyd has noted many times that he was writing a line of dialogue for Belushi's character when he received word of his friend's death.[133] The story regarding who Aykroyd envisioned as the third Ghost Smasher has changed throughout the years. At some points, he's said it was always meant for Bill Murray.[134] Other junctures have found Aykroyd insisting his original third pick was Eddie Murphy, the audacious and effortlessly funny *Saturday Night Live* cast member credited with saving the program from cancellation during its abysmal early '80s seasons.[135] Common history dictates that the tragic circumstances allowed Murray to simply inherit Belushi's role. Yet a *Variety* blurb from April 1982 announced that comedy legend Richard Pryor was the figure Aykroyd was initially after to replace Belushi in *Ghost Smashers*, which jibes with a comment Aykroyd made to the press in 1984 that Belushi's part was "[rewritten] for a black guy."[136]

There are long-standing rumors regarding who else was considered for *Ghost Smashers* before it was clear that Murray would fill Belushi's vacancy. Michael Keaton, then a fledgling comic with a devil-may-care edge akin to Murray's, is a name often raised in these discussions. Chevy Chase has said he turned down a role in the movie but has never elaborated about the details (storyboard artist Thom Enriquez says that when he was brought aboard to work on the film in June 1983, he was asked to draw a scene in which a ghost seduces Chase).[137] Murray was surely one of the first people to read what Aykroyd had written for *Ghost Smashers* in 1982, and the actor found himself engaged with the concept. He wanted to be involved, even though the script was only a third of the way done.

Aykroyd, emboldened by Murray's interest, contacted a director he thought would be perfect to bring this movie to life: Ivan Reitman.[138] Aykroyd, Murray, and Reitman all shared an agent in Michael Ovitz, but Aykroyd knew Reitman from working together a decade earlier in Canadian television. *Greed* (a game show) and *Sweet City Women* (a talk show) were two programs Reitman briefly produced for Toronto's CITY-TV; Aykroyd served as an announcer on both.[139]

In addition to his own paranormal experiences and some contemporary reading he'd done on parapsychology, Aykroyd said *Ghost Smashers* drew influence from the zany spook comedies of Hollywood's golden age (the most famous of which may have been 1940's *The Ghost Breakers* starring Bob Hope).[140] Reitman couldn't detect that element in the forty-some pages he first received from Aykroyd. In truth, the director was flummoxed by what he read.

"It was set in the future—not far in the future, but far enough," Reitman explained. "And it took place on a number of different planets or dimensional planes. And it was all action. There was very little character work in it. The [heroes] were catching ghosts on the very first page—and doing it on every single page after that, without respite. . . . By the 10th page, I was exhausted. By the 40th or 50th page . . . I was counting the budget in the hundreds of millions of dollars. And there really weren't very many laughs. Although I could detect a comic attitude, the whole thing was written rather seriously."

Reitman set *Ghost Smashers* aside and forgot about it.[141]

THIS IS A PIECE OF CAKE

By December 1982, Dan Aykroyd's futuristic ghost-chasing fantasy was generating a small buzz around Hollywood. Bill Murray's name was in the mix, and studios were placing bids. The project had been rechristened *Ghost Busters*,[1] which felt like a stronger, more potent name than *Ghost Smashers*. It was also a name that was already taken, twice over.

Comedian Gil Lamb anchored a 1952 theatrical short called *Ghost Buster*, which is centered on his bumbling detective persona Slim Patterson.[2] In 1975, CBS aired fifteen episodes of live-action farce *The Ghost Busters* during its Saturday morning lineup. *The Ghost Busters* was a broad affair produced by the Filmation Associates that reunited *F Troop* funny men Larry Storch and Forrest Tucker.[3] Meant to evoke the serials of yesteryear (right down to the actors' 1940s attire), the series paired its leads with a man in a gorilla costume and squared them all off against specters like Erik the Red and the Canterville Ghost.

Erika Scheimer, daughter of Filmation founder Lou Scheimer, insists that the Aykroyd *Ghost Busters* was no case of parallel thinking. "[Our] 'Ghost Busters' was a teenage or college kid cult show," she says, "and the guys on 'SNL' loved it. They absolutely stole the concept and refused to get the rights until we contacted them."[4] A corroborating story came from Kathy Burns, who worked as a secretary at Universal Studios in the early '80s. As Burns told filmmaker Anthony Bueno, one day during that period she overheard a visiting Aykroyd talking about the paranormal comedy he was planning.

When Aykroyd referred to this project as *Ghost Busters*, she had to interject; Kathy was married to Bob Burns, the actor who played the gorilla on the Filmation "Ghost Busters." She told Aykroyd he couldn't use that name because of the tv show. Allegedly, Aykroyd replied, "Yeah, but we'll just give 'em a million dollars and that'll be the end of it."[5]

Filmation didn't learn about the *Ghost Busters* movie until cameras were rolling the following autumn. Company attorney Ira Epstein inadvertently walked through one of the shooting locations in New York and did a double take when he caught the production's name.[6] Aykroyd has never spoken about the genesis of his *Ghost Busters* title, but there was awareness prior to filming that it might be blocked. Thom Enriquez kept a diary while he created storyboards for the film; as he recalls, "When I was hired on June 2, 1983, [the movie] was called *Ghost Chasers*. It changed back to *Ghost Busters* on June 17."[7] During the first week of shooting, the lead actors filmed scenes in which they substituted names such as "Ghost Stoppers" and "Ghost Blasters" for the titular business.[8]

The title issue was a blip on the horizon in January 1983, which is when Aykroyd polished off his elementary draft of *Ghost Busters*.[9] This script, colloquially known as "the *Ghost Smashers* draft," has transformed into an object of folklore thanks to the handful of outrageous details that have been published about its narrative. Three spirit eradicators—Stantz, Venkman, and Ramsey—capture ghosts in our dimension and several others for an eccentric boss figure named Ivo Shandor. Shandor causes issues across time and space when he imprisons an entity called a Zuul. This enrages Gozer, "the absolute ruler of the sixth dimension," who considers Zuul his most beloved pet. It's suggested that the extremely powerful Gozer normally appears with the nonthreatening looks of a 1950s game show host (Bert Parks, specifically),[10] but this villain can assume any identity it chooses.[11] The heroes drive a black ambulance with white and purple lights that can also dematerialize upon command.[12] During their escapades, the gas station headquarters of the Ghost Busters is blown up, setting most of northern New Jersey on fire.[13] As of 2016, this first *Ghost Busters* script is lost; no one associated with it can find a copy in their collective archives.[14]

The most popular movie in the country when Aykroyd finished his *Ghost Busters* script was a far cry from the fantastical world he had put to paper. Sydney Pollack's *Tootsie* is the story of a struggling male actor who disguises himself as a woman to earn fame and fortune on a soap opera. Dustin Hoffman plays the title role, and his non-plussed roommate is an uncredited Bill Murray. Murray, who rewrote the majority of his character's lines,[15] steals many a scene in *Tootsie* with comedy that the *San Diego Union*'s David Elliott likened to "an elegant jazz in-joke."[16] Concerned that people might see his name in commercials for *Tootsie* and assume this more dramatic outing might offer wackiness in the vein of *Meatballs* or *Stripes*, Murray asked that his credit be omitted.[17] It was a smart move considering the fervor of his loyalists. Dan Aykroyd's fans were of a similar ilk.

"I would go to see anything starring Aykroyd just to watch him in motion," critic Joe Baltake admitted in the *Philadelphia Daily News*.[18] Universal Studios understood many Americans shared Baltake's opinion, which is why they paid Aykroyd seven figures to play a meek college professor who moonlights as a ruthless street pimp in *Doctor Detroit* (a big-screen rendition of Bruce Jay Friedman's short story *Detroit Abe*). Aykroyd also received a percentage of *Doctor Detroit*'s gross profits, though there'd be no windfall to divvy up upon its May 6, 1983, release. The $3 million *Doctor Detroit* soaked up that weekend couldn't oust the previous month's *Flashdance* from the number one box office spot.[19] Business was hurt by sour reviews with headlines crying "'Doctor,' Heal Thy Jokes" and "Doctor Detroit Needs a Transfusion."[20] Even Baltake admitted his beloved jester was performing a "rescue job" and that the premise "wouldn't work without him."[21] Aykroyd later pegged *Doctor Detroit* as an "ill-starred, ill-fated, not very well-written piece of material that got made and put out purely on gumption."[22]

Off-screen, Aykroyd persisted with Ivan Reitman regarding *Ghost Busters*. He sent Reitman the completed script with hand-drawn examples of the fictional technology he envisioned (Aykroyd also videotaped himself wearing prototype equipment). The highly involved futuristic setting and "fantasy elements" continued to bother Reitman. In his estimation, they weakened the core idea. Reitman thought a story set in current times showing how these paranormal exterminators came together would be more fascinating and ripe for comedic potential. That was the film he'd be interested in producing and directing. Reitman told a receptive Aykroyd as much over lunch at Art's Delicatessen in Studio City. He suggested Harold Ramis not only as a writing partner who could help turn *Ghost Busters* around but also as a potential costar. Aykroyd and Reitman grabbed the nearest phone and put in a call to Ramis's office on the Burbank Studios lot. Once they confirmed Ramis was there, they headed over.[23]

There is another version of this story where Aykroyd and Reitman returned to Reitman's office before meeting with Ramis so they could consult Joe Medjuck, a producer who'd worked with Reitman on *Stripes* and *Heavy Metal*. Medjuck assured them that Ramis wouldn't turn down the *Ghost Busters* rewrite if there was also a leading role on the table.[24] Ramis was still stinging from the reviews of *Stripes* that suggested his acting was subpar, and he was searching for the right opportunity to prove himself.[25] Coincidentally, when Reitman and Aykroyd arrived at Ramis's office that day, they found Ramis perusing Aykroyd's script for *Never Say Mountie*,[26] an adventure comedy about the Royal Canadian Mounted Police that had a buyer in MGM/UA.[27] Ramis, Aykroyd, and Reitman had a brief chat about *Ghost Busters*, and after Ramis looked at the first draft, he agreed to come aboard. Striking while the iron was hot, Reitman called his agent Michael Ovitz later that day to obtain a meeting with Columbia Pictures head Frank Price.

Reitman has ascribed these events to an afternoon in mid-May 1983, but various documents show that Columbia Pictures was drawing up contracts for the headlining actors as early as May 10.[28] Regardless, there was a two- or three-week interim between Reitman phoning Price and the meeting they scheduled. During that period, several other studios tried to poach *Ghost Busters*. "As soon as everyone heard that me and Dan and Harold and [Ivan] were involved, they all wanted it," Bill Murray said. "All of a sudden everyone's your buddy again. There was a bidding war, and I always wanted to be in a bidding war. It was great."[29]

The war ended after Reitman gave Price a five-minute *Ghost Busters* pitch in person.[30] One would imagine this pitch was akin to a summation Aykroyd provided Ovitz in a separate conversation around the same time: "Me and Bill Murray running around New York 'Saturday Night Live' style, catching ghosts."[31] Price liked what he heard but had concerns about the cost. A budget no higher than $25 million was agreed upon, though reports differ as to who threw out the numbers. Price also wanted the film to be ready for a June 1984 release (it felt important to get it out ahead of the 1984 Summer Olympics, which were being held that year in Los Angeles). Reitman knew this would be a tricky deadline. Nevertheless, he steeled himself and said okay.[32]

Murray was never too concerned with where *Ghost Busters* would end up. He loved the idea so much, he "would have done [it] under any circumstance" and his immediate reaction to the script was, "Holy

God, I gotta do this. This is a piece of cake. This is not just going to be a big movie, this is going to be a *major* social event."[33] The actor was also very enthusiastic about his part as written, describing *Ghost Busters* as "the only movie I've ever had lines in that were good enough to say."[34]

That said, Murray already had a project languishing at Columbia, and *Ghost Busters* would help push it into gear. Previously the studio bought Murray's idea for a dramatic turn in an adaptation of W. Somerset Maugham's postwar novel *The Razor's Edge*. The 1944 story about a traumatized pilot and his search for life's meaning deeply resonated with Murray when he first read it in 1982. The book was actually a gift to his wife Mickey following the birth of their first son, given to her by the couple's director friend John Byrum (Byrum had been trying to film *The Razor's Edge* for years; he was chosen as this version's director).[35] Murray was excited about breaking away from comedy, but Columbia didn't view *The Razor's Edge* as a priority. "Nobody was getting in to work early to find out how the rewrites were going," he lamented.[36]

Ghost Busters was still up for grabs when Murray complained about the *Razor's Edge* situation to Aykroyd. Aykroyd sensed Columbia would do anything to secure *Ghost Busters*, especially if Murray was attached. He suggested offering them the supernatural comedy with the proviso that *The Razor's Edge* move forward immediately. Aykroyd's hunch was correct. The studio jumped at this pitch and within the hour major decisions were finally being made about *The Razor's Edge*.[37] Columbia agreed to pay Murray $3.5 million to star in *Ghost Busters*, twice as much as they paid Aykroyd (though Aykroyd earned additional monies as the movie's cowriter).[38] In further deference to Murray, no one pushed the issue when the actor refused to sign paperwork connecting *Ghost Busters* with *The Razor's Edge*. "We couldn't pin him down on that," Frank Price says. Price was worried hectoring Murray about contracts might jeopardize *Ghost Busters*, so instead they had a meeting. "I asked Bill to explain to me what version of *The Razor's Edge* he would do. Would it be funny? He said, 'It'll have humor. Don't you trust me?' 'Of course I trust you, I'm just trying to understand what the picture's going to look like.'"[39]

What if *The Razor's Edge* bombed? Price imagined that *Ghost Busters* would pay it off.[40] There was some measure of doubt among Price's coworkers. When Columbia's New York–based CEO Fay Vincent caught wind of the $25 million special effects movie being green-lit, he panicked. He didn't want a *1941* on his hands. A lawyer was dispatched to Los Angeles to try to nix *Ghost Busters*. Vincent and Dick Gallop also met with Price directly, but Price couldn't be swayed. He felt his defense was ironclad.

"I've got Bill Murray."[41]

Dan Aykroyd was still writing the first draft of *Ghost Busters*—soon stylized as *Ghostbusters*, all one word—when he began filming scenes for *Trading Places*, a sociological comedy that cast him as a sniveling prince to Eddie Murphy's streetwise pauper.[42] Murphy's big-screen career had been jumpstarted in 1982 when his agent Hildy Gottlieb suggested her brash young client for a vacant position opposite Nick Nolte in her boyfriend Walter Hill's action movie *48 Hrs.*[43] Executives at Paramount Pictures were so bowled over by Murphy during previews for the film that they scrambled to get him into a long-term development deal.[44] *48 Hrs.* was a massive hit when it was released that December, and just a few weeks later Murphy was exchanging barbs with Aykroyd on the Philadelphia set of *Trading Places*.[45]

When *Ghostbusters* went into rewrites during the summer of 1983, Aykroyd and Ramis invented a Black character named Winston who was meant to act as the Ghostbusters' skeptical and wise-cracking security expert. A popular rumor is that Winston was tailored specifically for Eddie Murphy. Reitman has refuted this, saying that Murphy was only ever considered as a possibility for the original multiple-dimension *Ghost Busters* and that he "never spoke to Eddie about being in the film."[46]

Murphy himself has remained tight-lipped over the years regarding his potential involvement with *Ghostbusters*. When *Tonight Show* host Jimmy Fallon asked Murphy point-blank in 2019 if he turned the movie down, the actor replied that he received an offer but he was already busy making *Beverly Hills Cop*.[47] This contradicts reporting from years earlier that places Murphy's involvement with *Beverly Hills Cop* no earlier than April 1984, four months after *Ghostbusters* wrapped principal photography. *Cop* wasn't even on Murphy's radar until two days before the contracts were presented to him; original star Sylvester Stallone dropped out at the last minute.[48] It seems plausible that Murphy skipped out on *Ghostbusters* because he was waiting for an opportunity like *Beverly Hills Cop*, where he could try carrying a movie as opposed to being a costar or ensemble player. That gamble wound up paying off, to put it mildly.

A second draft of *Ghostbusters* was completed in early June, the same week *Trading Places* was released (the *New York Times* hailed *Trading Places* as "the funniest American movie comedy of the year" and praised Aykroyd for giving "the best performance in his film career").[49] Aykroyd, Ramis, and Reitman retreated to Aykroyd's home on Martha's Vineyard to work on the third revision, toiling away in a basement the home owner called "depressing" in part because the walls were painted a "Third Reich green." The surroundings did not affect workflow. All three men were confident in *Ghostbusters*, and the revisions came together briskly.[50] Aykroyd, who could churn out pages eight times quicker than Ramis, thought up settings and circumstances while Ramis homed in on dialogue and specific jokes. Reitman's contributions included helping Ramis break his habit of overstuffing jokes and birthing the idea to establish the Ghostbusters as long-in-the-tooth college students.[51] Only one plot point was difficult to hash out—how the demonic possession of two characters could accelerate humanity's end.[52]

As the trio continued working, the July release of Ramis's sophomore directorial effort *National Lampoon's Vacation* was met with wide acclaim. It was the biggest hit yet for Ramis and star Chevy Chase.[53]

By this point, Joe Medjuck had signed on to *Ghostbusters* as an associate producer along with Michael C. Gross.[54] Gross held the same production title on *Heavy Metal*, but his work as an art director for *Esquire* and *National Lampoon* magazine was better known (he was responsible for the *Lampoon*'s most famous piece of imagery, the January 1973 "We'll Shoot This Dog" cover). Aykroyd's manager Bernie Brillstein was named executive producer of *Ghostbusters*, a credit that left founding producer Reitman confused and frustrated.

"In a deal I don't understand, [Dan] sold a treatment of *Ghostbusters* to Brillstein for $1," Reitman said. "So in return for allowing us to use the screenplay, he became an executive producer." Brillstein didn't do much of anything during the production, according to Reitman, beyond occasionally glancing at footage and remarking that everyone was "doing a wonderful job." For this minimal work, while Medjuck and Gross sweated everything out in the trenches, Brillstein earned "hundreds of thousands of dollars." Brillstein argued that Reitman barred him from taking a more hands-on role. "I would always like to earn my money, and [he] didn't let me," Brillstein said.

"That's his problem. If I hadn't prodded Danny, the movie wouldn't have been made."[55]

Script revisions continued though early fall, and the story fell into place: In a New York City where ghosts are real, a spiritual encounter in a library convinces three wise-cracking academic washouts to follow through with their plans to invent ghost-catching technology. Detached troublemaker Peter Venkman (Murray), earnest believer Ray Stantz (Aykroyd), and emotionless brainiac Egon Spengler (Ramis) create a business model similar to a pest control service, with matching jumpsuits and an easily identifiable paddy wagon. Their no-nonsense security guard Winston Zeddemore becomes the de facto fourth Ghostbuster, and the quartet quickly find themselves overwhelmed with customers. It turns out their very first client, a woman named Dana Barrett, is at the center of a world domination plot hatched by an evil figure from another dimension named Gozer. Gozer's minions, a pair of snarling beasts called terror dogs, possess Dana and her sleazy womanizing neighbor, Louis Tully. This leads to a showdown on a Manhattan rooftop that climaxes with the arrival of the Stay Puft Marshmallow Man (a once cheerful and tiny advertising mascot, now an unhinged leviathan who looms over buildings).[56]

Alternate planes of existence, extrasensory perception, dark sorcery, and pyramidology are just a few "real life" metaphysical concepts *Ghostbusters* delves into during its outlandish adventure. There are direct references to famous unexplained incidents as well; Aykroyd liked to joke that he took the name Gozer from a Chevrolet dealership, but it was actually spoken by a possessed medium during the Enfield disturbance of 1977.[57] Less frightening is a theory that the Stay Puft Marshmallow Man was inspired by a cartoon from the 1970s called "Ultra Ghoul vs. The Abominable Doughman" in which a Poppin' Fresh knockoff grows several stories high and stomps through Detroit. Created by Dave Ivey, the "Doughman" cartoon aired on syndicated horror host program *The Ghoul Show*. Aykroyd's "Ghoul" fandom was suggested when he appeared to imitate "Ghoul" character Froggy during a scene in 1982's *Neighbors*.[58, 59, 60]

When it came to the basic ghost-busting tools devised for the main characters—bulky nuclear backpacks with laser rifle attachments—Ramis hoped for scientific plausibility. "I was very concerned throughout this film that the physics of it make some sense," he said, "and that intelligent people wouldn't look at it and say it was ridiculous or totally impossible. We even went to the trouble of having physicists tell us what the real physical qualities of a ghost might be so that our equipment would be suited to the real physical phenomenon."[61] Reitman, who worked with Aykroyd and artist Stephen Dane on the aesthetic of the backpacks, was satisfied with their utilitarian construct: "There's none of that 'Star Trek' gloss to the equipment. It may look crude and dirty, but it looks like it works."[62]

Michael C. Gross worked with Thom Enriquez and fellow artist Brent Boates to realize the most important design element of *Ghostbusters*—the "no ghost" emblem that became the branding for both the heroes in-universe and the film itself. Aykroyd's college pal John Daveikis dreamed up the logo, which parodied increasingly prevalent "no smoking" signs by trapping a globular spirit behind the divide of a red circle.[63] Aykroyd and Reitman nicknamed their ghost Moogly. Bill Murray liked showing off the Moogly patch sewn onto the sleeve of the beige flight suit he'd wear battling spirits as Peter Venkman. Murray was less enthused about the suit itself. "Can you believe that an actual designer *designed* these uniforms?" he cracked to one reporter. Ramis agreed, likening the aesthetic to thrift shop. Aykroyd countered: "Actually, they do look the part. Assuming for the purposes of argument that we know what a Ghostbuster should look like."[64]

Aykroyd was the paranormal expert on staff keeping things "authentic," but even he had lines he wouldn't cross. A Ouija board the actor kept with him on the *Ghostbusters* set was never used. "It is a choice that I consciously made not ever to conjure anything up," Aykroyd explained. "It wouldn't do John [Belushi] any good, and it certainly wouldn't do me any good."[65]

The *Ghostbusters* team envisioned their lead female character Dana Barrett as a bicycle-riding actress with pronounced glamour.[66] In fact, British thespian Anna Maria Monticello (then known as Anna Jamison) remembers her agent specifically telling her that she should "look glamorous" for Ivan Reitman when she auditioned for the role. Dana's possession in the latter half of *Ghostbusters* also necessitated a specific brand of energy. "The audition I did is when [Dana] was freaking out or something," Monticello says. "It had to be over the top and I'm not an over the top actress. I'm quite minimalistic. But Ivan was very respectful and fairly quiet. I didn't feel uncomfortable. Some directors make you feel like you're just a number. He wasn't like that."[67]

Dutch model Merete Van Kamp says Harold Ramis was just as calming during her read. "I felt a really good connection with him and he made me work very well that day," she says. Van Kamp adds that Ramis was curious to hear Dana's lines performed in a variety of European accents.[68] Several models went out for the Dana part, including Joanna Pacuła, Kelly LeBrock, and Ronnie Carol.[69] Carol felt the eyes of the room on her when she arrived for her audition. "A few people looked at me and looked at [Ivan Reitman] and said, 'Wow, you look exactly like Ivan's wife!' I said, 'I hope you love your wife very much!' Everybody said I had a really nice reading and that I'd knocked them out. I came back maybe four times but they never put me on film."[70]

Daryl Hannah, Kelly McGillis, Denise Crosby, Cynthia Sikes, and Kathryn Harrold were some of the other talents considered, as was *Girlfriends* star Melanie Mayron (who first auditioned to play Ghostbuster secretary Janine Melnitz).[71] Donna Dixon claimed the Dana part was offered to her outright. "I said no because I wanted to establish a solid foundation for my marriage," she said. Dixon had recently wed her *Doctor Detroit* costar Dan Aykroyd.[72]

Aykroyd and Ramis thought *Ghostbusters* should at some point reveal Dana Barrett to be "an alien fugitive from another dimension" who has merely taken the form of a human woman in our realm. This angle was dropped entirely once talks began with Sigourney Weaver. As Ramis put it, "[Sigourney] has such dignity, there is just no way to treat her as an object."[73] He admitted that he and Aykroyd viewed the romance in *Ghostbusters* as just another gag before Weaver's involvement. "I remember watching her and thinking, 'Wow, this can really work and not get in the way of the comedy!' She added a whole new dimension, and we rewrote the picture to take it into account. She inspired Bill's conscious choice to play sincerity, tenderness. He'd always shied away from that."[74]

Weaver was a Manhattan native who spent her youth on the Upper East Side ensconced in affluence (mother Elizabeth was an actress; father Sylvester was the president of NBC for many years). This tall, composed young woman matriculated at Stanford before moving to Yale's School of Drama, where she was told during her second-year evaluation that she had zero acting skill. Weaver survived this abasement with humor, turning up for her third-year evaluation wearing a target on her chest.[75] The naysayers were proven wrong in 1979 when she starred as the heroine of Ridley Scott's blockbuster sci-fi thriller *Alien*. The reviews often singled out her distinct appeal as they rhapsodized about the thrilling space odyssey. "Weaver manages to act tough, efficient and sexy all at the same time," Vincent Canby cheered in the *New York Times*.[76] Canby reiterated how "compelling" Weaver was when he critiqued 1982's *The Year of Living Dangerously*, in which she plays a love interest to Mel Gibson.[77]

The stars of *Ghostbusters* held Weaver in unquestionable esteem. She recalled them touching base: "Bill, Danny, [and] Harold all came up to me and said things like, 'Are you sure you read the script? You're a serious actress. Shouldn't you be doing something with Merchant and Ivory?'"[78] Weaver, however, was more than game, growling during her audition to prove she could play an evil dog and preparing for her role by reading *Pet Sematary*. "[Dana] is a nice person, a sturdy person and then something awful happens to her. Something jumps into her body. I was trained to take everything seriously that I play, so I played her problem for real. Yet, I didn't want to be overly serious. An interesting balance was required."[79]

"Sigourney is this very tall, attractive girl who's an imposing figure to a lot of people," Murray said. "But she's really silly—she's like 14 years old. To get to that, you have to play with her. If you don't take her seriously, then she becomes very funny. She says some of the funniest things I've ever heard anyone say. She's real fast, like Dorothy Parker."[80] Murray's appreciation for Weaver, whom he nicknamed "Goulash," reached back to at least 1980. That's when he took in multiple performances of the off-Broadway comedy *Das Lusitania Songspiel* that Weaver appeared in and coauthored with Christopher Durang. At the time, the actress recognized Murray only as the man who lurked outside the theater after final curtain to "[make] faces at Chris and me through the window." A friend assured her he wasn't a threat.[81] Weaver wasn't so sure after her first encounter with Murray. "He came up on me from behind on a New York City street, and in front of thousands of people, he picked me up, and started shaking me, as if to say hello."[82]

Zany antics aside, Weaver found her costars to be generous, supportive, and open creatively (it was her suggestion to make Dana Barrett a musician instead of an actress). "There's that Second City attitude of sort of making the other person do their best, you know, helping them, and that's how you do your best," she remarked. "I mean, they really live that . . . There was just no competition between anyone on this film. It was just a joy."[83] Weaver would receive third billing in *Ghostbusters*, but she was still a few years away from the million-dollar paychecks enjoyed by Aykroyd and Murray (her first arrived with the 1986 sequel to *Alien*).[84] Although Weaver has never publicly disclosed what she was paid up front for *Ghostbusters*, it is known that she was granted a 2.5 percent cut of the movie's net profits.[85]

Not much was ever established about Dana Barrett aside from the fact she's an artist living in New York City. Winston Zeddemore, on the other hand, was introduced in the August 1983 draft of *Ghostbusters* as a former Air Force pilot with a litany of impressive credentials (including a black belt in the Wing Chun style of kung fu). Aykroyd and Ramis were aware they'd never scripted a person of color before, and they went out of their way to build Winston up. In addition to the rich backstory, Winston was given a handful of defining character moments. He's the victim of a messy ghost attack during the outfit's first major investigation at a swanky hotel. Later in the script, he bewilders his coworkers and the entire city by accidentally summoning the Godzilla-like Stay Puft Marshmallow Man.[86] Winston was a meaty part, and it caught the eye of Broadway star Gregory Hines.[87] Negotiations stalled, however, and Hines opted to headline Francis Ford Coppola's period drama *The Cotton Club* instead.

It's easy to imagine Yaphet Kotto playing Winston Zeddemore. Kotto says he was offered $2 or $3 million to appear in *Ghostbusters*, but he can't remember if that was the role in question. Whatever was on the table, Kotto passed. Some might consider his reasoning unconventional. The actor, known for indelible turns in *Live and Let Die* and *Alien*, was concerned that appearing in *Ghostbusters* might exacerbate the extraterrestrial encounters he'd been experiencing since he was ten years old. "Aliens are here. They're among us," Kotto swears. "This stuff is real. After I did *Alien*, I started having these experiences again. So when I got the script for *Ghostbusters*, I couldn't do it. I didn't want that stuff in my life. It's the same reason I turned down *Empire Strikes Back* and *Star Trek*. People say, 'Wow, how can Yaphet Kotto turn this stuff down?' Because I don't want this stuff happening to me! *Ghostbusters* was no fantasy. It was written by someone who knows."[88] It should be noted that period reports cited Kotto's commitment to the NBC military drama *For Love and Honor* as the reason he shunned *Ghostbusters*.[89]

Future sitcom star Reginald VelJohnson appears in *Ghostbusters* as a prison guard, a bit part he claimed was a consolation prize after losing the Winston role to Ernie Hudson.[90] Hudson auditioned for Winston six times and has commented that Reitman cast another actor in the role before him (though Hudson was not forthcoming with a name).[91] Hailing from Michigan, Ernie Hudson traced his career back to the late '60s, when he was a playwright with the esteemed Black institution Concept East Theatre. Later, he founded his own theater, the Actors Ensemble, and as a student at Wayne State earned a bachelor's degree in acting and English composition. Hudson's talent was such that Yale granted him one of their three annual graduate playwriting scholarships.[92] It was a full ride, but he only lasted a year. Hudson dropped out when a small part in the 1976 biopic *Leadbelly* put him a thousand miles southwest of his classes.

Hudson resumed his studies at the University of Minnesota for his master's and a doctorate in playwriting and acting. Opportunity interrupted once more, however. A chance to portray pugilist Jack Johnson in a local staging of *The Great White Hope* quickly consumed Hudson. He abandoned school again to devote himself to the show, even helping with financing.[93] *The Great White Hope* birthed a new minority-based acting community in Minneapolis, and it also proved Hudson's greatest success to date.[94] The production toured nationally; after playing Los Angeles, Hudson was crowned Best Actor of 1977 by the city's Drama League.[95] Emboldened, he decided to take on Hollywood. "I was quite cocky then," Hudson said. "I couldn't have written better reviews for myself. I'd tell the [movie] producer, 'Look, you're putting millions into this production. I assume you're serious. So, how can you not cast me?' I can't believe I had that kind of nerve. But it worked."[96] Parts arrived in high-profile affairs such as Barbra Streisand's *The Main Event* and the Neil Diamond remake of *The Jazz Singer*.

Hudson's most recent gig prior to *Ghostbusters* was a film coproduced by Reitman—the convoluted fantasy *Spacehunter: Adventures in the Forbidden Zone*, which opened a few weeks before *Trading Places* to unenthusiastic reviews. An earlier job as a cretin named Half Dead in the 1982 shocker *Penitentiary II* earned Hudson some praise but also motivated him to be more considerate of his work. "I hated everything [Half Dead] represented, and I didn't want to be that kind of actor anymore," he said. "I was trying to be a father to two young boys, trying to be responsible, and the stuff I was putting out on the screen was just the opposite of the values I was trying to teach. So I made a conscious decision that I would stop and make sure the jobs that I took represented people I could let my sons see."[97]

Like his neighbor Dana Barrett, Louis Tully began life on the *Ghostbusters* page as a mere disguise for some stronger, multidimensional being. Tully's human facade, that of a libido-driven party animal, was tailored for *SCTV* star John Candy. There has been disagreement over the years regarding why Candy ultimately passed on *Ghostbusters*. Some stories cite conflicting work or contention over the character's nuances.[98] In a 1986 interview with Gene Siskel, Candy admitted the real problem was money. "At the time I was under contract to Disney for $350,000 a picture, and the producer of *Ghostbusters* wouldn't pay me that kind of money," Candy said. "We had a dispute, but I didn't think it was right that I lower my price for him, and then go back and work for more at Disney."[99]

Laverne & Shirley actor Michael McKean auditioned to replace Candy before the part went to Candy's *SCTV* costar Rick Moranis. Moranis was a onetime radio deejay bred in Toronto whose nebbishy, nonthreatening looks hid a wickedly sharp comic mind. Hired as a writer and cast member during *SCTV*'s third season, in his first episode Moranis debuted an impression of George Carlin that skewered the stand-up legend for the banality of his recent material.[100] Moranis went after other perceived sacred cows, including Woody Allen and Dick Cavett, but his most popular character was a dim bulb he created called Bob McKenzie. Bob was the brother of Dave Thomas's equally boneheaded Doug, and together they hosted a cheap, lazy talk show on *SCTV* called "The Great White North." Audiences went wild for the bickering, beer-logged brothers who were only conceived to eat up time and fulfill a "Canadian content" edict from the CBC. Moranis and Thomas soon found they couldn't go out in public without being mobbed.

McKenzie mania spread to the States in 1981 after NBC started airing *SCTV* on Friday nights. The pair's comedy LP *The Great White North* sold hundreds of thousands of copies in both countries and even cracked the Billboard top 10 in America.[101] MGM released a McKenzie Brothers movie called *Strange Brew* in August 1983, a quirky parody of *Hamlet* that was not as successful as expected. That was fine by Moranis and Thomas; they were ready to move on.[102]

Around this time, both men got involved with Dan Aykroyd's project *Never Say Mountie*. Thomas took a pass at the script and was cemented as sidekick to Aykroyd's headlining lawman, while Moranis took the heel role (had he lived, John Belushi would have been cast as *Never Say Mountie*'s indigenous firebrand).[103] *Never Say Mountie* was largely a spoof targeting culture specific to Canada's

Yukon Territory, but purchasing studio MGM/UA had misgivings about these themes. They stalled the film and sent it into rewrites to make it "more American."[104] As for *Ghostbusters*, Moranis was over the moon when they asked him to play Louis Tully. "There was no way I wasn't going to do this role," he said.[105] Louis transformed with Moranis from lecherous creep to wounded nerd, one fruitlessly pining for Dana Barrett.

Gozer, the chief villain in *Ghostbusters*, retained elements of a benign Caucasian man through rewrites, earning comparison in one draft to *Marcus Welby*'s Robert Young.[106] The filmmakers considered asking character actor Paul Reubens to play the part, but Reitman decided Gozer needed more of a sexless, cutting-edge look. Ramis concurred: "There is something rather terrifying and slightly sadistic in some of these New Wave styles."[107] One person who auditioned for Gozer was Anne Carlisle, best known for a gender-bending turn in *Liquid Sky*. "I came in with a lot of fury," she says. "I made a loud noise. [Reitman] said, 'Well, I like the loud voice.' He liked something else, but then I didn't get hired." Carlisle dismisses the claim that Gozer was offered to her and she turned it down due to the sexist tone of the script, as Ramis stated years later. "I don't know why he'd say that. I guess that just proves how unreliable memories can be."[108]

Gozer was found in Yugoslavian actress Slavitza Jovan, whose large, hypnotizing eyes rested above unmistakable cheek bones and were as dark and striking as her shortly shorn hair.[109] Jovan spent her formative years appearing in various landmark productions that challenged the propaganda generated by her homeland's socialist dictatorship, including a 1969 production of *Hair* that was the first of its kind behind the Iron Curtain.[110] In 1971, Jovan had a memorable role in *Mlad i zdrav kao ruža* (*Young and Healthy as a Rose*), a nihilistic crime movie soaking in flagrant drug use and casual sex.[111] *Mlad i zdrav kao ruža* only screened twice before it was banned for being part of Yugoslavia's boundary-pushing Black Wave of filmmaking.[112] The repercussions for Black Wave artists could be harsh; the director of *Plastični Isus* (*Plastic Jesus*), another film featuring Jovan, spent years in prison for his efforts in general.[113]

Jovan started popping up in American news blurbs in 1976. She was living in the United States as Slavica Jovancic when *Kojak* star Telly Savalas selected her to play his love interest in a never-realized biopic of poker legend Nick Dandolos titled *Nick the Greek*.[114] Three years later, Jovan married Los Angeles restaurateur Michel Yhuelo, which is why she's credited as Slavitza Yhuelo for her brief role in

Gregory Nava's renowned 1983 drama *El Norte*.[115] Jovan plays a model in *El Norte*, and that's a profession with which she had experience. In fact, her statuesque figure was revered enough in the early '80s to be copied by the Decter company for a series of mannequins.[116] Jovan's physicality made for an imposing Gozer, but her voice was another matter. A thick accent made her impossible to understand—there is a famous anecdote regarding Jovan's on-set reading of "choose and perish" sounding like "Jews and berries"—so Reitman had her lines dubbed by television actress Paddi Edwards.[117]

The Ghostbusters had an earthly antagonist in Walter Peck, an irritable representative from the Environmental Protection Agency who is out to prove these spirit eliminators are polluters and charlatans. William Atherton, a fixture of New York theater who also appeared in dramas like *The Sugarland Express* and *Day of the Locust*, was hired for the part.[118] *Heartaches* actress Annie Potts won the role of the Ghostbusters' secretary Janine Meltniz after comedian Sandra Bernhard turned it down.[119] Potts was previously seen in 1978's *Corvette Summer* and once appeared in a stand-alone piece for *Visions* (the same television series that presented the TVTV comedy specials written by Harold Ramis).[120]

"It has always been my nature to go after whatever I wanted with full force," Potts told the *Los Angeles Times* in 1979. These words could describe the actress's ascent in Hollywood after leaving her hometown of Franklin, Kentucky. Specifically, Potts was talking about her role in the made-for-TV movie *Flatbed Annie and Sweetiepie: Lady Truckers*, which includes the first and only acting bow from Billy Carter (brother of US president Jimmy Carter).[121]

Director John Byrum's decision to film the World War I battle sequences for *The Razor's Edge* that are only alluded to in the original novel helped put his movie behind schedule when it began filming in Paris in July 1983. A month later, the production moved to India for three positively grueling weeks. Alcoholism, food poisoning, and altitude sickness plagued the cast and crew. Leading man Bill Murray managed to avoid any problems, however, proving "indestructible" in Byrum's words.[122]

Murray cherished being in India and grew especially fond of his experiences with a sect of monks in the region of Ladakh. Fraternizing with the holy people afforded Murray a newfound tranquility in his approach to life, an experience he later likened to "a light [coming] on in my head. I just sort of 'woke up,' you know?"[123] This peace was occasionally interrupted by messages from Columbia Pictures reminding him about *Ghostbusters*. Second unit photography for that film got under way two weeks into October; principal photography was supposed to start shortly thereafter, but a postponement couldn't be avoided due to *The Razor's Edge*.[124]

Murray couldn't start filming *Ghostbusters* in mid-October, but he did slip back to New York around that time for an extremely brief costume fitting. Harold Ramis and Ivan Reitman picked him up at La Guardia (where they found him amusing his fellow travelers with a bullhorn) and spent an hour watching him try on outfits. Murray, who hadn't read any of the *Ghostbusters* rewrites yet, had little to say about the movie before flying back to Paris to finish *The Razor's Edge*. "[Bill] said maybe two words about the whole script," Ramis remembered. "Then he took off again. But it was trust. *Ghostbusters* was the first film he'd ever committed to without fighting like crazy, and he'd just decided we couldn't fail."[125]

Such resolve had to carry Murray into *Ghostbusters*, which started for him on October 27. *The Razor's Edge* left him physically drained and thirty-five pounds lighter. Unfortunately, there was no time to rest. "I got off the Concorde from *Razor's Edge* and drove to 62nd Street and Madison to work on [*Ghostbusters*]," he said. "I left Paris at 9:30 in the morning and went to work at 11 o'clock in the morning in New York. I will never do that again. That was terrible. I mean, I was asleep the whole time."[126]

Nerves kept Peter Giuliano from doing anything but sleeping his first day on *Ghostbusters*. Giuliano was hired as the film's first assistant director just days before going to work. "I get a call on a Friday—I don't know anything about this movie," Giuliano recalls. "I interviewed that day with Ivan Reitman and it went well, I feel. I sit outside for about an hour. Then a production man comes out and says, 'You're hired. We have no schedule but you start Monday.' 'Well, what's this movie about?' 'It's about ghosts!'" Adding to Giuliano's unease was the fact he was replacing Newt Arnold, an esteemed first assistant director known for *The Getaway* and *Blade Runner*. Arnold had been fired earlier that week after doing some work with the second unit, but Giuliano never learned the cause. Today he guesses that it had to do with Arnold's lack of experience shooting in New York. "It's always been one of the toughest filming environments."

A first assistant director's job involves overseeing the nuts and bolts of a shoot, including scheduling, management, and problem solving that can't be addressed by the director. Giuliano read the *Ghostbusters* script and it dawned on him what a gigantic operation stood before him. Reality hit even harder the following Monday, when he showed up to a sea of bodies in green Eddie Bauer jackets. As Reitman and cinematographer László Kovács began discussing the first shot, Giuliano's knees buckled. "László, a wonderful human being, realized what was going on," Giulano says. "He grabbed me and said, 'Stay by my side until lunch and you'll be okay.' He introduced me to the crew. He saved my bacon that day."[127]

Kovács, a veteran of movies such as *Easy Rider* and *Paper Moon*, was excited to work on a horror-comedy and felt especially pleased when Reitman told him *Ghostbusters* shouldn't look "funny." "He wanted it to look just like a dramatic piece of film," Kovács said. "Automatically, everybody shoots comedy in the traditional approach. Very high-key photography, bright, cheerful, and all that . . . But, when you think of it, comedy is really a piece of drama. . . . It's harder to do than drama. Especially with this subject matter—ghosts getting loose in New York, which is kind of a silly idea. So, if you don't treat it seriously visually, as you would a drama, it's not going to have any credibility."[128] Kovács also realized early on that the black ambulance the Ghostbusters were to drive would be too difficult to distinguish on-screen because so much of the movie takes place at night. At his suggestion, the vehicle's color changed to white.

Ghostbusters spent three and a half weeks shooting in New York,[129] and the metropolis proved as difficult as Giuliano attests. A staggering $3 million insurance policy had to be purchased by the filmmakers when they decided to visit the roof of the RCA Building to obtain a shot of the city's skyline (a plan to shoot the film's finale on top of an actual skyscraper was quickly discarded).[130] The co-op board at 1 Fifth Avenue in Greenwich Village denied *Ghostbusters* the right to use their building for exterior shots of Dana Barrett's apartment, scuttling a visually rich concept wherein the Stay Puft Marshmallow Man could waddle past Washington Square Park's famous arch.[131]

When another location was discovered uptown at 55 Central Park West, city bureaucrats tried to squash *Ghostbusters* at the last minute. "Four days before we were scheduled to film there, somebody in the city woke up and said, 'You cannot film here,'" says Giuliano. "We were building the matching facade in L.A., so this sent everyone into a giant panic. The next day, we were filming in City Hall . . . the scene with the mayor. All of a sudden, we can't find Bill Murray or Dan Aykroyd. They've disappeared. There's a frantic search. Forty-five minutes go by before they pop up and walk into the set. 'We went down to talk to Ed to convince him to let us use Central Park West.'"[132] The "Ed" in question was New York City mayor Ed Koch, who let the ex–*Saturday Night Live* stars and adopted sons of the Big Apple get their coveted location.

Central Park West is a vital traffic artery that's overflowing even on the best of days. Dropping a film production into the equation created unheralded chaos. "It was just insane," Giuliano says. "That's an incredible intersection. You gotta go there and experience it. We closed Columbus Circle. People don't do that. The cops were losing their minds. The movie division was like eight cops, total. You get like three hundred for a parade."[133] Officers started brandishing their guns at irate, uncooperative drivers, and at least one person was yanked from their vehicle and told to walk. Producer Michael C. Gross was atop the apartment building that day and saw that *Ghostbusters* was causing gridlock "all the way [down] to Brooklyn."[134]

Amy Friedman, Reitman's personal assistant on *Ghostbusters*, said the director actually had a choice between the Central Park West building and an "identical" facade "on a quiet, dead end Uptown" street. The opportunity to generate hype convinced Reitman to go with the former. "He knew parking the big, gaudy Ghostmobile there, holding up traffic every afternoon from 3 to 5, utterly destroying the city's rush hour traffic patterns, would be publicity," said Friedman. "Everyone in town [would know] that a movie with those funny guys driving a big white hearse with that [ghost] symbol emblazoned on its side was being made—months and months before it was released."

Ghostbusters created more traffic strife one morning outside City Hall when Reitman delayed a complicated shot involving four hundred extras and two hundred army reservists for ninety minutes so his wife and two children could see it. "[László Kovács] was furious with Ivan, threatening to quit," Friedman said. Tension ticked upward as every minute passed. "The sound was deafening. Every car in Manhattan, it seemed, was honking its horn; the National Guard were fingering their rifles, and the crew members were praying that those guns weren't loaded."[135] *Ghostbusters* was a major disruption for hundreds if not thousands of New Yorkers, but the city got a last laugh of sorts by imposing heavy taxes on the production. Aykroyd called these taxes "rapacious." "When the checks are down to five dollars, I'll be sending them a buck-sixty."[136]

Bill Murray wasn't always trying to smooth things over with bureaucrats when he vanished from the set. Friedman recounted an incident while *Ghostbusters* was filming at Columbia University where Murray wandered off with "a beautiful Chinese undergraduate" who was his guest that day. Tomas, the production assistant assigned to Murray, frantically searched for the pair until he found them canoodling in an empty classroom. An agitated Murray instructed him to "get lost." A day later, crew members were instructed not to interact or even look at Murray for the rest of the shoot. "Bill would walk by, or sit down beside a production staffer at the lunch table, and the PA would look sideways, or up at the ceiling or the sky," said Friedman. "If Bill caught someone looking at him, by the next day, they were gone."[137]

When *Ghostbusters* was shooting interiors in Los Angeles, Murray disappeared to chat with locals who were milling around outside the Skid Row firehouse being used as the Ghostbusters' headquarters. Crew members were apprehensive about trying to retrieve the actor from this dicey neighborhood. A brave production assistant steeled himself to coax Murray back inside. Before the break, Murray kidded Aykroyd for needing multiple takes to slide down the firehouse pole. "My work has never, *ever* been sabotaged like this. . . . Not in New York, not in India, not in Lexington, Kentucky."[138]

Los Angeles is also where the filmmakers erected Gozer's temple, the ominous foreign structure that materializes atop Dana Barrett's apartment, inside Stage 16 at Burbank Studios. Created by production designer John DeCuir, this set was an honest full-size temple that reached a height of six stories with thirty-foot-tall doors. On top of that, the surrounding stage was cloaked in a glimmering panoramic backdrop of the New York City skyline. Three hundred hours and $1 million were spent crafting this behemoth, and a town of four thousand could have been powered by the electricity it used. The inherent danger of so much wattage in such a confined area kept Gozer's temple a restricted set. It was a massive fire hazard, and a short circuit did touch off a small blaze as cameras were rolling in early January. Power was cut, the stage evacuated, and after an hour the area was declared safe. This is somewhat remarkable when one considers the fact that Stage 16's sprinkler system had been shut off prior to filming. There was concern the lights would trigger it and ruin a shot. In lieu of sprinklers, four firemen kept an eye on the temple from Stage 16's rafters.[139]

Meanwhile, Ernie Hudson was facing his own struggles. He found it difficult to gain the trust of his tightly bonded costars, whom he said used "that language that families use when they know each other very well." The walls came down eight weeks into shooting and only then did Hudson "[start] to enjoy being there."[140] Something larger nagged at Hudson, though. Winston's role was pared down considerably just before cameras rolled, his introduction postponed until much later in the film and his robust background eliminated entirely. Aykroyd, Ramis, and Reitman never explained this minimization, so Hudson suspected it was a studio mandate.[141] In was, in fact, the writers' decision to scale Winston back, giving many of his lines and beats to Murray (whom they felt didn't have enough to do).[142] Hudson has been wary of citing racism as a root cause in this instance. "If I go to the racial side of it and blame that, it takes all my power away," he said. "Because if I blame racism there's nothing I can learn from it, and the message to my sons becomes really blurred. . . . So what I have to do is say, maybe there are other reasons. . . . Had I been as big a star as Eddie Murphy, I don't think the part would have been cut."[143]

One of the most vital bits taken from Winston was his awakening of the Stay Puft Marshmallow Man, which went to Aykroyd's character after some protest from Aykroyd. "We had to talk Danny into it," Ramis said. "He saw it as Winston's big moment. But Ivan and I both felt very strongly that it should be Dan's line. . . . [The] marshmallow man was, after all, his creation in reality. So why shouldn't he create it in the film?"[144]

Not only did *Ghostbusters* call for over two hundred special effects shots, but it also required almost every kind of visual trick in the book. Optical effects, puppets, people in costumes, and matte paintings were just some of the illusions the filmmakers would have to employ.[145] At first it wasn't clear what effects company could take on the project. The larger organizations like Industrial Light & Magic were booked solid, and the smaller houses didn't seem equipped to handle *Ghostbusters*. Fortunately, Reitman soon received word that Richard Edlund, an ILM veteran, was exiting that company to set up his own business, Boss Films.[146] Edlund's work on *Star Wars* earned him an Oscar and the praise of actual space travelers ("[I] believed it all," an astronaut told Edlund after seeing the movie).[147] Edlund also created award-winning effects for the two *Star Wars* sequels and *Raiders of the Lost Ark*.

Though smaller in scale than *Star Wars*, the effects workshop for *Ghostbusters* had to be larger than the shop Edlund worked in for the third *Star Wars* film, *Return of the Jedi*, because the ghosts had to be more articulated.[148] Eight weeks alone were devoted to sculpting a puppet for the putrid green ghoul known as Onionhead (a name borrowed from the Todd Rundgren song "Just Another Onionhead; Da Da Dali"). Reitman perceived this turkey-sized ghost as a successor to John Belushi's *Animal House* character, but no one could agree how Onionhead should look.[149]

Artist Steve Johnson was tasked with bringing Onionhead to life, and he found himself extremely irritated by "the circus of art directors, production designers, writers, and all of their wives and girlfriends" who continually interrupted his process with suggestions. Johnson crafted eleven Onionheads; just before his deadline, Aykroyd and Ramis asked him to make the vapor look more like Belushi. Cocaine kept Johnson on track for his final design. This story is colored by the artist's claim that he was snorting lines directly off an 8-by-10 of Belushi when the actor's ghost materialized before him ("That looks nothing like me, Steve").[150] Puppeteer Mark Bryan Wilson operated Onionhead on set.[151] The spirit moves like Belushi, but his marbly eyes and enormous mouth owe more to Carol Channing.

Reitman subscribed to a "domino theory" in filmmaking, where one starts small and gradually increases the zaniness so as not to overwhelm viewers with anything too bizarre too early.[152] He applied this to *Ghostbusters* but still worried that the Stay Puft Marshmallow Man would be a bridge too far. Ramis shared these concerns. Would an enormous confection-based monster wading through the streets of Manhattan be scary and funny or cutesy and dumb?[153] Aykroyd's father read the script and didn't believe there was any plausible way the Marshmallow Man could exist; he told his son to cut it.[154] The filmmakers believed, however, that this behemoth was worth the gamble for the metaphor: humanity's fear of the intangible proven to be, in Ramis's words, "as insubstantial as marshmallow."[155]

Special effects man Bill Bryan, who worked on the sculpting of Stay Puft, was the primary actor in the large white costume (stuntpersons Bill Couch Jr. and Tony Cecere also wore it for certain scenes).[156] "I spent some time just figuring out what the walk was going to be," Bryan said. "Would it be a fat man waddling, leg and hand moving at the same time, or would it be more of a Godzilla swing? We ended up with the swing." Stay Puft was filmed at a higher frame rate than normal to make his movements slower and convey his enormity; the miniature rooftops he strode past were filled with realistic details like empty wine bottles, discarded mattresses, and pigeon coops with tiny pigeons inside.[157]

The time and budget constraints on *Ghostbusters* forced the abandonment of several scripted sequences, including Egon's interrogation of a hotel guest just out of the shower (*Eating Raoul* star Mary Woronov was cast as that guest) and a set piece in which a pack of ghosts attack an audience viewing a 3D movie.[158] Truth be told, there wasn't always enough time to shore up the aspects of *Ghostbusters* that did make it into the completed film. "The final design for the terror dogs was a 'maybe,' not an 'okay,'" says Thom Enriquez, who also says an exact blueprint for the canine demons never existed. "They said 'terror dogs,' so my first pass on the design was two skinless dogs. I gave it to them and they said, 'No, they're not dogs.'"[159]

Indeed, these monsters were given a more ursine physicality and purely satanic visage, complete with jutting devil horns. Ghost shop leader Stuart Ziff and his art team needed so much time to craft the terror dog models and puppets that the monsters weren't ready until the very end of the shoot; the set for Dana Barrett's apartment, already wrecked from the events of the movie's finale, had to be rebuilt for a single terror dog shot. And though they looked invincible, the terror dogs were actually quite delicate. Bill Murray gave one of the dogs a pat on the head the first time he saw it but the weight of his hand knocked off a horn, which fell to the ground and shattered.[160]

Normally it took approximately twelve to fourteen weeks to edit a feature-length film in 1984. The editing team on *Ghostbusters*, which included Sheldon Kahn and Saul Saladow, had only half that time when they received the footage that January.[161] Another problem they faced was having to estimate how long certain special effects might last. As Kahn noted, "Bill Murray may be talking to [a ghost] but you have to use a piece of blank film in place of the [ghost] who has to be manufactured later. . . . You had to guess 99%, 99.7% correct, because the material given back to you by the optical house would be exactly as long as the leader you put in. Like shooting the guns, you had to be pretty accurate about how long it took for the ray to hit something, and they would draw it that way. If you made a mistake by making it too short or too long, especially if you needed more of something, you were stuck because there was no more."[162]

None of the visual effects were ready when Reitman screened *Ghostbusters* in Projection Room 12 on the Warner Bros. lot in February 1984. The audience booed when Reitman revealed the film's incomplete state, but that didn't matter—he was more interested in testing the comedy. As it happened, the horror elements may have been incomplete but they were still effective. Saul Saladow remembers, "[The scene where] Sigourney opens the refrigerator . . . at this screening, there was just a title card that said 'scene missing' where the refrigerator shot [of the monster] should be. Well, the audience jumped out of their seats. They were screaming! What they imagined was more vivid than what we ended up with in the movie. And the ending, where the Ghostbusters are in Sigourney's apartment at the top of the building, it was all scaffolding. You saw the crew in those shots, you saw the lights, but the audience loved it."[163]

As with any movie, there were scenes filmed for *Ghostbusters* that Reitman had to remove for aesthetic purposes. A pair of quarreling honeymooners who are accosted by Onionhead had to be cut because, in Reitman's estimation, something about the bit "stopped the movie cold."[164] A lengthy sequence at a military base was trimmed down to retain only the core joke of Aykroyd's character receiving oral sex from a ghost, which is briefly seen during a montage.[165] One of the stranger segments edited out of *Ghostbusters* involved Aykroyd and Murray briefly portraying exaggerated hobos whose conversation about heavyweight boxers fighting "Karate guy[s]" is interrupted by a terror dog attack. "As soon as I saw it on the screen, I knew I would have to cut it," Reitman said. "The audience would have been left wondering why [Aykroyd and Murray] were dressed up like bums, talking funny." Before scrapping these characters entirely, Reitman tried recasting with actors Joe Schmieg and Robert Englund but the chemistry wasn't the same. Schmieg took another role in *Ghostbusters* as a police officer; Englund moved on to play iconic bogeyman Freddy Krueger in the *Nightmare on Elm Street* films.[166]

As *Ghostbusters* entered the home stretch, its title was still in question. Columbia Pictures had yet to reach an agreement about licensing the phrase from Filmation Associates. Columbia's marketing department circumvented this problem by creating advertisements with no title. The anti-ghost logo was placed on a black canvas, sometimes by itself, sometimes with the tag "Coming to Save the World This Summer." The campaign, on which Columbia spent $7 million, was hailed as bold and savvy. Filmation did finally agree to license the word "Ghostbusters" to the studio for $500,000 plus 1 percent of the movie's net profits. The deal was reportedly struck at the last possible minute, just before the film's release that June.[167]

The music of *Ghostbusters* had to offer its own verisimilitude when coupled with the narrative and visual tones. To that end, Reitman teamed again with composer Elmer Bernstein, whose scores for *Animal House* and *Stripes* were rousing without being farcical or obvious. Bernstein's robust scoring career stretched back to the '50s and included work on such monoliths as *The Magnificent Seven*, *The Great Escape*, *The Ten Commandments*, and *Thoroughly Modern Millie* (for which he won an Oscar). The composer understood that with *Ghostbusters* he had to strike the perfect balance between comedy and horror, and that prompted him to employ an ondes Martenot as one of his main instruments. The ondes Martenot is an obscure cello/piano hybrid that produces otherworldly sounds not dissimilar to a theremin (though a theremin affords its operator more control). Bernstein discovered the instrument while attending a seminar in 1981 with assistant Cynthia Millar. Millar took up the ondes Martenot, playing it on Bernstein's scores for *Heavy Metal* and *Spacehunter* and returning to it once more for *Ghostbusters*.[168]

Every draft of *Ghostbusters* that Dan Aykroyd and Harold Ramis worked on included lyrics for a jingle the Ghostbusters would use in television commercials. "If you have a ghost, but you don't want to play host . . . You can't sleep at all, so who do you call? Ghostbusters, Ghostbusters."[169] No one had written any music for this jingle by the time of principal photography, which was just as well, as Reitman's ear was bending toward something on the pop charts.

Huey Lewis and the News released their breakthrough LP *Sports* a month and a half before *Ghostbusters* started filming; the album yielded hits like "I Want a New Drug" and "The Heart of Rock & Roll" and quickly became a staple of its era. Reitman felt that the casual blues-rock sound of the News would complement his movie and birth a perfect Ghostbusting jingle. The director was already editing footage to "I Want a New Drug," but Lewis and his band weren't interested. After years of struggle, they were touring the country on the heat of a famous album. They didn't want to break for Hollywood. "We were enjoying ourselves," Lewis said, "so we politely declined."[170]

Reitman, who acted as music supervisor for *Ghostbusters* alongside Joe Medjuck and Columbia executive Gary LeMel, continued using the News as his guide when soliciting other musicians for a *Ghostbusters* title song. The Alessi Brothers, a pair of singing twins from Long Island who had appeared on albums by Barbra Streisand and Art Garfunkel, received a videotape from Reitman after record producer Phil Ramone put the two parties in touch. "[It was] the car driving around, and the song playing [on the tape] was 'I Want a New Drug,'" says Billy Alessi. "We tried a couple different things, mimicking the beats and the rhythm of the Huey Lewis song." The Alessis' theme ideas were rejected, but another composition they gave to Reitman, "Savin' the Day," was placed in the finished film and on the corresponding soundtrack album. Air Supply, the Thompson Twins, the BusBoys, and Laura Branigan were also included on the *Ghostbusters* soundtrack. Alessi says each one of these artists submitted their own jingle idea. "Everybody who wound up on that soundtrack was fighting for that theme song."[171]

Dan Aykroyd's younger brother Peter was recording an album in Los Angeles around this time and connected Reitman with two of the musicians he was working with, Glenn Hughes and Pat Thrall (who comprised the hard rock duo Hughes/Thrall). Thrall remembers the director telling them he'd been cutting his film to "I Want a New Drug." "That's what he wanted," the guitarist says, "but I think lyrically it didn't make any sense with the film. He loved the music, though, and wanted to have that same vibe. So we said, 'Alright, we'll kind of borrow from that, but kind of do our own thing.'" Hughes/Thrall struggled with fitting the word "ghostbusters" into their music but eventually found a way to make it work. "The song was melodic . . . [with] hints of the Huey Lewis sound. It had a groove rock vibe, very '80s, with an overly big drum sound." Reitman liked the Hughes/ Thrall demo and asked them to flesh it out. The subsequent recording began replacing the Huey Lewis song in Reitman's edits, leading Hughes/Thrall to believe they had *Ghostbusters* in the bag. Then the duo was called in for a sushi lunch with Reitman, Dan Aykroyd, and Bill Murray during a break from filming in downtown Los Angeles.

"It was the day they were shooting the slime scene in the hotel," Thrall recounts. "Bill and Dan go into this restaurant completely slimed. We're sitting there having this meeting and these guys are completely slimed out in their Ghostbusters uniforms. People were staring at us like, *What the hell?* Anyway, Bill Murray didn't like our song. You just think of Bill Murray as a jokester all the time. He was totally the opposite of that at this lunch. He was all business. His whole thing about the theme was he wanted it to be credible, not gimmicky. I think his favorite band was NRBQ. I think he wanted them to do the theme. So we were like, 'Man, we submitted ours, whatever.' Also, the only thing Bill Murray ate through this whole lunch was uni and sake. He was downing sake like crazy, and he had more filming to do. And he was just emphatic about the NRBQ thing." Hughes/Thrall tried to author a new theme that might appease Murray, but in the end they weren't satisfied with their own results and threw in the towel.[172]

Reitman and Medjuck heard around sixty potential theme ideas for *Ghostbusters*, but none of them clicked.[173] Established names were also turning them down. Fleetwood Mac veteran Lindsey Buckingham, author of the bouncy anthem "Holiday Road" for *National Lampoon's Vacation*, passed on *Ghostbusters*, citing the desire to avoid soundtrack work as "a repetitive part of my identity."[174]

Filming for *Ghostbusters* wrapped in January 1984, and the months rolled along. As April turned to May, they were still without a suitable piece of music. It was at this point that a Columbia employee working under LeMel suggested a musician she was dating: Ray Parker Jr.[175] Parker was an accomplished instrumentalist and singer who'd been playing at a professional level since adolescence (a bicycle accident at the age of twelve sequestered Parker in his room, where he practiced guitar for up to ten hours a day).[176] Motown legends the Spinners hired Parker when he was just fourteen.[177] Four years later, Parker joined Stevie Wonder's touring band without even having to audition.[178]

Parker became one of the most in-demand session guitarists of the 1970s, and his smooth style helped define records from Barry White, Marvin Gaye, Tina Turner, Chaka Khan, and Herbie Hancock.[179] When Parker told the *Miami News* he earned $1,000 a day in 1977, he was sure to clarify, "I don't mean $1,000 a day and then four weeks off. I was earning $1,000 a day, six days a week, week in and week out. Month after month after month." Eventually the guitarist grew tired of answering to other people, so he launched Raydio, a more or less one-man band that secured a deal with Arista Records (a subsidiary of Columbia Pictures, as fate would have it).[180] Raydio sailed into the '80s on four albums of gentle and romantic funk, all of which went gold. "I feel I can do anything," Parker remarked in 1978, a seemingly justified sentiment.[181]

A collaboration with boy band New Edition is what Parker was working on when he received LeMel's call about *Ghostbusters*. "He offered me a [nice fee] to work on it," Parker said. "Gary said, 'We only need 20 seconds [of music] for a library scene. If you turn in some music and we don't like it, you keep the [money]. That was his big bait—You've got the money whether we like it or not. Just give us the music and make sure you have the word 'Ghostbusters' in it."[182] LeMel issued two other directives for Parker: the song had to include a saxophone, and the deadline was in forty-eight hours.[183]

As Parker began focusing in his studio, he received a visit from keyboardist Martin Page and guitarist Brian Fairweather of the British group Q-Feel. Page and Fairweather were in Los Angeles trying to capitalize on the success of Q-Feel's spacey synth hit "Dancing in Heaven." They'd met with Parker's manager Diane Poncher, who insisted they get together with her client, as Parker was trying to move his light soul sound into something more modern. Page and Fairweather were excited; as fans of Parker, they were happy just to meet him. "We had only been in America two weeks," Page says. "We didn't know we'd be doing anything the day we met [Ray]." Parker explained to his visitors that he was working on "a twelve-bar blues, bar type of song" and invited them to contribute. Then he left.

"[Ray] said, 'I'm going to lunch, just play something.'" Page says. "'Play me some good steady blues licks. Do your keyboard thing. I love the new wave approach. Give me the quirkiness you have in England . . . and make it creepy, as creepy as you can.' I didn't know what the fuck he meant. Brian played rock guitar and I just doodled around on my keyboard. I thought we were doing a commercial for Corn Flakes or something. We didn't think it was a good track. We thought we'd be playing on a soul song. [Ray] came back and said, 'I love this!' . . . [but] we went back to Diane and said, 'We played on this god-awful track, it's really a shame.'"[184]

Like Hughes/Thrall, Parker discovered that the phrase "ghost-busters" was cumbersome in a musical context; he spent a day and a half trying to massage it into his creation. Eventually Parker realized that a call and response was the perfect solution. He turned to a girlfriend for help—not the girlfriend who worked with Gary LeMel, but a seventeen-year-old the twenty-eight-year-old Parker was simultaneously seeing.[185] "I told her my idea and she quickly got a bunch of her high school friends to come by and yell on it."[186] The teenagers came in the next day before their classes to sing the chorus to "Ghostbusters." They've never been credited, partly due to Parker's belief that these women are somehow not actually a part of the recording. "I realized I had to say, 'Who you gonna call?' If

I do that, it allows me to never say the word 'ghostbusters.' Then I'm gonna have a crowd answer, 'Ghostbusters.' . . . Because it's a crowd, they're not really in the record. They're not musical. So that takes away the word 'ghostbusters.' That gets it out of the song. So we can have a song. And I could sing, 'Who you gonna call?"[187]

It only took ten minutes for Parker's girlfriend and her classmates to complete their part for the "Ghostbusters" theme. While they were working, a messenger arrived from Columbia Pictures to collect the recording. Unfortunately, it wasn't done—Parker still had absolutely no lyrics beyond the chorus. He improvised the verses on the spot as the messenger waited.

Reitman called Parker the following morning to issue his verdict: he loved "Ghostbusters" and wanted a longer version with an accompanying music video. The singer wasn't sure about that latter aspect. "I was thinking . . . *me in a video, singing to a ghost? I don't know about all that.*"[188] Parker didn't sing to a ghost in the video but to actress Cindy Harrell, whom he chases around a haunted house. "I was ten years younger than [Harrell]," Parker recounted decades later. "So I was like, 'Why didn't they get a cute chick? Who's the old girl?' Now I look at her and it's like, 'Ooh, she's kinda sexy.'" Reitman interspersed clips from the movie and also filmed celebrities like Melissa Gilbert, Carly Simon, and George Wendt shouting the "Ghostbusters" refrain.

"I think they were just looking for people who were around on the Columbia lot," said Wendt, who was pulled aside while filming *No Small Affair*. "Nobody had even heard the song. I was just praying I would come in on the right beat. Looking back, I can see the panic in my eyes." Wendt was paid in *Ghostbusters* promotional items (a button, a T-shirt, an eventual copy of the video). Music videos at that time were nonunion work, so he also received an angry letter from the Screen Actors Guild.[189]

The "Ghostbusters" clip ends with Parker dancing through Times Square with the stars of the film. This shoot gave Reitman another opportunity to cause maddening congestion in the heart of New York City. So many people stopped to try to catch a glimpse of Dan Aykroyd and Bill Murray that cops forced the entire production back in their vehicles until the crowd dispersed. The Times Square dance was filmed in the last week of May, three weeks before the movie's release.[190] Parker couldn't believe how quickly this had moved. Of course, the filmmakers were up against the wall and they had no fallback option.[191] This afforded the singer one incredible advantage, allegedly: it's rumored that Parker was able to retain majority rights to his "Ghostbusters" song after it went into the film, ensuring he'd make the most money from its success.

Many people loved Ray Parker Jr.'s "Ghostbusters" the minute they heard it. Previous theme authors Glenn Hughes and Pat Thrall were not among those people. "We went over to Peter Aykroyd's house and he played it for us," says Thrall. "And we were like, 'This is basically the music for "I Want a New Drug."'" The thing Ray Parker got away with, though—he came up with the 'Ghostbusters' chant allegedly, but that's from an old song from the late '60s called 'Soul Finger.' It's the exact same phrasing, the group chant. It was by the Bar-Kays. He completely ripped that off, too."[192]

The Alessi Brothers were also taken aback by the similarities between "Ghostbusters" and "I Want a New Drug." As Billy recounts with a chuckle, "When we heard what Ray Parker did, we were like, 'Oh, you didn't tell us you just wanted us to *steal* it!'"[193]

While reflecting on his career in 1993, Harold Ramis touched on the confidence he and others felt while creating some of their most popular hits. "We were so arrogant about [*Animal House*]. We thought we were going to be the biggest comedy in history. It was really a delusion. . . . [With *Ghostbusters*] we were even worse in our arrogance, because we felt no one had done a big special effects comedy in a long time, and our writing, we knew, was in a good groove with a strong technical overlay."[194]

Ramis believed enough in *Ghostbusters* to buy a new house just before the movie's release.[195] Bill Murray's convictions went beyond even that. Once he saw a few minutes of edited footage, he knew *Ghostbusters* was going to change everything.

"Not only did I go back to work with a lot of attitude, I was late," he said years later to *Rolling Stone*. "I didn't care—I knew that we could be late every day for the rest of our lives."[196]

BIBLICAL PROPORTIONS

Nine hundred million dollars is a staggering amount of money to spend on anything that doesn't involve multiple space flights, but that's roughly what Coca-Cola paid to acquire Columbia Pictures in January 1982. The business world was turned on its ear when this deal was announced. Why would a relatively conservative beverage manufacturer spend so much capital to wade into an industry as volatile as film? Coca-Cola CEO Roberto Goizueta and president Don Keough remained undaunted even as their company's stock dipped in reaction to the buyout. These relatively new leaders were interested in audacious strategies to diversify holdings and increase profits for the American institution now under their charge. A smattering of industry insiders recognized the acuity in absorbing Columbia, a company with an extensive entertainment library, just as cable television and home video were on the rise. In fact, Columbia already had a lucrative deal in place with cable network HBO wherein the channel could license material for broadcast so long as they were helping to finance the studio's newer productions.[1]

Coca-Cola made it clear, however, that they were very taken with Columbia's theatrical market, doling out praise for the studio's "fantastic track record over the past few years." Goizueta simultaneously promised that his organization understood "the creative process" of filmmaking and would adopt a "totally non-hostile supervisory attitude toward that process."[2] The beverage makers certainly had no personal acumen for recognizing potential box office winners. A crystalline example exists in *Ghostbusters*. Goizueta saw the movie ahead of its June 8, 1984, release and was convinced Columbia and Coca-Cola were about to weather a costly misfire. Speaking later with the *Wall Street Journal*, he admitted, "When I came out of [the theater] I thought, *Gee, we're going to lose our shirts*."[3]

Ghostbusters was entering the fray during a landmark competitive stretch for Hollywood. Untold fortunes would hang in summer 1984's balance as new movies arrived from crowd favorites like Indiana Jones, *Star Trek*, the Muppets, and Conan the Barbarian. In such a climate, analysts believed a comedy like *Ghostbusters* had to enjoy record-breaking success to be accepted as anything other than a bomb. This was especially true considering the film's reputed final budget of $38 million (a number that factored in marketing costs).[4]

Columbia had been in a similar position two years earlier when they bet their summer bundle on a big-screen version of Broadway's *Annie*. Fifty-two million dollars was spent on that film, and although *Annie* eked out a profit, it was nowhere near the nine-figure returns the studio projected. *Annie*, a comedy about a Depression-era orphan, was written off as a failure because it could barely keep its head above water next to *Rocky III* and *Star Trek II*. There was also Steven Spielberg's *E.T.*, the touching story of a boy and his alien that ran off with the 1982 box office when it was released two weeks after *Annie*. Columbia had been offered *E.T.* but passed because they felt it lacked commercial value. At its zenith, *E.T.* was grossing an unprecedented $3.5 million dollars a day.[5]

Frank Price wasn't worried about *Ghostbusters*. As Columbia's chairman, he knew the picture couldn't lose any money because of the aforementioned ancillary deal he put together with HBO. Similar contracts with NBC and RCA Records actually prepaid the negative costs for *Ghostbusters* up to 135 percent.[6] Besides, *Ghostbusters* had not been as expensive to produce as *Annie*, and it had greater demographic appeal. Dan Aykroyd and Bill Murray shared this care-free attitude, so much so that they both skipped out on a week of *Ghostbusters* promotional activities in late May.[7] Aykroyd explained to a reporter on June 2 that if this movie fizzled, it would be a drop in the bucket: "Coca-Cola can make it up with a week's sale of orange juice."[8]

The film's producers had their doubts. What if *Ghostbusters* did go sideways somehow? They looked for ways to minimize potential damage. Sixty thousand dollars in printing fees were saved once the names of fifty special effects technicians were eliminated from the end credits.[9]

Ghostbusters had its world premiere at Westwood's Avco Cinema on June 7, 1984. Michael Ovitz, talent agent for several stars of the film as well as its director, organized the Los Angeles showing with his wife as a $250-a-ticket charity event to raise money for St. John's Hospital.[10] It was a lively affair, with acclaimed break-dancing crew United Street Force performing for a sea of celebrities that included Dolly Parton and Robert Duvall (Sean Penn was so mesmerized by these break-dancers he couldn't entertain the advances of Debra Winger or Beverly D'Angelo). Before the movie started, Bill Murray tried to cajole the crowd into a round of calisthenics.[11] The mirth apparently ended once the lights went down. Ovitz said not a single laugh was heard that night as *Ghostbusters* screened.[12]

The movie had a second "premiere" four days later to benefit Santa Monica's pluralistic school PS1, which naturally left St. John's Hospital feeling discontent. Columbia Pictures president Guy McElwaine acknowledged their complaints but refused to cancel PS1's *Ghostbusters* fund-raiser. Harold Ramis had spearheaded this repeat premiere because his daughter was enrolled in the school. Also, at only $25 a ticket, the PS1 screening could be billed as "family-oriented."[13]

Squaring off against *Ghostbusters* on its nationwide June 8 rollout was *Gremlins*, a horror-comedy produced by Steven Spielberg and directed by Joe Dante. Dante's penchant for crafting sinewy fright streaked with droll parody brought filmgoers subterranean classics like *Piranha* and *The Howling*. "[Dante] seems to make his movies and the *Mad* magazine parodies of them at the same time," raved *Film Comment*. "He's turned self deprecation into a weird new form of fun."[14] *Gremlins* would be no different, weaving a tale of tiny adorable cryptids who evolve into murderous reptilians and take over a suburban enclave. Dante's clever marketing gimmick was not allowing any images of the monsters to be seen prior to the film's release—not even by the company editing the trailer (they received a print of *Gremlins* that edited out every gremlin).[15]

One element handicapping *Gremlins* was a controversy that began brewing a couple weeks earlier with another film bearing Spielberg's name. Watchdog groups expressed discontent with *Indiana Jones and the Temple of Doom* because they believed the movie's PG rating was too lenient for some of the intensities it depicted, such as human sacrifice. Even Spielberg, *Temple of Doom*'s director, admitted there were portions of *Doom* he'd never screen for kids; he called for a new rating between PG (parental guidance suggested) and R (restricted; no one under 17 admitted without parent or guardian).[16] The debate remained in heat when *Gremlins* arrived to stoke the fire. Of objection in Dante's film was a morbid beat where a character explains in vivid detail how her father snapped his neck trying to impersonate Santa Claus.[17] The Motion Picture Association of America relented to the outcry by adding a new ratings category on July 1: PG-13 (parents strongly cautioned).[18]

Ghostbusters avoided being swept up in the furor because it was deliberately softer. Though the movie was, in the words of Harold Ramis, "the most outrageous" that he and his peers had done in terms of concept, it was also their "most restrained in terms of taste level." "We wanted this to be the first film in which we didn't patently accept the notion that crude is good," he said. "There was a general confusion in Hollywood that it was the vulgarity which really sold [our] films. Raunch behavior became a focal point."[19] Aykroyd and Ramis massaged impropriety out of *Ghostbusters*, excising drug references, excessive perversion, and a few rough expletives.[20]

The team behind *Ghostbusters* also took a lesson from *An American Werewolf in London*, the 1981 John Landis movie that had difficulty mixing wry, weird humor with intense gore. *Ghostbusters* producer Michael C. Gross remembered watching *American Werewolf* with theatergoers who were unsure if they should laugh or scream. *Ghostbusters* was purposely broader and generally subscribed to cinematic attitudes of the 1940s, à la *Abbott and Costello Meet Frankenstein*. "There's no blood," Gross noted. "There's no people turning inside out. We don't want to put things on the screen that people can't look at."[21] One of many scenes cut from *Ghostbusters* directly references these older films Dan Aykroyd cited as an influence. CBS newscaster Diane Sawyer was scripted to interview the Ray Stantz character, remarking that his job "sounds like an old Bob Hope movie." Stantz politely reminds Sawyer that the 1940 movie she's thinking of is actually called *Ghost Breakers* (CBS policy forced Sawyer to turn down the cameo—their journalists were not allowed to appear in commercial films).[22]

The *New York Times* noted in their *Ghostbusters* review that the movie earned its PG rating with nothing more than "a little strong language and the occasional good-humored leer."[23] The paper was far from enamored with *Ghostbusters* in general. "This film hasn't gotten very far past the idea stage," wrote Janet Maslin. "Its jokes, characters and story line are as wispy as the ghosts themselves."[24] Maslin's coworker Vincent Canby noted in a later piece that *Ghostbusters* "elicited only a couple of smiles" from him, commenting that "our [national] sense of humor seems to have become as bland as a salt-free, low-cholesterol diet. . . . [Maybe] it's difficult to make comedies within and about a society when everything is going well or, at least, when everything is widely perceived to be going well." Canby followed this line of thought to blame President Reagan for boosting our economy and flooding the marketplace with intellectuals, thereby defeating skepticism ("the basis of comedy").[25]

Variety also expressed disappointment with *Ghostbusters*, calling the film "lavishly produced but only intermittently impressive" and noting that its haunted building plot was borrowed from straight-faced horror opus *The Sentinel*. This paper of Hollywood record predicted *Ghostbusters* would enjoy "good but not smash" box office returns.[26] Jay Scott of the *Globe and Mail* dismissed *Ghostbusters* as "Summer twaddle" that couldn't live up to the pioneering television comedy its stars turned in years earlier: "You may enjoy it and then find you have forgotten it before your theater seat has had a chance to snap back into place."[27] The *Boston Globe*'s Jay Carr was less generous, dubbing *Ghostbusters* "a dead battery" that might be "the biggest bust" of the summer thanks to a "juvenile screenplay" and "cementlike" pacing and editing. "It's never loose enough, crazy enough, spontaneous enough," Carr wrote. He also described Bill Murray as "greasy" and noted that Dan Aykroyd had grown "tubbier" since *Trading Places*.[28]

Scores of critics would disagree with these early assessments and, more importantly, so would the popcorn-chewing public. *Ghostbusters* became an unparalleled phenomenon. In fact, its monstrous success would prove too difficult for some cast members to handle.

Vincent Canby was correct when he observed that life was basically on the upswing for America in the early to mid 1980s, though New York City was a notable exception. The doldrums of the '70s were failing to evaporate in the five boroughs. In fact, 1980 saw the highest crime rate in the history of the city's annual tally, with over seven hundred thousand incidents cataloged (experts agreed since many crimes go unreported that this number was possibly twice as high).[29] The chairman of the Metropolitan Transit Authority, Richard Ravitch, admitted in 1982 that he didn't allow his fourteen-year-old son on the subways after dark because it was too dangerous.[30] Economic woes saw New York tagged that same year as "the youth unemployment capital of the nation" by the city's own Department of Employment.[31] These issues remained prevalent through 1984, and they're reflected in *Ghostbusters* via the thin layer of grime László Kovács captured in his documentary-style cinematography.[32] All the fantastical elements of the movie and the jocular tenor are juxtaposed against harsh realities of a metropolis coping with crippling, unshakable problems. It underscores and complements the fabricated horror perfectly.

Ghostbusters earned plenty of glowing reviews and champion financial figures upon its release, but there's much more tangible evidence that speaks to its immediate, immense popularity. The film hadn't been in theaters for a full week yet when a merchant selling bootleg *Ghostbusters* buttons on a Chicago bus was mugged for his entire supply.[33] A handful of teenagers in Lincoln, Nebraska, converted a 1964 Cadillac to look like the car in the movie and spent their June and July nights "[cruising] Lincoln's main street . . . looking for deadly ghosts."[34] The "Fritzbusters," several college-age right wingers, traveled to the Republican National Convention that August in Dallas with their own replica car and uniforms bearing a "No Walter Mondale" logo (Mondale, the Democratic nominee for president, was nicknamed Fritz).[35] A *Ghostbusters* fan club started when Pittsburgh residents Mark Lister and Jim Garvey bought the right to do so from Columbia Pictures for $10,000. The club's $8.95 membership fee granted fans an ID card, a patch, an "anti-paranormal proficiency" certificate, and "an insurance policy protecting them from 'sliming.'" In just a few months, Lister and Garvey signed up twenty-five thousand members.[36]

There was also the case of Jeff Nichols, a high-schooler in Hackensack, New Jersey, who found himself a hometown hero when friends began noticing him in the background of a brief scene *Ghostbusters* filmed at Rockefeller Center. Nichols had been on a school trip to New York City in the fall of 1983 and had no idea he'd been caught on camera. No less than the *New York Times* caught up with this accidental star. "It's strange to think that I'm in a movie that's playing all over the country," Nichols said. "I guess it's like being a part of history."[37]

Preeminent critical voice Roger Ebert offered a succinct explanation as to exactly what made *Ghostbusters* such a resonant achievement. "This movie is an exception to the general rule that big special effects can wreck a comedy," he wrote in his three-and-a-half-star review for the *Chicago Sun-Times*. "Special effects require painstaking detail work. Comedy requires spontaneity and improvisation; or at least that's what it should feel like. . . . *Ghostbusters* has a lot of neat effects, some of them mind-boggling . . . [and] they're placed at the service of the actors; instead of feeling as if the characters have been carefully posed in front of special effects, we feel they're winging this adventure as they go along." Ebert also noted the complexity of the humor involved: "[The actors] are funny, but they're not afraid to reveal that they're also quick-witted and intelligent; their dialogue puts nice little spins on American clichés, and it uses understatement, irony, in-jokes, vast cynicism, and cheerful goofiness. Rarely has a movie this expensive provided so many quotable lines."[38]

New York magazine's David Denby agreed, further explaining that *Ghostbusters* contains "about eighteen layers of joking media reference: We're reminded of the solemnly lurid, siren-blasting radio crime serials of the '30s, and such early '50s TV exercises in technological suspense as 'The Atom Squad,' with its actors in diving suits waving Geiger counters at innocent plants. *Rosemary's Baby* and *The Exorcist* are taken for a ride, and also the dreadful gothic-religioso *Omen* series . . . yet *Ghostbusters* doesn't live off parody, the way a sketch on 'SCTV' might. The movie has abundant personality of its own."[39]

Ghostbusters earned the number one box office spot the weekend it debuted with $13.6 million in earnings, a new record for Columbia Pictures. That total was also a crown jewel in what was cited as cinema's most lucrative weekend to date—*Gremlins* raked in $12.5 million behind *Ghostbusters*, squeaking past *Temple of Doom*'s $12 million (and handily beating *Star Trek III*'s $9 million).[40] It's rare for a film to make even more money during its second week of release, but that's exactly what both *Ghostbusters* and *Gremlins* managed, taking in $15 million and $13 million, respectively, the following weekend.[41] During these early days of commercial screening, *Gremlins* did in fact best *Ghostbusters* in several major cities, including Pittsburgh, Los Angeles, and New York.[42] Some have attributed the latter upset to lingering resentment over the traffic jams the filming of *Ghostbusters* caused in Manhattan. It's a moot point; *Ghostbusters* eventually won the top dollar in the Big Apple, not to mention everywhere else.[43]

A third comedy had been scheduled for June 8, 1984, but Paramount Pictures blinked at the last minute and rescheduled their espionage farce *Top Secret!* for June 22. *Top Secret!* was the latest spoof from *Airplane!* masterminds Jim Abrahams and David and Jerry Zucker.[44] *Airplane!* had left *National Lampoon* figurehead Doug Kenney despondent in 1980; he knew the cartoonish Abrahams/Zucker brand would supersede the deft satirical style he'd labored so hard to popularize in print and on-screen.[45] What Kenney couldn't foresee was an evolution of his work into *Ghostbusters*, which takes an irreverent *Lampoon*-ready concept and handsomely combines it with clever storytelling, showstopping special effects, and firm strokes of humanity to create something totally unique. *Top Secret!*, though extremely funny, lacks the special qualities that define *Ghostbusters*. The *Top Secret!* filmmakers admitted as much when they announced the release delay. "We don't have big stars or a smashing new concept," said producer Jon Davison. "All we have is jokes."[46] *Top Secret!* didn't set the box office aflame and went largely unappreciated until decades later.[47]

For seven straight weeks, *Ghostbusters* reigned as America's most popular movie. The streak was only broken by the release of Prince's musical drama *Purple Rain* in late July.[48] A week after that, *Ghostbusters* returned to number one, sailing into August as 1984's highest-grossing film with a tally of $162 million.[49] For the first time in five years, the year's most celebrated film was not affiliated with either Stephen Spielberg or George Lucas.[50] *Ghostbusters* didn't stop making money there, however; by December, its totals rose to $221 million.[51]

The success story repeated overseas. *Ghostbusters* did explosive business in South Africa, Singapore, Malaysia, Australia, the UK, New Zealand, Denmark, and Finland.[52] Some markets, like West Germany, witnessed the popularity of *Ghostbusters* rescue their entire film industries from inertia.[53] In Japan, eight thousand people packed into Tokyo's Budokan arena to see the movie's premiere.[54] "We were surprised by the success of *Ghostbusters*," said Kunikazu Sogabe, general manager of Columbia Films Ltd Japan. "No foreign comedy-oriented movie has ever had that degree of success here.... Comedy is difficult, especially as in Japan we always use subtitles, which effectively cover only one third of the dialogue. The culture gap also means a big difference in the sense of humor.... Fortunately, a lot of the humor was visual. Nevertheless, we didn't sell it as a comedy, but as [a special effects] movie."[55] Ivan Reitman observed that Japanese audiences "really understood the Marshmallow Man. It'll be the Marshmallow Man versus Godzilla next."[56]

Ghostbusters was Columbia's biggest hit ever in foreign markets by a sizable margin, validating the $15 million spent in Coca-Cola advertising tie-ins to break the film in forty European and Asian countries.[57] The movie didn't always exhibit the same staying power it had in the United States, though. In Norway, *Ghostbusters* quickly took a backseat to the political thriller *Orions Belte* (*Orion's Belt*), a domestic production that spoke more clearly to the country's heritage and pride.[58] Italian audiences were just as smitten with Roberto Benigni's *Non Ci Resta Che Piangere* (*All We Can Do Now Is Cry*) as they were with *Ghostbusters*—the two films tied for largest box office take of the year.[59]

And there were outright rejections of *Ghostbusters*. One of the more memorable of such incidents came when the movie screened at the London Film Festival. Reitman was on hand, and *London Times* critic David Robinson described a moment wherein "a gentle Scandinavian lady in the audience stood up, hurt and near to tears, to ask Mr. Reitman if he were not ashamed to use so much money for a film that only tended to degrade the audience." Reitman's response was not recorded, though Robinson noted the director "was so fervently supported by the National Film Theatre audience as a whole that any of us who felt inclined to support the lady were in the event far too cowardly."

Robinson's review of *Ghostbusters* coupled it with *Gremlins*, panning both movies as "far from being extraordinary, innovatory or in any way elevating to the imagination. . . . They are costly and calculated industrial products, garish plastic toys for grown-up infants."[60]

As big as *Ghostbusters* was, Bill Murray was even bigger. Nearly every review of the film, good or bad, rhapsodized about Murray's part. "He makes [Bob Hope's] vintage movie cool look sweaty by comparison," David Elliott wrote in the *San Diego Union*.[61] *Time*'s Richard Schickel embraced Murray's Peter Venkman as "a brilliantly observed caricature of the contemporary urban male. . . . His utter imperviousness to anything that cannot be comprehended in those basic materialist terms is finally a more potent weapon than all the atomic gadgetry he and his friends carry."[62] Murray was likened to comedy legends Groucho Marx and W. C. Fields in David Denby's

New York review: "[He] doesn't pretend to be scared when facing the demons and specters. He jokes and plays, spinning his own smarmy, hip patter off the chunky surfaces of the plot. . . . He's a great American muttering wit."[63] "Essentially [Murray's] talking to himself [in *Ghostbusters*]," *Newsweek*'s David Ansen said, "yet somehow he's able to make smugness totally endearing (unlike, say, Chevy Chase)."[64]

New Yorker mainstay Pauline Kael found *Ghostbusters* to be an empty, amateurish exercise but further lionized Murray in her recap, writing that his "patent insecurity makes him the perfect emblematic hero for the stoned era. He has a genuine outré gift: he makes you feel that his characters are bums inside—unconcerned and indifferent—and he makes that seem like a kind of grace (he's always an onlooker; he won't commit himself even to being in the movie). . . . He turns burnout into a style."[65] Gene Siskel went so far as to personally thank Murray in his write-up for the *Chicago Tribune* after several paragraphs of effusive praise. "*Ghostbusters* is the movie that confirms Bill Murray as one of our funniest comic actors. He's funny doing absolutely nothing in this overblown, special-effects-filled, $25 million comedy. . . . In fact, more of Murray doing less would have made *Ghostbusters* an even funnier film than it is."[66]

When asked directly about his contributions to *Ghostbusters*, Murray was nonchalant. "I was just doing what I do," he told the *Los Angeles Times*. "I just had better material than usual. They gave me *all* the lines. I was resisting it—I didn't think it was right not to have it all balanced. But nobody wanted to hear about it. Dan didn't want any more lines, and Harold was the same."[67]

Thanks to Peter Venkman, Murray watched his already established fame mushroom overnight. Before, there was a chance he could slip through a crowd unnoticed. *Ghostbusters* changed that forever. "I could not go anywhere," he said. "Not to a restaurant. Not to a store. Not to walk down the street. You cannot overstate too much the inability to go out to a restaurant and have a meal. . . . I couldn't get away from it." The pressure got to him. Murray cracked one morning at around 5:00 a.m., driving to the airport and hopping a plane to Montreal. There, he rendezvoused with Aykroyd for a getaway in Quebec City. The duo's cover was quickly blown, so they journeyed south to Wisconsin to try to hide out with some of Aykroyd's relatives. Once again, the situation got "extremely weird," according to Murray. Gossip about the A-list celebrities in these rural confines prompted throngs of people to take to the streets, tying up traffic and generating chaos.[68]

One might argue that the consolation prize for the actors' loss of privacy was wheelbarrows of money. In addition to their up-front salaries, Aykroyd, Murray, Ramis, and Reitman all received a portion of the gross profits from *Ghostbusters*. Michael Ovitz said his four clients took 30 percent of the movie's overall revenue; internal documents from Columbia suggest the split was not even. Still, even a short straw like Ramis's alleged 1¼ percent generated an extra $3 million by 1985. If Murray held on to the 10 percent stipulated in his May 1983 agreement, his profit payout was closer to $20 million.[69]

People adored Murray because they either identified with or aspired to the utter detachment that was the foundation of his artistic expression, an emotional avoidance that stood in savory contrast to the childlike enthusiasm of Dan Aykroyd and the quiet dedication of Harold Ramis. So he doomed himself, perhaps, by even admitting he had a passion project, let alone following through with it. *The Razor's Edge*, the period drama Murray made before *Ghostbusters*, was released in October 1984, the first post-*Ghostbusters* entertainment bearing his name to whet a now insatiable public hunger. Murray conceded during the film's promotional cycle that transitioning out of comedy was a personal struggle. "I feel funny making [*The Razor's Edge*]," he told the *Globe and Mail*, "because I know I'm basically just an idiot who wants to drive down highways throwing beer bottles out of cars."[70] Murray insisted he took the work seriously, however, just as seriously as any comedic endeavor. He said it was his goal with *The Razor's Edge* to present a more rounded, whole person in lead character Larry Darrell.[71]

The actor also promised levity wasn't entirely absent from his dramatic foray. "We weren't trying to make a funny movie, but the intention was to show that this [spiritual] search doesn't mean you lose your sense of humor," he explained. "I'm not funny some of the time in the movie. But for every person who thinks it's too funny, there will be a quarter of a million people who are going to sit through it because at least there's some humor. . . . Whether or not the audience reacts well is not going to drive me crazy. Because I really got enough out of it just doing it. If they don't like it, it's really not going to kill me."[72]

The Razor's Edge was not the birth of a new dynasty for Bill Murray. Reviewers complained that the film's tone was upset by its star, who couldn't drop his glib modern style to comfortably play a philosophical 1920s roustabout. "Murray's inventive riffs give too many scenes an odd, jarring rhythm, as if we were watching Charlie Parker sitting in with the Boston Pops," Patrick Goldstein wrote in the *Los Angeles Times*. *The Razor's Edge* was judged as a misfire in several other departments as well, including scripting, direction, and scoring. "Perhaps the Maugham story just isn't meant for the movies," the *Wall Street Journal*'s Julie Salamon surmised, insisting that Hollywood's 1946 interpretation was also "a groaner."[73]

It may not have killed Murray to watch *The Razor's Edge* sink away that autumn, but surely he felt some disappointment. He poured more of himself into Larry Darrell than most viewers realized (a speech Murray delivers in the film to a deceased soldier mirrors his own emotions regarding the death of John Belushi).[74] Murray also gave up his several-million-dollar acting fee for *The Razor's Edge*, taking only $12,000 for cowriting the script.[75] About a decade after the fact, the actor admitted to *Entertainment Weekly* that *The Razor's Edge* was a blunder. "I kind of deluded myself that there would be a lot of interest," he said. "I made a big mistake. The studio wanted to make it a modern movie, and I said, 'No, it should be a period piece.' I was wrong and they were right."[76]

The failure of *The Razor's Edge* didn't have much effect on Bill Murray's popularity. Lynda Rose Obst summed up the prevailing attitude toward Murray in *Vogue* that December when she wrote that he was "a dissipate Little Rascal" and a "major part of the Zeitgeist," fawning over his "big, innocent eyes, morning-after demeanor, and harmless lechery."[77] Murray was turning into a folk hero, but the man himself sought reprieve. Thus, he departed for France with what some saw as a measure of permanence. When speaking about family in an April 1985 newspaper profile, younger brother John Murray was already using the term "expatriate" to describe Bill.[78]

Murray spent half a year in France,[79] dodging a fame he felt wasn't commensurate with his talent. "I was considered the biggest star in movies, and it was something I don't think I completely earned or deserved," he said. "I was proud of the work, but I think my success was actually beyond my ability." Murray would later joke that he "learned how to eat with a fork and knife" while living abroad, but in truth he dedicated himself to becoming a better, more informed actor. He studied not just comedy but film in general, taking classes at the Sorbonne and watching a pair of movies each day. Murray was enormously affected when he attended a screening of D. W. Griffith's long-lost 1919 drama *A Romance of Happy Valley*. He considered it the greatest film he'd ever seen, even though the print he watched had no sound and was subtitled in Russian (this remains the only version of *A Romance of Happy Valley* in existence).

"I didn't know what the hell they were saying, but this movie destroyed me," he said. "I thought, *How the hell could somebody make* The Love Bug *if they've seen this?*"[80]

The cultural moment *Ghostbusters* carved out for itself in 1984 was pocked by a handful of legal problems. In October of that year, Columbia Pictures won permanent injunction against several companies responsible for flooding the market with counterfeit *Ghostbusters* merchandise.[81] Official licensees had been blindsided by the film's monolithic success and couldn't get their product onto shelves quickly enough (Galoob's Stay Puft Marshmallow Man toy wasn't available until a month after *Ghostbusters* was released).[82] Bootleggers prospered before the injunction, which finally staved off the majority of hats, shirts, and other tchotchkes illegally bearing the "no ghost" logo.

The emblem itself became part of a more serious dispute a month later. The team who designed the *Ghostbusters* symbol had labored to make sure their drawing wouldn't be mistaken for Casper the Friendly Ghost, but Harvey Comics, Casper's creators, still filed a lawsuit, believing the *Ghostbusters* logo infringed upon a secondary character they owned called Fatso. Harvey wanted $52 million in damages. They also asked that every copy of *Ghostbusters* be confiscated and destroyed.[83]

Harvey's case ran into trouble when it was determined that Fatso's likeness was rooted in a series of comic books that were no longer copyrighted. Furthermore, the court decided that the "tremendous consumer demand for [*Ghostbusters*] merchandise bearing the logo" was a result of "the goodwill created by the film and the theme song, rather than any possibility of confusion with the Casper characters." Manhattan federal judge Peter K. Leisure took further issue with Harvey's evidence—clippings from magazines that "suggest a general association" between *Ghostbusters* and Casper. "It is clear from reading these articles," Leisure said, "that there was no confusion whatsoever on the part of the authors."[84]

The judge dismissed the lawsuit in 1986. When pressed to compare the two ghosts at hand, Leisure opined that Fatso displays "evil or mischievous facial expressions" whereas the *Ghostbusters* ghost appears "bewildered."[85] Harvey pursued litigation, and a settlement was reached in 1989.[86] Coincidentally, one of Harvey's lawyers in the original complaint was named Egon (Egon Dumler of Dumler & Giroux).[87]

It's telling that Judge Leisure's statement about *Ghostbusters* generating demand specifies both the movie and its title music. Ray Parker Jr.'s "Ghostbusters" theme became just as celebrated as the film; insiders believed the song helped bring in an extra $20 million in box office receipts.[88] As 1984's summer drew to a close, Parker's "Ghostbusters" was topping the charts, besting Prince, ZZ Top, and Bruce Springsteen.[89]

Another artist Parker bested was Huey Lewis, who with his band the News was still riding high on their enormously popular LP *Sports*. *Sports* contained "I Want a New Drug," the song Ivan Reitman used when he was first editing together footage from *Ghostbusters*. Many people believed Parker simply copied "Drug" for his own composition. Lewis certainly felt that way. During the week of August 29, he and his publishing company filed suit against Parker, Parker's publishing company, Reitman, Columbia Pictures, and Arista Records.[90] The plaintiffs were seeking $5 million plus all profits from and a permanent injunction against Parker's song.[91] Lewis only told the media he felt "Ghostbusters" and "Drug" shared "remarkable similarities." The defendant had more to say.

"To me it doesn't sound like the same song," Parker said in an interview with the *Daily Breeze*. "But I tell you, I like Huey Lewis and the News. . . . [The lawsuit] just means I'm popular. I mean, if this were a number 80 record, then fell off the chart, I'm sure nobody would say a word. It's kind of flattering. I wish Michael Jackson would sue me, though, so then I could get famous."

Parker's insinuation that he wasn't famous after landing a number one pop song is bizarre, as is another statement he made about the case. "I think both records sound like [M's] 'Pop Musik,'" he said,[92] referencing a new wave hit from five years earlier. It's true that the primary rhythm of "Pop Musik" is akin to the signatures of both "I Want a New Drug" and "Ghostbusters." It's unclear, however, why Parker would mention this as if he was a neutral third party and not, in fact, the very figure at the heart of this infringement complaint. Legally, invoking the name of a second composition surely did Parker no favors. When discussing the controversy during a separate interview with *Billboard*, Parker volunteered that "Ghostbusters" had similarities with a third song. "Remember 'Soul Finger' by the Bar-Kays?" he asked the interviewer. "At least there the chorus comes in at the same time."[93]

Proceedings between Huey Lewis and Ray Parker Jr. dragged on for a year. Just before the start of trial in the summer of 1985, the defendants agreed to settle.[94] Financials were never disclosed, but it's been heavily suggested Lewis received the $5 million he was after.[95]

Reitman later admitted that the "Ghostbusters" theme has "basically the same kind of riff" as "I Want a New Drug" but insisted it's "a totally original song [with] original lyrics, original everything, . . . The fact that it had the same kind of bass hook doesn't in itself mean a copyright infringement."[96] Surprisingly, the legal situation didn't dampen Reitman's Huey Lewis fanaticism. The director used Lewis's music again in the early editing stages of 1986's *Legal Eagles*.[97]

Plagiarized or not, Ray Parker Jr.'s "Ghostbusters" was one of numerous catalysts that helped reestablish the motion picture soundtrack as a viable commercial entity. The movement began in 1983 after the romantic drama *Flashdance* yielded several chart-breakers. Business solidified when music from *Against All Odds, The Woman in Red, Purple Rain*, and *Ghostbusters* all found similar success.[98]

The new soundtrack boom was great news for everyone except the classical musicians whose orchestral scores for films now had to compete with contemporary rock and pop. *Ghostbusters* composer Elmer Bernstein was definitely upset over the way the music for the film panned out, as stretches of his material were excised to make room for Parker, the BusBoys, and Mick Smiley. "I have nothing against rock n' roll, per se," he said. "I think if it's appropriate, then fine. What bothers me is that it's a shame that in a film like *Ghostbusters* one feels compelled to put in a rock n' roll tune for public acceptance. There isn't any real reason why *Ghostbusters* had to have rock n' roll music—after all, it's not *Footloose*! I'd rather handle the whole thing myself and, ultimately, I don't think it's as good for the film as having a completely composed score."[99]

With the ethereal sounds of the ondes Martenot often employed as a centerpiece, Bernstein's *Ghostbusters* score conveys a proper amount of fright, whimsy, and heroics for three academic washouts battling paranormal evils. The orchestral work was not released in full at the time, and only two selections from Bernstein's score were included on the corresponding *Ghostbusters* soundtrack album.[100] Frustrating, but even Bernstein had to admit "it's very hard to argue [against rock n' roll] when [the Ray Parker Jr. song] is up in the top ten."[101]

Ghostbusters solidified its headliners as comedy establishment, a cadre of stars in the upper deck who from that moment forward were only competing against their own résumés. Fourth Ghostbuster Ernie Hudson did not enjoy a similar ascent. "[*Ghostbusters*] made people aware of me, but it did not get me the kind of stuff I wanted to do," he said years after the fact. "I learned what it means to be poor and popular."[102]

Hudson's work as Winston Zeddemore, of course, is absolutely vital to the film. He delivers the only character grounded in our reality, the only character who's not a caricature or a cartoon or a victim of cartoonish possession. It's reductive to call Winston a mere straight man, though—he has nuance and emotion and generates plenty of his own substantial, satisfying laughs. Winston's ability to adapt to increasingly bizarre landscapes is just as admirable as any of the sci-fi gadgetry on display or Peter Venkman's weaponized dispassion.

Critics in 1984 took very little note of this. *Ghostbusters* write-ups in the *New York Times*, *Boston Globe*, *Los Angeles Times*, and *Wall Street Journal* neglected to even mention Ernie Hudson or his role.[103] Some reviewers, like Gene Siskel, viewed the Winston character as mere tokenism since he doesn't arrive until *Ghostbusters* is almost halfway over.[104] Strangely enough, *Saturday Night Live* was the only mainstream outlet to offer direct commentary on Hudson's value in *Ghostbusters*. The November 10, 1984, episode aired a sketch in which Consuela, a guest on a *Ghostbusters*-themed talk show, says her favorite Ghostbuster is "the black one" and laments that "they didn't give him enough to do." A problematic layer of irony exists in the fact that the Latina character discussing fair opportunity for persons of color was played by a white woman (*SNL* cast member Julia Louis-Dreyfus).[105]

Television offered Ernie Hudson a fair amount of work following *Ghostbusters*. He appeared on several episodes of the hospital drama *St. Elsewhere*,[106] lent his voice to comic book hero Cyborg on *The Super Powers Team*, and even filmed a pilot for his own sitcom called *Full House* about a suburban Chicago family (which was of no relation to the Bob Saget *Full House* that was a hit for ABC just a few years later).[107] The actor was not exactly enamored with this medium. "TV is limiting in terms of expression," Hudson said. "It's great exposure. But television doesn't create; it manufactures. They assume people want to see stereotyped characters, so that's what they give them."[108]

Hudson's career may not have been moving upward, but *Ghostbusters* did earn him respect from viewers of color who were thankful that

Winston Zeddemore did not fall prey to damaging racial stereotypes. Hudson remembered an encounter with venerated contemporary Denzel Washington after the film's release: "I ran into him at a bank and he said, 'Wow, man, I really loved the character and you didn't embarrass me.' And I knew exactly what he meant because a lot of times, you go, 'Oh, okay, here's a black guy. Here we go . . .' In the big films, the blockbuster adventure movies, a lot of times if there is a black character, it's really the cartoon. He's doing something that makes people kind of cringe. 'Okay, you're representing us in a way.' And nobody should have to represent [everyone], but they see that, and this is going to be a reflection on me. [But] I didn't think about that when I played [Winston]. It wasn't about trying not to be something. It was just about trying to be true."[109]

Further validation arrived when Hudson's turn in *Ghostbusters* was nominated for an NAACP Image Award. Sadly, Hollywood's systematic refusal to create space for Black talent was reflected in the way the Image Awards structured their categories. The seven people qualified for either Best Actor or Best Supporting Actor were condensed into one field. Hudson lost his statuette to Prince's showcase in *Purple Rain*.[110]

As the 1984 awards seasons rolled on, Ray Parker Jr.'s "Ghostbusters" theme was the only element from the film to be consistently recognized. The song was nominated for an Image Award, a BAFTA, a Golden Globe, a Grammy, and an Oscar.[111] The Oscar telecast for that year opened with Parker performing a jazzy rendition of "Ghostbusters" in an elaborate staging that included a floating forklift, an assortment of dancing ghouls, and an interruption from Dom DeLuise. *San Francisco Chronicle* scribe Terrence O'Flaherty called the performance "interminable" and likened it to "amateur night at the Continental Baths."[112] Parker only won the BAFTA and the Grammy but he believed the industry attention exacerbated problems between himself and Ivan Reitman, who received zero nominations for his directing.[113]

"People kept writing in the newspaper that the song made the film, and I think it made some people crazy," Parker reflected. "We sold over 10 million records immediately, even before the movie came out. Then I got nominated for an Oscar and the movie didn't. I won a BAFTA and the movie didn't. I don't know where the resentment [on their part] came from, but there was a lot of emotion. . . . I'm thinking, *Wow, every movie Ivan Reitman directs, it's going to be like Steven Spielberg and John Williams!* I never got a call again."

Parker also said that "there was a point where they asked me to return some of the money [from 'Ghostbusters']."[114] This seems to confirm rumors that Columbia tried (and failed) to renegotiate Parker's contract following the enormous success of the song so the singer would no longer have the largest controlling stake and corresponding monetary payout.

Arista Records wanted to stick with Ray Parker Jr.—they'd been in business together since Parker's first Raydio album in 1978. The label didn't count on a competitor swooping in to poach their "Ghostbusters" siren. Geffen Records signed Parker to a seven-figure deal shortly before the release of his June 1985 Arista LP *Sex and the Single Man*. Parker kept the whole thing to himself, so Arista never had a chance to match or better Geffen's offer. Arista founder Clive Davis expressed disappointment at this turn of events. "When people talk about the big R&B artists of the late '70s and '80s, you hear about Michael Jackson, Prince, Rick James," he said, "and there's no denying that they're the pinnacle. They changed everything radically, made history. Still, for a long stretch of time, Ray Parker, Jr. was right there in the mix, consistently generating hits with independence and single-mindedness."[115]

Parker was ready to branch out from R&B hitmaking, however, and around this time he began publicly expressing a desire to break into acting. "I like seeing myself on TV," he said. "I feel more comfortable in front of the camera in front of millions of people than I do onstage." Yes, he had a dream role. "The Billy Dee Williams part in the *Star Wars* movies. That's heaven. I'd probably retire after that. There wouldn't be anything else left to do."[116] Parker would have to make do with lower-profile opportunities, like a guest shot on the NBC sitcom *Gimme a Break!* and a showcase in the opening of Richard Pryor's short-lived CBS kids' show, *Pryor's Place*.[117] In 1987, Parker was cast as a lead in the gritty gang movie *Enemy Territory*. A blaxploitation entry ten years too late, *Enemy Territory* was condemned ("Like any other garbage, it deserves to be thrown out," said the *Philadelphia Inquirer*) and did nothing for Parker's screen career.[118]

After Dark, Ray Parker Jr.'s debut album for Geffen Records, was met with similar appraisal when it was released the same year. Despite contributions from Natalie Cole, Carole Bayer Sager, and Burt Bacharach, the *New York Daily News* pegged *After Dark* as "depressing" while the *Tampa Bay Times* wrote it off as "too generic and bland to matter."[119]

History is always rapidly rewritten at the box office. Although *Ghostbusters* was confirmed as Hollywood's most successful comedy ever in January 1985, having amassed a domestic gross of $225 million, its successor was already lunging forward.[120] A month earlier, Paramount Pictures fostered a new eminence of hysteria when they released Eddie Murphy's *Beverly Hills Cop*. The action-comedy played to all of its young star's strengths; reviewers were breathless, comparing Murphy to legends like James Cagney, while crowds snapped up tickets in Herculean numbers.

Although there was some strategy involved—*Cop* opened on a Wednesday, allowing two extra days to bring in its $19 million start—the film's appeal was organic.[121] No one could engineer what Murphy was generating. *Beverly Hills Cop* was the first movie to play on over two thousand screens throughout the country, and at certain points it was making more money than all three of its closest challengers combined.[122] Two years earlier, *E.T.* pulled in $3.5 million a day over the July Fourth weekend, but *Cop* managed the same feat for nearly an entire month.[123] 20th Century Fox studio head Tom Sherak spoke for every jealous executive when he called *Beverly Hills Cop* "the Grinch [who] stole Christmas."[124]

Beverly Hills Cop ended 1984 as the seventh-most-popular movie in the United States with a gross of $80 million.[125] Eddie-mania stormed through 1985 and brought in a final tally of $234 million for *Cop*, crowning Murphy as laughter's new king.[126] His reign continued on the fledgling home video market. At the time, home video was geared more toward sales than rentals, and *Beverly Hills Cop* sold over 1.4 million VHS tapes after its October 1985 release. These sales figures were aided by what was then considered an inexpensive retail price of $29.95 for the *Cop* tape.[127] The *Ghostbusters* VHS, released during the same period, was offered for a more standard $79.95. Although it only moved 410,000 units, *Ghostbusters* was still the number one title in its price bracket.[128]

Videocassette dealers faced direct competition from cable television, this period's other burgeoning home entertainment field. Experience suggested sales of VHS tapes were always negatively affected after a movie ran on a pay station. So the dealers were especially irate when HBO treated their subscribers to *Ghostbusters* on Christmas Eve of 1985, airing the film months ahead of its scheduled premiere on the channel. The only advance warning was in newspaper television listings that showed "HBO Christmas Present" for the 11:30 p.m. time slot.[129] HBO pulled this very same stunt two years earlier with *Annie*. VP of programming Seth Abraham told *Variety* that the positive feedback they received from the *Annie* "Christmas Present" encouraged them to try it again. Abraham said they were adding a "touch of serendipity" to HBO, a quality he believed was absent from the rest of the TV landscape.[130]

Columbia knew about HBO's surprise *Ghostbusters* airing ahead of time. They took no issue with it, probably because of the astronomical amount of money the channel was paying for it. HBO had been so desperate for content in 1981 when they inked their deal for exclusive broadcast rights to the Columbia library that they accepted potentially bankrupting terms. The channel and their parent company, Time Inc., agreed not only to cover 25 percent of production costs for every theatrical release Columbia made through 1984 but also to pay 25 percent of whatever a film earned in theater rentals. On top of that, there was a 25 percent equity buy-in. These figures had no ceiling; when *Ghostbusters* attained $144 million in theater rentals, HBO and Time had to write Columbia a check for $36 million. Rivals gleefully observed this bath was about as much as the film itself cost to make. The studio had offered HBO a price break if they agreed to hold off showing *Ghostbusters* until 1986, but they didn't take it. A contract renegotiation added ceilings to this legendarily awful deal to prevent future embarrassments.[131]

Even more embarrassing is the fact that HBO wasn't the first pay station to bring *Ghostbusters* to the small screen. SuperTV, an obscure subscription model specific to the greater Washington, DC, area, aired the movie on November 1, 1985.[132] Not that there was a breakneck race to beat network television. *Ghostbusters* wasn't scheduled to air on a network until 1987. ABC purchased those rights for $15 million just a few months after the movie's debut.[133]

As the videocassette and cable television markets expanded, so did film piracy. The MPAA spent millions every year trying to thwart illegal VHS distribution in the United States. Quite often the source of this piracy was the video retailers themselves—too cheap to purchase multiple copies of an in-demand title, they simply dubbed extra cassettes.[134] However, there were numerous bootleg tapes circulating in the mid-'80s that had been recorded directly from cable broadcasts. Piracy ran absolutely rampant in foreign markets, especially in regions where American cinema was scarce.[135]

Ghostbusters was one of the most pirated titles across the globe, and Columbia Pictures did what they could to halt it. Complaints to federal police of individual countries often resulted in successful raids of bootleg operations.[136] In the United Kingdom, the studio tried introducing "piracy-proof" cassette packaging.[137] Sometimes, films would be passed around on VHS before they even hit theaters. Thus, as illicit copies of *The Karate Kid* and *Dune* flooded the streets of Rome in early 1985, twenty-four-hour security was hired to protect the Italian dub of *Ghostbusters* in the weeks prior to release.[138]

Ivan Reitman visited Columbia Pictures shortly after the release of *Ghostbusters* to thank the studio's executive staff for the support they'd given the film. One former employee remembered this as a disingenuous and awkward encounter, one that perfectly illustrated Reitman's often unpleasant demeanor. "He stood up and looked at the ceiling and said, 'I know I'm rough, and I can't thank you enough for the job you did for me.' But he couldn't even look at anyone.'"[139]

Being weird and impersonal is not an egregious offense in the arts. In fact, many would consider it requisite behavior. Reitman's personality quirks certainly did not bar him from conversations about *Ghostbusters II*, a sequel everyone was frothing over. December 1984 gossip columns suggested the sequel might revolve around the "franchise outlets" briefly mentioned in the first movie. In response, the filmmakers would only confirm that a sequel was being discussed.[140] According to Reitman, everyone from the first movie was committed to another chapter, but he added that they might reteam to make something else entirely if the mood struck them.[141]

Ghostbusters II was definitely not what the marquee talent wanted to work on in the immediate future. Reitman was diving into an adaptation of the venerated sci-fi tome *Hitchhiker's Guide to the Galaxy* (a film he started putting together before *Ghostbusters*).[142] Harold Ramis signed on to direct the tropical resort farce *Island Jack*, aka *Club Paradise*, aka *Club Sandwich*, a Warner Bros. release starring Robin Williams and Peter O'Toole.[143] Bill Murray's decision to spend the majority of 1985 on vacation put the brakes on a San Francisco–based comedy called *The Night People* he was considering making with Dan Aykroyd.[144] That was fine with Aykroyd, who had coals burning all across Hollywood.

Aykroyd's espionage caper *Spies Like Us* was moving ahead for Warner Bros. with costar Chevy Chase just as Columbia was readying a team-up with John Candy about security guards called *Armed and Dangerous*.[145] *Empire Man*, a long-gestating script about an evangelical preacher, was being tailored for Aykroyd by Orion Pictures and Britain's Hemdale Leisure Corp.[146] Simultaneous to all that, the actor convinced Universal Studios to make a film based on the '60s TV show *Dragnet* starring himself.[147] Universal was also trying to revive Aykroyd's *Never Say Mountie* as another pairing with Murray.[148]

Nineteen eighty-five sailed by and the work Aykroyd planned to do on a *Ghostbusters II* script didn't happen. As the new year loomed, he admitted he only had "a few notes and some ideas" pertaining to the sequel.[149] This wasn't good news for Columbia. Their theatrical fortunes for 1985 were down compared to the previous year, the result of too much product and not enough diversity.[150] Columbia's decision to churn out eighteen movies instead of the requisite twelve or thirteen did nothing to bring in extra profit. In fact, Columbia was one of 1985's worst-performing studios (inexplicably, the market research that established parent company Coca-Cola as savvy in the beverage industry wasn't utilized during this tenuous stretch).[151] There was also enough executive turnover at Columbia to give outsiders the impression their hierarchy was mired in chaos.[152] The projected windfall from a *Ghostbusters II* couldn't come soon enough for this beleaguered studio.

In a maddening bit of irony, Columbia Pictures threw up its own roadblock to *Ghostbusters II* in 1986 when they hired as their chief executive and chairman an altruistic film producer from England who came to Hollywood hell-bent on elevating commercial motion picture as an art form. His violent resistance to *Ghostbusters II* was just one of a million issues that doomed his brief tenure to adjectives like controversial, notorious, and infuriating.[153]

THE TYRANNY OF THE
BOX OFFICE

David Puttnam wanted a career defined by his principles. As a twentysomething in the 1960s, he left a cushy advertising job in his native London after being assigned a campaign for cigarette maker Benson & Hedges. "I'm sure they thought I was being very pretentious," Puttnam said, "but I've never smoked, I don't agree with smoking, and I just wasn't prepared to spend my life urging other people to smoke." Puttnam moved forward as a business representative for famous photographers like Richard Avedon and David Bailey. It was another successful endeavor, but his heart was truly in film.[1] So this resolute young man who paired a trim beard with shaggy hair quit photography to cofound the Goodtimes Enterprises production company.[2]

Ironically, Goodtimes experienced some of its earliest popularity with two documentaries about Nazi Germany. Both 1973's *Double Headed Eagle* and 1974's *Swastika* were championed for conveying Hitler's devastation through meticulously edited newsreel and propaganda footage.[3] Puttnam and his producing partner Sandy Lieberson simultaneously enjoyed a more upbeat hit with the rock 'n' roll drama *That'll Be the Day*. Ringo Starr and Keith Moon had supporting roles, and *That'll Be the Day* made enough money to warrant a sequel, *Stardust*.[4]

In 1976, Goodtimes put their cash behind *Bugsy Malone*, a musical from Alan Parker that softened the titular gangster's blood-soaked story with a cast composed entirely of children. This gimmick made

Bugsy Malone seem like a joke. When the movie was offered to the Cannes Film Festival, they refused it on the grounds that it wasn't "esoteric" enough. A livid Puttnam went to the press, insisting that *Bugsy Malone* was "a film for *everyone* that just happens to feature a cast of kids." Cannes relented; *Bugsy Malone* screened to great acclaim, paving the way for a successful general release.[5]

Puttnam's first international film hit arrived in *Midnight Express*, a 1978 prison drama he helped produce for Parker and Casablanca FilmWorks (an offshoot of US record label Casablanca). *Midnight Express* was showered with critical praise and earned several Oscar nominations—winning one statue for Best Screenplay—but the triumphs came at a specific price for Puttnam. Namely, the realization that his perception of *Midnight Express* and its grim realities differed wildly from that of the average moviegoer. Sitting in a crowded theater for an early screening, Puttnam was shocked when patrons ate up an attack scene that culminates with the protagonist chewing off an aggressor's tongue. "We thought they'd be under their seats, but instead they were cheering!" he marveled. "That's the depth of misjudgment I realized I was capable of." This led Puttnam to feel hoodwinked by the whole enterprise.[6]

There's been some disagreement regarding the genesis of Puttnam's involvement with *Midnight Express*. While Puttnam's claim is that he was asked to join up, Peter Guber, one of the movie's founding producers who acquired the script for Casablanca, has said Puttnam invited himself.[7] Discrepancies of this nature would pop up throughout Puttnam's career, standing in marked contrast to his own alleged moral code. Director Hugh Hudson was especially irritated with Puttnam's truth-bending upon completion of the 1981 drama *Chariots of Fire*. Puttnam did fight an uphill battle bringing *Chariots* to screens; a movie focusing on the religious struggles of Olympic distance runners in 1924 was a tough sell for everyone.[8] Still, Hudson was aghast when Puttnam took credit for aspects far removed from his influence.

"He voraciously grabbed anything he could for himself from *Chariots of Fire* and denigrated my position many times to the extent that people wondered what I had to do with the film," Hudson complained. The director was incensed after hearing Puttnam say during a radio interview that he had chosen the memorable and moving Vangelis theme music for *Chariots*. "*I* chose the music for the film, Vangelis was my collaborator on many of my projects, someone I'd know for ten years. . . . David was determined to grab everything, didn't want to share the glory."[9]

The press gushed over *Chariots of Fire*, declaring it refreshing, uplifting, and a much-needed return to a certain brand of cinematic integrity.[10] A Best Picture win at the Academy Awards minted *Chariots* as the year's most esteemed entry.[11] Puttnam exercised his flair for incendiary remarks minutes ahead of that ceremony when he commented on the Best Director category to gossip columnist Marilyn Beck. He did nothing to mask his contempt for nominee Warren Beatty, whose direction on the biopic *Reds* was up against Hudson. "Hugh is without a doubt a better director than Warren is, or ever will be," Puttnam announced. "And so are Steven Spielberg and Louis Malle" (Spielberg and Malle were also nominees, for *Raiders of the Lost Ark* and *Atlantic City*, respectively). Puttnam believed if Beatty won it would only certify that he was profitable. Beatty did win and responded to Puttnam by calling his remarks "absolute chickenshit."[12]

Puttnam's next projects carried on the prestige legacy he was trying to build. Released in 1984, *The Killing Fields* adapted the gripping story of two journalists escaping Cambodia's genocidal Khmer Rouge; it was recognized as another work of eminence.[13] *Cal*, a romance starring Helen Mirren set against the violent unrest of Ireland's Troubles, made less of an impact the same year. However, *Cal* was just as important to Puttnam. "I love the picture," he enthused. "If pictures like *Cal* don't work at the box office, all we'll be left with is *Ghostbusters*."[14]

Moving into the second half of the 1980s, Puttnam began to wonder about his future. He felt at odds with the British film industry and needed advancement of some kind to secure a proper retirement fund. As fate would have it, an executive offer from Paramount Pictures soon arrived. Puttnam couldn't accept, though, because the position didn't offer enough creative autonomy. Shortly thereafter, in April 1986, Guy McElwaine resigned as chairman and CEO of Columbia Pictures with no successor in line.[15] The studio's first pick for replacement, NBC president Brandon Tartikoff, wasn't interested.[16] Columbia bosses began working down a list of names.

David Puttnam wasn't on that list. No one at Columbia thought a British producer of his stature would have any interest in moving to Hollywood.[17] They were wrong. Puttnam was familiar with Columbia (they coproduced *Midnight Express*), and the empty chair position looked like the perfect opportunity. He sent his attorney Tom Lewyn to meet with Columbia executive vice president Fay Vincent.[18] Lewyn expressed desire on behalf of Puttnam to an excited Vincent and presented Puttnam's three conditions for acceptance: total authority on what films to green-light, at least $3 million in net capital after taxes, and a tenure no longer than three years. Vincent agreed to it all.[19] Despite the ease of this brokerage, Puttnam couldn't avoid jamming in one small chunk of rigmarole.

"I'm telling everyone you made the approach [to me about this position]," Puttnam told Vincent when they first met face to face. "It sounds better." Puttnam clung to this lie so voraciously, even his official biographer Andrew Yule couldn't get the truth out of him. "No. *I* didn't make the approach," he told Yule in 1989. "Tom Lewyn did." An incredulous Yule pressed: "Well, he's your lawyer, after all, isn't he?" Puttnam replied, "You'll have to talk to Tom about it."[20]

Regardless of this introductory quirk, Fay Vincent was confident in David Puttnam. He believed Columbia's new head would usher in an era of prosperity and class and that Puttnam would ultimately stay in the position beyond his allotted three years. Patrick Williamson, figurehead for Columbia International, strongly disagreed. He tried to warn Vincent.

"Puttnam will self-destruct. . . . I really know him and you don't."[21]

Once you reach the top, the only direction you can go is down. The personalities responsible for *Ghostbusters* were probably familiar with this musty axiom. They certainly lived through their own varied examples in the years immediately following their commercial apex.

Dan Aykroyd's first screen appearance following *Ghostbusters* was a tiny role in the 1985 John Landis film *Into the Night*, which follows a modest insomniac as he becomes ensnared in a string of violent escapades. The *New York Times* blanched at this "supposedly light-hearted comedy in which throats are slit, chests are stabbed, stomachs are shot, and artificial blood flows like beer at a fraternity house homecoming weekend."[22] The gore felt exceptionally tone-deaf considering Landis made *Into the Night* while under indictment for involuntary manslaughter. Three years earlier, a gruesome helicopter crash killed actor Vic Morrow and two children during a segment Landis was filming for *Twilight Zone: The Movie*.[23] An NTSB investigation found Landis had ignored safety precautions and the entire lurid case was slowly moving to trial.[24] *Into the Night* vanished that February beneath a thicket of *Twilight Zone* headlines, though not before the *Wall Street Journal* could declare it "the worst kind of bad."[25]

Aykroyd, who worked with Landis six months after the *Twilight Zone* deaths on *Trading Places*, echoed prevailing Hollywood attitudes when he dismissed the tragedy as "an industrial accident, nothing more."[26] Although Landis had to cancel his cinematic take on *Dick Tracy* because he was afraid it would conflict with legal proceedings, he did find time to helm Aykroyd's intelligence farce *Spies Like Us*. *Spies Like Us* was the big gambit for Christmas 1985, but Landis, Aykroyd, and costar Chevy Chase learned they didn't have a *Ghostbusters* on their hands when their comedy failed to claim the box office. Critics from California to Quebec raked *Spies Like Us* over the coals. "*Rocky IV* has more laughs," the *Los Angeles Times* announced under the headline "Saturday Night Dead." The *New York Times* dismissed the movie as another example of humor-averse "New Comedy."[27]

Ivan Reitman's next effort was a throwback to "old comedy," as it were. Once *Hitchhiker's Guide to the Galaxy* collapsed (in part because he couldn't convince his friend David Cronenberg to direct it),[28] Reitman began focusing on an urbane caper called *Legal Eagles*. The script, penned by Jim Cash and Jack Epps Jr., offered wit and mystery befitting of Hollywood's golden age as it laid out a story inspired by the fraud case that embroiled the estate of painter Mark Rothko.[29] Reitman's plan to reunite Bill Murray and Dustin Hoffman on *Legal Eagles* collapsed when Murray objected to story revisions and Hoffman booked himself elsewhere. Rakish idol Robert Redford, who admired Reitman's work, read *Legal Eagles* over Labor Day weekend in 1985 and agreed to star in it for Universal so long as his costar was a woman.[30]

Academy Award nominee Debra Winger took the other leading role in *Legal Eagles*, a venture that transformed into a protracted headache due to numerous personality clashes. Redford and Reitman, for instance, bickered over the director's instinct to go broad. "We kept having these high road–low road arguments," Redford explained. "I'd say 'that's corny' or 'that's cheap' or 'that's dumb,' and he'd do things to ensure the audience was laughing, going for laughs to build a character or build a scene. But I loved arguing with him. He's very stubborn, very strong-minded, and he'd just hang in." For his part, Reitman found it difficult to get Redford to loosen up and rediscover the charm he'd brought to career-defining movies like *Butch Cassidy and the Sundance Kid*.[31] Redford and Reitman both experienced friction with Winger, who later claimed she was forced into *Legal Eagles* by CAA, the talent agency that represented her,

Redford, and Reitman (Winger eventually likened the shoot to a POW experience).[32] On top of all this, *Legal Eagles* had serious script problems. Veteran screenwriter Tom Mankiewicz called it "all concept and no high" when he was asked to help doctor the screenplay.[33]

More tongues wagged about the budget. The A-list talent hired for *Legal Eagles* all commanded large paydays, pushing expenses to nearly $30 million.[34] This hefty price tag appeared to be the only element the film had in common with *Ghostbusters*. Released in June 1986, *Legal Eagles* took nothing by storm and was routinely lanced for its baffling story and inept direction.[35] One of the harshest critics was Debra Winger, who voiced her distaste for the movie when she was meant to be promoting it. "I was horrified to see it edited with a chainsaw," she told one reporter. "*Legal Eagles* is the kind of film that takes audiences and shakes them up until $6 falls out of their pockets." Winger had specific complaints about the superfluous action sequences that were added as filming progressed. "I never planned to be in a pyrotechnic movie. It was intended to be a movie like *Adam's Rib*, a sophisticated romantic comedy about relationships. Imagine my dismay to find myself jumping in the East River while I'm thinking about *Adam's Rib*. I had a lot of disagreements with Ivan as the film changed character. But he's a very strong personality, and he made the movie he wanted to make."

"I would have liked less pyrotechnics myself," Reitman admitted when asked to comment for the same article. "Looking back at the movie, there are things I would do differently." He tried to be fair when discussing his conflict with Winger, but not before blaming her. "She's historically been a difficult actress to work with. Talk to her other directors. Debra works out of a nervous tension, and she thrives on that tension. Ultimately, though, our disagreements are irrelevant. What counts is what happens onscreen, and I like her performance in the film."[36] In a *Rolling Stone* interview several years later, Reitman reflected that he "was trying to make [*Legal Eagles*] too many things" and he realized when they were editing the movie that it didn't make sense."[37]

Opening a week ahead of *Legal Eagles* was *Back to School*, the Rodney Dangerfield comedy written and produced by Harold Ramis that debuted to top-grossing business. *Back to School* enjoyed popularity all summer long, but for Ramis this victory was tempered by the cratering of two other projects.[38] *Club Paradise*, the tropical resort comedy he directed, received an icy reception that July despite a talented cast including Robin Williams and Peter O'Toole. Ramis disagreed with the rejection of that film but he couldn't defend *Armed and Dangerous*, a stale security guard send-up based on one of his scripts.[39]

The weird, convoluted history of *Armed and Dangerous* is more captivating than the movie itself. Columbia Pictures bought the script in early 1982, hoping to use it as another vehicle for Dan Aykroyd and John Belushi. *Armed and Dangerous* was revisited after Belushi's death, and Aykroyd agreed to star with John Candy under the direction of John Carpenter.[40] Carpenter was in the mood to "try something nutty," as he put it, after primarily making horror films. He didn't get to try anything at all. For unknown reasons, Aykroyd soured on Carpenter and had Columbia fire him.[41] Aykroyd then left *Armed and Dangerous* himself during what was supposed to be the first week of filming.[42]

Carpenter never learned why Aykroyd had him removed from *Armed and Dangerous*. Aside from a pleasant introductory conversation at the start of the project, the actor never spoke with him. Aykroyd's behavior left Carpenter furious, but the director understood Columbia's follow-through: "They were afraid he wouldn't do *Ghostbusters II* for them if they didn't keep him happy."[43] John Candy, on the other hand, felt duped by the studio. He considered legal action before realizing it would be cheaper to just make the movie. Eugene Levy was hired as Candy's costar, *Roller Boogie*'s Mark L. Lester was brought in to direct, and Ramis was so disillusioned by the end result he lobbied to have his name removed entirely (he was unsuccessful).[44]

Several other films Aykroyd was working on around this time, including the televangelist satire *Empire Man* and his Canadian police adventure *Law of the Yukon* (previously known as *Never Say Mountie*), stalled or petered out entirely.[45] Aykroyd wasn't present on screen at all in 1986, but he did serve as executive producer for the quasi–teen comedy *One More Saturday Night*. His old *Saturday Night Live* cohorts Al Franken and Tom Davis wrote the movie, which follows the various goings-on in a small Midwestern town on one specific evening. Franken and Davis cast themselves as a fictional rock group called Badmouth, and bad mouth is all *One More Saturday Night* received as it died a quick death that September. *Variety* said the film "deserves to be deep-sixed into Lake Superior."[46] "The more time you spend at the concession stand, the happier you'll be," remarked the *Chicago Tribune*.[47] A month later, Aykroyd was back in front of the camera filming the semi-parody *Dragnet* with costar Tom Hanks. *Dragnet* spent two weeks at number one the following summer.[48]

Sigourney Weaver's visibility was high in 1986 as she reprised her heroic Ellen Ripley role for James Cameron's *Aliens*. *Aliens* was a box office smash that summer, and it also earned Weaver an Academy Award nomination for Best Actress. This was a first not just for Weaver but for the Academy as well; never before had they recognized a lead actress in an action/adventure or science fiction film.[49] Though it appeared Weaver had effortlessly moved from one hit to the next, she had in fact made two unremarkable entries between *Ghostbusters* and *Aliens*. The 1985 French-language comedy *Une femme ou deux* (*One Woman or Two*) cast her with Gérard Depardieu and sex therapist Dr. Ruth in a story of mistaken identity. Europeans gave *Une femme ou deux* the cold shoulder, and upon its US release in 1987, Roger Ebert declared there wasn't a single element that made the film worth seeing.[50] *Half Moon Street*, an erotic thriller Weaver made just before *Aliens*, received mixed reviews in fall 1986 and disappeared in the shadow of *Crocodile Dundee*.[51]

There were plenty of supporting dweeb roles for Rick Moranis after *Ghostbusters*, and he took them in standard to poor fare such as *The Wild Life*, *Brewster's Millions*, *Head Office*, and *Club Paradise*.[52] Moranis had dreamed of a different trajectory. Just before *Ghostbusters*, the comic tried a more dramatic part in Walter Hill's rock 'n' roll opus *Streets of Fire*. Hill was beloved in Europe, and Moranis hoped *Streets* would prove big enough to break him into that continent's film industry.[53] Ironically, it was *Ghostbusters* that afforded Moranis a movie across the Atlantic. Director Frank Oz was so taken with the warmth Moranis displayed in *Ghostbusters* that he hired him as the lead for an adaptation of *Little Shop of Horrors*, which was shot in England.[54] A musical about a lovelorn nerd forced to do the bidding of a bloodthirsty plant, Oz's *Little Shop* was hailed as a delight when it was released in December 1986 (the film also earned two Oscar nominations). Among *Shop*'s zaniness is a cameo from Bill Murray as a lunatic dental patient. *New York Times* critic Janet Maslin called Murray's appearance "perfect."[55]

At this juncture, Bill Murray was spending most of his time at home in Upstate New York with his growing family, remaining in a state Harold Ramis described as "semiretired." "He loves his life the way it is right now," Ramis said. "Bill was ambitious, but now he's got all the goodies. . . . He can travel all over the country and watch minor league baseball games to his heart's content."[56] Murray explained later that his absence from celluloid was inadvertently extended when he turned down *Legal Eagles*. "That put me a whole season behind," he said. "There are actual moviemaking seasons. . . . and the three weeks before every season, I would get 20 phone calls a day from people wanting to do a movie, and there would be this incredible amount of pressure. On Friday, I'd get like 30 phone calls, and then on Monday, no one would call, and I'd look in the paper, and someone else was doing the movie because I didn't say yes."[57]

Bill Murray may have considered himself a man out of season, but there were plenty of people trying to hand him work. Murray remained Murray, though—difficult to pin down even for a conversation. His own agent Michael Ovitz never got a response after forwarding Murray the script for sibling drama *Rain Main*, which Ovitz envisioned as the perfect vehicle for Murray and Dustin Hoffman.[58] That autumn, Steven Spielberg and Robert Zemeckis were mounting their production of the live-action cartoon hybrid *Who Framed Roger Rabbit* and imagined Murray might be good for the lead; the pair gave up after they couldn't get a hold of him.[59] A miracle occurred for *Mad Max* director George Miller when he managed to speak with Murray in 1987 about playing the heavy in *The Witches of Eastwick*.[60] There was also an offer to join *Three Men and a Baby* that Murray said he considered.[61]

At one point, a story went around that Murray would sign on for a remake of *His Girl Friday* with Dan Aykroyd and Debra Winger (this project mutated into *Switching Channels* with Burt Reynolds, Kathleen Turner, and Christopher Reeve).[62] But it was a different script with a similar milieu that actually galvanized Murray for his return to moviemaking. *Scrooge* was a modern-day twist on *A Christmas Carol* that reimagined its main character as the ruthless head of a TV network. Written by Michael O'Donoghue and Mitch Glazer, *Scrooge* enticed Murray with its satirical humor and intelligence, but he also saw importance in the script's lessons about ethics, hope, and the human condition. These were the themes Murray wanted to address in his work going forward. It was time to shift away from the sarcastic slob persona and make films that, as he put it, "you wouldn't be afraid to let your kids' kids discover decades from now. Like I discovered *A Tale of Two Cities* or even Mr. Magoo."[63]

Scrooge was eventually renamed *Scrooged*.[64] By the time production wrapped, that's certainly how Murray felt about the experience.[65]

When Columbia Pictures licensed the phrase "Ghostbusters" from Filmation Associates for their big-budget effects comedy, they agreed to cut Filmation in for 1 percent of the film's net profits. Erika Scheimer, daughter of Filmation founder Lou Scheimer, is resolute: Columbia never honored that deal. "We saw not one penny," she says. "They had some very creative bookkeeping. They claimed [the movie] *Ghostbusters* never made a profit, which you and I both know is bullshit."[66]

A more pointed defeat came from within Filmation's own house. By the 1980s the company was primarily known for creating animated hits like *Fat Albert and the Cosby Kids* and *He-Man and the Masters of the Universe*—in fact, no other studio in the United States was creating as many cartoons as Filmation was at that point in time.[67] However, when Filmation's lawyer Ira Epstein was negotiating the *Ghostbusters* title license, he neglected to secure the rights to any potential cartoon spin-off from Columbia's property. Granted, there was no way of knowing just how popular the film would be, but one would assume those rights would be part of a fair exchange for the name. As Scheimer puts it today, "Ira really fucked up on that one."[68]

Scheimer dismisses reports that her father offered to produce an animated *Ghostbusters* series for Columbia after the fact. In truth, when rumors began circulating that Columbia would launch a cartoon based on the movie, Filmation decided to issue a direct challenge by giving their own mid-'70s *Ghost Busters* sitcom an animated revival. Filmation's new *Ghostbusters* was sold into approximately forty US television markets for daily syndication by August 1985. Columbia easily doubled that number when their spin-off *The Real Ghostbusters* (produced by DIC Enterprises) was ready shortly thereafter. Some television stations purchased both cartoons. Herman Ramsey, vice president and general manager of WGNX in Atlanta, echoed many of his contemporaries when he said, "I wanted to make sure I had both so that if there's any confusion, it wouldn't matter."[69]

On top of syndication deals, *The Real Ghostbusters* had a network contract. ABC ordered thirteen episodes to be created for their Saturday morning lineup and set a premiere of September 13, 1986—mere days after Filmation's *Ghostbusters* was set to start airing. Columbia Television Distribution president Joseph D. Indelli was mostly diplomatic when discussing the competing programs. "If the kids don't like the other 'Ghostbusters,' they have a place to turn to. We hope both of them will work . . . [but] we have a stronger show."[70] *Real Ghostbusters* marketing was not as polite.

Print ads screamed: "When you want the REAL one, who ya gonna call?"[71] There was a major caveat to this authenticity: Dan Aykroyd, Bill Murray, and Harold Ramis all kept their distance from *The Real Ghostbusters*, refusing to allow their likenesses to be copied for the cartoon. Thus, the characters were reimagined. Ray Stantz transformed into a redhead, while Peter Venkman was drawn like a classically handsome everyman. Ramis's Egon Spengler was the most radical departure—he was now a platinum blond with a rat tail.[72]

There was a fine line to walk when it came to the voice acting on *The Real Ghostbusters*. "We knew we didn't want them to sound like the guys," said voice casting director Marsha Goodman, "but they had to have the same attitude and the same kind of personalities. They couldn't do impersonations of Murray and Aykroyd but they had to have certain personality qualities like that."[73] Maurice LaMarche, the actor hired to voice Egon, ignored this directive when he auditioned. "They asked me not to do Harold and I still did it because I didn't know anything else to do with the character," he said. "They decided they could let that slide and Egon was such a specific character they really had to honor Harold Ramis's unique take on that character."[74] Journeyman voice actor Frank Welker was hired to create the earnest sound of Ray Stantz, while drowsy-sounding Garfield star Lorenzo Music became Peter Venkman.[75]

Unlike his *Ghostbusters* costars, Ernie Hudson was happy to try to get involved with *The Real Ghostbusters*. He met with the show's staff to perform a reading for the character he originated in the film, Winston Zeddemore. Hudson was thrown by the director's feedback. "The guy said, 'No, no, no, that's all wrong! When Ernie Hudson did it in the movie . . .' And I'm like, 'Well, wait a minute. I *am* Ernie Hudson.'" *The Real Ghostbusters* never followed up with Hudson, and the actor eventually learned Arsenio Hall was cast. "I was really disappointed because the thought of someone else doing Winston was not something I felt great about," he said. "Arsenio's a friend, so there's no disrespect to him. But they had me come in and read, and even though they said I wasn't auditioning, I dunno, I guess I was just there to have the director get on my nerves."[76] Today, Goodman sheds light on Hudson's loss: "It wasn't a matter of liking Ernie's reading. I felt terrible. He's a wonderful actor. The producers said, 'Use Arsenio. He's funnier, he's sillier.'"[77]

Over at Filmation, Lou Scheimer's urge to sue Columbia for infringing on his copyright with their *Real Ghostbusters* cartoon was doused by corporate parent Westinghouse–Group W, who wanted to avoid any costly and time-consuming litigation. Scheimer faced enough of a battle trying to establish pre-broadcast merchandise. "Licensees are very, very unwilling to make commitments until they see which show is going to work," he told one reporter. "If you're going to put up $25,000 for the license to produce watches, you want to know which ghost to put on that watch. That murders you." Scheimer also found it impossible to sell his *Ghostbusters* series into foreign markets that had no knowledge of his history. "It's pretty hard to explain, especially if the guy you're dealing with can only speak French."[78]

Things got tougher once both programs were airing. *The Real Ghostbusters* made a splash when it debuted and was seen as the better of the two shows, even by those who worked on the rival *Ghostbusters*. "They had better scripts and such evocative talent," says Pat Fraley, who voiced numerous characters for Filmation's series. "It was a more interesting show. [Filmation] just wasn't that unique. [Our show] was good, it was fine, but we didn't expect it to last more than a season. And it didn't."[79]

Filmation had a grind approach to making cartoons that did not leave much room for creativity. Other studios might spend ten weeks crafting one minute of commercial animation; Filmation cranked out fifty to seventy-six half-hour cartoons in the same window. This schedule prompted massive turnover as writers and animators burned out from the workload.[80] J. Michael Straczynski left the company for different reasons. While working as a staff writer on *He-Man and the Masters of the Universe*, he helped cocreate the spin-off series *She-Ra: Princess of Power* and was subsequently vexed when he received zero credit for his world-building. Straczynski had also felt stymied by how often *He-Man*'s episodes were influenced by its corresponding toy line. He found a job at DIC, a company that placed emphasis on art and innovation (and outsourced much of its animation to studios overseas).[81]

Straczynski was thrilled when DIC placed him on *The Real Ghostbusters* as a story editor and writer for both the syndicated and network versions. "I loved the movie enormously," Straczynski said. "[The producers] said, 'We want to do the movie. We don't want to cheapen it. We don't want to bring it down in quality. We want this to be as good as the movie was and as sophisticated in its storytelling.' Which was music to my ears, and I signed on to do that." *The Real Ghostbusters* offered Straczynski liberation, allowing him his first chance to write about mature topics for a cartoon and work obscure references into the dialogue. The joyride was short-lived.[82]

Although the debut thirteen episodes of *The Real Ghostbusters* had been a hit for ABC, the network still insisted on hiring the Q5 consulting group to help broaden the show's appeal. A September 1987 *Los Angeles Times* profile of Q5 highlighted specific changes they implemented to *The Real Ghostbusters*, with great attention paid to the character of secretary Janine Melnitz. In the center of the article was a large "before and after" comparison of Janine showing what Q5 did to strip away her allegedly confrontational elements. "Hair softer, glasses rounder . . . no necklace, no bracelets," reads the handwritten scrawl between the drawings. "Generally less harsh and 'slutty' and her face and expressions are prettier." ABC vice president of children's programming Jennie Trias had no issue with this "warmer" version of Janine, who would have a more motherly presence on the show. Straczynski was outraged. "Janine was one of our most popular characters," he wrote decades later in his memoir. "Strong, smart, hip, witty, and independent . . . [Q5's assessment] said more about how they viewed strong women than it did about Janine."

Q5 had plenty of other notes for *The Real Ghostbusters*. They wanted to rub out all the arcane references and urbane humor that was probably lost on young viewers. The consultants also felt the show needed more child surrogate characters. They suggested re-centering the series around Slimer, the globular green ghost from the movie previously known as Onionhead who was now a friend to the Ghostbusters, and adding a group of preteen Junior Ghostbusters. The writers could only laugh when Q5 said the Ray Stantz character should be removed entirely because he didn't "benefit the program." Straczynski's final straw arrived when it was revealed that Q5 wanted Winston Zeddemore, the only Black character on *The Real Ghostbusters*, to be demoted to the role of chauffeur for the other heroes.

"I said, 'You're out of your mind. I will not do that, and if you and try and push that through, I will leave' . . . and I went." Straczynski concluded that Q5 was an "evil" and "insidious" organization and said as much to the press. "Their research and theories are strictly from voodoo. . . . I think they reinforce stereotypes. . . . They are not helping television, they are diminishing it." The network version of *The Real Ghostbusters* adopted the majority of Q5's notes, eventually rebranding as *Slimer! and the Real Ghostbusters*. Meanwhile, the sixty-five episodes of *The Real Ghostbusters* DIC created for syndication aired as originally conceived.[83]

This behind-the-scenes warring remained entirely unknown to the legions of children who were captivated by both versions of

The Real Ghostbusters and whose religious devotion kept ratings high.[84] The hottest gifts for Christmas 1987 were any of the Kenner brand toys adapted from the cartoon. Demand for handheld ghost zappers and bright blue proton packs outpaced supply to such a degree that Kenner senior vice president Peter J. Kelly guessed an extra $20 million could have been sold had they been able to produce it. The company was besieged by thousands of phone calls every day from customers desperate for tips on where to find *Real Ghostbusters* merchandise. Occasionally they'd show up outside Kenner's headquarters in Cincinnati, Ohio, flying from different parts of the country, hoping they could pay several times the retail price for whatever was available on-site.[85]

Two seasons into *The Real Ghostbusters*, Dave Coulier was hired to replace Lorenzo Music as the voice of Peter Venkman. Maurice LaMarche gave his understanding of the recasting in 2006: "Legend has it Bill Murray finally came forward and said, 'How come Harold's guy sounds just like him and my guy sounds like Garfield?' And they say, 'Well, Bill, that's because the guy who does the voice of Garfield is doing your character.' Now, Bill's not asking [Lorenzo] to be fired or anything. But this one comment from Bill Murray . . . somebody in the machine said, 'You know what? Bill's unhappy. We got to get a guy who sounds like him.'"[86]

Coulier's understanding was that Murray had nothing to do with Music's dismissal, that it was an independent decision reached by the producers of *The Real Ghostbusters*. Marsha Goodman says otherwise. "Yeah, it was Bill," she asserts with a laugh.[87]

Shortly before David Puttnam started as head of Columbia Pictures on September 1, 1986, the energetic and self-assured Englishman met with executives at Columbia's parent company, Coca-Cola, to feel them out. Puttnam wanted everyone within the corporate structure to understand that cinema had touched his life and he was not at all passive about the state of the North American film industry. He literally spelled it out in copies of a "manifesto" he handed to each Coca-Cola figurehead. "The medium is too powerful," Puttnam's statement read, "and too important an influencer on the way we live, [and] the way we see ourselves, to be left *solely* to the tyranny of the box office or reduced to the sum of the lowest common denominator of public taste; this 'public taste' or appetite being conditioned by a diet capable only of producing mental and emotional malnutrition!" The specific example Puttnam cited was *Rambo* as the type of movie he'd never make "no matter what the size of the built-in profit guarantee." The Coca-Cola executives were visibly stunned by the presentation but they didn't disagree. In fact, a few were emotionally affected by this newcomer's passionate rhetoric.[88]

A calmer Puttnam spoke with *Screen International* a month into his tenure and explained his plan to reinvent Columbia as a venue of greater maturity. He wasn't interested in chasing the teenage demographic considered so essential to the industry at large. "Perhaps that means a different way of making money," he conceded. "Maybe making less money from more moderate films, not necessarily needing or expecting the through-the-roof blockbusters." The interviewer countered: "But you wouldn't turn your back on a blockbuster?" Puttnam gave an analytical, noncommittal response. "I have inherited a very healthy situation because in the inventory of Columbia there exists the opportunity to make a sequel to *Ghostbusters*, and there exists the opportunity to make [*The Karate Kid III*]. Now these are wonderful opportunities. It would be economically foolish not to very carefully look at that potential."

Puttnam wasn't really concerned about the economics of his job, of course. He admitted as much in the same interview when he declared that it didn't matter if he made "a mess" of Columbia since the studio wasn't Coca-Cola's primary source of revenue. Far more important was Puttnam's belief that "the person who runs the company embodies the soul of the company."[89]

Franchise filmmaking wasn't in David Puttnam's soul. He certainly wasn't enthusiastic about signing off on *Ghostbusters II*. As it happened, the principal talent behind *Ghostbusters* had their own qualms. The original *Ghostbusters* represented a creative and financial pinnacle. Could lightning strike twice in a medium where diminishing returns were the rule, not the exception? To that end, there was a round of talks between Dan Aykroyd, Bill Murray, Harold Ramis, and Ivan Reitman about setting aside *Ghostbusters II* and reuniting for an entirely different concept that would have centered on "space cadets."[90] Specifics regarding this alternative project have never been confirmed; maybe it's no coincidence that between 1984 and 1987 Murray was attached to a scripting of Kurt Vonnegut's galactic comedy *The Sirens of Titan* that was being written by Tom Davis and Grateful Dead guitarist Jerry Garcia.[91] Davis worked on another cosmic project with Aykroyd around the same time, a television pilot called *Mars: Base One* about an Earth family living on the Red Planet.[92]

Nevertheless, it was hard to ignore the public's appetite for *Ghostbusters II*, and there could be artistic opportunity in a sequel. Ramis spoke words to that effect while promoting *Club Paradise*, emphasizing that he and his friends didn't feel much pressure regarding the whole endeavor.[93] The more pragmatic executives working at Columbia were in a different frame of mind—they needed *Ghostbusters II* to make up for the fiscal barrens of 1985 and as insurance against Puttnam's gamble on the highbrow.

Puttnam thought about it. Adding the actors' salaries to the proposed special effects budget gave *Ghostbusters II* a price tag he found offensive. Puttnam also took issue with the fact that all the marquee players were represented by the same talent agency, CAA. The practice of packaging, or filling out a movie with clients from one agency so that agency could reap maximum profit, was an industry-wide abhorrence Puttnam wished to end (thanks to packaging, CAA made a bundle on *Legal Eagles* even though the movie tanked). Replacing Aykroyd, Murray, Ramis, and Reitman with incipient comedy figures would fix these problems. After all, Columbia owned *Ghostbusters* and its characters. Puttnam suggested he'd be willing to bankroll five sequels under such a plan.[94] With that in mind, he had no reason to ingratiate himself with the stars of *Ghostbusters*. And he didn't.

One project that started moving forward at Columbia simultaneous to Puttnam's hiring was *Vibes*, a comedy about psychics starring pop singer Cyndi Lauper. Surprisingly, Puttnam loved both the script and Lauper and was convinced Dan Aykroyd had to take the costarring role. Aykroyd wasn't interested; the inexperience of both Lauper and director Ken Kwapis bothered him too much. A determined Puttnam refused to accept defeat. In January 1987, he sent Aykroyd a lengthy missive defending *Vibes*. "Of the dozen or so scripts that I read before I joined the company *Vibes* represented one of the two or three home runs. . . . Is [Cyndi] right for the film? Off the page the answer for me is unquestionably 'yes.' Can she act? Again the answer is also a conclusive yes. . . . The only video test I've ever seen which similarly excited me was the one for Haing Ngor when we were seeking a lead for *The Killing Fields*."

Aykroyd didn't respond to Puttnam's letter, but it left him outraged. The comedian felt "maligned" by the pushing of the issue. "[Puttnam] tried to get me to do a horrible film," Aykroyd said. "He actually tried to exert pressure on me to do a movie that I knew was bad."[95] Jeff Goldblum took the male lead in *Vibes*; the film was DOA upon release the following year.[96]

Puttnam ignited a messier, more public feud a month after the Aykroyd letter while speaking at a British-American Chamber of Commerce luncheon. Following a round of praise for Robert Redford's philanthropy, Puttnam leveled some harsh criticism against Bill Murray. "Bill Murray exemplifies an actor who makes millions off movies but gives nothing back to his art. He's a taker." The quote exploded in the press. Murray was livid: "What the hell's it got to do with him how I spend my money?"[97] Later the actor told *The Times* of London, "I think it was hysterical that David Puttnam singled me out as an example of an old Hollywood robber baron or something. . . . I don't do lousy movies and I don't do material I don't believe in, and that to me is giving something back to Hollywood."[98]

Puttnam denied making the remarks and asked numerous lawyers who were present at the luncheon to testify on his behalf. One lawyer told the *Los Angeles Times* that Puttnam's words were not "fabricated" but "misconstrued." Nigel Sinclair, the luncheon's host, said the reported commentary was "absolute balderdash." Another lawyer explained to *Variety* that Puttnam was answering a question about the high pay of actors and actually said, "You don't see people, for example Bill Murray, putting back any dollars from *Ghostbusters*."

Murray eventually heard from Puttnam, who told him in a letter that he had been misquoted. Murray replied through an intermediary and said he had never truly believed the comments had been made. Regardless, it was a headache of an affair, and in the heat of it all Murray allegedly told CAA's Mike Ovitz that he would never appear in *Ghostbusters II*. This was dismal news for Ovitz, who had been working hard to finesse Murray into joining his more eager comrades for one more round of spook chasing.[99] Ovitz has said that in the wake of the luncheon comments there was a mutual decision among the *Ghostbusters* creatives to halt work on a sequel until Puttnam was out at Columbia. At the same time, a legally binding tontine was drawn up by Ovitz and lawyer Ray Kurtzman that stated Columbia could not make another *Ghostbusters* without the consent of Aykroyd, Murray, Ramis, and Reitman.[100]

There's no doubt that experiences both past and present influenced the filmmakers' decision to draft this accord. A few years earlier, Reitman let go of the sequel rights to his summer camp comedy *Meatballs* only to watch Tri-Star Pictures slap the name *Meatballs II* on a completely unrelated *E.T.* rip-off.[101] As difficulties with Puttnam were compounding, Ramis was being forced to confront *Caddyshack II*; he'd agreed to cowrite the script only after it became clear there was nothing he could do to stop Warner Bros. from putting the sequel into motion ("The classic argument came up," Ramis noted, "which says that if you don't do it, someone will, and it will be really bad").[102] Shoring up the rights to *Ghostbusters* as something the actors and director had to sign off on would protect the brand from similar cheapening. Columbia was desperate enough for *Ghostbusters II* that they agreed to this arrangement, killing Puttnam's dream of a cost-efficient franchise dotted with unproven talent.

The *Ghostbusters* humorists were far from alone on the list of filmmakers Puttnam alienated or angered while running Columbia. Norman Jewison severed ties with the studio after Puttnam kept the director at arm's length regarding the development of future projects (one of those projects became MGM's Oscar-winning *Moonstruck*). *Roxanne*'s Daniel Melnick turned sour after Puttnam reneged on a contract renewal and blamed the decision on a subordinate.[103] It didn't take much to upset veteran producer Ray Stark, who counted *Funny Girl* and *Annie* among his entries for Columbia, and Puttnam's blunt script rejections left Stark apoplectic ("Fuck you," he snarled over one breakfast meeting, "[you] think I need you?").[104] Puttnam was no schmoozer and he also admitted to struggling with the favor-based nature of Hollywood. "It's absolutely the opposite of the British ethos," he said. "If you do me a favor, I will go out of my way not ever to be seen doing you a favor back. If I do, you have to assume that what you did for me was something other than a favor—it's become a deal."[105]

Concern grew that Puttnam was burning too many bridges.[106] The production slate he curated for 1987 brought Columbia a number of intriguing boutique titles, including Spike Lee's Black collegiate comedy *School Daze* and an adaptation of the award-winning novel *Housekeeping*, but only a commercial smash could excuse Puttnam's foibles.[107] No such hit came. Instead, David Puttnam presided over two of the biggest embarrassments in Hollywood history.

To be fair, Elaine May's geopolitical comedy *Ishtar* was already causing financial headaches for the studio when Puttnam took over; unfortunately, his arrival only complicated the matter. *Ishtar* producer and star Warren Beatty hated Puttnam for knocking his directing skills in the press years earlier. Beatty's costar Dustin Hoffman wasn't a fan either, having fought viciously with Puttnam while making 1979's *Agatha*. The actors were furious over his hiring.

Would Puttnam cancel *Ishtar* out of spite?[108] Puttnam didn't try to kill the movie, but he also didn't bother trying to make amends with its stars or combat the negative publicity weighing down the title prior to release. Instead, Puttnam ignored *Ishtar*—he never even watched the completed film.[109] *Ishtar* didn't come close to recouping even half of its $51 million budget in theaters that May, and only the faintest of critical praise was doled out. Beatty cited Puttnam's lack of support as one big reason this quirky comedy turned into a punch line.[110]

Ishtar was nothing compared to the catastrophe of *Leonard Part 6*, a James Bond spoof that struck Puttnam as a license to print money when it was pitched to him by television star Bill Cosby. Columbia granted Cosby a wide berth that included authority over everything from music to costumes. Script concerns were assuaged by Coca-Cola's agreement to underwrite *Leonard Part 6* as well as a general assumption that Cosby could spin gold from straw. British director Paul Weiland was hired because Cosby had expressed interest in altering his comedic sensibilities but Weiland found Cosby insulated, combative, and unwilling to break from proven formulas.[111] The toxic fumes rising from *Leonard Part 6* couldn't be ignored. Columbia thought they were spending $40 million on a sure thing for Christmas 1987, the first in a lineage of hits Cosby promised to deliver. What they received was a movie so stupid and indulgent, its star ended up on CNN begging people to not see it: "I don't want [people] to go see this movie thinking that I'm saying to them this is a great picture or that this is even a good picture."[112]

Leonard Part 6 took in a heart-stopping pittance of $1.3 million during its opening weekend. The film landed in tenth place, trumped by several movies that had been in release for an entire month.[113] Puttnam weathered this indignity at home, ostensibly. He had resigned from Columbia months earlier, in September, likening the studio to Poland as he exited. "An awful lot of people over the years have felt they've owned it," he remarked, "and it continually gets knocked backward and forward and sideways by continuous invading forces."[114]

A nightmare meeting with Coca-Cola's executive board shortly after the release of *Ishtar* all but promised Puttnam would depart long before his three years was up. When executives broached the subject of Puttnam's control issues and the damage he was doing to assets like *Ghostbusters II*, Puttnam lost it. He angrily ranted that the problem with Hollywood was fear, and that everyone at Columbia lived in fear of Coca-Cola CEO Roberto Goizueta. Then he turned to Coca-Cola president Don Keough. "I would become less of a man if I looked at myself in the mirror every morning and wondered whether Don Keough still likes me," Puttnam sneered. Goizueta exploded in response.[115]

Naturally, there is debate as to whether Puttnam resigned of his own volition or if he was forced out, but it doesn't matter. The Englishman couldn't bend Hollywood to his altruistic will. The establishment was too powerful and Puttnam too stubborn. And yet, his regime had its success stories, though they were all critical and after the fact. Roger Ebert bestowed four stars on the version of *Housekeeping* that Puttnam put together and admitted the movie left him "quietly astonished."[116] Others scoffed when Columbia picked up the Serbo-Croatian-language *Dom za vešanje* (*Time of the Gypsies*), but the movie earned its helmsman Emir Kusturica Best Director at Cannes as well as a five-minute standing ovation after it screened.[117] Most notably, Puttnam bought US distribution rights to *The Last Emperor*, a British biopic of Chinese leader Puyi, after seeing only forty minutes of footage. *The Last Emperor* went on to sweep the Academy Awards with an incredible nine wins, including Best Picture.[118]

Puttnam was replaced by Paramount Pictures veteran Dawn Steel, whose hiring at Columbia marked the first instance of a woman presiding over a movie studio. Steel wrote in her memoir that, despite his eccentricities, much of Puttnam's troubles at Columbia could be attributed to "the usual Hollywood backbiting and stabbing." That said, the difference between Steel and Puttnam was night and day. And she knew how her time at Columbia had to start.

"The first thing we had to do was to put *Ghostbusters II* back together."[119]

According to Ivan Reitman, David Puttnam wasn't the one to blame for a *Ghostbusters* sequel delay. In fact, there was a point during Puttnam's tenure when Columbia executives in New York circumnavigated their chairman and tried to establish a secret deal for *Ghostbusters II*. They suggested Reitman tie the film to an independent corporate entity created specifically for the sequel, thereby shielding it entirely from Puttnam. This plan never came to fruition because Dan Aykroyd, Bill Murray, and the other figureheads couldn't line up their schedules.[120]

Scheduling remained an issue once Puttnam was gone and *Ghostbusters II* got on track in November 1987. Aykroyd was already booked through the middle of 1988, committed to productions like the John Hughes comedy *Big Country* (later retitled *The Great Outdoors*), the celestial romance *My Stepmother Is an Alien*, *Caddyshack II*, and a cop comedy with Gene Hackman.[121] Reitman's projects included *Rain Man* and the drama *Random Hearts*, though he wound up abandoning those movies so he could focus on something he was developing for Danny DeVito and Arnold Schwarzenegger, both of whom expressed an interest in working with Reitman during separate chance encounters.[122]

Bill Murray started filming *Scrooged* that December under the direction of *Superman*'s Richard Donner.[123] Murray and Donner didn't get off on the best foot. They met when Murray paid an unscheduled visit to Donner's home late one evening before Donner had agreed to make the movie. Murray was on a mission of persuasion but his target was annoyed—it was almost midnight, and Donner considered his time after 10 o'clock to be off-limits. Tensions subsided and a warm conversation was enjoyed that resulted in Donner's commitment.[124]

The warmth froze up once shooting commenced. Donner favored a voluminous style of comedy directly at odds with Murray's quiet deadpan.[125] When asked in 1990 if he and Donner experienced any disagreements, Murray joked, "Only a few. Every single minute of the day."[126] Arguments extended to *Scrooged*'s TV commercial and programming parodies, which were meant to spoof the increasingly graphic nature of the medium. One clip Murray fought for included "a kid committing suicide, another kid shooting up, and AIDS patients in a hospital scene." "[It's] really rough," the actor said, "but not much rougher than today's horror movies or even the nightly news." These scenes were ultimately altered to appear less graphic.[127]

Also gnawing at Murray was an anxiety over how to play the heartfelt concluding sequences of *Scrooged*, something that bothered him right up to the second cameras rolled. He decided to improvise a new ending on the spot. Writers Mitch Glazer and Michael O'Donoghue were both on set that day, and they couldn't believe the manic performance unfolding before their eyes. They thought Murray's impromptu sing-along was disturbed.[128] Murray tried to explain the ending he winged: "I hate sentimentality. I prefer sincerity. It's also the hardest thing in the world to achieve one without the other. Also, the problem with today's audience is that there's so much cynicism stored up. But when the real spirit of Christmas grabs you, that's really great."[129]

Elsewhere, Murray admitted that being away from work for so long had left him feeling rusty. "It took me weeks [on *Scrooged*] to get back into it. I wasn't really sharp at all," he said. "Usually, just before lunch there's a big shot, and they like to get it. For two or three weeks, I blew the take just before lunch and they said, 'That's okay, Bill, go eat, maybe that will help.' I wasn't amusing anybody for weeks."[130]

At least Murray was being well compensated for his troubles. *Scrooged* paid him $6 million, a hefty sum for a comedian but still a few million shy of the echelon enjoyed by the likes of Jack Nicholson or Arnold Schwarzenegger. As plans for *Ghostbusters II* solidified, gossip columns barked that Murray would take nothing less than an eight-figure paycheck to thrust him into a more rarified class.[131] Rumors also flew about profit sharing. It was said that Aykroyd and Ramis resented Murray for snatching such a huge portion of the gross on the first *Ghostbusters* when he had so little script input. They wanted their colleague to scale back his percentages. Murray, allegedly, wanted an even bigger cut for *Ghostbusters II*. When asked about all this, Ramis would only say, "There was a little air to clear before we got going [on the sequel]."[132]

Murray may have been intentionally pricing himself out of *Ghostbusters II* to avoid confrontation. He claimed the monetary benefits of screen acting never motivated him anyway. "It would queer everything to make a movie just for money," he said. "We make 'em for fun. . . . If I worked with Dan or Harold [for the money] we'd all look at each other like, *Yes, we did kill that little boy and bury him in the woods. . . .* We'd have our little dark secret."[133] It was only the comedic potential of *Ghostbusters II* that convinced him at last to make the sequel. "I kept saying no to it. But finally they told me a scene that was such a killer. There were five of the biggest, hardest laughs in it that you'd have to batten down the hatches for them."[134] This scene discussion may have occurred during the four-hour lunch Mike Ovitz set up between the three stars of *Ghostbusters* and their director in December 1987 at Beverly Hills eatery Jimmy's. Murray was certain at the start of the meal that *Ghostbusters II* would never be made. Then, as he put it, "We had so many laughs and so much fun that it became clear we'd really enjoy working together again."

The spirit was rekindled, but no one was working for free. It took a year to finalize the talent's compensation for *Ghostbusters II*, and there are conflicting reports as to how everything shook out.[135] The prevailing story at the time was that the key players all gave up their million-dollar advances to spare the film's budget, agreeing to cull their earnings from *Ghostbusters II*'s gross profits. Some outlets reported that Murray earmarked 15 percent of those future monies, seizing the biggest slice away from Reitman (10 percent), Aykroyd (8 percent), and Ramis (5 percent). Other write-ups suggested that each of the four negotiated a 15 percent profit take, suggesting their sum was greater to Columbia than the individual parts.[136] Ovitz revealed no specifics when discussing *Ghostbusters II* profit sharing in his memoir, but he did state the collective take among stars and director was similar to the first movie in that it didn't exceed 30 percent. Ovitz also revealed that no one actually eschewed their "big up-front fees."[137]

Ancillary monies would come in from *Ghostbusters II* merchandising. Documents leaked in 2014 showed that the lead actors were by this point all being cut into revenue generated by officially licensed products. These percentages worked on a sliding scale, though Murray's 44 percent stake would actually go down as the other participants' numbers slightly increased. Aykroyd and Reitman started at 20 percent each, while Ramis had 15 percent. After sales broke $56 million, those three men would have 22.5 percent of merchandise sales against Murray's 32.5 percent.[138]

Reitman acknowledged the financials before shooting. "If the movie's a success, we make a lot. If it's not, well, we don't deserve to profit."[139]

SOMEWHERE IN BETWEEN

Dan Aykroyd completed the first *Ghostbusters II* script by himself in September 1986. In keeping with his style, the story was rife with bizarre imagery and outlandish concepts. "It opened in Scotland," Harold Ramis explained, "with Sigourney [Weaver's character Dana Barrett] touring with an all-girl orchestra. They were all sucked into the ground through a Druid fairy ring." Subtitled *The Seed*, this version of *Ghostbusters II* also contained a sequence in which the Ghostbusters become trapped in a two-thousand-mile-long tube for three days. Aykroyd's premise was not met with enthusiasm. "No one really got behind it," said Ramis. "So, we sat down together and came up with the new idea."[1]

Violent crime was on the rise in cities across the United States in the late 1980s. There were concrete explanations—economic inequality, drug epidemics[2]—but what if the real cause was simply bad vibes? Aykroyd and Ramis theorized that anger and negativity might build up over time among humans and lead to dire consequences in densely populated areas. Applying this to *Ghostbusters II*, the writers imagined New Yorkers generating so much misery that it all sinks into a giant paranormal cauldron beneath the city. One of the many ghosts this conduit attracts is the spirit of an evil monk named Vigo the Carpathian. Vigo is looking to possess a baby so that he may be reborn to rule the Earth on the heels of our society's collapse. In their attempts to thwart Vigo and lower the negative energy pulsating under New York, the Ghostbusters implore denizens of the boroughs to dial back their attitude and actively employ positivity.

Ramis spent some time scripting this iteration of *Ghostbusters II* by himself in early 1987 while Aykroyd filmed his version of Ken Kolb's satirical 1970 novel *The Couch Trip*. Then the pair hunkered down in Aykroyd's bungalow on the Universal Studios lot for rewrites.[3] Initially they believed the infant targeted by Vigo should be the son of Dana Barrett and Bill Murray's Peter Venkman. Murray liked this angle; the opportunity to work again with Sigourney Weaver made *Ghostbusters II* especially attractive to him.[4] Giving Venkman a family created a few problems, however. It tore him away from the other Ghostbusters, and it also neutered the comic possibilities. Furthermore, was having Dana as the primary victim too similar to the first movie? And would loyal viewers of *The Real Ghostbusters* cartoon be confused to see Dana in *Ghostbusters II* since she was never on the show?

By August 1988, Dana Barrett had been dropped entirely from *Ghostbusters II*. A disappointed-sounding Weaver cited some of the aforementioned creative problems when explaining to the press shortly thereafter why she'd be absent from the sequel.[5] There was a larger, thornier issue at play for the actress, though, one that made it slightly easier to leave *Ghostbusters II*: Columbia Pictures was withholding a large chunk of her earnings from the first *Ghostbusters*.

Weaver had been contracted to receive 2.5 percent of net profits from *Ghostbusters* in addition to her up-front salary. Net profits are the monies left over from a film's gross profits once every other expense is paid. These expenses include production, marketing, distribution, and whatever gross profit percentages have been earmarked by other talent. (Aykroyd, Murray, Ramis, and Reitman each took their own slice of the *Ghostbusters* gross.) When Weaver attempted to collect her percentage, she was told that *Ghostbusters*, the highest-grossing comedy in movie history, had zero net profit. This was especially surprising as the film's negative cost (i.e., its basic cost) was in theory completely paid for by a handful of ancillary deals Columbia Pictures made several years prior. "Actually, I got a little bit," Weaver revealed to *Newsday* that September, "but then I got a letter saying I have to send it back because they forgot to deduct such and such. I can't believe it. I'm thinking of maybe having them audited."[6]

Accounting mysteries like this were nothing new in Hollywood and they could befall anyone, regardless of stature. Sean Connery launched several lawsuits over missing profits throughout his career, the most famous of which was the $225 million case he brought against MGM/UA for nonpayment on five James Bond films.[7] Marlon Brando, Richard Donner, and Mario Puzo all went after the producers of 1978's *Superman* in search of their compensation (Brando was so certain he'd have to fight for the 11.3 percent gross cut he was promised, he filed his lawsuit on the day the movie was released in the United States).[8] Sigourney Weaver followed through with her audit request for Columbia Pictures; she also threatened a lawsuit.[9]

Meanwhile, Aykroyd and Ramis simply created a new set of parents for *Ghostbusters II*. The August 5 draft presents unassuming mother Lane Walker and her estranged partner, the mysterious Jason Locke. When Lane notices bizarre phenomena occurring around her child, she seeks help from cable access talk show host Peter Venkman.[10] The Ghostbusters are no longer operating at the start of this story. They've been bankrupted and legally curbed from paranormal investigation after losing numerous lawsuits related to their activities five years earlier (Aykroyd and Ramis considered presenting the Ghostbusters as so popular and successful at the start of *Ghostbusters II* that they had their own line of souvenirs sold directly from their headquarters, which was a cute idea but not narratively fertile).[11] New career paths for our heroes have dawned: Venkman has his talk show, *World of the Psychic*, while Egon Spengler is a college professor. Ray Stantz owns an occult-themed book store and makes personal appearances in his old Ghostbusting gear alongside Winston Zeddemore.[12]

Jason Locke is eventually proven to be the human avatar of Jalmar Litvinov, aka Vigo the Carpathian, a genocidal Russian abbot who immigrated to the United States in 1917 with a powerful triptych that houses his spirit.[13] Since Vigo and the other ghouls haunting New York draw their power from an accumulation of negative human energy resting under the city, the Ghostbusters make a televised appeal to the citizens of New York: be nicer to one another (a computer program determines that the 1970 Ray Stevens song "Everything Is Beautiful" is the perfect composition to help calm everyone down).[14] This plot allowed for colorful illustration based around two of New York City's most cantankerous figures. A stand-in for icy hotel queen Leona Helmsley named Leona Wellesley ignores growing tensions in her household and is met with a swarm of cockroaches. Billy Martin, the unpredictable manager of the New York Yankees, had a cameo written for him in which he fights with an umpire as cheerfully as possible.[15]

A handful of supporting characters from the original *Ghostbusters* were scripted to return for the sequel. Louis Tully transitions from accountant to lawyer when the Ghostbusters need legal representation following an indictment for reopening their business. Tully is promoted to fifth Ghostbuster toward the end of the story and helps lure Jason to Ellis Island for a final confrontation by appearing in drag as Lane. He also enjoys "a long and passionate kiss" with Janine Melnitz, who has returned as the Ghostbusters' feisty secretary.[16] During the courtroom scenes, Walter Peck is called to testify for the prosecution and repeats his claims that the Ghostbusters actually engineer the hauntings they police.[17] This edition of *Ghostbusters II* ends with Jason possessing the Statue of Liberty and fighting the Ghostbusters near Battery Park. Jason is excised from the statue, leaving the monument "sprawled across Wall Street with her toga up over her knees." "And we just had it restored," the crestfallen mayor remarks.[18]

The writers felt *Ghostbusters II* had to end with some sort of massive entity as a complement to the earlier film's Stay Puft Marshmallow Man. Ramis described this discussion as "the only really crass conversation we had about the script." They also had to consider Slimer, the gluttonous green blob who became the Ghostbusters' pet on *The Real Ghostbusters* cartoon. There was disagreement among the creatives about whether or not Slimer had any part to play in *Ghostbusters II*. And yet it was difficult to ignore the character's growing popularity.[19] While Aykroyd and Ramis were swimming through sequel rewrites, the staff of *The Real Ghostbusters* were preparing to relaunch their show as *Slimer! and the Real Ghostbusters*, now doubled in length to accommodate Slimer-specific stories. Though Slimer is absent from the August 5 rewrite of *Ghostbusters II*, he is featured in the September 29 revision. In one scene, Slimer plays the hero when he alerts Lane and Venkman to the fact that Lane's baby has somehow wandered onto the ledge of Venkman's high-rise apartment.[20]

Also added into that September draft was a cameo for Dana Barrett. Venkman bumps into Dana while taking Lane out for a New Year's Eve dinner. It turns out Dana and Lane know each other from school years before. The awkward moment for Venkman is compounded when Dana's partner for the evening is revealed to be pop music superstar Sting.[21] It's unknown if this brief moment for Dana was a sign of detente between Sigourney Weaver and Columbia Pictures. Perhaps the writers were trying to let Weaver know that despite the business problems they still cared about her. At any rate, there were reports that Weaver was "delighted" with this cute little scene and that same month she told the *Daily News of Los Angeles* she "might be involved" with *Ghostbusters II*.[22] A month later, the story was different—Dana Barrett is completely absent from an October 29 revision.[23]

By this point, the October 31 start date for filming of *Ghostbusters II* had been pushed back roughly one month. Ivan Reitman didn't want to get behind the cameras again until he'd finished post-production on his separated-at-birth farce *Twins*.[24] *Twins*, due for release that Christmas, was one of 1988's most anticipated movies thanks to its gimmicky pairing of Danny DeVito and Arnold Schwarzenegger as the titular brothers.[25] Reitman believed Schwarzenegger could shed his steely action hero persona and succeed in comedy, describing the muscular star as a "really intelligent guy with a sweetness to him, a kind of goofy, naive quality."[26]

Bill Murray's much-ballyhooed "comeback" movie *Scrooged* was released that November to healthy business and mixed reviews. The *Boston Globe* applauded the film for having an "emotional center" and rhapsodized about Murray's "pale blue eyes . . . the eyes of a troubled searcher, even when he's dispensing one of his hip, loosy-goosy [*sic*] comic routines."[27] Roger Ebert found *Scrooged* "unsettling" and gave it one star: "The movie's overriding emotions seem to be pain and anger."[28] Murray appeared to agree. When a reporter that month asked him if he liked the finished film, the star replied, "[That's] like asking Reagan if he's happy with the results of Hinckley's assassination attempt."[29]

Murray fielded plenty of questions about *Ghostbusters II* while promoting *Scrooged*. Principal photography on the sequel was to begin Monday, November 28; in conversations held just days prior, Murray insisted he didn't know who had been cast as the movie's female lead. "I had to audition with some actresses," he told *Starlog*, "but we all like Sigourney." Well, what *about* Sigourney? Murray, per a *Houston Chronicle* interview printed November 27, said, "[Sigourney Weaver's role] is still a question mark." Then he added a cryptic tag: "I understand she's considering being paid very well for this one."[30]

In truth, Sigourney Weaver had inked a costarring role in *Ghostbusters II* the previous week.[31] Her profit dispute with Columbia Pictures had been settled—the studio, eager to avoid a high-profile legal spat, scrounged up the money to pay Weaver what she was owed from the original *Ghostbusters*. The actress then asked if Dana Barrett could be reinstated as the baby's mother in *Ghostbusters II*. The filmmakers said yes, paying her $1 million up front for the privilege.[32]

Of course, Weaver deserved far more. As Ivan Reitman's wife Geneviève once bluntly put it, "The female roles [in Ivan's movies] have been so stupid. He was not interested in etching a female character. What was good about Sigourney [in *Ghostbusters*] was Sigourney, not the character. She cannot be stupid. She takes this nothing character and gives it dignity and intelligence."[33] At the time of her *Ghostbusters II* signing, Weaver was the subject of serious Oscar buzz thanks to her recent starring role in the Dian Fossey biopic *Gorillas in the Mist*. Fossey was a preservationist who lived a complex, controversial life; critical consensus held that Weaver's work in *Gorillas* was nothing short of astounding.[34]

The story in *Ghostbusters II* was still lacking clarity when Weaver came aboard. At the behest of Murray, the writers booked time with innovative comedy scribe Elaine May. May did uncredited work on 1982's *Tootsie* that included creating the oddball character Murray plays; more recently, Murray had been impressed when May took just one night to entirely rescript and improve *Scrooged*. "She really has a major coconut on the top of her head," raved Murray. "When you've been writing a script for a year and someone comes in and says, 'Why don't you do this?' and it's something as simple as changing the way the door opens, you sort of go, 'Oh, yeah, right.'"[35]

May read what Aykroyd and Ramis had for *Ghostbusters II* and spent six hours picking their brains. "[She was] just asking questions," Ramis explained. "'If the guy can do this why can't he do that?' or 'What does the photograph have to do with the painting?' It made it all clear, at least in our own minds."[36] Murray may have had script concerns, but he also wasn't losing sleep over it. He knew history was on their side. "*Caddyshack* was all made up after we started," he reminded one newspaper that month. "I signed for *Meatballs* eight days before it started and that was the same with the writing."[37]

Instead of reverting back to the marriage storyline for Dana Barrett and Peter Venkman, the filmmakers decided to use Dana in the Lane Walker role. "Bill looks great hitting on women," Weaver said. "One of the funniest things about the original was the manner in which Peter hit on Dana. If they were married, Peter would have to hit on other women, which would risk losing audience sympathy for the character."[38] Dana, Peter, and the other Ghostbusters would be protecting Dana's infant son Mikey from his father Justin Locke, an art historian who becomes possessed by Vigo the Carpathian after working with a painting of the centuries-old madman.[39] For Justin, the filmmakers talked about trying to get Murray's pal Dustin Hoffman. They definitely envisioned the character as dark-haired with foreboding energy. That changed when they saw jittery redhead Peter MacNicol guest starring on *The Days and Nights of Molly Dodd*.

MacNicol's agent had sent an episode of *Molly Dodd* to *Ghostbusters II*'s producers, but only because they also represented a regular from the NBC sitcom who fit the casting notice for Justin. Reitman and associates found themselves drawn to MacNicol in his *Dodd* appearance as a wacky Manhattan jingle writer. MacNicol received a script; he wasn't impressed. Justin had no hook or angle to savor. *Anyone could play this*, he thought. The actor phoned his agent and told them to pass. Moments after hanging up, he reconsidered (in part because he couldn't really afford to turn down work). "I thought, *What can I do with the Carpathia connection? Why does this art restorer know so much about this particular painting? Maybe there's some kind of kinship of country involved there.* This is all in a matter of seconds. . . . I called back the agent and said I'd go in."[40]

Peter MacNicol was a native Texan who chose acting over pale-ontology, getting his start in the late '70s as a repertory player at the Guthrie Theater in Minneapolis. The aptitude was there, but MacNicol's passion for the craft was far from endless. "I only love acting when the situation is perfect, which it so rarely is," he said in 1982. "I'm not one of these people who can just love doing it for the sake of doing it. It takes you into areas of your own experience that can be unpleasant, even awful."[41]

MacNicol found that the repetitious nature of theater left him tense as he obsessed over performances and the fine-tuning of his characters. Still, he worked steadily and found major successes, such as a breakout role in the 1981 Pulitzer-winning *Crimes of the Heart* and a lauded turn as Richard II in Central Park. But there were times when MacNicol's delicate emotions almost prompted him to quit acting entirely. The rigorous demands of starring in the 1981 special effects fantasy *Dragonslayer* throttled his psyche.[42] MacNicol's second movie, *Sophie's Choice*, grew turbulent when costars Meryl Streep and Kevin Kline started bullying him off-camera as part of their method technique. It was ugly and upsetting, though MacNicol admitted the trio later blossomed into "great, great friends."[43]

A lifelong horror fan, MacNicol once looked into vacationing in Transylvania. The authority he met from Romania's tourism board became the basis for his *Ghostbusters II* audition. "When I read for the part, I said, 'Anything goes?' Because I had seen the guys out in the waiting room, they were young John Carradine types," he said. "This thing, this character, came full-blown like Athena out of my skull. Judging from the looks in their eyes, they were thinking, *We can use this guy—we got to use this guy.*" Justin Locke became Janosz Poha, the figure who supervises Dana Barrett in her new restoration job at the art museum. Janosz falls under Vigo's spell, turning into a Renfield-type devotee. MacNicol invented an entire backstory for Janosz that included a flag for the character's never-identified homeland. The flag was emblazoned with the image of "a snake stepping on a man."[44]

Vigo the Carpathian was meant to remain within the confines of the painting that controls Janosz,[45] so the actor playing Vigo had to project malevolence even at a standstill. Orthodox students of boxing were probably not surprised that the man hired for the job was "Prince" Wilhelm von Homburg. Homburg was a hulking blond Berliner whose pugilistic heyday came twenty years earlier. He made headlines on both sides of the Atlantic, not so much for his athleticism but for the arrogant, showboating attitude Homburg borrowed from wrestling (in which he also dabbled). "[Homburg] sneers insolently at reporters and treats others in his own profession with contempt," wrote Sid Ziff in a 1963 *Los Angeles Times* report. "He has only to make an appearance and he is the villain."[46] In 1969 Homburg generated one of Germany's most talked about cultural moments when he refused to answer any of presenter Rainer Günzler's questions during a televised interview. Homburg had lost a bout the night before, and Günzler was intent on making a fool of his subject. The livid pugilist would have no part. A prolonged silence from Homburg was coupled with an icy smile that barely masked his rage.

Born Norbert Grupe in 1940, the foul persona Wilhelm von Homburg cultivated for the boxing canvas was not much different from his true nature. Petulance, cruelty, and menace were his guiding life principles. Homburg spared no one from his abuse, not even his own family members. The most despicable example comes from 1959 when Homburg, then barely an adult, raped his stepmother Ursula while his father Richard was away from home. For years afterward, there was a question as to whether Homburg's half-sister Rona was actually his daughter (a blood test eventually proved Rona's father was Richard). Homburg could never reform, regardless of the highs and lows he experienced over the years. He always squandered his money and mistreated everyone in his orbit. As Rona put it, "None of his friends ever wanted anything to do with him once they got a good dose of him."

When Homburg's boxing career started to fizzle, he transitioned to acting with sporadic results. There were small roles in the late '60s on American TV westerns and in military movies like *The Devil's Brigade* and *The Hell with Heroes*. In 1977, experimental auteur Werner Herzog gave Homburg a role as an imperious pimp in his grim character study *Stroszek*. Herzog, no stranger to the unsettling, admitted Homburg's imposing aura left him "absolutely terrified." *Ghostbusters II* producer Michael C. Gross wasn't afraid of the man hired for Vigo, he was merely disgusted by him. "I can only say he was a crude bigoted asshole," Gross commented years later. Though Homburg was spiritually aligned with the sour Carpathian, his voice did not have the theatrical quality Vigo necessitated. At least that's what Ivan Reitman decided. Like Slavitza Jovan's Gozer in the first *Ghostbusters*, Homburg's lines were dubbed. Max von Sydow, star of *The Seventh Seal* and *The Exorcist*, provided Vigo's frightening bellow.[47]

Fiery EPA rep Walter Peck was cut from *Ghostbusters II* after producers couldn't satisfy the financial demands of Peck actor William Atherton. A new bureaucratic thorn was created in Jack Hardemeyer, an assistant to New York's mayor who openly taunts the Ghostbusters and does everything he can to keep them at arm's length. Actor and Los Angeles real estate agent Kurt Fuller found his way to the part thanks to Harold Ramis's first wife, Anna Plotkin. Fuller spent portions of 1986 and 1987 appearing on stage in a dark comedy called *Kvetch* that Plotkin loved so much she saw it eight times. Ramis caught the show on her recommendation and became a great fan of Fuller's style; he suggested Reitman put the actor somewhere in *Ghostbusters II*. Fuller initially auditioned to play a banker named Ed Petrosius whose irate nature is causing his office to periodically catch fire. The producers were looking for Gilbert Gottfried energy and that's who got the part of Ed Petrosius over Fuller, though the sequence featuring the character was ultimately cut from the movie.

On his first day meeting with the *Ghostbusters II* team, Fuller ran a scene with Bill Murray. He didn't realize this moment was his make-or-break audition. "It was this scene where I confront him," Fuller said, "and if it didn't go well, or if he or someone else didn't like me, I'd be on a plane the next day going back to L.A. . . . Thank God I didn't know, because I would have blown it. I would have been so nervous I would've thrown up on Bill's shoes, I'm sure. But it went okay. Well, they stuck with me, anyway."[48]

"It's amazing how much writing it takes to make a dense comedy."

That was a remark Harold Ramis made in an interview after admitting that he and Dan Aykroyd churned out "10 or 11 drafts" of *Ghostbusters II* in total.[49] The draft they finished the day before principal photography began on November 28, 1988,[50] included most of what crowds would see on-screen the following year. In this edition, the Ghostbusters have disbanded; public opinion has turned against them since Gozer's defeat and a judicial order prevents them from plying their trade.[51] Where else can Dana Barrett turn, though, after the baby carriage holding her infant son Oscar propels itself into traffic one afternoon?[52] The Ghostbusters reunite, but just as they discover a subterranean river of slime seemingly responsible for the carriage incident, they're arrested and put before a judge. Sentencing is interrupted by two maniacal ghosts, whom the Ghostbusters quickly thwart to win back their glory.[53] Soon their attentions turn to a painting of sixteenth-century madman Vigo the Carpathian that has recently arrived at the museum where Dana works. Vigo possesses Dana's boss Janosz and commands him to find a baby. Janosz decides to zero in on Oscar.[54] Realizing that positive emotions can also affect the slime, the Ghostbusters use it to coat the Statue of Liberty—New York's enduring symbol of hope and freedom—bringing the landmark to life for a final showdown against Vigo.[55]

Like its predecessor, *Ghostbusters II* called for a wide number of eye-popping special effects. Richard Edlund's Boss Films effects company expected to be hired for the job since they created all the memorable spirits in the original installment. Everyone at Boss was shocked when Industrial Light & Magic was hired for *Ghostbusters II* instead. "They felt blindsided," says Ned Gorman, ILM's chief visual effects coordinator for *Ghostbusters II*. "They felt the spirit of the first movie was due to their work and also they needed *Ghostbusters II*, financially. But Ivan brought *Ghostbusters II* to ILM, we didn't poach it. Ivan asked us if we wanted to bid on some of the work for the movie, and who wouldn't? There was a feeling at Boss that we were taking bread out of their mouths. . . . but I don't think Ivan was dissatisfied with their work on [*Ghostbusters*]. It's really important to remember that in 1988, worldwide, there were only four or five world premiere effects places and, at that time, we were kind of the world champions. There weren't many places you could get a big show done. And I think there was some sense that Ivan wanted a different feel for the film [from the first *Ghostbusters*]."[56]

ILM had their work cut out for them from the moment they started on *Ghostbusters II* in August 1988. The film was scheduled for release the following July, giving the ILM artists less than a year to complete everything.[57] "The schedule on that show was so tight," Gorman remembers. "At that time, [*Ghostbusters II*] was in the running for having the tightest schedule ever. We were in all phases of production at once. And there were so many changes to the script and so much was amorphous."[58]

As Dan Aykroyd, Harold Ramis, and Ivan Reitman solidified their vision for the sequel, they were open to suggestions from ILM, a rare disposition for established filmmakers to offer an effects house and one that alleviated stress on both sides. One idea from ILM that Reitman in particular loved was art supervisor Harley Jessup's belief that Janosz should fly out of the sky dressed like an undead Mary Poppins when kidnapping Oscar late in the film. This scene replaced a scripted sequence involving a giant two-headed avian creature that Peter Venkman fends off with a baseball bat.[59] The advantage of using a costumed actor over a complicated and time-consuming special effect was obvious. The ghost nanny also beat out a more imaginative concept from storyboard artist Thom Enriquez.

"I couldn't see kids playing with a nanny toy," says Enriquez. "My idea was, what if the baby wakes up because the clock stops ticking and all the toys in the baby's room come to life? The baby's eyes open, he looks left and right, and then a stuffed rabbit and a stuffed bunny come to life. They're animated. Then the baby starts moving towards the window because something's happening outside. The buildings have faces and there's a flying clown, all these happy things. I said to them, 'Think of the possibilities of the toys!' They just said, 'No.'"[60]

Slimer was included in the final draft of *Ghostbusters II*, and history repeated itself in the sense that no one could agree how the ghost should look. "We kinda got mixed messages," Gorman recalls. "They'd say, 'We want him to look like the first movie, but better.' Well, what does that mean?"[61] The filmmakers worked out a design that incorporated aspects of Slimer's child-friendly rendering on *The Real Ghostbusters* cartoon. Though his visage was less menacing, the

Slimer of *Ghostbusters II* went a step beyond the original puppet to include servo motors and pneumatics so the ghoul's facial expressions could be articulated with greater nuance.[62] This iteration of Slimer was also larger; actress Robin Shelby slipped into a full body costume to play the ghost in his various scenes.[63]

"We shot so much more [with Slimer] than was used," said ILM Creature Shop supervisor Tim Lawrence, who cited a sequence where Slimer is revealed to be driving an MTA bus as the puppet's shining moment. Striking a "typical bus driver pose," Slimer greets a disbelieving Louis Tully, whom he waves on board before reminding him to pay his fare. Later, Slimer follows Tully off the bus and has to be dissuaded from joining the battle against Vigo. "Michael Gross said it was the best rubber performance he had seen," Lawrence recalled, "and in the same breath said they couldn't use it. He told me a story about watching dailies in Burbank and after screening some [of our] Slimer shots, Bill Murray's voice droned from the dark: 'It's called *Ghostbusters*, not *Slimer*.'" The bus scene was cut down to a seconds-long Slimer cameo.[64]

One of the most difficult visual tricks demanded from ILM on *Ghostbusters II* was also one that absolutely couldn't be cut—the haunted painting of Vigo the Carpathian. For Michael C. Gross, this effect seemed like an insurmountable task, one that left him rattled as he couldn't conceive how it might be accomplished. After months of labor (and many weeks into shooting), the filmmakers found their solution in Laguna Beach. Since 1933, that city's Festival of the Arts had played host a unique project called the Pageant of the Masters in which famous works of art like *The Last Supper* and *Little Boy Blue* were presented as "living reproductions" with human volunteers.[65] Pageant director Glen Eytchison was a fan of *Ghostbusters* and the pioneering work of ILM, so he was more than happy to get involved.

Eytchison and his team created a look for Vigo and his painting that was accurate to sixteenth-century Carpathia (earlier renderings of the villain were dismissed for their resemblance to Conan the Barbarian). Artist Lou Police painted a full-figured Vigo in oil, standing amid a dreary landscape of ruination and skulls, that Eytchison re-created in the third dimension to photograph with Wilhelm von Homburg. The photograph was then blown up and treated to look like a painting so it could more accurately match live-action shots of Homburg.[66] At one point it was suggested that Vigo should be seen escaping the confines of his painting in some kind of dramatic fashion, but no one could figure out a satisfactory method. "About two or three years later, with digital compositing, we could have done the painting stuff so much better," laments Gorman. "Vigo was actually gonna peel himself off the canvas. But ultimately, Ivan lost confidence in the painting coming to life. He told us, 'Guys, it's not your fault.' So it changed to a magic window." Indeed, in the completed film, Vigo simply fades in and out of the painting with less-than-commanding results.[67]

Additional uncertainty surrounded the movie's voluminous amounts of "mood" slime. Reitman still hadn't chosen the ooze's color when shooting began. "I mean, we knew it would be pink," Gorman concedes, "but not the exact hue. And [cinematographer] Michael Chapman had to know what light to put on the actors' faces."[68] Second assistant director Christine Larson-Nizsche corroborates with a story about lighting the slime. "It was the scene where Dan Aykroyd is being lowered into the pink slime river," she says. "We got everything ready . . . we're two hours into the day now. All of a sudden Ivan turns to Michael Chapman. 'How long would it take if we wanted to have a pulsating glow over Dan or the set?' Chapman said, 'Mmm, four hours.' Ivan said, 'Okay.' Everybody stopped and went back to their trailers."[69]

Michael Chapman, a seasoned professional who shot both *Taxi Driver* and *Raging Bull* for Martin Scorsese, was happy to defer to Reitman or the actors. "They knew the first movie better than I ever could," he reasoned. "They knew exactly what they were doing." (*Ghostbusters* cinematographer László Kovács couldn't return for the sequel because he was busy working with Cameron Crowe on *Say Anything*.) Easygoing by nature, Chapman didn't get angry when a slime cannon misfired and drenched one of his cameras. "They're just pieces of metal with glass in them," he said. "They're not anything sacred and you mustn't take them too seriously."[70]

Ghostbusters II transformed the Statue of Liberty into a sentient being by filming actor Jim Fye in a Liberty costume and superimposing him over New York street footage. To convey the proper gait, Fye walked to the beat of a metronome.[71] For a shot of the statue's foot crushing a police cruiser, a miniature car was made from wax and filled with margarita salt to simulate the window breaks.[72] Replicas of Liberty's interior and crown were built, the latter being full-scale and placed atop a gimbal to simulate motion as the Ghostbusters lean out the windows.[73] Interestingly enough, even the establishing shots of the main characters arriving on Liberty Island would be achieved via matte paintings and blue screens. Matte painter Mark Sullivan remembered the time crunch was such that for the first time ever he worked on a piece simultaneously with another artist—an overhead shot from above Liberty's crown. "I worked on the right side of the painting and Caroleen Green worked on the left," Sullivan said. "She helped draw a lot of it in, and blocked in a lot of the colors. It worked out pretty well because our painting styles are pretty similar."[74]

The tight deadline didn't worry everyone. "I felt like we had plenty of time and plenty of money," says Larson-Nizsche. "It was fun working on that show because you knew you were already on a hit. The hardest part for me was getting all four Ghostbusters to the set at the same time. Bill was such a character you'd never know when he'd show up, first or last."[75]

Kim Masters was a senior writer with *Premiere* when she visited the set of *Ghostbusters II* for a feature-length article. In her experience, the Hollywood magic left something to be desired. "It was very clear it was not a happy set," Masters says. "You can get a vibe on a set a lot of the time. Whether the crew feels good, whether they feel they're working on something good. Even on the set of *Titanic*, which was an arduous shoot—shooting with Jim Cameron isn't easy—they sensed something was going on that was going to be really great. With *Ghostbusters II*, there was just a bad vibe, honestly."

Masters found most of the cast and crew accommodating as she conducted her interviews. The glaring exception was Bill Murray. "He was very uncooperative and in some cases wouldn't come out of his trailer. He was just balky." She was eventually escorted into Murray's trailer but even then the actor was, in her words, "just not doing the interview."[76]

Masters wrestled a few quotes out of Murray when the actor interrupted one of her talks with Ivan Reitman in Reitman's trailer. Murray's attention was drawn to a series of *Ghostbusters II* promotional posters. "These are really terrible," Murray remarked. "This is really high school stuff. I swear to God, this is exactly the kind of thing we used to make for football posters for next week's game." He turned to Reitman. "Do you ever keep the stuff that's so bad? I got a little trunk, and the stuff that's just unbelievable, that stuff I save." Murray teased Reitman about not getting along with his film crews: "[Ivan's] made great progress this year . . . he had trouble expressing himself in the past. And a little bit of lightness goes a long way with the crew. If you cheer them up a little bit, they don't steal as much and they work hard. . . . I don't know where it happened. Did it happen on *Twins* or something?"[77]

When Masters returned home from the set she managed to get Murray on the phone, though she remembers "it seemed like someone was leaning on him to do it. I asked him, 'To what do I owe the pleasure?' He said, 'I guess I'm just a nice guy.' 'No, try again.'"[78] Tensions aside, Murray spoke to Masters about the appeal of working with Reitman. "There are [directors] who take a strong hand but a dumb hand. It doesn't make me any more creative to be bullied. You end up miserable, and you end up with rage that takes years and years to go away. Ugly rage. But I've never had that experience with Ivan."[79]

Ghostbusters II's first assistant director Peter Giuliano remembers differently. Giuliano says Murray derailed one of the movie's videotaped rehearsals with a lengthy tirade about some unspecified indignity Reitman forced upon him years earlier during the making of *Stripes*. A more serious incident occurred on the *Ghostbusters II* courtroom set one day after filming. "The prop master was having an argument with Murray," Giuliano begins. "I have no idea what they were arguing about, but Murray slapped him. Suddenly there was all this kicking and punching. And this guy was so much bigger than Murray. I got between them and started talking to the prop master to figure out what's going on. All of a sudden his eyes got gigantic. I turned around and Murray was running at us with a big wooden chair, like it was a wrestling match. A set costumer, a woman, got involved to help me. That night when I went home I was fuckin' black and blue all over my body!" Giuliano declined to identify the prop master by name, citing "a big lawsuit" that broke out after Murray had the individual fired, but call sheets from that week list a "MacSems" filling the position.[80] It was Bill MacSems, a veteran in his field whose credits included *Chinatown*, *Marathon Man*, *All the President's Men*, and *RoboCop*.[81] Now retired, Bill MacSems declined to be interviewed for this volume.[82]

Sources who wish to remain anonymous say the courtroom altercation started because Murray was angry about the weight of his proton pack, the cumbersome piece of equipment all three lead actors had to wear like a rucksack during their ghost-busting sequences. Murray wasn't fond of wearing the fifty-pound apparatus while shooting the first *Ghostbusters*, and it remained an issue on the sequel, even though he was scripted to spend less time with the proton pack and the prop department had crafted a more lightweight device.[83] Livid that the straps were cutting into his shoulders, Murray allegedly tore the proton pack off his body, threw it to the ground of the courtroom set, and then knocked over a nearby table filled with other proton packs before accosting MacSems. In light of this story, it's understandable why Murray wasn't asked to wear one of the much larger and heavier slime-shooting backpacks created for *Ghostbusters II*.[84]

During a 1990 interview with the *Toronto Sun*, Murray acknowledged that there had been some kind of donnybrook involving Giuliano on one of the *Ghostbusters* movies, but explained the incident had to do with the security detail Columbia hired to keep tabs on him and the other actors between takes. "Whenever they'd yell, 'Cut,' [Dan Aykroyd] and I would go off, y'know, just walking the streets, looking around," Murray said, "and we'd turn around and there'd be someone ducking in a doorway. I flipped out. I physically abused the first assistant director. Like if we make them wait 15 minutes it costs them $600 or something—penny wise and pound foolish. When you're dealing with that kind of mindset all you can do is hurt them. They won't listen to reason, they won't listen to intelligence. And anyone that treats me like that gets it. . . . We hurt them, I won't say how, but I remember even saying, 'This is for the tail!'" Murray conceded in the same conversation that doing so many big-budget special effects films in a row had worn him down. "[*Ghostbusters II*] was just so loaded with effects I really felt like I was trapped in some level of Super Mario Brothers that I didn't know how to get out of."[85]

Whatever frustrations Murray experienced while making *Ghostbusters II* were probably exacerbated by the fact that they weren't using the story idea he'd been pitched in which he and Sigourney Weaver's character are married. Murray employed terms like "outfoxed" and "false pretenses" when discussing the situation decades later. "Harold had this great idea, but by the time we got to shooting it, I showed up on set and went, 'What the hell is this? What is this thing?' But we were already shooting it, so we had to figure out how to make it work."[86]

There are many individuals who worked on *Ghostbusters II* who only saw the pleasant side of Bill Murray. "Bill was so nice to me and my staff," says second assistant director Christine Larson-Nizsche. "We were people on the lowest rung of the totem pole but he took our entire staff out to dinner. When we were shooting in California, he took us to his beach house. We just sat around while he made us coffee."[87] Rebecca Baehler, Murray's personal assistant for *Scrooged* and *Ghostbusters II*, concurs. "He was not difficult at all. He was really funny and a super-nice guy. I booked flights for him, booked his hotels, got him dinners, picked up his laundry, but I mostly kinda hung out and was Bill's friend on set. He was very generous and honestly, *Ghostbusters II* was the most fun I've ever had in my career."[88] Cinematographer Michael Chapman was another person who worked on both *Scrooged* and *Ghostbusters II* and he described Murray as "an absolute gentleman." Said Chapman, "He's a complicated man but a great talent and [he was] always extremely kind and good to me."[89]

Sigourney Weaver told the press she adored working with Murray and enjoyed the ribbings he would give her, saying, "He keeps me from taking it all too seriously."[90] Murray's "Goulash" nickname for Weaver carried over from the first *Ghostbusters*; he'd tease her about revealing attire she was sometimes scripted to wear and liked to carry on about her critical success. While *Ghostbusters II* was filming, Weaver earned not only a Best Actress nomination for *Gorillas in the Mist* but also a Best Supporting Actress nod for her turn in the romantic comedy *Working Girl*.[91] A reporter from *Rolling Stone* visiting the *Ghostbusters II* set caught one of Murray's faux outbursts: "I say if she blows this scene, maybe she doesn't *deserve* the awards. You know, you're not such a big deal when you're working with actors as tall as you are."[92] Weaver told *USA Today* that everyone needled her about the recognition. "Were they irreverent? Wonderfully so! And I'd just tell them that they were jealous. My trouble is that I'm not as good at teasing as they are. But I'm learning."[93]

Weaver also valued working with Reitman, whom she described as a grounding force between her acting style and the improvisation of Aykroyd, Murray, and Ramis. She had further praise for the director's foresight. "He isn't looking for the perfect take [when we're filming], although I may be," Weaver said. "He's seeing how he can put different things together." (Reitman had to operate this way on *Ghostbusters II*, as the shortened schedule forced him to begin editing the movie long before filming was over.)[94]

Dan Aykroyd had a similar appreciation for Reitman's clarity of vision. "He's very confident, and that confidence translates onto the set," Aykroyd explained. "You're not running around going, 'What does he want from me?' 'Cause he knows what he wants. The trouble with directors that I would not work with again is that they have you try things fifteen different ways, six of which are a waste of time and one of which they pick and they aren't sure of. Ivan comes in, he tells you what to do, you do three or four takes of it, and he's happy."[95]

When Reitman was asked about "getting the most" from his comic stars, he replied, "After knowing them for fifteen years, I know how good they are, but I'm not easily impressed by their first thought."[96]

As with Murray, there were those who had more to say about Reitman's difficult personality. The *Ghostbusters II* piece Kim Masters turned in for *Premiere* included quotes from coworkers and associates who derided Reitman as "demanding," "unpleasant," "unreasonable," and "arrogant." "He treats people rather arbitrarily and high-handedly," said one anonymous colleague. Dan Goldberg, Reitman's collaborator on *Meatballs* and *Stripes*, went on record: "I've been an apologist for him for a long time, saying, 'He's a nicer guy than you think.' Yes, he's been an incredible jerk to me. I've been a jerk to him. But it just happens in the process."[97]

Masters touched on a thorn in Reitman's side—for all his financial success, the director was never granted the same artistic appreciation as a George Lucas or a Steven Spielberg. Reitman accepted he was a populist and couldn't argue that his movies were, as Masters put it, "high-concept, low-IQ product dedicated to the proposition that any wiseass loser can be a hero." "I take what I do very seriously," he said, "intellectually and emotionally as well. I'd like to think the films are carefully crafted. I have kind of a middle-class sensibility that's very easy to belittle." Harold Ramis offered a humorous take: "They didn't bring *The Last Emperor* to Ivan, and if they did, it would have taken 102 minutes, and it would have had a big chase at the end."

Reitman's attention to the craft was captured while shooting a scene with Rick Moranis and Eugene Levy that was ultimately cut. Moranis was asked to alter his line from "Do you believe me now?" to "Do you believe me now, Sherman?" "This is a very minor point," the director confided to Masters, "but one's much funnier than the other. It's sort of like distilling it and pushing it. These are the little things that accumulate into stuff." Reitman stopped himself.

"I hate to describe these things. You always sound like you're full of shit anyway."[98]

New York City's attitude toward Ivan Reitman and his *Ghostbusters* production was friendlier the second time around. Bureaucrats didn't interfere with shooting, and even though *Ghostbusters II* was on location during the frantic lead-up to Christmas, there were no major problems. Regardless of what the script dictated, the Ghostbusters were heroes to New York. "The people love it," said Ramis. "They bring their kids and hold them up to us like offerings."[99] According to Rick Moranis, the children who showed up to watch them film had a clear favorite.

"We're in downtown New York," Moranis recalled, "and these 4-year-olds with blue Ecto-pacs [*sic*] and their guns, all they want to see is Winston—Ernie Hudson—the fourth Ghostbuster, because he's got the best character on the cartoon show. They've never watched 'Saturday Night Live,' they don't care who Bill Murray is, they don't know me—they don't know anybody. They want to see Ernie."[100]

Ernie Hudson met with his *Ghostbusters* costars before agreeing to appear in the sequel because he wanted to make sure his character Winston Zeddemore wouldn't be kept on the fringes of the story. Aykroyd, Ramis, et al., offered their assurances,[101] but in the end Hudson found little difference between making the *Ghostbusters* films. "In the first one . . . they had hired [Winston] at a certain salary, he was not one of the Ghostbusters, he was not part of the franchise," the actor explained to the *Boston Globe*. "He thought these Ghostbusters guys were a little bit weird. In some ways, it mirrored my own life. When they hired me, I was not getting the money they were getting and all the other perks. . . . I think with this one, [Winston] enjoys being a Ghostbuster, he likes the guys as opposed to thinking they're a little weird . . . [but] he's still not full-fledged. He's a Ghostbuster, but he's not part of the franchise. He's not getting the money those guys are getting."

"This is me and the character," Hudson said with a laugh, adding that, regardless of how or why the filmmakers utilized Winston, he was "very proud to be a part" of *Ghostbusters*. "I love the guys and say that in all sincerity. . . . I'm very happy as a black male that they have a black male as one of the Ghostbusters." Yet Hudson had mixed feelings about a scene he was given where a ghostly locomotive would charge full speed through his body. "As a black man in America, I don't want to do stuff that's going to be embarrassing. And black people tend to get embarrassed by black guys getting on a bus with pink curlers in their hair. I don't feel I can take the same liberties with a character that, say, Rick Moranis can take. I become aware that I'm going to be run over by a train, okay? Now a train's going to run me over, right? But, man, I don't want to open my eyes too wide. Yet, the reality as an actor . . . I was very happy to be the one chosen to be hit by the train because it's a great bit. You don't get many bits, let's face it." Reitman promised Hudson the train would look real. Hudson was blunt with the director about his concerns: "I don't want to lose my membership in the NAACP over this."[102]

The train scene was part of a larger sequence that culminated in Hudson, Aykroyd, and Ramis turning on each other while covered head to toe in slime. Reitman filmed eleven takes of the slime fight on a bitterly frigid evening. Hudson couldn't believe how cold he felt. "We shot for hours," he said, "and we couldn't go into the trailers because they were too far away. So we had to sit outside between takes without the luxury of heaters. Danny was there and Harold was there and *they* weren't complaining, so I figured I shouldn't either . . . [but] at one point I had to ask them, 'Wait a minute. You guys wrote this scene? What the hell were you doing? Didn't you think you were going to have to *do* this stuff?'"

Everyone was relieved when a wrap was called for the night. That is, until it was discovered that a camera motor had been off-speed. The entire slime fight had to be filmed again the next evening.[103] Incredibly, this was not Hudson's most difficult tangle with the slime. A grueling sixteen hours were spent filming a brief scene wherein he, Aykroyd, and Ramis, all dripping with the viscous goo, interrupt Bill Murray during a meal at a fancy restaurant. "All day long . . . it's in your hair, in my eyes," remembered Hudson. "It's lunchtime and they say, 'Don't take it off [because] we're gonna come back in a half hour.' They have buckets of it! It's not like, 'We'll dip some on.' It's, 'Pour it over him.' And it soaks into your clothes."[104] Peter MacNicol also had a scene where his body was slathered in slime and discovered later that a shower did little to rinse it off. "It shifts like a slick moving to another harbor," MacNicol complained. "You have to wipe it off with coarse towels. It leaves a pink glow. I looked like a Chernobyl victim for hours."[105]

Ernie Hudson struggled with the slime, but at least he was choosing to be a part of *Ghostbusters II*. As he told one reporter, "The good news is that I [have] been able to make a fairly good living without *Ghostbusters*. The worst thing that could have happened in my career was to have done a *Ghostbusters* and not have worked afterward and really have to do the sequel."

"I think there are a lot of wonderful, positive things in it," Hudson concluded. "Kids especially find things in it. I think our biggest audience will be kids who weren't born when the first *Ghostbusters* came out."[106]

Ghostbusters II music supervisor Peter Afterman found himself in an advantageous position as numerous large record companies were vying for the right to curate and release the sequel's pop music soundtrack. Afterman had his eye on MCA, the major label that was home to a singer enjoying what looked like the prelude to his own empire—Bobby Brown. A few years earlier, Brown tasted the limelight as a part of chart-topping kiddie R&B quintet New Edition. By the time *Ghostbusters II* was in production, the nineteen-year-old's second solo effort, *Don't Be Cruel*, had exploded, selling two million copies and spending several months on Billboard's Top 10 ("He's starting to put up numbers like Whitney Houston," bragged one MCA rep). Musically, *Don't Be Cruel* and its hit singles like "My Prerogative" were hailed as an important step in the nascent subgenre of new jack swing (a blending of rap, funk, and R&B). Afterman wanted to co-opt Brown's new jack swing for *Ghostbusters II*. MCA was offered the film's entire soundtrack on the condition Brown get involved. A savvy, starry-eyed Brown countered with a demand for a role on-screen, which he would receive in the form of a very brief cameo.[107]

In concert, Brown coupled his singing with a lewd, raunchy persona that resulted in at least one arrest for gestures that were too suggestive.[108] He was outspoken, and this enfant terrible with a hi-top fade couldn't stop himself from taking a swipe at Ray Parker Jr. when announcing his *Ghostbusters II* job in April 1989. "We're going to do the *Ghostbusters* tune over again," he said, "but we're going to make it Bobby Brown's version. It's going to be more like 'Prerogative' and not use Huey Lewis's lick too much."[109] Brown actually decided to forgo remaking the famous *Ghostbusters* theme in favor of contributing two original songs, "On Our Own" and "We're Back." "On Our Own" was first slated for inclusion on the Babyface album *Tender Lover*—Babyface cowrote the track with L.A. Reid and Darryl Simmons—but the singer/songwriter became convinced Brown could to a better job with it.[110] Brown cowrote "We're Back" himself with gospel singer Dennis Austin.

Oingo Boingo, Elton John, Glenn Frey, and Brown's former group New Edition were some of the other MCA recording artists who were granted slots on the *Ghostbusters II* soundtrack. One of the few non-MCA acts to be included was Run-D.M.C., who accepted the responsibility of covering Ray Parker Jr.'s hit from the first movie. There was some amount of strife getting this pioneering hip-hop crew on board, but stories differ as to the problem. Cory Robbins, the head of Run-D.M.C.'s label Profile, said he spent a week trying to convince the eager group members that covering "Ghostbusters" was beneath them. "It's a stupid idea," Robbins said, "and it's not cool for Run-D.M.C. You guys are much cooler than this."[111] According to vocalist Darryl McDaniels, Run-D.M.C. didn't want to make music for *Ghostbusters II* or any other movie because they were trying to focus on the growth of their art. "It was an ill time," McDaniels said. "We didn't wanna do no side projects because [1988] was one of the most powerful years in hip hop. . . . I think the only reason that we did it was because we was tryin' to be nice to our management."[112]

As for Ray Parker Jr. himself, the original "Ghostbusters" hitmaker was not invited to participate in any way with the *Ghostbusters II* soundtrack. When Parker was eventually asked why that was, he replied, "Because I made too much money on *Ghostbusters I*."[113]

The *Ghostbusters II* soundtrack was devised long before the film was complete. When Ivan Reitman was getting close to the finish line, he and Peter Afterman realized the majority of their songs simply wouldn't work as part of the movie. They squeezed them in where they could or, as was the case with Elton John's "Love Is a Cannibal," omitted them entirely. Oingo Boingo singer Danny Elfman was furious when he saw how his band's song "Flesh 'n Blood" was used in the completed film. "It was supposed to fit the scene, but it's in the background for no reason, coming out of a radio for 10 seconds," Elfman griped. "I was really [mad]. I'd given up the song for nothing."[114] Afterman understood the frustration: "Looking back, we probably shouldn't have had a soundtrack, but the producer and the record company wanted the added promotion of what they thought would be the summer's megahits."[115]

Elmer Bernstein chose not to provide an orchestral score for *Ghostbusters II*. The composer turned down two other comedies during that same period, deciding instead to write music for the drama *My Left Foot*. He hoped it would lead to more work in that vein. "You know this town," Bernstein said. "You become typecast. I sometimes think this is the only place in the world where it's harder to fight your way down from the top than up from the bottom. You figure it out."[116] Reitman hired *Twins* composer Randy Edelman in Bernstein's place. In the 1970s, Edelman had been what the *New York Times* dubbed a "singing songwriter"—while he authored material for Barry Manilow and the Carpenters, the classically trained Edelman also released several albums of his own. The transition to film and television scoring was made once Edelman began feeling restricted by the three-minute pop song. "In a film," he said, "you can write whatever you want to enhance the scene." Edelman's most recognized creation at this point was probably the rousing theme to TV's *MacGyver*.[117]

While *Ghostbusters II* was in production, trade magazines would occasionally list or refer to it as *The Last of the Ghostbusters*. This alternate title was conceived by Bill Murray, who wanted, in his words, to "make sure there won't be anything like a *Ghostbusters III*."[118] Whatever they were calling the sequel, Columbia Pictures was banking on it to help reverse their various misfortunes. *Variety* dubbed the summer of 1989 "make-or-break" for the ailing studio and said that if they didn't score big with something, "the future looks bleak."[119] Columbia president Dawn Steele was honest, emphasizing to the press that *Ghostbusters II* was "a priority" and that "in the dollars-and-cents point of view, it's probably the most important, eagerly awaited sequel in the history of Columbia Pictures."[120] *Ghostbusters II* was originally slated for a July release until Ivan Reitman became convinced the weekend of June 23 would be a more ideal release window. No one was thrilled that two weeks had suddenly been shaved off, but there was a general commitment to making the deadline.[121]

Then *Batman* swooped in.

A Batman movie had been in development since 1979 when producers Michael Uslan and Ben Melnicker purchased the motion picture rights to the vigilante hero from DC Comics.[122] The pair sold their idea for a serious noir version of Batman to Casablanca FilmWorks, which had recently been absorbed by PolyGram. Casablanca chairman Peter Guber and his "karmic brother" at PolyGram, Jon Peters, loved the concept so much that they signed on as producers themselves, wrestling away the majority of ownership and bringing the concept to Warner Bros. in 1982. Script issues and the search for the right director grounded *Batman* for several years.[123] Ivan Reitman had actually been approached shortly after completing *Ghostbusters*, but the idea of walking right into another big-budget special effects movie didn't excite him.[124] There was also creative disconnect regarding the project's tone. When speaking about this period in *Batman*'s development, screenwriter Sam Hamm commented, "We were talking at one point about Bill Murray as Batman and Eddie Murphy as Robin."[125]

In 1987, Warner executive Bonni Lee realized Tim Burton would be the perfect director for *Batman*.[126] Burton had a striking style, one that existed somewhere between nightmare and dream, and he mined humor from pure weirdness. Once aboard, Burton made the expected casting decision when he hired Jack Nicholson to play infamous Batman villain the Joker but surprised everyone by hiring comic actor Michael Keaton for the title role.[127]

Batman was two months away from filming in August 1988 but public excitement was already ticking up—stores in New York City couldn't keep T-shirts featuring the famous Batman bat emblem on the rack. Some theorized that Batman's popularity was growing because people were beginning to relate more to his troubled "everyman" persona as opposed to an invincible, patriotic symbol like Superman. The nuclear age was over, Communism had fallen; American minds were now focused on surviving domestic blight.[128] "I think the mood of the country is fairly grim at the moment," said DC Comics rep Dennis O'Neil that October. He was commenting specifically on the reader survey in which comic fans voted to kill off longtime Batman sidekick Robin the Boy Wonder instead of sparing his life during a dangerous tussle with the Joker.[129]

A ninety-second trailer for *Batman* released in December thrust North America into a fever. The *New York Times* called it "the most talked-about 'coming attraction' in recent memory," one that "elicits applause and often cheers with its succession of electrifying images." "You hear 'Oh, boys' when the trailer runs," said one theater owner in Colorado. "It's not kids, it's young adults." Moviegoers were so rabid for *Batman*, they would buy tickets for whatever film had Burton's footage in front of it. Over a thousand extra prints of the trailer had to be created to meet viewer demand. Bootleg VHS tapes of *Batman* film clips had a street value of $25. By February, everyone knew when this Caped Crusader was coming: June 23, 1989.[130]

Ivan Reitman knew as well as anyone that putting anything up against *Batman* was a fool's gamble. However, no one expected him to suggest releasing *Ghostbusters II* a week earlier. As Michael C. Gross remembered, "Ivan said to the studio, 'It would make a huge difference if we could come out on [June] 16th, right?' And the studio said, 'We'd love you if you come out on the 16th. Can you make it?' Ivan said, 'Sure, we can make it.' Then he looked around the room, and [producer] Joe Medjuck and I were turning pale. Our editor, Shelley Kahn, I think he fainted. We just looked at each other and said, 'Yeah, well, if you say we'll be out on the 16th, we'll be out on the 16th.' But on paper it did not look possible. . . . It was a real killer. It meant the editing schedule had to be pushed [ahead], and it meant that ILM's dates had to be pushed [ahead]—and they were already dying. But we had to do it."[131] Even more surprising: Reitman told gossip columnist Marilyn Beck that they'd also considered bumping *Ghostbusters II* up to May.

Ghostbusters II was scheduled to complete filming on March 18, but shooting and reshooting continued well into the following month.[132] A preview screening had convinced Reitman that the movie's ending didn't work. "[It] just died a horrible death," he said (newspaper reports described the director fielding a bevy of "complaints from a baffled audience" at this showing). Four days were spent filming a new twenty-five-minute conclusion for the movie, though it was entirely Reitman's decision—the studio took no issue with his original ending. "The Columbia people were happy, and we said, 'Y'know, it's too easy for [the Ghostbusters] at the end," Medjuck recalled. "The delay was because of us, the actors and Ivan deciding to do it."[133]

The early screening also helped the filmmakers identify better ways to connect the ghost activity and the river of slime to Vigo the Carpathian. Interestingly enough, the test audience was not thrilled with Slimer. "We had an ongoing confrontation between Louis [Tully] and Slimer in which Louis was constantly trying to catch him," said Gross. "We expected the audience to cheer and laugh when they saw [Slimer] again. But [there was] nothing. No reaction."[134]

Peter Giuliano will never forget the final day of New York City location shooting on March 30 because it was almost literally an entire day; the crew worked for twenty-two hours straight. They were also almost trampled by out-of-control extras. "It was the sequence where all the ghosts are chasing people through Washington Square Park," Giuliano says. "We started at six in the morning and finished the next morning, straight through. I don't think it was set up that way. We had about a hundred extras, and man, it's New York. The first time we rolled on that scene, probably two hundred people came running out of the park. The third time we did it, seven hundred or eight hundred people came running out. We got pulled away from the camera by the mass of people running past us. That was the last time we did it because the police shut us down. The cops came over and said, 'We're done.' Ivan and Joe lost that 'discussion.'"[135]

Toward the end of May, 25 of the movie's 180 special effects shots were still absent and the actors were continuing to work on additional dialogue recording. In a blurb that ran May 21, Ernie

Hudson assured the *Los Angeles Times* that *Ghostbusters II* would arrive on time: "The movie will definitely be released on June 16th but I know Ivan will be working on it up to the last minute."[136] Meanwhile, *Batman*'s grip on society tightened. The *Los Angeles Times* reported that over 1,200 *Batman* posters were stolen during a two-month period that spring from public transit depots in New York, Los Angeles, Chicago, St. Louis, and San Francisco. Gannett Transit, the billboard company behind the advertisements, told the *Los Angeles Times* that theft on this scale was "unheard of." The same article noted that "a special order *Batman* catalogue . . . was as thick as the one that lists comic book material and merchandise for the entire industry."[137] Retailers everywhere were stocking up on Bat paraphernalia, from J.C. Penney and Macy's (who opened their own Batman boutique in their flagship Manhattan store) to normally trend-averse counterculture stores like Philadelphia's Zipperhead.[138] Some places, such as Hollywood's Golden Apple Comics, had to hire extra security to protect their Batman wares.

Warner Bros. boasted about *Batman*'s "awareness level," noting that the buzz was greater than anything *Ghostbusters* had ever generated.[139] There was more direct competition between *Ghostbusters II* and *Indiana Jones and the Last Crusade*, however, as soft drink rivals Coca-Cola and Pepsi had advertising deals with each film, respectively. *Last Crusade*'s cowriter and executive producer George Lucas announced Pepsi's tie-in with the film earlier in the year by declaring, "This is the summer that we're going to beat *Ghostbusters II*."[140]

This wasn't just a three-way race, though. Numerous popular franchises were entering the seasonal fray with new installments, including *The Karate Kid III*, *Star Trek V*, the sixteenth James Bond entry *License to Kill*, and *Lethal Weapon II*. The majority of these films would open in no less than two thousand theaters apiece, and with rising ticket prices, studio executives were salivating over potential financials. They all hoped to continue the trend of besting the previous year's record-breaking summer. 1988's seasonal take was $1.7 billion, nearly $100 million more 1987's unprecedented haul.

Sequels were considered one of the safest bets in Hollywood; an audience's familiarity with a proven brand worked to the filmmakers' advantage. The headlining talent of *Ghostbusters II* felt differently.[141] "We are *not* over-confident," Reitman told *BoxOffice* magazine. "If anything, we're scared, because we know that people are going to come to the movie with extraordinarily high expectations. And to me, that's much more frightening than having an audience come to a brand new movie, not knowing what to expect, and having the chance to be pleasantly surprised. Living up to expectations has kind of frightened all of us, and forced us to work as hard as we can to make the film as good as we can."[142]

During his set visit, *Rolling Stone* reporter Patrick Goldstein asked Harold Ramis about the social conscience of *Ghostbusters II*. Ramis spoke about using humanity to reverse urban decay. After a pause, he spoke again. "Hey, it's pretty deeply buried in the script. It's not like we're sending a lot of messages here. There are some comedies that satisfy the requirements of art and some that are gratuitous and pandering, and we like to think [laughing] that we're somewhere in between."[143]

David Giammarco from the *Toronto Sun* was also dispatched to the *Ghostbusters II* set. Like many, he was curious about the possibility of a *Ghostbusters III*. Dan Aykroyd was enthusiastic. "I'd do ten of these," he said. "But it's up to Billy and Harold and Ivan. If it was up to me, I'd be on the bullhorn saying, 'Boys—show up for work next week.' I'd love to do it again."

Murray was less gung ho. "Maybe if one of us is going to die or something, we'll do it again. You know, if somebody comes down with leukemia, we'll try to do one more."[144]

I HATE THAT PAINTING

"I just want to remind you that we're all very sensitive and delicate, and we would really appreciate it if you only wrote really nice things about us that won't hurt our feelings."

Ivan Reitman lobbed this half-joke to an assembly of reporters in the State Room of New York's Plaza Hotel, kicking off a *Ghostbusters II* press conference on June 10, 1989. The sunny weather outside stood in contrast to the State Room's atmosphere as Reitman, Dan Aykroyd, Ernie Hudson, Bill Murray, Annie Potts, Harold Ramis, and Sigourney Weaver fielded questions about the sequel. "The conference was an awkward and unwieldy affair," wrote *Houston Post* critic Joe Leydon, "apparently designed more for the guests of honor to rib one another and crack wise than for reporters and critics to ask in-depth questions and receive straight answers."[1, 2, 3]

Murray, who was several minutes late to the panel, tried to be forthcoming. "I think we all saw the negatives of making a sequel and the problems we'd have trying to explain why we bothered to do it again," he explained. "It took a few years to decide to do it again. The determining factor was that we realized how much fun we had doing [the first one] together. . . . And I think it took a lot of courage on Ivan's part, and Dan and Harold's part, to say, 'Okay, we're gonna face the fan now and see if we can make a sequel that can live up to the first one.'"[4, 5]

"We made a pact," added Reitman, "that we were going to do the film for the fun and not the money, and we'd do it all together or not at all." A reporter countered: "Yes, but you did take percentage points [on] the film." Reitman: "Well, we're not crazy."[6]

Aykroyd described *Ghostbusters II* as the summer's "only really hard, hard comedy." "There are laughs in *Batman*," he said, "there are laughs in *Indiana Jones*, no question. Jim Cameron's movie *The Abyss*, we're all gonna see that, I know I will. Everybody is gonna see everything, it's that kind of summer. But we are the only comedy." The actor also gushed about the franchise potential for *Ghostbusters*. "There's a lot of places you can go with these characters. Myth, mysticism, metaphysics—man, you got the limits of the universe, inner and outer, man, you can do all kinds of things. I guess I sound like Dennis Hopper. That's what it provides. The hardware we've got, the characters, there's no limit, there's no end to it."[7]

Aykroyd turned sour when a journalist asked about the upcoming movie version of *Wired*, Bob Woodward's controversial 1984 John Belushi biography.[8] Belushi's widow Judy first hired Woodward to investigate the mysteries surrounding her husband's fatal overdose, but the famed *Washington Post* reporter decided Belushi deserved an entire book. Friends and family who agreed to help were appalled by Woodward's end result. He failed to capture what was special about Belushi, focusing instead on tawdry details. Aykroyd never read *Wired* but denounced it as trash just the same and said he once burned a copy he'd found at his parents' house.[9] Aykroyd's major comment on the *Wired* movie up to this point was that he was paying witches to jinx it. Additionally, Aykroyd had actor J. T. Walsh fired from a film they were working on together called *Loose Cannons* after learning Walsh had taken a role in *Wired*.[10]

"Let me straighten you out on this thing," Aykroyd replied to the inquiring reporter, jumping out of his seat. "They're saying there is censorship and that we're trying to hide drug use and the lifestyle in Hollywood. But the people I know who are opposed to this thing don't do drugs—their lifestyles are quite open. I've got nothing to hide. Everybody knows the vagaries of my life. The fact of the matter is that John was a friend of mine. My stance has to be to be against those who are exploiting his death with a product." Aykroyd grew even more agitated with a follow-up question asking if he'd ever see *Wired*. "Man, that's it. I don't have to say another word. And for you to presume I'd see it, sir, undermines the general impression of the relationship between John and I. I *never* want to see that movie."[11]

Murray, who egged Aykroyd on with a "Get 'em, Dan!" at the top of his rant and chimed in with a "Hear, hear!" after the statement on exploitation, now rose. "This means a duel," he said to the reporter. "You die!"[12] Murray offered his take on *Wired* shortly after the tome's publication: "[John] paid his own price. The sentence has been given, so there is no need to write a book about it."[13]

Another voice rose up at the press conference. "Bill, your character Peter Venkman is so much warmer this time through." Murray deadpanned: "I was asked to be less like myself." He went on, joking about an operation. "Actually, I was neutered here in New York. I'm just easier to get along with now. I don't chase buses or cars. . . . it was really the writers' idea to have me neutered. Sigourney went to a special handling school. She's probably the best I've ever worked with. I ate right out of her hand." The actor had to clarify here to one confused reporter that he was being facetious. Murray also spoke a bit about how his views on comedy had changed.

"I used to be a lot more particular about what I might enjoy. There are certain comedians who'd have a hit movie, and I'd think, *Yeah, it's terrible*. I didn't like it, and I decided only stupid people could laugh at it. Now I feel whomever makes anyone laugh is okay. It doesn't matter if someone is laughing at someone else, but not at me. . . . What's really important is the laughter." A *New York Times* critique from Vincent Canby published that April prompted reassessment, Murray said. Titled "Comedy That Smirks at Itself," Canby railed against Murray and his fellow *Saturday Night* graduates for pushing "comedy of disconnection," a "new kind of cool" that avoids emotional commitment to the material. "[*Scrooged*] is funny only for the way in which Mr. Murray successfully says a lot of nasty things without having to be held accountable, either as a character or an actor." Though it gave Murray much to consider, he was touched the following month when the *Times* printed a rebuttal from Sigourney Weaver that cited Groucho Marx and Bob Hope as earlier purveyors of so-called "disconnection." Weaver simultaneously praised Murray and Chevy Chase for finding "direct communion" with their audience.[14]

Did the future of Columbia Pictures depend on the success of *Ghostbusters II*? "We think the future of America depends on it," Harold Ramis joked, "not to mention our futures." Would there be a *Ghostbusters III*? Aykroyd and Murray remained at odds on that issue. "I'm always ready," Aykroyd said. "I'd love to work with these guys again and I have ideas for stories. . . . We'll come back. Why shouldn't we? Look at *Return of the Jedi*. That was a good sequel."

"I think many things come in threes," Murray began, "but I think some things come in twos. Leopold and Loeb, Hitler and Mussolini.

It's a little early. We're not going to say we're going to repeat in '91. We're going to enjoy this championship right now. Harold and Dan have something to say in this one, but we're not going to do it if there's not anything to say. We didn't do it for five years because there was nothing to say."

The junket ended abruptly with an announcement from Aykroyd: "We've got to go do a video with Run-D.M.C." The crowd chuckled, assuming it was a joke. "No, really."[15]

If the reporters who visited the Plaza for this media event found their subjects difficult, they could take solace in the fact they got the jump on screening the movie. Columbia made special arrangements so Plaza attendees could see *Ghostbusters II* ahead of their media colleagues. Cleveland film critic Joanna Connors cited this to *Plain Dealer* readers in the June 17 issue when explaining why they had no *Ghostbusters II* review to print.

"Columbia Pictures arranged the one and only local preview screening of it for 11:45 last night—a trifle late for deadlines," wrote Connors. "'They just can't get [prints of the movie] out here in time,' a local representative said. Uh-huh. As someone who saw the movie at the screening for the junkateers last weekend said, 'Why should Columbia care about reviews? People who loved *Ghostbusters* are going to see it no matter what. . . . The rest pretty much know what it will be."[16]

Nineteen eighty-nine's summer movie season blasted off on Wednesday, May 24, when Steven Spielberg's *Indiana Jones and the Last Crusade* opened to mammoth business. The third and ostensibly final *Indiana Jones* adventure earned $5.6 million on its first day; only *Return of the Jedi* ever did better in a midweek spot prior to Memorial Day. A *Last Crusade* write-up in the *Los Angeles Times* spent seventeen paragraphs on fan reaction. "On a scale of 1 to 10, I give it a 12," declared Fred Chytraus. Gloria Brown raved: "It was absolutely the most wonderful, exciting movie I have seen in years. You lose yourself in it. . . . No message, no nothing, just a very wonderful adventure story."[17] Over the four-day weekend, *Last Crusade* captured a gross of $37 million.[18]

The loyalty Spielberg and *Indiana Jones* writer/producer George Lucas engendered was critic-proof. "I can't be disappointed by this film," Shankari Patel insisted while waiting in line for the movie.

"Lucas has never disappointed me!" That's what helped *Last Crusade* reach the $100 million mark in nineteen days, a new record. The film's distributor, Paramount Pictures, was thrilled to read reports of theatergoers finishing a screening and immediately getting back in line for the next showing.[19]

Paramount scored another number one in early June when *Star Trek V: The Final Frontier* enjoyed a $17.4 million debut. It was the best opening for any *Star Trek* film, though *Star Trek V* owed some success to inflation. Admission prices had risen by 11 percent since 1986's *Star Trek IV: The Voyage Home* and *The Voyage Home* actually sold 300,000 more tickets.[20] Advance word for *The Final Frontier* hadn't been stellar, but disciples of this franchise have always exercised cult-like devotion. Linnea Fairbanks and Paul Ramos set up a tent outside Fresno's Festival Cinemas four days before tickets went on sale. Almost two hundred Trekkies and Trekkers lined up for opening day at Pensacola's University Mall theaters, some of whom flashed Star Trek–themed credit cards.[21]

America's natural enthusiasm for movies wasn't the only reason lines were growing at cinemas. A disagreement between United Artists (the largest theater chain in the country) and Touchstone Pictures distributor Buena Vista over business protocols resulted in UA banning all Touchstone entertainment from their screens. Independent theaters were then allowed to show some of the year's most anticipated films, though they often couldn't accommodate the overflow. Santa Fe's Jean Cocteau Cinema was overwhelmed with massive lines and had to turn away thousands during the first ten-day run of the Robin Williams drama *Dead Poets Society*.[22] *Ghostbusters II* was expected to scare up even larger crowds. Insiders predicted this sequel would easily break $150 million to be 1989's most popular film. "[They] will never have to work another day in their lives," columnist John Griffin assumed of the movie's cast.[23] Bill Murray didn't disagree, telling *Starlog* that "even if it's a dog, the sequel's going to make money because so many people are going to say, 'Let's see if they ruined it' or 'Let's see if it's any good.'"[24]

Sure enough, audiences swarmed to see *Ghostbusters II* when it went into general release on June 16, and the $29.4 million the movie brought in that weekend was the biggest three-day take in box office history. This more than doubled the opening numbers of the first *Ghostbusters*, though as with the *Star Trek* franchise, shifting economics were at play. Ticket prices were up, and *Ghostbusters II* had been booked into over one thousand more theaters than its predecessor, which allowed two million extra sales on opening day.[25] Another similarity *Ghostbusters II* shared with *Star Trek V: The Final Frontier* was that critics were not especially taken with it.

"Much of the charm (and considerable commercial power) of the original film was due to its way of unselfconsciously projecting childlike emotions and childlike pleasures onto adult characters," wrote David Kehr of the *Chicago Tribune*, "not only the clubhouse bonding, but also the thrill of campfire ghost stories, the satisfaction of smarting off to authority figures and the forbidden scatological delight of messing around with disgusting substances. *Ghostbusters II* is a bit more knowing and bit more tired." Kehr noted that the opening scene in which the Ghostbusters are shown relegated to birthday party appearances "is funny enough but also suggests that the filmmakers themselves are ready to put their creations out to pasture. The story that follows . . . recaps the original film without equaling the audacity of its effects."[26]

Reviewing for *Newsweek*, David Ansen said, "The most interesting question about *Ghostbusters II* is not 'how good is it?' (not very) but 'can it possibly fail?' . . . Audiences today seem so hungry to recreate their cinematic highs that they may convince themselves they're having a great time watching *Ghostbusters II*. The preview audience was cheering when the first title appeared: '5 Years Later,' and they let out a victory hoot every time one of the flying specters got zapped by Our Boys. But what you didn't hear much of was precisely what made the first movie a smash: the honest, steady sound of laughter." Ansen felt the film wasted a "host of satirical possibilities" by not thoroughly exploring the concept of New Yorkers having to be polite to one another. "Where are the jokes showing the legendary incivility of the Big Apple? There are none. Nothing *builds* in Ivan Reitman's movie, nothing pays off. Why isn't Sigourney Weaver, a juicy comedienne, given anything funny to do? Why is there no tension in her romance with Murray?"

"The filmmakers seem so cocky about the appeal of the Ghostbusters that they forgot to notice their script doesn't add up," Ansen continued. "Basically what you have is an enormous, special-effects-laden movie resting on Bill Murray's ability to toss off a few low-key improvisational ironies. Sure, Murray is funny. You laugh when, under interrogation in a witness stand, he calls the female prosecutor 'kitten.' But he could do that in any movie."[27]

Some critics went for the jugular. "*Ghostbusters II* is a cynical swipe at the idea of movies as art, as pleasure, or even as simple amusement," Joanna Connors wrote in the *Plain Dealer*. "[It] ends up looking like an assemblage of halfhearted schticks and special effects, put together by the Phil Collins of directing, Ivan Reitman. . . . The script has many clever lines; unfortunately, the flatfooted Reitman cheeses most of them by getting the timing wrong, and what he doesn't step on with bad cuts he steps on with astoundingly bad, loud music. . . . [Writers] Aykroyd and Ramis don't have a fresh idea between them: The movie climaxes with a skyscraper-sized being stomping through the streets of Manhattan, and with crowds of New Yorkers watching a building as the Ghostbusters battle slime and the supernatural inside. Sound familiar? That's the sound of money clinking into Columbia's coffers."[28]

Boston Globe critic Jay Carr expressed identical complaints. In describing Reitman's directorial style, he said, "Imagine a dumpster filled with wet cement falling from a great height."[29] Mick LaSalle of the *San Francisco Chronicle* lambasted Murray for "trying to be cuddly and lovable" by goofing around with a baby. "As for Sigourney Weaver," LaSalle wrote, "she's either a very nice lady or they paid her a small city, because she doesn't have to play in movies like this anymore."[30]

"Don't listen to the TV and newspaper reports where the cast and crew of *Ghostbusters II* claim they actually tried to make a good, honest sequel," warned *St. Petersburg Times* writer Perry Clark. "They didn't. They're in it for the money and the evidence is up there on the screen."[31] *People* magazine also turned in a pan: "Who you gonna call? Try your local videotape dealer, to see if they have copies of the first *Ghostbusters* to rent. This comedy sequel is life after death warmed over."[32] On their TV show, Gene Siskel and Roger Ebert agreed *Ghostbusters II* was disappointing. "The film contains little comic energy or invention," said Siskel. "I know this isn't true, but the movie comes across as if the guys were filming the first draft of a script." Ebert added, "No thought went into it, no effort went into it. . . . This is a demonstration of the bankruptcy of sequels." When Siskel began to say he was surprised, Ebert cut him off: "I was shocked."[33]

Positive reviews were often tempered with dismissive remarks pertaining to the movie's overall value. "Hammered together out of the junkiest of elements, [*Ghostbusters II*] rattles along with a pleasing rambunctiousness," surmised the *Washington Post*'s Hal Hinson. "It's a mishmash, like the first film, big and dumb and clunky. But the dumbness has personality and invention, much more so than in the first film, and the jokes spring right out of the heart of America's long trash heritage. It's classically dumb."[34] The *Orlando Sentinel's* Jay Boyar began a favorable review by saying, "Movies like this defy criticism. I might as well review a whoopee cushion."[35] Vincent Canby of the *New York Times* doled out praise so faint it was laughable: "*Ghostbusters II* certainly isn't all bad. . . . [It] strikes me as being far easier to take, funnier even, than the first film. . . . It has the weight and stylishness of designer toilet tissue, but it doesn't offend."[36]

Ticket sales for *Ghostbusters II* dropped by 53 percent during its second weekend of release, a plunge normally indicating poor word of mouth.[37] June 23 was no normal weekend, though. After almost a year of hysterical buildup, Tim Burton's *Batman* finally arrived to tantalize moviegoers. Excitement and curiosity over what was now a pop culture milestone helped *Batman* rinse the competition with a record-shattering $42.7 million opening.[38] The movie flew past both the $100 million and $200 million sales marks faster than any other on record, evoking powerful responses with its urgent, arresting, and highly stylized approach.[39]

Roger Ebert derided *Batman* as "a hostile, mean-spirited movie about ugly, evil people."[40] Science fiction writer Harlan Ellison found it exhilarating. "Remember how you felt the first time you saw *Star Wars*? It's that 'Oh my gosh, all bets are off' feeling? Well, that's what happens when you see this movie."[41] Jennifer Chlebek, a viewer who saw *Batman* at Mann's Chinese Theater, was similarly gobsmacked. "There are no words to describe it," she gushed.

"I wish Batman was real. I want to live in Gotham City."[42]

Ghostbusters II had no hope of being as striking or uncanny as *Batman*, but the sequel also couldn't even match the dirt-stained irreverence of the 1984 *Ghostbusters*. This was partially by design, as the filmmakers felt the need to court young devotees of *The Real Ghostbusters* cartoon.[43] Thus, the constant cigarette smoking that marks the original film is all but absent from *Ghostbusters II*, as is any coarse language (when confronting Vigo the Carpathian, Peter Venkman can think of no greater pejorative than "bonehead"). Ivan Reitman and company were so committed to pushing a warm, "feel good" message that they also skirted reality. A scene was lopped off the film's ending where the main characters gaze up at the Statue of Liberty and speak in wistful tones about their lineages. Ray Stantz mentions the photographs his great-grandparents took when their boat arrived in front of the statue. Winston Zeddemore interrupts: "My people weren't taking any pictures from those slave ships, man."[44]

Decades after the fact, Reitman admitted the gentrified touch of *Ghostbusters II* was a reflection of this comedy troupe's less than enthused disposition. "None of us [were] in the mood to do another one," he said. "Our problem was we made too much money on the first one and were too successful. Everyone was kind of on to other stuff in their own lives."[45] Reitman explained that *Ghostbusters II*'s humor quotient was also handicapped by the very fact it was a sequel. "In comedy, the element of surprise is everything. And I think once that element of surprise is gone, once people know there's going to be ghosts, there's going to be big ghosts, and they're expecting something big at the end, a lot of the tools that are at your disposal are gone."[46] Reassessing *Ghostbusters II* in 1991, Dan Aykroyd said he thought the Statue of Liberty was the wrong device for the movie's conclusion. "There could have been a better way out of that," he lamented. "I believe everybody connected with the film regrets the way we did it."[47]

Fatal flaws aside, there is a meta textuality to *Ghostbusters II* that lends it an intriguing hue (although this facet of the movie is somewhat muted by modern standards). It is proven in this sequel that Ray Parker Jr.'s theme song from the first movie's soundtrack exists in-universe when the Ghostbusters deliberately play it on a stereo; later, Murray's Venkman character uses Parker's famous "Who ya gonna call?" refrain when testifying in court. Once the Ghostbusters officially revive their business in *Ghostbusters II*, they adopt the same redesigned "no ghost" logo flashing two fingers that the filmmakers used in promotional materials for the movie. Is this supposed to signal that the Ghostbusters know they're in a sequel? Logo codesigner Thom Enriquez says the fingers were never contested as unrealistic but there was slight disagreement over the ghost's foot, which is outside the red circle and therefore breaking the fourth wall.[48]

"We're the best, we're the beautiful, we're the only Ghostbusters," Venkman announces in *Ghostbusters II* just before a flashy montage showing the heroes' triumphant return to everyday casework. In another blur between fiction and reality, this line is a variation of a motto Murray ascribed to himself, Aykroyd, and Ramis while promoting the original *Ghostbusters*. "We are the brave, the best . . . the only," Murray bragged to Roger Ebert in 1984. "We notice, however, that sometimes a little Three Stooges stuff creeps in. We try to guard against that."[49]

One component of *Ghostbusters II* almost universally praised in reviews both approving and disdainful was Peter MacNicol's turn as Janosz.[50] "He blows the others away in every one of his scenes," Bill O'Connor wrote in the *Akron Beacon Journal*. "When he is on screen, you mentally lean forward for you can sense the comic energy and inventiveness."[51] In the *Miami Herald*, Rene Jordan sang, "There has not been such a creative creepiness on the screen since Renfield sucked spiders to please master Dracula. Possessed or dispossessed, MacNicol is a ghost you'd never want to bust."[52] British publication *Screen International* fairly criticized Janosz, however, for perpetuating "the American taste for ridiculing accents."[53] Critics also praised Rick Moranis for the laughs he generates as Louis Tully during *Ghostbusters II*'s courtroom sequence. *New Yorker* mainstay Pauline Kael raved that these scenes resembled "a perfectly achieved edition of 'Saturday Night Live.'"[54] Word even has it that a generation of attorneys count Tully's limp defense work as "a minor classic" of legal comedy.[55]

Moranis took a lead role in the only movie that summer daring enough to open against *Batman*—*Honey, I Shrunk the Kids*, a live-action fantasy from Disney in which Moranis stars as the scientist patriarch committing the titular screwup. Disney executives were shocked when *Honey* earned $14.3 million that weekend, putting it in second place ahead of *Ghostbusters II*'s $13.9 million draw.[56] That $14.3 million was actually the highest opening any Disney movie ever achieved, and the studio believed this was proof that you didn't need established brands to succeed at the box office.[57] Contradicting this logic is the fact every screening of *Honey, I Shrunk the Kids* was prefaced by a Roger Rabbit cartoon called *Tummy Trouble*, the first animated short Disney had made in twenty-four years. Roger Rabbit enjoyed great popularity through his own feature a year earlier and some thought Disney was attaching him to *Honey, I Shrunk the Kids* to rescue a weak movie.[58]

A brief, tongue-in-cheek rivalry appeared to develop between *Honey, I Shrunk the Kids* and *Ghostbusters II* during the films' promotional cycles. "It's going to be the end of a friendship if [Rick] outdraws our movie," Bill Murray joked during a *Ghostbusters II* cast appearance on *The Oprah Winfrey Show*. "But actually, we hear that movie is very good," he quickly added, "and that's the only one we like and the only one we recommend to anyone."[59] Moranis was absent from the *Oprah* episode, but he turned up a week later on *Late Night with David Letterman*. Letterman opened the conversation with *Ghostbusters II*. "No, no, no," Moranis interjected. "They made $30 million last week, we gotta talk about *Honey, I Shrunk the Kids*." The guest eventually yielded. After swearing he still hadn't seen *Ghostbusters II*, Letterman asked Moranis if he got "a good hunk" of the movie financially. "Me? Are you kidding?" the actor replied while laughing. "No, no. But I got a big piece of *Honey, I Shrunk the Kids*! Hey, alright!"[60]

Moranis was shielding his truths about *Ghostbusters II*. "I didn't like the experience in shooting the second one, or the final product," he told Ghostbusters fan website Proton Charging in 2006.[61] Murray agreed about what ended up on-screen and was lodging public complaints once the obligation to sell tickets was over. Reitman cut out too much comedy, the actor said, turning *Ghostbusters II* into an action movie.[62] Also, the special effects were too abundant and the film's thesis was obscured. "We tried to do something and it didn't work," Murray said a year after the film's release. He went on to note that making any kind of sequel "was always going to be like painting plywood. No matter how many coats of paint you put on it, or how great the paint is, it's still plywood. It's never gonna look right."[63] Harold Ramis concurred, calling *Ghostbusters II* "a worthy attempt." "We gave it a good shot, but we weren't really together on it."[64]

Bobby Brown's *Ghostbusters II* theme "On Our Own" had its moment in the sun. *Billboard* praised the single's "consummate street savvy" before the song earned gold and platinum sales that summer.[65] Like Ray Parker Jr.'s "Ghostbusters," "On Our Own" was accompanied by a star-studded music video featuring cameos from Christopher Reeve, Jane Curtain, Lori Singer, Malcolm Forbes, two of the Ramones, and Donald Trump.[66] Another characteristic "On Our Own" shared with Parker's song is that it spawned a plagiarism lawsuit.

Minneapolis musician Derrick Moore filed suit against Columbia Pictures, MCA Records, and "On Our Own" songwriters Kenny "Babyface" Edmonds and L.A. Reid on June 14, 1989, claiming that Brown's hit was infringing upon a song he'd written called "She Can't Stand It." The complaint alleged that Moore's agent sent MCA a selection of his material the previous March and that the label responded favorably, zeroing in on an instrumental of "She Can't Stand It." MCA asked for a full version; they also asked to keep the tapes, which Moore's agent agreed to despite his better judgment.

Moore never heard from MCA again. His complaint was asking for $50,000 in damages plus "an unspecified portion of the profits" from "On Our Own."[67]

Derrick Moore was not entirely unknown. Nicknamed Dezzraye, he was the front person for a funk act called Exotic Storm that was put together by one of Prince's former bodyguards. Exotic Storm landed a deal with Epic Records almost immediately after forming (a testament to the fact that any connection to Prince could get you somewhere) and they released their debut LP, *In the Beginning*, in October 1986.[68] The album received fair reviews, but in concert, Exotic Storm was considered a joke. *Star Tribune* writer Jon Bream said the group had a live act that was "embarrassingly bad" and gave them an F.[69]

In 1991, a US District Court dismissed the Moore complaint on the grounds that the plaintiff had no plausible evidence.[70] Moore appealed, and the case went before a three-judge panel the following year.[71] One of the judges, Gerald Heaney, acknowledged a lack of musical aptitude. "I have played the tape which contains the two musical compositions," Heaney said, "and although I do not know the difference between be-bop, hip-hop, and rock and roll, the tunes all sound the same to me. This may be because I have no ear for music other than reflecting my generation's preference for the more soothing rhythms of Glen Miller [*sic*] and Wayne King or the sophisticated beat of Woody Herman playing the Wood Chopper's Ball. Obviously judges have no expertise to resolve this kind of question—which is why jurors should tell us whether a composite vote of reasonable minds can or cannot find similarity of expression."[72]

While the court decided there was "a reasonable possibility Edmonds and Reid heard Moore's work before composing 'On Our Own,'" they also found no "substantial" likeness between the songs.[73] Legal opinion suggests Moore's case was done in by Michael McCormick, the music expert who testified on his behalf. When pressed, McCormick admitted it was possible "On Our Own" was not based at all on "She Can't Stand It." McCormick also said he couldn't describe the exact genre of either song.[74] A separate court upheld the ruling in 1993.[75]

Columbia Pictures was met with another *Ghostbusters II* lawsuit in 1991 when an extra from the movie named Jody Oliver demanded a $1 million judgment over injuries sustained when she was trampled during the crowd scenes filmed at Washington Square Park. Oliver explained that "careless, reckless and negligent" behavior on the part of the filmmakers led to "riotous and unruly conditions" that left her "incapacitated from her employment and incapacitated from the normal pursuits of life." Among the injuries Oliver claimed were multiple body contusions, a sprained cervical spine, and a host of joint and ligament maladies.[76] Columbia denied any wrongdoing and said Oliver "knew the hazards . . . and inherent risks" of appearing as an extra; "such risks were assumed and accepted by her in performing and engaging in said activities."[77] The case dragged on for years until it was finally dismissed in 1998.[78]

A controversy much more publicized than either the Moore or Oliver complaints involved the promotional fast-food tie-in for *Ghostbusters II*. Hardee's was ten days into their *Ghostbusters II* campaign in July 1989 when reports surfaced that eleven children had accidentally swallowed the lithium batteries that powered a Ghostblaster noise toy the restaurant was selling. John Merritt, vice president of public affairs for Hardee's, offered comically bad damage control: "Every year at Christmas, children ingest all kinds of small parts and are none the worse for wear. But it's not good for you."[79] At first, Hardee's put up warning signs in their restaurants and pledged to spend $1 million to seal every battery compartment of their remaining Ghostblaster stock. With 2.8 million of the toys already sold, however, the restaurant realized they had to announce a recall. All Ghostblasters could be returned for a refund of $1.79 and a free dessert.

The documented cases of Ghostblaster battery swallowing totaled forty-six, but none of the children experienced serious medical repercussions. Another public relations figure for Hardee's, Jerry Singer, tried to put some spin on this PR nightmare. "[The recall is] going well, but I can't say how many [Ghostblasters] have been returned," he said. "We've had a lot of people saying they wished we still sold them. We were on target to sell out of the Ghostblasters." Singer refused to say how much this debacle might cost Hardee's. "In the short term it's going to have an impact because you're disappointing customers. Their repeat business was cut short. Now they may be going to get [Taco Bell's] *Batman* cups."

Singer added that Hardee's planned to "go after" the company that made the Ghostblasters for them, but it is unclear if such a legal avenue was ever actually explored.[80]

Cinema's history is littered with examples of audiences seeing things that aren't really there. In the 1990s, a rumor began circulating that a brief pattern of ill-defined movement spotted during *The Wizard of Oz* was a cast member hanging themselves. Eventually it was clarified that viewers were witnessing the movements of a bird that was purposely on set for atmosphere.[81] A cardboard cutout of Ted Danson that was misplaced during the filming of *Three Men and a Baby* convinced many people they were seeing the apparition of a young boy.[82] More risible was the belief that a male extra on the set of *Teen Wolf* exposed his penis during the very final scene of the movie. An investigation proved the extra in question was actually a woman who forgot her pants were unbuttoned, revealing a small portion of her underwear.[83]

Ghostbusters II is a special case in this rarefied class thanks to a viewer subset (both domestic and international) who swear that when they saw the movie theatrically in 1989, the very last shot during the credits included Slimer flying out of the Statue of Liberty's crown toward the camera. There are also those who insist Slimer was nowhere to be seen in the conclusive vista that looks from Liberty Island across to Manhattan's financial district; home media releases of *Ghostbusters II* have always presented a Slimer-free ending.[84] People who believe they saw Slimer at the end are usually written off as victims of the Mandela effect. What they must be remembering is Slimer flying toward the camera at the end of the first *Ghostbusters*.

There were definitely plans to have Slimer emerge from Lady Liberty at the end of *Ghostbusters II* as the sequence was scripted and storyboarded.[85] From there, the details get hazy. Only one day was spent filming on Liberty Island—December 5, 1988—and although the call sheet lists special effects company ILM, there are no effects shots detailed.[86] "I cannot answer with certainty," says chief visual effects coordinator Ned Gorman when asked whether or not the Slimer scene was filmed. "I remember a meeting about it and people talking about what a nice little button it would be . . . but then somebody, I can't remember if it was Ivan Reitman or [editor] Shelly Khan, said, 'Should we really do the same gag twice?' I think we shot a blue screen for it. I know it was never used in a preview."[87] Robin Shelby, the actress inside the Slimer costume, says she doesn't recall shooting anything for a Statue of Liberty bit. "I don't remember seeing it composited either," she adds. "But we shot so much stuff over a period of six weeks, they could have used some of that footage to make it look like that."[88]

Slimer's escape from Liberty's crown isn't the only discrepancy people claim to have noticed between *Ghostbusters II*'s theatrical and home versions. A Eugene Levy cameo was allegedly intact when the film screened in Calgary and a viewer in Alabama noticed changes during the mid-movie montage.[89] One theory suggests that numerous test prints of *Ghostbusters II* were accidentally shipped to theaters instead of the final cut. It is also plausible that the movie was re-edited for home release, though that doesn't seem to jibe with Ivan Reitman's style. He never really embraced the post-theatrical "director's cut" mentality like so many of his contemporaries. Besides, the major alterations that were made to *Ghostbusters II* just before its debut were his decision, not the studio's.[90] That said, there were *Ghostbusters* higher-ups who weren't satisfied with the final edit. "Harold [Ramis] was disappointed by some of the cutting decisions," says Gorman. "He was proud of the film but wished they had another month to edit."[91]

If the so-called "Slimer ending" of *Ghostbusters II* was completed and lost, there is always a chance it will be found. Missing film resurfaces all the time. Alternate versions of Fritz Lang's *Metropolis* were located nearly eighty years after the fact. It took 108 years, but historians finally uncovered the rare French comedy *Défense d'afficher*.[92] As of this printing, Reitman himself can claim two entirely vanished movies—1970's *The Columbus of Sex*, every copy of which is said to have been destroyed or completely re-edited, and 1971's *Foxy Lady*, an entry that has dematerialized without much explanation. In 2005, *Foxy Lady* costar Andrea Martin said she thought the master print fell victim to a fire. "It was a happy accident," she noted, touching on *Foxy Lady*'s reputation for being less than entertaining.[93]

Even though Slimer didn't have much of a presence in *Ghostbusters II*, his popularity endured thanks to his starring role in *The Real Ghostbusters* cartoon show. Toys based on that show remained hot around Christmastime in 1989. Some toys were hotter, though, like the Nintendo Entertainment System and anything related to recent animation smash *Teenage Mutant Ninja Turtles*.[94] Like *The Real Ghostbusters*, *Ninja Turtles* was often lumped in with what critics called "kidvid," the cheap and usually crude programming network television was aiming at children. Kidvid was called "brain-rotting" and "a national embarrassment" and there was a serious demand for reform. A congressional bill was drafted, the Children's Television Act, which asked that youth-oriented shows meet "the educational and informational needs of children." The CTA also sought a limit to advertising during these shows. President George H. W. Bush signed the bill into law in 1991 over the protest of numerous other Republicans who believed the advertising constraints to be unconstitutional. Bush actually had the same concerns but said he believed "wholeheartedly" that children deserved higher-quality entertainment.[95]

There was no question that at least one broadcast of *The Real Ghostbusters* was inappropriate for young viewers. On September 12, 1989, San Antonio station KABB-TV accidentally aired a portion of the rape scene from the 1977 film *Looking for Mr. Goodbar* during a 7:00 a.m. showing of the cartoon. A station technician pressed the wrong button while a KABB producer was editing the rape scene for later broadcast, cutting into the *Real Ghostbusters* satellite feed.[96] Program director Sam Bickel lamented, "We try to do a good thing and we wind up doing a bad thing. It was real quick. But it was a mistake."[97] Luckily, not many people were watching at the time. KABB only received fifteen viewer complaints over the *Goodbar* snafu.[98]

Slimer! and the Real Ghostbusters drew to a close in 1991, though the lovable glob lived on during the new decade thanks to a popular tie-in beverage. Two years earlier, the Hi-C juice brand decided to rename its Citrus Cooler flavor Ecto Cooler and put Slimer on the packaging to help promote *Ghostbusters II*.[99] Ten million dollars was spent rolling out Ecto Cooler, which was half of Hi-C's annual advertising budget, but it was money well spent. The "new" drink attracted a loyal fan base that kept it on shelves until the early 2000s.[100] Kiddie juices aren't usually subject to serious culinary review, but Ecto Cooler occasionally received such treatment. In 1989, the *New Haven Register*'s Supermarket Samplers gave it a pan.

"The very least you can ask of a drink is that its taste reveals its contents," Sampler scribe Carolyn Wyman wrote. "Ecto Cooler fails even this basic test. Is it made of apricots, pineapple, oranges, tangerines or any combination of these? It's hard to say from the taste and when you drink it out of an aseptic carton, you get no clues from its looks either. The only thing I can be sure of is that Ecto Cooler contains water and sugar."[101]

Saturday Night Live entered its fifteenth season in 1989, a milestone celebrated with a two-and-a-half-hour prime-time special reviewing the program's legacy thus far. Such a retrospective might have been satirical fodder for the original faces of *Saturday Night*. Now the show was less intrepid, less outrageous, more clearly the branch of a corporation (and it could still be incredibly funny thanks to cast members like Jan Hooks, Phil Hartman, Jon Lovitz, Mike Myers, and

Dana Carvey). *SNL* creator and executive producer Lorne Michaels acknowledged this progression: "Like the early days of rock n' roll, the innocence will never come back."[102]

Founding *SNL* writer Michael O'Donoghue had a sharper critique, dismissing the newer edition as "ossified" and likening its stars to "utility outfielders." "Lorne doesn't like confrontation and strife in his life," O'Donoghue explained to *SPIN*. "And the very people that make good comedy are the very people that make a hellish life around you, because they're always misanthropes and misfits and sad fucking people. Now he's got socially acceptable people around him." O'Donoghue continued: "There's no one in America who couldn't write 'SNL' now. It's a sitting target. First, there's the cold opening, then they say 'Live from New York it's Saturday Night,' then they go to that sort of 'the night belongs to Michelob' crawl—then the host monologue, commercial parody, then their first big piece, then a smaller piece, then the music act—I mean we all know the formula. And we could all write the formula."[103]

Some of *Saturday Night*'s most famous graduates also seemed to be losing their edge. "If you spend three minutes with Eddie [Murphy] you would laugh harder than in an hour-and-a-half of an Eddie Murphy movie," observed Mary Gross, one of Murphy's castmates in the early '80s. "The things he said around the office made me laugh more."[104] To that end, for many viewers *Ghostbusters II* was just another underwhelming entry in the Dan Aykroyd canon, which now included *The Couch Trip* and *The Great Outdoors*. Aykroyd knew those two specific films weren't classics and said as much not long after they were both released in 1988 ("Funny, but could have been better," he remarked about *The Couch Trip*; as for *The Great Outdoors*, "the director was inept"). Of course, Aykroyd believed he'd only ever been in one outright bad movie: 1982's *It Came from Hollywood*, a compilation of 1950s schlock clips.[105] Aykroyd must have been repressing memories of his supporting role in *Caddyshack II*, another film from 1988, one so egregious it inspired pull quotes like "for people in comas" and "dumber than grubs."[106]

"I am doing movies for the pure joy of doing them," Aykroyd told one reporter, insinuating that critical appraisal or being "hot" wasn't a career motivator.[107] And yet, when he fired longtime manager Bernie Brillstein in early 1988 to let his talent agency CAA handle all of his business exclusively, rumors swirled CAA curried Aykroyd's favor with promise of an Oscar nomination.[108] As improbable as that may have sounded, it became reality after the Academy saw Aykroyd's supporting role in Bruce Beresford's December 1989 adaptation of *Driving Miss Daisy*. The producers were wary of even meeting with Aykroyd, as surely his wacky persona would undermine the integrity of this racial drama. Aykroyd surprised them by approaching the part of Daisy's put-upon son with sincerity and commitment. "He made more money from *Ghostbusters II* than we spent on this whole picture," said producer Lili Zanuck. "[But he] didn't even want to know about the money or the billing. He just wanted to do it."

Aykroyd's nomination shocked a few cinephiles. "Maybe Academy voters thought they could use the nomination as a bribe to keep him from making *Ghostbusters III*," cracked John Jarvis in the *Marion Star*.[109] *Driving Miss Daisy* took home four Academy Awards the following March, including Best Picture. Aykroyd was not among the winners.[110] "Frankly, I had some hope of winning at the start," he said, "but then I saw *Glory* and I knew Denzel Washington was going to win. I even voted for him. But it was really good enough to be nominated. It was good enough to know that I was in the best movie of 1989."[111]

Ghostbusters II concluded its domestic run with a $112 million gross, placing it seventh on the list of 1989's most lucrative movies.[112] International box office wasn't any better. *Back to the Future II* was the motion picture that triumphed in the UK, Japan, and most other overseas markets against everything else (including *Batman*).[113] In Yugoslavia, *Ghostbusters II* was one of the weakest foreign imports, falling behind *Dead Poets Society* and *Born on the Fourth of July*.[114] One country that did go crazy for *Ghostbusters II* was the Philippines, so much so that even the Category 5–equivalent super typhoon simultaneously threatening to make landfall during the film's opening couldn't keep patrons away. *Ghostbusters II* earned more Philippine pesos in four days than the first movie made there in three weeks of release.[115]

Columbia Pictures had to view this as a small, almost meaningless victory. The studio spent $30 million making *Ghostbusters II* and they burned through another $15 to $30 million marketing it. With so much of the gross profits being divvied up among the actors, it was speculated that Columbia's take was under $10 million. Former Columbia head David Puttnam believed studio profits couldn't be higher than $5 million. And there were others who estimated that

Columbia made zero profit on *Ghostbusters II*. "[They] might actually be the first studio to lose money on a film that earned nine figures," wrote Bob Strauss in the *Daily Breeze*."[116]

Nevertheless, Columbia distribution president James Spitz insisted everyone at the company was pleased with *Ghostbusters II*'s performance. "I can count on one hand the films that have grossed more than $100 million while I have been at Columbia Pictures," Spitz said. "No one can be disappointed with a film that earns over $60 million in [theater] rentals. I hope Ivan Reitman makes *Ghostbusters III*. I'm eagerly awaiting it, and I think exhibitors are as well."[117]

Columbia did ask Reitman about making a *Ghostbusters III* before the year was out. The director told them, "I don't think so." Reitman was more interested in tackling something with greater humanity, something like his previous film, the Arnold Schwarzenegger / Danny DeVito comedy *Twins*.[118] Released in December 1988, *Twins* made roughly the same amount of money as *Ghostbusters II* and was considered a major success thanks to its relatively meager budget and the payoff of a risky concept (Schwarzenegger doing comedy).[119] As fate would have it, Reitman's next movie would be a re-teaming with Schwarzenegger for the action-comedy *Kindergarten Cop*. This story about a police officer who goes undercover as an elementary school teacher was being produced by Ron Howard and Brian Grazer's company Imagine Entertainment. "To turn something that abstract into a movie with Arnold and Ivan—that's the biggest rush there is," said Grazer.[120]

Bill Murray said he didn't know what to make of Reitman's "Schwarzenegger thing," as he called it. "I don't think I'm muscular enough for Ivan anymore," Murray joked, or half-joked.[121] At least they still agreed on one fundamental, which Murray reiterated in a July 1990 interview with the *Dallas Morning News*.

"There definitely will not be another *Ghostbusters* movie."[122]

THE LONG WINTER

Ghostbusters became part of a new vanguard on June 7, 1990, when a theme park attraction based on the film was included in the grand opening of Universal Studios Florida. A stage show called *The Ghostbusters Spooktacular* reimagined the rooftop battle against Gozer with laser effects and animatronics, and it was one of the few attractions in the park that wasn't based on a Universal property. This was acknowledgment that *Ghostbusters* was as culturally relevant as *Jaws*, *American Graffiti*, *Psycho*, or *King Kong*, all of which had their own USF spotlights.[1]

Ernie Hudson was one of the celebrities on hand to help open this motion-picture play land, but appearances by Hudson, Janet Leigh, Jimmy Stewart, and Michael J. Fox were overshadowed by technical malfunction. Numerous rides broke down within hours of the ribbon cutting, including those based on *E.T.* and *Earthquake*, and the premier *Jaws* attraction never opened at all.[2] Glitches of this sort plagued Universal for the remainder of the summer and *The Ghostbusters Spooktacular* was not immune. "Ghostbusters broke down in the middle both times I tried to sit through it," reported visiting *Seattle Post-Intelligencer* critic William Arnold.[3]

The curious streamed in anyway, eager to try to experience the interactive enshrinement of their favorite blockbusters.[4] Simultaneously, the masses were turning a blind eye to the latest starring vehicle from Bill Murray. *Quick Change*, a comedy about a clown who faces numerous difficulties making his escape after robbing a Manhattan bank, went belly-up against *Die Hard 2* and *Ghost* that July. Murray's decision to codirect *Quick Change* with writer Howard Franklin was born out of necessity; he couldn't find anyone else. "I asked all the top [directors]," the actor explained. "They said they only had so many movies left and they didn't want a clown comedy about a bank robbery as one of them. I mean, after you've done *Last Temptation of Christ* it's hard to do a clown with a gun."[5] Murray blamed *Quick Change*'s box office failure on parent studio Warner Bros., accusing them of neglecting promotion. "I think in 10 years people are going to say, 'That was a really good movie,'" Murray predicted.[6]

Warner Bros. was also the studio that agreed to make *Valkenvania*, a bizarre horror-comedy starring (and partially conceived by) Dan Aykroyd. "[It's] sort of like *Texas Chainsaw Massacre* meets *Wall Street*," Aykroyd said of *Valkenvania*'s premise, in which two New York yuppies become ensnared in a rural nightmare. Chevy Chase and Demi Moore were lined up as the yuppies and Aykroyd volunteered to direct. Like Murray with *Quick Change*, he was worried *Valkenvania* wouldn't get made otherwise.[7] Aykroyd proved he wasn't kidding with his *Texas Chainsaw Massacre* comparison as *Valkenvania* transformed into a more grotesque special effects demonstration than anyone was anticipating. Aykroyd wore heavy prosthetics to play the foul-looking elderly judge who traps the protagonists in his dilapidated, booby-trapped mansion. He also disappeared into a fat suit to play one of *Valkenvania*'s enormous slimy infants.

Aykroyd's inexperience as a director was more worrisome to Warner Bros. executives. He was attempting to direct by committee—each actor on *Valkenvania* was given a video monitor so they could provide feedback after takes.[8] Production crawled across most of 1990; autumn and Christmas release dates were rescheduled for February 1991. An anonymous source told *People* magazine the movie was "so bad it's unreleasable."[9] By this point *Valkenvania* had been retitled *Nothing but Trouble*, which was probably just as much a comment on making the film as watching it. Reviews published ahead of *Nothing but Trouble*'s opening weekend were scathing ("It is the cinematic equivalent of leprosy," said the *Richmond-Times Dispatch*).[10] In the end, Aykroyd's $30 million backwoods gross-out movie could only drum up a $3.5 million debut.[11] Although Aykroyd said he enjoyed making *Nothing but Trouble*, he knew he'd never direct again. "By my choice," he said, "and mutual choice of the industry."[12]

Ivan Reitman's career faced no peril after *Kindergarten Cop*, the Arnold Schwarzenegger action-comedy he directed in 1990 that enjoyed sizable popularity at the end of the year (the movie did even better in other countries like the UK and Australia).[13] Nevertheless, Reitman had his insecurities. Plans to direct a biopic about the Marx Brothers were abandoned because the director said he was simply "afraid to do it." "I couldn't imagine casting it in a way that would give me confidence to make the movie." Shortly after Reitman gave up on that project, in January 1992, Columbia Pictures touched base about another *Ghostbusters*. As he told one reporter, "They've gone back and checked the records and realized that three of my films were Columbia's most successful: *Stripes* and *Ghostbusters* and its sequel, and that piqued their interest about *Ghostbusters III*."[14]

Columbia Pictures wasn't just Columbia Pictures in 1992. They were a subsidiary of Sony Pictures Entertainment, which is how Eastern electronics firm Sony rebranded Columbia's multitiered empire after buying it three years earlier.[15] The figures cited in that unprecedented sale could hardly be believed. Sony paid $3.2 billion for Columbia, the largest amount a Japanese company ever spent on a US business, while simultaneously absorbing $1.3 billion in debt and buying $100 million shares of Coca-Cola stock.[16] For all their successes in cinema, it was Columbia Pictures Television that was most attractive to Sony. CPT was booming in the late '80s by producing and distributing sitcoms like *Designing Women*, *Married . . . with Children*, and *Who's the Boss?* (*Who's the Boss?* alone earned the studio $250 million in syndication monies over four years). Columbia also had the era's most popular soap opera, *The Young and the Restless*, as well as several profitable game shows.[17]

Sony's purchase of a legendary Hollywood studio exacerbated fears that American culture was becoming grist for Japan's indestructible economic machine.[18] A few years later, the deal looked like it was curdling for the buyers. An advertising depression cooled off success in the television market. On the film side, Sony was being run through with their own sword. Peter Guber and Jon Peters, the red-hot *Batman* producers Sony installed as Columbia's new heads shortly after the buyout, were sinking too much money into movies with not enough return. Some notable examples were actually distributed by partner studio Tri-Star, like Warren Beatty's gangster biopic *Bugsy*. *Bugsy* cost almost $40 million and lost nearly that much when it bottomed out at the box office in December 1991. Steven Spielberg's Peter Pan sequel *Hook*, another Tri-Star release from that month, was an $80 million fantasy that was very popular but not quite lucrative enough to make up for *Bugsy* and other duds.[19]

Guber and Peters, whose indifference toward money was only out-done by their disregard for other humans, burned through so much capital at the start of their Columbia tenure that analysts predicted a $300 million negative cash flow annually for the studio over the next several years. The pair needed as many blockbusters as they could get, not just for their own reputation but to justify the extra half billion Sony spent poaching them from Warner Bros.[20] So why not try to set a *Ghostbusters III* into motion? The last one earned over $100 million. It was a safer bet than the Mountie comedy Dan Aykroyd was still pushing, which he now wanted to make with Bill Murray and John Candy (Murray briefly touched on the plot that May: "[Dan] plays a Canadian Mountie, I'm an Alaskan State Trooper, and Candy's an escaped convict. It would cost about $700 million to make, but we're hopin' to get the Eskimo Nation to put up some of the dough").[21]

The unique rights agreement that split control over all future *Ghostbusters* movies among Reitman, Aykroyd, Murray, Harold Ramis, and the studio made a *Ghostbusters III* slightly more complicated to bring to life than the average sequel. And that was when every member of this quartet was getting along. Soon, two of these famed mirth-makers would have an incredible falling-out that lasted well into the next century.

In 1993, Harold Ramis described what it was like to make movies with Bill Murray. "When Bill is up, he's up. At other times it's like working with Vincent Van Gogh on a bad day. He seems so tortured by the demands on his creative resources, so plagued by public attention, you might think he was on the verge of cutting off his ears or one of yours. When something works for Bill, you're talking magic. At times he has to dig and mine his deepest reserves to come up with something good. That must be draining."[22]

It was February and Ramis was promoting the imminent release of *Groundhog Day*, his latest directorial effort starring Murray as cranky weatherman Phil Connors. Connors is a misanthrope who winds up embracing humanity after becoming trapped in an unexplained twenty-four-hour time loop. There would be no such redemption for Murray while making *Groundhog Day*. Van Gogh took over, driving a wedge between himself and Ramis, who was clearly being polite and deferential while doing press for the movie. When reflecting on

Groundhog Day decades later, Ramis made it clear the experience left him exasperated. "What I'd want to say to [Bill] is just what we tell our children: 'You don't have to throw tantrums to get what you want. Just say what you want.'"[23]

Ramis and Murray initially agreed that *Groundhog Day* was incredible. Ramis believed the story, conceived by rookie screenwriter Danny Rubin, was on par with a fairy tale like *The Frog Prince* or one of Frank Capra's movie. Murray was astonished that the narrative maintained excellence the whole way through. "Every person should be forced to read 25 scripts a year just to see how bad they can be," Murray said. "When you get one like [*Groundhog Day*], you have to do it. It sounded like life."[24] Problems began when Murray, who had previously disengaged with nearly every script he agreed to make, took an obsessive interest in reshaping *Groundhog Day*. Ramis had already done a rewrite to establish clarity and a traditional Hollywood script structure and that was the draft Murray signed on for, but Murray wanted something more philosophical. He recruited Rubin to help him breathe life into his vision. Ramis would call to get updates on their progress, and Murray refused to get on the phone. "I'm not here," he silently mouthed to Rubin.

Ramis and producing partner Trevor Albert were shocked when they read Murray's revisions. "Some new lines were good," Albert admitted, "but mostly it was like a grenade had been thrown into the middle of everything." Tempers flared at a meeting between Ramis and Murray a week and a half before *Groundhog Day* began shooting, setting the tone for the entire production. "I never really understood what was going on," said Rubin. "And it wasn't really between Harold and Bill—it was Bill. There was something going on with him. Because Harold seemed as bewildered by the whole thing as I was." In addition to his nasty disposition and uncooperative behavior, Murray pulled cruel stunts. When Ramis asked Murray to hire a go-between to help them communicate with minimal conflict, the actor hired a person who was hearing impaired.[25] At least one physical altercation broke out, when the normally even-tempered Ramis grabbed Murray by the shirt collar and threw him into a wall.[26]

Retellings of the *Groundhog Day* discord usually cite Murray's disintegrating marriage to Mickey Kelly as an explanation for his foul actions, or a sudden resentment of Ramis's hand in his success. Yet the anecdotes here aren't much worse than what has been relayed about Murray in general. When a photo shoot didn't go well, he hurled a dinner plate at the photographer.[27] He got so angry while filming *Ghostbusters II* that he tried to smash a chair over the prop master's head.[28] While making 1991's *What About Bob?*, Murray attacked producer Laura Ziskin several times, intentionally breaking her sunglasses at one point and shoving her into a nearby lake at another (Murray also threw an ashtray at costar Richard Dreyfuss after screaming, "Everyone hates you! You are tolerated!").[29] *Groundhog Day* was certainly not the last motion picture to include behind-the-scenes stories centered on Bill Murray's unchecked anger.

Too many people in Murray's community just accepted this as the price to pay for the laughs. Murray was another "tortured genius," like Jerry Lewis or Buddy Rich. And there was no reason for those in power to try to quash his infantile violence because his name was still incredibly valuable. See Ramis's explanation of how *Groundhog Day* was green-lit: "I went to Columbia Pictures with *Groundhog Day*, said 'Bill Murray' and I got their blessing. Period."[30]

Ramis held the line on *Groundhog Day* despite Murray's bullying, benching the esoteric in favor of warmth. Murray admitted that was the correct move upon the film's release and the world agreed—*Groundhog Day* was embraced as a classic, albeit slowly.[31] There was some rapture up front, like a *Washington Post* write-up that hailed the movie as "brilliantly imaginative" and "multilayered and rich without pretension," but the indelible mark of *Groundhog Day* wasn't fully realized until years later.[32] "Certainly I underrated it in my original review," Roger Ebert wrote in 2005. "I enjoyed it so easily that I was seduced into cheerful moderation. But there are a few films, and this is one of them, that burrow into our memories and become reference points. When you find yourself needing the phrase 'This is like *Groundhog Day*' to explain how you feel, a movie has accomplished something."[33] The film also achieved legitimacy as religious text; leaders from varying devotions hailed *Groundhog Day* as an affirming testament to faith.[34]

Groundhog Day's triumph did not smooth things over between Ramis and Murray. The two did not speak again for twenty-one years, save a handful of superficial exchanges at public events. Ramis, who would occasionally reach out to no avail, was hurt but not surprised. "I watched him turn on people before for virtually no reason," he told his daughter. "Maybe it was only a matter of time."[35] If Columbia Pictures was aware of the serious rift between Ramis and Murray, they didn't let it get in the way of asking the pair about *Ghostbusters III*. Ramis spoke about that briefly while doing press for *Groundhog Day*. "They haven't yet said, 'We'll do it with you or without you.' So far they're still anxious to do it with us, almost on any kind of basis. They wouldn't mind if we just showed up for five minutes and introduced the new Ghostbusters."[36]

In a separate interview from the same period, Murray made a face when asked if there would be a *Ghostbusters III*. "Yeah, if you write it," he replied. "Nobody else will."[37] Murray must have gotten wind of Dan Aykroyd's plans. That summer, Aykroyd announced a decision to retire in two years, citing fatigue. "I've done this an awful long time," he said. "It's enough . . . [Acting is] not art, it's work. It's punching in and punching out. I wouldn't miss it." Aykroyd's grand finale would include a *Blues Brothers* sequel and a "bridge-burning" tell-all memoir that would, in his words, "get all the jerks who jacked me around in this town." (At the same time, the actor was writing a satirical novel about moviemaking that was set in the year 2003.)[38]

When it came to *Ghostbusters*, Aykroyd said he didn't think they would "further exploit" the brand. "It looks like that's about had its run. . . . Although we made a good movie, [*Ghostbusters II*] just wasn't as commercially successful as everybody thought it would be." In the same breath, however, Aykroyd admitted it would be "a real dream" to make *Ghostbusters III*. "I think there's a great story to be told."[39]

Aykroyd had a change of heart about retiring in 1996. In public, fans were starting to recognize him mostly from his supporting role in the recent Chris Farley comedy *Tommy Boy*, which prompted Aykroyd to try to launch a comeback.[40] The book projects were put aside, the *Blues Brothers* sequel moved forward, and the comedian started discussing a *Ghostbusters III* script with Sony Pictures that September. The story involved new, younger Ghostbusters and Aykroyd had casting choices. Namely, his *Tommy Boy* costar Farley (who was also a linchpin of early '90s *Saturday Night Live*) and sitcom-star-turned-action-hero Will Smith. "I've already talked to Chris about the casting and have told him I'll be drafting the part for him."

Would Bill Murray be involved? No, said Aykroyd, and neither would Ivan Reitman. "They want to concentrate on other things."[41] Harold Ramis was on the fence. "Dan won't give up," he jokingly complained that July. "I know Bill won't do it, and I don't know whether I would. I think we milked that thing twice already." Ramis was uncertain about even trying to cowrite a *Ghostbusters III*, though he did pitch a few ideas for the story.[42] Aykroyd turned to Tom Davis, another longtime collaborator, to help flesh out this new paranormal adventure. Aykroyd's chief concept: send the Ghostbusters to Hell, literally, and have them square off against the Devil.[43]

Ahead of that, however, the Ghostbusters were being prepared for a return to television.

"We really wanted to make as much of a horror show as we could make without crossing a line. We wanted to push the envelope as much as we could."

Jeff Kline was an executive in the drama department at Columbia Pictures Television before he decided to join up with the children's programming division the company launched in 1995. "The first show I got involved with there was 'Jumanji,'" he explains. "They said the next show they wanted to do was 'Ghostbusters.'" According to Kline, this was not because Columbia or Sony had plans for a new *Ghostbusters* movie (the children's unit was never entirely privy to those matters anyway). "The toy company Trend Masters may have been the driving force," Kline says. "They came to Sony and said they wanted to make a toy line for Ghostbusters. That's my memory of it. But you know, a lot of those animated shows were meant to be bridges from what came before and what was next."

Kline and *Real Ghostbusters* veteran Richard Raynis were named executive producers for the new series, which would revolve around Egon Spengler teaching several rookie Ghostbusters the ins and outs of the trade. "Richard is the one who had the idea of making Egon a carry-through character," Kline says. "He may have also had the idea to make Egon a professor. He thought Egon was the character kids most related to." Like *The Real Ghostbusters*, founding *Ghostbusters* authors Dan Aykroyd and Harold Ramis had no creative involvement with this cartoon. "They just had [producer] credits," Kline says. "I really don't remember them giving us any rules with our show, either. We had a pretty open playing field."

Trend Masters also never dictated how anything had to be on the program, though Kline does recall a donnybrook with the toymakers over the show's name. "They wanted to call it 'Super Ghostbusters.' Richard and I thought that made the Ghostbuster sound like super-heroes, which they weren't."[44] Though Columbia started promoting the show as *Super Ghostbusters* in early 1996, the name was changed to *Extreme Ghostbusters*, a fitting title for the show Kline, Raynis, and the other figureheads were trying to create.[45]

Extreme Ghostbusters pushed to be more severe and ghoulish than most children's entries, particularly in visual aesthetic (even beloved mascot Slimer had more of a traditional hobgoblin appearance in this edition). Raynis used designs and art from Australian illustrator Fil Barlow, with whom he'd worked on the *ALF* animated series, and *Duckman* creator Everett Peck. The bizarre, confrontational style of *Duckman* is reflected in *Extreme Ghostbusters*, though there was a deliberate blending in of aspects from *The Real Ghostbusters*. Barlow wasn't thrilled with that decision. "I disliked the original character designs for 'Real Ghostbusters.' . . . I felt that their faces were blobby and undefined. I still think that today."[46]

Kline reveals that the dynamic between newbie characters Kylie, Eduardo, Roland, and Garrett was influenced by coming-of-age classic *The Breakfast Club*. "I'd also like to point out, for the record, that Kylie was named after Kylie Minogue, Roland was named after a FOX Kids executive named Roland Poindexter, and Garrett was named after the son of a woman I was dating. Eduardo was just a languid name I liked." The voice cast, which included Tara Strong (Kylie), Jason Marsden (Garrett), and Alfonso Ribeiro (Roland), got along slightly better than the kids in *The Breakfast Club*. "We recorded in the evening, I'm sure for budgetary reasons and maybe availability," says Kline, "and they'd all hang out for hours afterwards. That cast really loved each other."

Budgeting did prove a difficult issue for *Extreme Ghostbusters*. In order to make their finances work, the show had to record two episodes a week.[47] This was particularly difficult considering some of the staff's prior commitments. "Richard Raynis had very high standards," says producer Audu Paden, "but he was still working on *The Simpsons* or *Family Guy* and he wouldn't be available to approve stuff. We'd be waiting around until eleven at night." Then there was the theme song. According to Paden, there was an incredible delay with Ray Parker Jr. approving use of his "Ghostbusters" music. "It got down to the wire. We had maybe thirty hours before the first mix was due before we finally got his okay."[48] Jim Cummings, a journeyman voice actor known for his work with Disney, performed a new rendition of Parker's theme with a heavy metal edge.

The theme matched the dark, garish noir of *Extreme Ghostbusters*, which only ran for forty episodes in syndication in late 1997. What little notice it received wasn't positive. "'Extreme Ghostbusters' is the next generation of ghostbusters without cleverness or comedy," huffed the *Chicago Sun-Times*. "It trades on the name, giving us violence in return."[49] An impact or popularity similar to *The Real Ghostbusters* wasn't in the cards. "If I spend too much time thinking about that, I'll go crazy," Kline mutters with a laugh. "A big reason the other show is remembered so fondly is because it sold a crap ton of toys. And it was on a network, whereas we were a syndication block on at different times across the country."[50]

Yet for a small, specific generation of viewers, *Extreme Ghostbusters* was something to be cherished. This would become clear to the creators as our culture's general appreciation for animated fare deepened over the years. The show would also be praised for the diverse ethnic makeup of its characters as well as its depiction of differently abled character Garrett, whose wheelchair use was never the focus of his adrenaline-crazed personality.[51]

"There were no fans back then, we just did the work and got on with the next show," Barlow remarked. "Now it's a thing. I'm glad that our efforts affected so many people in such a positive way. Especially creatively. It's really good to see."[52]

Hollywood was littered with high-concept science fiction movies in the late '90s, and Columbia Pictures could claim one of the most popular with 1997's *Men in Black*. Released that July, the story of two federal agents hunting aliens in New York City starring Will Smith and Tommy Lee Jones couldn't be beaten that year with its domestic gross of $250 million (globally, *Men in Black* took in nearly $600 million).[53] *Men in Black* earned comparisons to *Ghostbusters*—"this is a comedy about cool dudes with daffy gizmos who serve as deadpan custodians of the absurd," said Brian D. Johnson in *Maclean's*.[54] David Ansen of *Newsweek* noticed other moves swiped from the Aykroyd bible: "Invent a *Ghostbusters*-like agency, add the poker-faced seriosity [*sic*] of *Dragnet* . . . dress your heroes in *Blues Brothers* fashions and you get, paradoxically, something that almost feels new."[55]

Aykroyd's own high concept that he was working on with Tom Davis, *Ghostbusters III*, had been ready to go before *Men in Black*'s release. A story treatment dated February 6, 1997, outlined with detail an unholy adventure for the paranormal eliminators. It opens at a funeral home in Yonkers, where the corpse of Mrs. Flora Burke gets out of her coffin and walks into the office to bum a cigarette from a stunned attendant. The Ectomobile arrives on the scene and three new Ghostbusters get out. Frank Stantz, nephew of founding Ghostbuster Ray Stantz, is the role that was obviously meant for Chris Farley: "a big cute-looking blonde [*sic*] man in his early thirties" who is "very nervous and physically ungainly. [He is] tense and ill-suited to the work." With Frank are Nicole, a "very tough no-nonsense ex-Airborne type," and a "blinking, mouth-breathing brainy kid" named Dwight. They enter the funeral home to discover the staff giving snacks to various restless corpses. The corpses, "wandering around like children who don't want to go to bed," wish to resume their lives. The attendant points out this is probably within their legal rights. So the Ghostbusters take Mrs. Burke back to her shocked family. "What's for supper?" she asks.[56]

Frank Stantz and his crew are one of several new teams in this treatment, as the Ghostbusting business has thrived in the years since *Ghostbusters II*. Winston Zeddemore is introduced as a company executive with his own fancy office. Egon Spengler is busy conducting telekinesis experiments in which people try to move pinballs and smoke with their minds. Ray Stantz is still active as well and tries to guide his nephew, who is a "problem employee." Peter Venkman is absent; a postcard reveals that he's in Indonesia mining gold.[57]

The Ghostbusters determine that death isn't taking for so many people because there's a blockage preventing souls from crossing over. Ray and Egon witness this firsthand when they visit the deathbed of their mentor Professor Wyance, "a charismatic man with beautiful soft gray eyes." Wyance discovered that life and death work like radio frequency with "two separate oscillating lines" for each state. One can move between these realms with a device called a "phase flux generator/shifter" that Wyance was working on before he died. Using this machine, the Ghostbusters must visit the afterlife and solve the blockage problem (the notion of Hell existing concurrent to reality was thought up by Harold Ramis).[58]

The Ghostbusters assume they'll need a car to get around in the afterlife, so they rig up one of the Ectomobiles to Wyance's phase flux invention in a Brooklyn warehouse. In a flash, Frank, Nicole, Dwight, Ray, Egon, and Winston find themselves in the grim reflection of New York City that exists in Hell. The streets are jammed with taxis from all different time periods. Traffic is so bad on the Brooklyn Bridge that cars are spilling over into the East River (the Ectomobile has been modified to hover above all this gridlock). At South Street Seaport, they see a crowded ferry governed by "four foot high leathery-skinned little demons using pitchforks to shovel the people off the barge into the river." The Ghostbusters are trying to gain an audience with the mayor when "a grizzled old guy in turn of the century clothing with rheumy alcoholic eyes and a gaping bullet wound in the side of his head" who claims to be a lawyer offers help. He can't save them from being imprisoned for trespassing, though they manage to use "their technology" to escape.[59] A summit with the mayor proves ineffectual; the lawyer then agrees to take the Ghostbusters to meet the person who actually runs the afterlife, Ron Lucifer.

Their journey to Lucifer Towers takes them through other exaggerated versions of famous New York locales, like a Greenwich Village where everyone has comically severe piercings and a Washington Square Park overrun with hell dogs. Ron Lucifer is likened to Alec Baldwin and described as "attractive . . . well-spoken, [a] smooth, corporate type, [but a] reasonable guy." Lucifer confirms that his realm is becoming overpopulated and that's why "souls are being denied entry." During their meeting, Frank notices a "warm, white beautiful glow" in New Jersey, an area that is out of Ron Lucifer's jurisdiction. Lucifer, who has a vested interest in the Ghostbusters' phase flux device, traps them in his office for a battle ("the building shoots up a thousand stories" as the fight commences). Our heroes give Lucifer the slip and decide they need to send as many souls as they can across the George Washington Bridge to what is obviously Heaven. Frank broadcasts to the citizens of Hell via Lucifer's PA: "If there's a God and He's the God He thinks He is, He's not going to turn you away. All you have to do is choose."

The Ghostbusters lead many souls over the bridge, and as they are admitted their grotesque figures transform into that of angels. One especially gorgeous angel moves toward Frank with arms open for an embrace. As Frank goes to return the gesture, the Ghostbusters phase themselves back into our world, where Frank ends up romantically hugging a New Jersey transit cop ("a fat black female Jersey transit cop," as the treatment puts it). At the very end, we see a newborn in a hospital who as the exact same soft gray eyes as the late Professor Wyance.[60]

This iteration of *Ghostbusters III* was rumored to be in development in November 1997, sharing gossip column space with *Men in Black II*, a fifth *Batman* movie, a *Superman* reboot, and a big-screen version of *The A-Team* starring Mel Gibson.[61] Whatever excitement there was over Chris Farley potentially slipping into a Ghostbusters uniform came crashing down a month later when the comedian was found dead from an accidental overdose in his Chicago apartment.[62] Shortly thereafter *Newsweek* reported that Sony was trying to move forward with *Ghostbusters III* but compensating the rights

Matty Simmons and Ivan Reitman on the set of *National Lampoon's Animal House*, 1977. PHOTOFEST

"Call the professionals—Ghostbusters." PHOTOFEST

Ecto-1 was originally supposed to be black with purple lights. PHOTOFEST

Rick Moranis as Vinz Clortho. PHOTOFEST

Sigourney Weaver. PHOTOFEST

Playwright and actor Ernie Hudson. PHOTOFEST

Ray Parker Jr. and friends dance through Times Square. PHOTOFEST

Bill Murray, Harold Ramis, and Dan Aykroyd on the first big case. PHOTOFEST

"Okay, who brought the dog?" PHOTOFEST

The real star of *Ghostbusters*, the Stay Puft Marshmallow Man. PHOTOFEST

Crossing the streams atop Spook Central. PHOTOFEST

The Gatekeeper and the Keymaster. PHOTOFEST

Hey hey, the gang's all here for *Ghostbusters II*. PHOTOFEST

Harold Ramis.
PHOTOFEST

Critics loved Peter MacNicol as the fussy Janosz Poha. PHOTOFEST

Aykroyd in his trademark ecto goggles. PHOTOFEST

A somewhat meta logo. PHOTOFEST

Deutschendorf twins William and Hank played baby Oscar. PHOTOFEST

Ghostbusters 2016: a new team answers the call. PHOTOFEST

Once an ambulance, now a hearse. PHOTOFEST

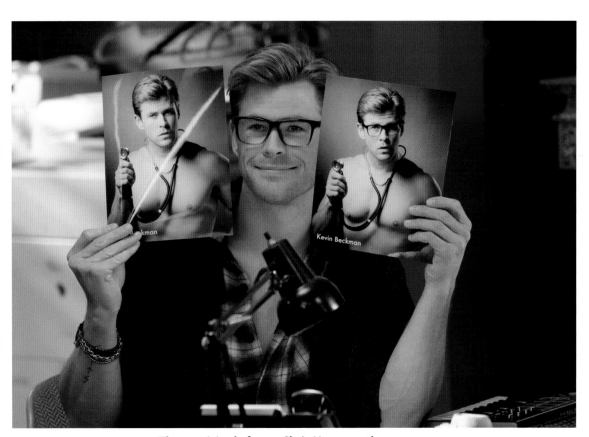

The suprisingly funny Chris Hemsworth. PHOTOFEST

Melissa McCarthy, Kristen Wiig, Kate McKinnon, Leslie Jones. PHOTOFEST

Leslie Jones, force of nature. PHOTOFEST

Director Paul Feig wanted the streams to look like lava. PHOTOFEST

Pure thrills: Logan Kim and McKenna Grace in *Ghostbusters: Afterlife*. PHOTOFEST

An unexpected avatar of the pandemic. PHOTOFEST

Paul Rudd as Gary Grooberson. PHOTOFEST

Muncher, based on a tardigrade and Chris Farley. PHOTOFEST

Egon's grandkids and Podcast in front of the Wrecto. PHOTOFEST

A darling Mini Puft before the chaos. PHOTOFEST

holders was an issue. "After demanding more than 40% of Sony's receipts, they all backed down to a more reasonable price, sources say. Except for [Bill] Murray. He still wants a hefty cut of the gross not to star in the movie."[63]

The Internet was paving a new path for showbiz hearsay in this era, and amateur movie news websites like Ain't It Cool and Dark Horizons were becoming daily must-reads thanks to their juicy anonymous spy reports.[64] *Ghostbusters III* tidbits were a staple of these sites no matter how outlandish they felt. "[Talk show host Conan O'Brien] is helping [Dan] Aykroyd write the movie, and will also have a significant part in it," read one report (O'Brien's assistant responded in July 1998: "Conan has nothing to do with the *Ghostbusters 3* script").[65] Another rumor, verbatim: "Aykroyd spoke with former 'Seinfeld' star Jason Alexander and he asked Jason to maybe consider playing a role as a ghostbuster" ("This is not true," Alexander confirmed for this volume through his publicist).[66] There were stories that the script for *Ghostbusters III* was so long, they'd have to divide it into two films and that Chris Farley's comedy partner David Spade would somehow be involved.[67]

There were also websites dedicated entirely to *Ghostbusters*, like Spook Central, GB Central, and Proton Charging. Though Michigan native Bill Emkow's The Ghostbusters Homepage is often cited as the first of these fan-based endeavors, Emkow insists his website was actually the second to appear when it came online in February 1996. "The first site was just a purple screen with the 'no ghost' logo in the center," he says. "I tried contacting whoever made it but I never got a response." The Ghostbusters Homepage grew to include separate areas for trivia about the original movie, schematics for building your own screen-accurate proton pack, and a section dedicated to *Ghostbusters III* news. "I encourage you to email me if you hear any verified news about *Ghostbusters III*," Emkow wrote on the site. "Unless, of course, you are Dan Aykroyd or Harold Ramis, I would take your word of mouth." Emkow had a message board on the Ghostbusters Homepage as well that allowed "ghostheads" (a term coined by fan and site user Norm Gagnon) to virtually speculate and commiserate with each other about *Ghostbusters III*.[68]

Harold Ramis eventually warmed up to the idea of a third *Ghostbusters*. In an interview with the *Chicago Sun-Times* in February 1999, he said, "Dan Aykroyd and I talk about a new *Ghostbusters* on a regular basis. . . . The studio would love to make a deal, but they're not sure who to make the deal with. Bill [Murray] is very elusive. Our director, Ivan Reitman, is also standing on the side. . . . The dream plan is that Danny would produce it. I would direct the next sequel, and we would recruit some newer, younger, popular ghostbusters." Asked if he had any actors in mind, Ramis said, "Yeah, Leonardo [DiCaprio]. We'll have Leonardo and Ben Affleck. Matt Damon would also be good. Maybe Will Smith is free. He did so well with those aliens."[69] In other interviews, Ramis said he also considered Chris Rock and Ben Stiller.[70]

Shortly thereafter, Bill Murray commented that he was only interested in *Ghostbusters III* if his character died at the start of the movie. "I read those stories," Reitman said, "but people should remember that Bill marches to his own drummer and he changes his tune an awful lot."[71]

Dan Aykroyd and Tom Davis made significant revisions as they turned their 1997 story treatment into a full-length *Ghostbusters III* script. The opening was changed to a complex special effects shot that moves into and beneath the grave of philanthropic financier J. J. Desseter. They emphasize a "deep black velvety blackness" under Desseter's body as we hear "the sound of deep grinding gears and screaming moaning grate of massive old rusted iron plates being ground and pushed against each other." Suddenly a door opens and Desseter is shoved into the black void by a pair of demonic-looking arms. He then bursts out of his coffin and levitates above the grave site, "part phantom, part corpse, three times the size he was in life and imbued with the power of the dark afterlife." Desseter floats over to a building he dedicated to the arts during his life that has now become a garish-looking modern bank. His rage shatters the bank's windows. At the same moment, fellow grave evictee Ulysses S. Grant is breaking windows and terrifying people as he cries out for whiskey.[72]

A "lowdown rap-rhythm tune" signals that *Ghostbusters III* has started; "I've seen it all between you and me," a rapper intones, "let me get down with it and set you free, leave it to the Master, the Master GB!" We're introduced to a new Ghostbusters crew as they respond to a call about Desseter's ghost haunting a bridge. There's Franky, a muscular "Jersey punkster" with purple hair and multiple piercings (unlike Frank in the story treatment, Franky is not related to any established character). Nicole and Dwight have been cut in favor of an uptight former gymnast named Moira, the "beautiful Hispanic college graduate" Carla, and "handsome FUBU devotee" Lovell.[73] As they engage Desseter, the script notes that these Ghostbusters "will use '90s versions of the same proton/neutrona throwers with separate trap until the conversion to muon reservoir technology." The team captures Desseter, but much of their equipment accidentally plunges into the river below. Their supervisor, Dr. Nat Colby, a ten-year-old with "a very prominent cranium," arrives to scold them for their clumsiness.[74]

The full-length script carries over the idea that the Ghostbusters have a larger operation now, one that's housed in a city sanitation garage with thirty Ectomobiles (though a scene with Louis Tully makes it clear the company is losing money).[75] Professor Wyance is replaced by Father Trenodius, a renowned theo-physicist who is also "the Church's leading authority on exorcism." He has theories about the afterlife but no magical invention to get there.[76] After numerous scenes of the dead returning and trying to resume their lives, J. J. Desseter's extremely wealthy descendent Marta summons the Ghostbusters to her office. Marta, who is described as looking like Lauren Bacall, demands to know what they're going to do about all the undead people. Ray Stantz says they can achieve "afterworld access through alteration of the planar frequency around the Five Boroughs by a gluon phase reversal" but they need to build a "Heisenberg-Feynmann loop provider," "muon pots," "particle grieves," and a "planar frequency attenuator." Marta asks how much that will cost. Spengler: "If we want it by next week, nine billion dollars." Marta balks at first but changes her mind after seeing J. J.'s ghost in her private bathroom.[77]

In Hell, the sky burns orange, the streetlamps glow red, police officers are large minotaurs with "translucent blue skin," and it is impossible to travel faster than six miles per hour.[78] The shady lawyer they meet is named Michael Taaaghaanikghh, "an orange-suited six-foot figure in a bad orange-brown wig over a heavily leathered sun/jerkied and olive mottled head behind Jim Jones shades."[79] The Devil is called Luke Siffler, and he actually manages to phase-shift over in our world for a few moments during the office battle.[80] Up to this point, Peter Venkman has been omitted from the story with no explanation. As the Ghostbusters discover that the heavenly area of New Jersey is partially a golf course, they see Venkman riding toward them in a golf cart. Ray Stantz starts to apologize to him for "what happened" but Venkman interrupts: "Wait. I'm not Venkman. I assumed this familiar form for you because it is the best way to communicate to you so many complicated matters. However Pete does say hello. He's in a very happy place and he forgives you for your part in the lab accident." God then invites all the overflow souls from Hell to Heaven to "be forgiven, redeemed and accepted."[81]

In a final confrontation, Siffler grows into his full demonic form, grabs Ray Stantz by the neck, and climbs to the top of his building with him. Moira and Winston Zeddemore work to save Ray while Lovell and Franky fight off giant hell hornets. Siffler is defeated, everyone escapes, and the souls cross over to Heaven. The adventure ends in a traffic jam in the real world. "It's beautiful, isn't it?" Lovell asks. "I love this city," replies Carla. "Unconditionally," adds Franky.[82] First completed in March 1999, this script was titled *Ghostbusters III: Hellbent*.[83]

Hellbent paints an intriguing picture, but the narrative is light on jokes and heavy on awkward dialogue. Complaining in his first scene about having to work overtime, Lovell huffs, "Yuh, like this is why I made straight As at the Bronx School of Science." Moments later, he refers to his assertive Ghostbusting partner Moira as "the Witch Queen."[84] When the Ghostbusters meet God toward the end of the script, Franky asks for an autograph. "No more autographs since Moses," God replies.[85] Luke Siffler is given a weird, feverish rant to reel off once he's been defeated: "Doll to the child, child to the woman, woman to the man, man to the devil. Bit sexist, but never mind. The point is, you won the day. THE! DAAAAAAY! Days are like seconds to me. How many minutes will it feel like until you're back here the old fashioned way?"[86]

Hellbent may not have been Shakespeare, but that wasn't a deterrent for Sony Pictures. That summer, the company purchased the Internet domain name Ghostbusters3.com, causing a new ripple of excitement.[87] *Ghostbusters III* would be part of a rebuilding effort for Sony, whose fortunes had fallen since the heady days of *Men in Black*. The anticipated sequel to that monolith was joining the likes of *Jumanji 2* in development hell. Simultaneous plans for a trilogy of big-budget *Godzilla* remakes collapsed after the debut entry was judged to be one of 1998's biggest embarrassments. Under Sony Pictures head John Calley, Columbia president and eventual chair Amy Pascal rolled out a slate of smaller films in 1999 that only did okay at the box office (one exception being Adam Sandler's *Big Daddy*). To try to win back stature, the company committed the immediate future to pricey spectacles like Mel Gibson's *The Patriot*, Arnold Schwarzenegger's *The 6th Day*, and a big-screen iteration of *Charlie's Angels*.

Most of these movies were projecting budgets in the $80 million to $100 million range (even *Stuart Little*, the family comedy about a talking mouse scheduled for Christmas 1999, cost $103 million).[88] This was Sony's expenditure comfort zone, apparently, especially after sinking a reported $130 million into *Godzilla*. Although *Godzilla* made money, it didn't bring in enough to vaporize the perception that it was a failure on all levels.[89] So when Dan Aykroyd proposed a $120 million budget for *Ghostbusters III*, Sony demurred. Aykroyd was persistent, insisting that it was a small price to pay for a sequel that would pull *Men in Black* numbers at the box office. The studio knew they'd get the short end of that stick, though. It was a foregone conclusion that huge gross percentage points would have to go to the actors just to get *Ghostbusters III* made.

The debate became heated, so much so that Aykroyd moved his offices off of the Sony lot. The actor unloaded about the squabble during an *Access Hollywood* interview that November. "[Sony's] trying to get bargains. They're trying to get the next *Blair Witch*," he said, referring to *The Blair Witch Project*, the 1999 indie horror film that raked in nine figures on a budget well under $1 million. "But, you know, sometimes you have to seed for the big harvest to come in. . . . I'm not angry at all. I'm just resigned. I'm passionate and I'm sorry I have to leave the lot because I like it there."[90]

Seven months later, *Hellbent* was pronounced dead. "There will be no *Ghostbusters III*," Ivan Reitman told a reporter. Financial hurdles were mentioned, but for Reitman there was a more pressing issue: "I can't solve all the script problems."[91] This was just as well for some of the other Ghostbusters.

"I can't say my heart was really in it," Harold Ramis remarked in 2005. "Making the third one."[92]

Dan Aykroyd and Tom Davis dusted off *Hellbent* in the summer of 2006 for a "limited revision." There were talks with Columbia Pictures around that time about reviving the script as a computer-animated feature. One of the most significant updates Aykroyd and Davis made to *Hellbent* added more color and weight to Peter Venkman's absence at the top of the story. After an experiment with a highly unstable artificial black hole goes awry, Ray Stantz looks up at a portrait of Venkman that graces a wall in the Ghostbusters headquarters. "I could have killed us all," he says. "Like my last mistake did to him."

"Ray, you did not kill Venkman," Egon Spengler counters. "It was an industrial accident. He lost his grip and slipped."

"But he was trying to help *me*."

"Peter Venkman was the Chairman of this company. He called the shots on what we were to research. He was obsessed with developing his foolproof love potion and it cost him his life. We were all merely instruments in his hands."[93]

Astute, considering how attempts to revive *Ghostbusters III* in subsequent years would play out.

I'LL TELL MY BROTHER

There was no shortage of wacky comedies bearing Ivan Reitman's name throughout the 1990s. In 1992, he produced *Stop! Or My Mom Will Shoot*, which paired Sylvester Stallone with Estelle Getty for a dud loathed by critics, moviegoers, and Stallone himself.[1] Reitman fared better directing Arnold Schwarzenegger as a pregnant man in 1994's zany outing *Junior*.[2] Then there was *Space Jam*, a 1996 live action/animation hybrid based on a series of TV ads starring Bugs Bunny and Michael Jordan. *Space Jam* was unbridled commercialism but *New York Times* writer Janet Maslin observed that the film's "loose, wisecracking style" was in line with producer Reitman's output. "The film also kids about its own crassness," Maslin added. "One character succeeds in plugging Hanes, Wheaties, Gatorade and a Big Mac in a single sentence."[3]

Reitman could have been accused of regression when he agreed to produce shock jock Howard Stern's 1997 biopic *Private Parts*, a movie as close to *Animal House* in raunch as the decade had seen. There were definite knocks for backsliding when Reitman directed 2001's *Evolution*. David Duchovny and Orlando Jones headlined this summer sci-fi comedy about hip, goofball scientists living in Arizona who fight an infestation of rapidly developing nightmare creatures (in this case, aliens) while federal officials try to interfere with their efforts. *Evolution*'s heroic quartet wind up in matching uniforms, the ending has a leviathan that explodes into viscous goo, and the soundtrack emphasizes an upbeat funk-rock hit. Dan Aykroyd also had a supporting part.

"Look, there's no way around the comparisons," Jones admitted. "On the poster that came out in December, all it said was, 'Coming this summer: *Evolution*, from the director of *Ghostbusters*.'"[4]

The reviews were savage. "Forced like chopped meat through a flagrantly self-reverential *Ghostbusters* template, *Evolution* seems to be producer-director Ivan Reitman's attempt to show he can re-create the success of his biggest comedy ever," wrote John Anderson in the *Los Angeles Times*. "What he proves instead is that, given time and money, a comedy director can devolve into a lower life form."[5] *Journal News* writer Marshall Fine said, "To get a sense of just how weak a film *Evolution* is, think of what *Ghostbusters* would be like without Bill Murray. That's right: a not-particularly funny Dan Aykroyd movie (is there any other kind?) [with] the latest in special-effects technology. . . . [The cast] is helpless without a good script—unlike Murray, who is funnier than this movie when he talks in his sleep."[6]

Evolution imitates aspects of *Men in Black* and *Jurassic Park* but the echoes of *Ghostbusters* are so pronounced, many people suspected it was a repurposing of an unused *Ghostbusters III* script. That wasn't true. *Evolution* was actually based on a tense, thrilling Don Jakoby script that contained zero humor. Reitman read it and thought he could make it work as a comedy. Jakoby said there was no subterfuge from the director: "He was upfront about it. [He said] 'This is what I intend to do if you sell me the script. If you can't live with that, don't sell me the script.'" After Jakoby tried writing his own funny version and writing duo Todd Phillips and Scott Silver took a pass, Reitman hired David Diamond and David Weissman to fully author his *Evolution*. "Our script *The Minutemen* was strongly influenced by *Ghostbusters*," says Weissman. "Ivan read it and asked us to come in. Todd Phillips and Scott Silver wrote a very good script but what Ivan was looking for was more akin to *Ghostbusters*. He felt we captured that tone in *Minutemen*."

"Ivan didn't think there was gonna be another *Ghostbusters*, which was very frustrating," says Diamond. "He had given up on it and wanted to do something different."[7] *Evolution* wasn't different enough, but certain aspects of this retread were appreciated. "[Duchovny and Jones] have a nice double-act together," Roger Ebert wrote in his two-and-a-half-star review. "Like the characters in *Ghostbusters*, they talk intelligently and possess wit and irony, and are not locked into one-liners. Jones even gets a laugh out of a significant nod, which is not easy in a movie with this decibel level."

Ebert summarized *Evolution* as "not good" but also "nowhere near as bad as most recent comedies."[8]

While promoting *Evolution*, costars Julianne Moore and Seann William Scott said they had to push Reitman to give their characters more depth. "I didn't like the script until Ivan said I could fall down," Moore explained, referring to her character's recurring clumsiness. Scott decided to flesh out the aspiring firefighter he was playing with characteristics borrowed from eccentric low-budget filmmaker Mark Borchardt. As Professor Harry Block, Jones was pleased to sidestep stereotypes. "Usually there's a black guy and a white guy in a movie, and one thing happens," he said. "The black guy is from the ghetto and the white dude is from Harvard, and the black dude says, 'You don't understand my people,' and the white dude says, 'Look, I don't want to hear your Ebonics, buddy.' The other thing is, the black dude usually dies in the first half hour, and then in the next half hour the woman dies. I just wanted to do a movie where there's a black and a female who are as much a part of saving the day as the main guy is."[9]

Despite poor reviews, *Evolution* was predicted to be the box office winner the weekend of its June 8, 2001, release. The movie landed in fourth place instead, taking in a mere $13.2 million and falling behind Michael Bay's World War II epic *Pearl Harbor*, the animated hit *Shrek*, and a number one debut from the John Travolta thriller *Swordfish*.[10] *Ghostbusters* producer Michael Gross revealed many years later that *Evolution*'s flopping stamped out whatever enthusiasm Sony had for an actual *Ghostbusters III*.[11] Not that sequel shareholder Bill Murray was helping matters. "We can't come to any agreements," Aykroyd said a few days after *Evolution* came out. "And even when we feel we might come to an arrangement we know in our hearts that Bill won't agree with anything. He simply doesn't want to re-explore the Ghostbusters concept."[12]

In a separate interview from the same month, Aykroyd said he'd finally "been able to let go" of *Ghostbusters III* and that it brought him "tremendous liberation." "For years I was consumed with trying to get that movie made and I wrote a script which is the best devil script or Hell script that has come out of Hollywood. . . . I know it's really good." The interviewer was dubious, remarking, "You don't sound like you let it go." Aykroyd laughed. "No, I have though, I really have. Now I can call Ivan and Harold and Billy and say, 'Let's work on something else.' But no, it will never happen."[13]

169

When Ray Parker Jr. settled out of court with Huey Lewis in 1985 over Parker's alleged theft of Lewis's "I Want a New Drug" for his hit "Ghostbusters" theme, both men signed an agreement limiting what they could say publicly about their legal fight. Anything beyond "[the suit] has been amicably resolved to the satisfaction of all parties" was considered out of bounds. Lewis couldn't help himself, however, when he and his band were profiled for a February 2001 episode of VH-1's *Behind the Music*.

"The offensive part was not so much that Ray Parker Jr. had ripped this song off," Lewis remarked on the program. "It was kind of symbolic of an industry that wants something, they wanted our wave, and they wanted to buy it. We were adamant about—look, it's not for sale. In the end, I supposed they were right, I suppose it was for sale because, basically, they bought it."

Parker responded by suing Lewis for breach of contract and public disclosure of private facts. The filing described Lewis's *Behind the Music* comments as "despicable, oppressive and fraudulent," adding that they were spoken "with conscious disregard" for Parker's rights. Parker was seeking the entirety of his original settlement with Lewis in damages, long rumored to be $5 million. No monetary amount is specified in these papers, as Parker was trying to follow the rules of the original confidentiality clause ("the terms of the confidentiality clause are themselves confidential," the suit reminds the reader at one point). Parker was seeking additional damages for "emotional distress."[14]

Lewis's attorneys fired back, calling Parker an "opportunist" looking for "an unthinkable windfall" of money for Lewis's infraction. Furthermore, they pointed out that "as a matter of law . . . emotional distress damages are not available for a breach of the settlement agreement. Such allegations are therefore irrelevant and improper and should be stricken from the complaint."[15] The court agreed. Parker's entire lawsuit was dismissed that December.[16]

The following month, Parker joined Sheryl Crow, Don Henley, Beck, Carole King, and members of the Deftones in Sacramento, California, to present the state's legislature with a bill aiming to amend labor laws in favor of recording artists. They were the only labor group in the state who didn't have the right to terminate an employment contract after seven years. The standard record label contract stipulated a seven-album minimum, which the artists on hand argued was impossible to fulfill in seven years. "[In seven years] I have only made two albums," said Crow. "At that rate it would take me 21 years to complete the contract. All we're asking for is fairness."

Henley revealed he was not supporting this bill for himself but for future artists who deserved an even shake.[17] One might surmise Parker's reasoning was the same. Industry scuttlebutt held that he enjoyed majority rights ownership of "Ghostbusters," his biggest hit by a country mile. Still, there must have been some issue with Columbia Pictures, Arista Records, or one of the other rights holders. Around this time, Parker rerecorded his vocals for "Ghostbusters" to create a new take of the song that he retained full ownership of and could therefore license for commercial use without paying anyone else. The practice of rerecording popular material to circumvent established contracts has a long history in the music business; everyone from Frank Sinatra to Taylor Swift has done it. For Parker, the re-creation was easy.

"If you told Led Zeppelin to re-record 'Stairway to Heaven,' that might be difficult," the singer explained, "because you've got to be in the same hall, the drums have got to sound the same . . . but 'Ghostbusters' is a computer-driven song. The bass and the drums came out of the sequencer, and I play guitar, and I got the same guy to play the saxophone. It sounds big, but you could cut 'Ghostbusters' on less than 16 tracks." The variation between the 1984 recording of "Ghostbusters" and Parker's update is indeed difficult to discern. Only when listening to the versions back to back is it clear that the newer mix is brighter with slight changes in instrumentation. Parker's singing is nearly identical.

Whatever prompted the rerecording, Parker held no serious grudge against the filmmakers. "I would love to work on *Ghostbusters III*," he said. "I hope they do call me. But if they don't call me, I won't be surprised. . . . They could call Beyoncé, or they could call Britney Spears. . . . I just think they should call me for *Ghostbusters III*, and they should put me in the film."[18]

"He's not malicious. He's just a ronin or a samurai in his commitment to no existing authority. I don't know what the standard is he's upholding, but when someone is acting outside of it, he will do whatever he feels is necessary to bring them into line."

Harold Ramis was speaking to *Time* magazine for a 2005 profile of Bill Murray that championed Murray as "the king of deadpan wit" and "the undisputed master of comedic strife." The strife Murray created off-camera was explored as well. Ramis defended his estranged friend: "It's also very hard being the kind of star he is. Few scripts are perfect, and every movie Bill's been in, he's put on his shoulders and made infinitely better. That's an incredible burden on his creativity and leadership, but he's so suspicious and his standards are so high that he allows very few people to help carry the weight."

"If you could please attach the words 'he said affectionately' to every quote of mine, I'd really appreciate it," Ramis added. "I had and have a great affection for Bill. It goes unexpressed and unconsummated at this point, but I'd love to do something with him again." When asked about Ramis for the article, Murray left it at, "We had a falling out."[19]

Ramis had reached out to Murray a year earlier to offer him a role in his crime comedy *The Ice Harvest*. Murray declined with no further comment.[20] Aykroyd and Murray remained friends only because Aykroyd stopped engaging about business; Murray made it too difficult. Aykroyd gave *Time* a specific example: "Getting him to read the script for the second sequel to *Ghostbusters*—I don't think he's ever read it, actually." Later, Aykroyd echoed Ramis when he said, "A lot of us work in whatever we can and let the locusts come in and clean our bones. Billy's different. He's off on another kind of journey that people, including me, don't always understand."[21]

Murray's journey was taking him through weightier roles that were garnering much more acclaim than his 1984 diversion, *The Razor's Edge*. A turn as a wealthy but miserable businessperson in Wes Anderson's 1998 oddball dramedy *Rushmore* won the actor an Independent Spirit Award and a Golden Globe nomination for Best Supporting Actor. The Academy Awards nominated Murray for a Best Actor statuette for his work in 2003's *Lost in Translation*, a romantic story about two guests in a Tokyo hotel. *Lost in Translation*'s director, Sofia Coppola, didn't have an easier time communicating with Murray than anyone else. She spent close to a year trying to get a response from him about the part. Murray no longer had professional representation; in 1999, he gave up his agent and manager in favor of an 800 number connected to a voicemail that he semi-regularly checked. Coppola dutifully called for eight months to no avail. Finally, a mutual friend connected them when they were both in New York at the same time.[22]

"They weren't helping me anymore," Murray said about the talent reps he cut loose. "They were complicating things for me because they tried to get me to do things I didn't want to do. Besides, the scripts still get to me somehow."[23] ICM Partners represented Murray for the last four years he had professional handlers, and one of the last movies they placed him in was Sony's 2000 *Charlie's Angels* reboot. Contract negotiations lasted at least six months; Murray kept dropping out because they weren't offering enough money.[24] During filming, there was an incident where Murray began verbally abusing costar Lucy Liu, allegedly calling her talent into question. Liu said Murray's anger stemmed from not being included in a rewrite of the scene they were shooting. In later interviews, Murray said Liu lacked professional decorum.[25] The actor denied a story that he also violently head-butted *Charlie's Angels* director McG while on set but did say "[McG] should be pierced with a lance, not head-butted."[26]

Ostensibly the 800 number was Murray's unshackling from the Hollywood system, allowing him to clear his own path through more films like *Rushmore* and *Lost in Translation*. So it came as a surprise in 2004 when Murray provided the voice for a computer-generated version of famous comic strip cat Garfield in an otherwise live-action film. *Garfield: The Movie* was written by *Toy Story* cowriters Joel Cohen and Alec Sokolow. Afterward, Murray said that *Garfield* sounded fun but the big selling point was the fact he thought it had been cowritten by Joel Coen of the Coen brothers. The actor didn't question why the auteur filmmakers behind subversive masterpieces like *Fargo* and *The Big Lebowski* would decide to make a Garfield movie, he just showed up when it was time to record and worked himself into a lather trying to improve the material he was presented. "And we managed to fix it, sort of," Murray said. "It was a big financial success." Perhaps for that reason, he voiced Garfield again in the 2006 sequel, *A Tale of Two Kitties*.

In 2014, Sokolow rebuked Murray's mistaken identity yarn. "He knew it was not Joel Coen well before he met Joel Cohen. It's a funny take. And it kind of defends him against the criticism of making such an overtly commercial film. But, it's complete horse shit." Referring to a derisive joke Murray made about *Garfield* while playing himself in the 2009 film *Zombieland*, Sokolow wondered, "If it's his biggest regret, why did he do it twice? Nobody on either of the *Garfield* movies ever thought they were making *Citizen Kane*." Sokolow added that Murray's "boorish behavior" alienated everyone who worked on *Garfield*. "It was on the third ADR [session] when [Joel Cohen] and I were asked by the studio to fly to New York and sit in because he had already beaten the director of the film and the producers and the studio into submission. . . . Nobody else in the hierarchy of the moviemaking wanted to be anywhere near him."

Sokolow comments were a direct response to Murray during an "Ask Me Anything" session the actor was conducting with the message board website Reddit. Murray had no follow-up.[27]

One of 2003's most popular video games was *The Simpsons: Hit & Run*, a clever parody of the immersive *Grand Theft Auto* series that puts players in the fictional world of Springfield so they can crash the Simpson family car into various buildings and characters from the beloved TV show.[28] *Hit & Run* was produced by John Melchior for Vivendi Universal Games, and the reviews and sales figures were so glowing that the company gave Melchior carte blanche on his next project. Melchior, whose years in gaming stretched back to the late '90s, told them he wanted to make *Ghostbusters*. There had been a handful of games based on the 1984 movie and its sequel during the "Super Mario" era, but nothing had been done that utilized the more realistic and expansive gaming techniques of the twenty-first century.

"I mean, that was the driving force behind me being in the industry," Melchior told *Playboy*'s Matt Paprocki in a lengthy 2016 interview. "There were a couple of games I wanted to make and that was one of them." Melchior took a cursory meeting with Sony where he learned that the company had discussed making a *Ghostbusters* video game but the license was dormant due to the number of rights holders. "Ramis, Aykroyd, Murray, and Ivan Reitman were the triumvirate who had to be impressed or notified. At that point, Sony didn't think it was possible for them to agree on something to do, but they said, 'Let's go down the road,' and the goal was if we could find a way the financials would work from Sony's point of view, maybe we take it to a vertical slice and we try to get Sony, the film side, along with Reitman and the actors on that. Like, show them something amazing. For that, we had to put about a million dollars to take that risk."

Melchior knew that, in addition to the original actors reprising their characters, his *Ghostbusters* game needed an impressive effect for the proton beams. While working with developer Terminal Reality on another project in 2006, Melchior was bowled over by a weapons demo meant for a Middle Eastern military game. "I was sitting with a guy named Pete Wanat who was helping me get this thing off the ground," Melchior remembered. "The military game was well enough but at that point it was probably more of a sensitive thing for a game in that region. As soon as we saw the destruction and the physics engine, [Pete] and I looked at each other, then got up to discuss it in the hallway, which is kind of funny. It was more like kids on Christmas morning . . . because *Ghostbusters* was only going to work if the proton beam destroyed everything." Wanat and Melchior went back into the room. "We asked them, like, 'This is a great demo . . . but what would you say if we turned this into *Ghostbusters*?' The room was silent for a good five to ten seconds. It felt like an hour. We didn't know if that was the stupidest idea they've ever heard or 'you just made my day.' Turns out they were as big of *Ghostbusters* fans as I was."

Sony was no help getting Melchior and his *Ghostbusters* gameplay demo in touch with Aykroyd, Murray, Ramis, or Reitman. "Sony told us, 'Look, we don't have relationships with the people,'" Melchior said. "'They're not exactly talking to everybody every day about this, so if you can't get the talent to say yes, you can't get the license.'" Vivendi CEO Bruce Hack gave Melchior a deadline of two weeks but offered "as many plane tickets as you need to get these guys to say yes." Melchior started with Aykroyd, whom he met at a House of Blues to show off Terminal Reality's concepts and prototypes. Aykroyd, who understood at a high enough level the ins and outs of video games, was immediately enthusiastic. "We could put you guys back in your 1991 body type and age to make you young again," Melchior told the star. "We can tell the third story, the third movie." Aykroyd jumped on that, and the game would be called *Ghostbusters III* through 90 percent of its development.

Harold Ramis was more hesitant. Video game creation was Greek to him. Melchior said Ramis had a few "What the fuck?" moments when they met about the project. One big hurdle was the length of the script, which had to accommodate the player's every potential move. "If a character walks through a door, they have to do four different instances," Melchior explained. "If he walks away from the door, if he opens it, or if he doesn't open it, or he just stands there. That's a lot of writing. He was daunted by that, but we left the meeting and it felt good." Melchior and Ramis met while the latter was on a break from directing an episode of *The Office* on the FOX lot, a mere twenty minutes from Vivendi headquarters. "I believe he called before we got back to Vivendi. . . . He was in."

Reitman came aboard as a consultant, and Ernie Hudson was hired to bring life to Winston Zeddemore. "From there, we did not approach Bill Murray because we know how difficult Bill Murray could be and we had to get that approach right," Melchior said. "So we had to think about it."[29]

The game creators went further down their list of *Ghostbusters* alums while the Murray plan was being devised. Annie Potts and William Atherton were secured. "They had conversations with Sigourney Weaver but they fell apart," says John Zuur Platten, one of the writers who worked on the video game's script.[30] Weaver countered this, sort of, telling MTV News, "I don't think they even asked me to be a part of [it]. If they did I don't remember it and maybe I was just busy." Weaver prefaced her statement by saying that she'd be interested in working on a "high quality" *Ghostbusters* game. The developers have said that the actress got back in touch much later in the process when it was clear they were making something legitimate, but by that point the game was too far along to add another character. A new female lead had been created in lieu of Weaver's Dana Barrett anyway—Professor Ilyssa Selwyn, voiced by Alyssa Milano.[31]

"We wanted to use Janosz from *Ghostbusters II*," Platten says, "but we knew we wouldn't be able to get Peter MacNicol."[32] Sure enough, the game makers didn't, and they almost didn't get Max von Sydow to reprise his role of Vigo the Carpathian. When Melchior called von Sydow at his home in Paris, the actor had no memory of dubbing Vigo's lines for *Ghostbusters II*. "I don't think I was in that movie," he replied. It took forty minutes to convince von Sydow otherwise.

A new fifth member of the Ghostbusters team was being created for the person playing the game to control. At first, the creators wanted to make this new character look like John Belushi, a sweet tribute to Aykroyd's friend who was meant to costar in *Ghostbusters* before his death. Aykroyd and Ramis were worried that Belushi's estate wouldn't approve this idea, so then they figured the playable character could be Rick Moranis's Louis Tully. Moranis was retired by this point, and as Melchior explained, "He wrote us a nice note saying if he was ever to come back to do anything, this would probably be it. But he made promises [when] he retired and he wanted to keep [them], which we respected."[33] In the end, the new character wasn't based on anyone famous; his likeness was borrowed from one of the game's associate producers, Ryan French, and he was given no name beyond Rookie.

Platten says Aykroyd and Ramis outlined where they wanted the video game's story to go, while he and writing partner Flint Dille worked out the script's nuts and bolts.[34] Drew Haworth, a Terminal Reality employee who helped create the Ghostbuster gameplay demo for Melchior, also made significant script contributions.[35] Haworth justified setting the game fifteen years in the past by saying, "We really wanted to preserve the idea of the do-it-yourself, junky looking technology. We didn't want cell phones and the modern conveniences that make script writing so hard now. Our biggest thrust throughout the whole game was to be as true to *Ghostbusters* as possible, even to the point of retreading stuff for fan service." Haworth also noted that Dan Aykroyd was very open to all the story ideas they were coming up with and never pressured them to consider using any of his own *Ghostbusters III* plot ideas.[36]

The writers constructed an experience that borrowed heavily from the original *Ghostbusters*, allowing the player to tangle with Slimer, the Library Ghost, and the Stay Puft Marshmallow Man while moving through a story involving Gozer cultists. Their assumption was Bill Murray would never be involved with this game. "We wrote it with Peter Venkman going to Los Angeles to open a new Ghostbusters franchise with new Ghostbusters," says Platten. "So literally, the first page of the script, he's out."[37] Vivendi shared the belief that Melchior could never get Murray, and they were blunt about it. "[A creative director] told me in a room full of executives that if I got Bill Murray to do this game, he would dig up his dead grandma and kiss her," Melchior said. This comment was made at some point in 2007 and was accompanied by news that Vivendi was slashing Melchior's budget. Murray would never happen, so the game was at best a value bin title.

"I don't think I've ever been so angry in my professional life," recalled Melchior, who wasn't about to be stopped in the midst of a dream project. "I went to war over that decision." He and Wanat held an emergency meeting where they filibustered for close to four hours, eventually patching in a call from Aykroyd. "We turned the table in that room, [but] it was like the first 20 minutes of *Saving Private Ryan.* . . . It was the most tension-filled meeting I've ever been in because this was it. If that decision holds, the game is a disaster."[38] Vivendi acquiesced, reasonably convinced they could get Bill Murray and that the *Ghostbusters III* video game might even be worth it without him. Ironically, in private Aykroyd and Ramis tried to deter Melchior from signing Murray.

"They told us not to hire him because the game had a shipping date. Harold specifically was warning us, 'This is what you're getting into.' And yeah, with Bill, it was quickly a rough road."[39]

The mysterious 800 number that Bill Murray used to get jobs was sparingly doled out by an attorney the actor retained. John Melchior communicated with this attorney for quite some time before he acquired the 800 number, a request that was granted even though it had been made clear through the attorney that Murray had "no interest" in the *Ghostbusters III* video game.

"The train is moving and Vivendi was really stepping on my throat about this," Melchior said, "because marketing and PR felt that if we couldn't announce it with Murray, we didn't have an announcement. It's as stressful of a time [as] I've ever been in . . . building a game on the anticipation that we're going to get someone that everybody in the world, including every doorman and valet in Los Angeles, would tell me was impossible to get, [it] almost made me physically ill at points. But we persevered."[40] With time running out, the team considered recasting Peter Venkman. Their first choice was Vince Vaughn, a deadpan presence in many of that decade's motion picture comedies who was cut from the same cloth as Murray. Melchior spoke with Vaughn's agent and hashed out how much it would cost. At the end of the day, however, the producer felt there still had to be some way to snag Murray.

At 2:00 a.m. one morning, Melchior figured out a "Hail Mary" plan: they would hire Murray's brother Brian Doyle to provide a voice for the game. Then Brian could appeal to Bill that the game was worth doing. Unfortunately, at that point every part in the *Ghostbusters III* game had been cast. The creators didn't want to fire anyone, but they had no other options. They chose to terminate David Margulies, who was reprising his role as the Mayor from the *Ghostbusters* films. Melchior felt there wouldn't be much outcry if Margulies was absent.[41]

Brian Doyle-Murray came in and Melchior's team lavished him with fantastic details about his character and the game. "Do you do this for everybody?" Doyle-Murray asked. "Because it's just 50 lines in a video game." The team laughed and assured the actor that yes, this is how we treat everyone. "What about my brother? Is me being here a plot to get my brother?" Melchior offered a nervous denial. Doyle-Murray agreed to play the Mayor, though he was still skeptical. He turned around as he was leaving the offices. "You did this so I would tell my brother that it's a good game, didn't you?" Melchior caved, admitting the truth. Doyle-Murray replied, "It's a good game and I'll tell him." Two days later, Bill Murray's attorney called Melchior: Bill was in. "There was a dog pile of producers in the hallway when we got that call," Melchior remembered. "It was almost like when a [player] charges the mound after winning the World Series."[42]

"The rumor I heard," John Zuur Platten says, "is that Bill Murray called Dan Aykroyd and said, 'Hey, I hear you're doing a video game?' And Dan Aykroyd said, 'Yeah, we asked you to do it!'" Murray came aboard "three or four weeks" out from the start of voice recording, Platten adds. "Writing Venkman back into the script was the most intense part of the process. That was really the biggest issue we faced in writing the game."[43] Drew Haworth said the script was "gigantic" by the time it was completely done. "For a game that's not *Skyrim* or *Witcher* where it's an open world game, for a linear game, my gosh," he marveled. "Probably 10,000 lines. Before we put all of the generic lines in, just the story was 600 pages. We had to move it onto a spreadsheet."[44]

The game was starting to generate buzz and Sony was paying attention. Suddenly, the name changed from *Ghostbusters III* to *Ghostbusters: The Video Game*. According to Melchior, "Once [Sony] thought there might be a chance for another movie because of this . . . and I'm speculating here, they were like, 'Holy shit, this is a viable franchise. Holy crap, the actors are working together and people are receptive to this.' So then they figured they can't let the video game be called *Ghostbusters III*."[45] *Ghostbusters: The Video Game* was announced in mid-November 2007 as a collaboration between the studio's consumer products division and Vivendi subsidiary Sierra Entertainment. A release date sometime in fall of 2008 was expected. "We will create the ultimate Ghostbusters experience," said Sierra president Martin Tremblay, "full of the characters, ghosts and other paranormal creatures so many have come to adore over the years."[46]

Dan Aykroyd discovered that returning to his world-famous role as Ray Stantz was something of a challenge. "I had to restore the enthusiasm, the passion, the energy, and the youth," he said. The night before his first recording session, Aykroyd watched the two *Ghostbusters* movies with his friend and collaborator Tom Davis to jog his memory. Davis also accompanied Aykroyd to one of his sessions to help refine the Ray Stantz tone as necessary. Melchior enjoyed recording Aykroyd and he also had a great time recording Harold Ramis. "The best conversation I've ever had in my Hollywood experience and making games is talking about 1980s comedies with him for two hours during a break," Melchior said. "He had my sense of humor. Like, he's it."[47]

Murray, on the other hand, was proving his usual difficult and elusive self. The actor didn't show up for his first scheduled recording session. Melchior and his team tried bringing the mountain to Muhammad, flying out to meet Murray with their equipment in Charleston, South Carolina, in May 2008, but Murray blew them off then as well.[48] Ramis was in the middle of a recording session when he learned how Murray was behaving. He exploded, eviscerating Murray in an angry twenty-minute rant that was caught on tape. Vivendi's marketing department wanted to leak the Ramis diatribe for extra publicity. Melchior implored them to can it.

"Personal issues" was the gentle term Melchior used to describe the problems Murray was facing at the time.[49] The same month the game team was in South Carolina, Murray's second wife, Jennifer Butler, filed divorce papers in which she accused her husband of emotional and physical abuse (she fled to that state from the couple's New York home; Murray followed her). A specific incident was described where Murray said Butler was "lucky he didn't kill her" after striking her in the face.[50] Melchior started leaning toward replacing Murray with his sibling Joel, who already did much of Bill's additional dialogue recording in movies. When they informed Murray they were going to use Joel instead, the actor only wanted to know if he'd still get paid. The answer was no. "Okay, when do you want me?"

Murray was still six weeks late to his two-day recording session, which took place in New York City. Melchior described it as the most nerve-racking session of his career. The first day began early on a Saturday, before 8:00 a.m. "We go to the engineer, who says, 'Who are we recording today?' 'Oh, it's Bill Murray.' His face turned so pale and he said if he knew that was the case, he would have called in sick. Already, I'm like, 'This is my own personal *Shawshank*.'" Murray arrived on time, but he would only read three or four lines at a time before burying himself in a magazine for minutes on end. The following day, Murray was more engaged; he'd listened to the *Ghostbusters* soundtrack to jazz himself up. In the end, however, Melchior said the actor only recorded 44 percent of his scripted material. Murray suggested he could finish recording his part in August. That wouldn't work; the game was supposed to ship that month. Aykroyd and Ramis volunteered to fill in gaps, each donating an extra seven to eight hours of their time.[51]

A much larger problem soon developed for *Ghostbusters: The Video Game*. Vivendi had merged with Activision the previous December to create Activision Blizzard, a new billion-dollar entity that took the second part of its name from the Vivendi subsidiary behind the immensely popular role-playing game *World of Warcraft*. Activision was already home to huge video game franchises like *Guitar Hero* and *Tony Hawk's Pro Skater*.[52] Thus, in summer 2008, Activision Blizzard decided some "streamlining" was in order for Vivendi's developing titles. *Ghostbusters* was omitted from press releases discussing what games would go forward.[53] This wasn't a mistake. "[Activision had] no interest," Melchior explained, "but it wasn't just *Ghostbusters*. There was no interest in any game [at Vivendi]. . . . Ninety percent of the games in development, including a Tim Burton original IP—they wanted none of those."[54] Although a playable demo made it to the floor of that year's Comic-Con, a showcase *Ghostbusters: The Video Game* panel scheduled for the convention was canceled.[55] It looked like the game would follow suit.

Activision's dismissal of *Ghostbusters* was another moment of irony, as they had published the very first *Ghostbusters* video game in 1984. Melchior knew that even if *Ghostbusters: The Video Game* somehow managed to survive the changing of the guard, there was no guarantee he'd remain on the project. He sent a good-bye email to everyone involved just in case he was fired. "Before I got home," he said, "and it was an hour drive to Irvine, both Dan Aykroyd and Harold Ramis called my wife to tell her it was going to be okay and they'll make sure I'm part of the game. I'll never forget that."[56]

Four months of uncertainty ended for *Ghostbusters: The Video Game* when Atari acquired the game for a 2009 release.[57] Though all involved were thankful the game was saved, there was disappointment since Atari was no longer a king of the industry. "Atari didn't have the resources and the capability to sell *Ghostbusters* as well as Activision could have," said Terminal Reality's John O'Keefe. "I think Activision could have made it into a franchise."[58] John Melchior agreed but noted that the producers from Atari who got involved with *Ghostbusters* were really good. "[They] wanted to make the game great," he said.[59] All told, this dream project of Melchior's cost $20 million to realize. Regrets were minimal, but they existed. "We way overpaid for the 'Ghostbusters' song," Melchior said of Ray Parker Jr.'s hit. "We paid $75,000 or $80,000 just for that song. It was horrible but how do you not have the song?"[60] Not surprisingly, the version Parker licensed to the game was his rerecording from a few years earlier.[61]

Ghostbusters: The Video Game sold a million copies in the month following its June 16, 2009, release, prompting some to hail it as a "blockbuster." Business wasn't strong enough to make the game a top 10 seller, though, which some might blame on a retail depression video games were experiencing at the time.[62] "If you dug the movies, you should dig *Ghostbusters: The Video Game*," Greg Miller wrote in a review for the website IGN. "There are some moments that cause the game to stumble, but you're getting a new tale in the *Ghostbusters* canon, fun gameplay, a whole bunch of stuff to destroy, and some cool ghosts to scan." Miller had some criticism for the game's animation during the in-game cut scenes: "Lip sync will seem off at places (laughably so in the cutscene after the library chapter), the characters are standing a bit too rigidly and so on. It's that double-edged sword of using a property people know so well—we know how the actors are supposed to speak and act, so when there's a miscue, it's obvious."[63]

Giant Bomb's Ryan Davis said that for "the first few hours" he was playing, he found all the fan service in *Ghostbusters* was "intoxicating." "Eventually, though, I realized that, while there were moments of amusement, there hadn't been an honest laugh in the game. The references and call-backs are relentless, but just saying 'hey, remember that?' isn't inherently funny." This went hand in hand with the gameplay for Davis, which he found repetitive and sloppy. "I won't deny that it's unique amongst third-person shooters, but even still, what was exciting the first few times eventually felt rote to me." Davis also pointed out that the artificial intelligence in the game wasn't all that intelligent. "Your AI-controlled teammates can get knocked down too, and it seems like that happens rather often, leading to a number of chaotic situations where it feels like you're spending more time babysitting the AI than actually bustin' ghosts."[64]

The reception to *Ghostbusters: The Video Game* was positive enough that John Melchior tried to produce a sequel. "Bill Murray said to me and on Letterman that he would do another game," he said. "Dan said he was in and we were going to ask Harold if we could reuse his dialogue for a minor role, but I couldn't get investors to bite." Although Melchior was deeply saddened that his *Ghostbusters* stopped at one game, he called *Ghostbusters: The Video Game* the greatest experience of his life. "That I got to live in the universe with the heroes I used to worship as a kid in a movie I think is one of the funniest movies of all time? [And] the creators are singing its praises? It doesn't get better than that."[65]

ALIVE AGAIN

Mainstream American film comedy throughout the 2000s was dominated by the Frat Pack, a loose collection of amusingly obnoxious schlub comedians like Will Ferrell and Ben Stiller who were churning out loud, silly crowd-pleasers at a steady clip. As analyst Brandon Gray put it, "They're almost like a comedy troupe with a new episode every few months. All of their movies seem to have the same goofy tone to them—they're very light, with a bit of parody, and often devoid of any connective tissue between the scenes." Adam McKay, who directed 2004 Frat Pack cornerstone *Anchorman: The Legend of Ron Burgundy*, could have been outlining any of the films when he described *Anchorman* as being about "someone who thinks they're a little bit better than they are, a neurotic guy who is playing a little bit above his game, the slightly dumb guy who thinks he's better than he is."[1]

The cartoonish Frat Pack comedies took obvious inspiration from what Dan Aykroyd, Bill Murray, Harold Ramis, and Ivan Reitman established twenty years prior. The line of demarcation wasn't always clear, however, especially when Reitman started getting involved with the newer movies himself. Reitman enjoyed the 1998 Todd Phillips documentary *Frat House* and agreed to produce Phillips's first two narrative features, *Road Trip* and *Old School*.[2] Critics who chastised Reitman for repeating himself with *Evolution* had more fodder with *Old School*, a 2003 college comedy owing much to *Animal House*. "Can you sue yourself for plagiarism?" wondered Elvis Mitchell in his *New York Times* review of the film.[3]

Seth Rogen was a Frat Pack minor leaguer until he took a well-received starring turn in 2007's *Knocked Up* (a more grounded entry that featured Ramis in a bit part as Rogen's father). The same year, a script Rogen started writing when he was thirteen with friend Evan Goldberg made it to cinemas as the riotous high school comedy *Superbad*. Rogen wasn't too different from the hilariously blunt outcasts he created, something he proved in October 2008 when he issued a denial that he was involved with the making of a third *Ghostbusters*. "It's hard to imagine that it would be good, isn't it?" Rogen mused to Collider. "I mean, just as a movie fan, I am the first guy to be skeptical of that. It sounds like a terrible idea when you first hear it. . . . I mean, that would have to be one motherfucking good script."

Rogen wasn't being asked about *Ghostbusters III* completely out of the blue. About a month earlier, news broke that Lee Eisenberg and Gene Stupnitsky had been hired to write a script for the long-awaited sequel. Eisenberg and Stupnitsky were Emmy-nominated writers on NBC's version of UK show *The Office* (their nominated episode "Dinner Party" is often tagged as the best of the series).[4] "They write dumb characters really intelligently," Ramis affirmed. "People can say the dumbest things but they're so clever and surprising it makes you laugh and not have contempt." Ramis enjoyed Eisenberg and Stupnitsky's work long before *The Office* and actually facilitated their partnership; the two scribes met when they were both working entry-level positions on Ramis's 2000 remake of *Bedazzled*. In 2006, Ramis invited Eisenberg and Stupnitsky to pen a Stone Age comedy he'd been thinking about for decades called *Year One*.

Year One wrapped filming in fall 2008, counting Judd Apatow among its producers. Apatow was a behind-the-scenes Frat Pack linchpin—producing *Anchorman* and *Superbad*, writing and directing *Knocked Up*—but he'd also enjoyed a robust career outside that bubble.[5] *Superbad* and another Apatow movie, *Talladega Nights*, had been released under the Columbia Pictures banner, and Columbia's parent company Sony was hoping that relationship coupled with Apatow's attachment to *Year One* might allow them to stack *Ghostbusters III* with the young bankable talent seen in so many Frat Pack films.[6] Ramis detailed this in a September 2008 email to *Chicago Tribune* writer Mark Caro that also scraped together what few facts there were about this third installment. "Aykroyd, Ivan Reitman, and I are consulting at this point, and according to Dan, Bill Murray is willing to be involved on some level." Per storyline, all Ramis could say was "the old ghostbusters would appear in the film in some mentor capacity."[7]

That same month, Bill Murray fielded a question about *Ghostbusters III* during a festival screening of his latest movie, *City of Embers*. Asked about "the possibility of strapping on another proton pack and kicking some ghost ass," the actor joked, "Well, I think the wounds from *Ghostbusters II* have healed."[8] Murray was more straightforward during a chat with the *Birmingham Mail*. "It's a great idea that they have these two [*Office*] guys do it because I think it could be a fresh look at it, and it could be funny," he told the newspaper. "It's all about the script. It's not like I have any obligation to the franchise or anyone. If the script was good and I thought we could do it, it could be fun."[9] Murray spoke about Eisenberg and Stupnitsky as if their work was familiar, but he admitted to MTV in October that he had no idea who they were (Murray had never even seen *The Office*). What stars should play new Ghostbusters? "I think it'd be funny to have a girl Ghostbuster," Murray suggested. "I mean, they say like, 'What if you passed it to Chris Rock?' And I go, 'Well, I dunno. Is Chris Rock gonna save us?' You know, I guess. He's funny."[10]

Apatow signed on to produce *Ghostbusters III* in early 2009, and there were hopes the cameras would roll later that year. As rumors circulated once more about Rogen's involvement and perhaps the casting of fellow Frat Packer Paul Rudd, the filmmakers were trying to figure out who might direct. "I'm sure we're all hoping someone else will do it," Ramis told MTV News in March, noting that Reitman wasn't keen on directing *Ghostbusters III* either. "It's a lot of work!" Regarding Murray, Ramis quipped that his old pal was "just waiting for the truckload of money to arrive" before reiterating Murray's stance that the script was most important.[11]

The year rolled on. In June, Ramis said he still only had "a sense" of *Ghostbusters III*'s story and that the film was "half in the works." "No one has ruled anything out and no one has committed to it yet. We'll see if it turns into a movie or not."[12] Four months later, Ramis spoke with more certainty, telling MovieWeb that *Ghostbusters III* would have new Ghostbusters and "inter-dimensional creatures visiting New York." He also had ideas for his character Egon Spengler in the twenty-first century—he'd be a Buddhist monk or a professor at "the Institute of Imaginary Science" in Switzerland.[13]

There are conflicting reports as to when Eisenberg and Stupnitsky completed their first draft. Reitman said he received the completed *Ghostbusters III* script in September and it looked "promising";

come December, Dan Aykroyd said the pair were still hacking it out.[14] There must have been something by that point because that's when Sigourney Weaver teased a few plot details in an interview. "I don't know if I'm going to be in it," Weaver said. "[But] I have had a couple of calls asking, 'Would you read the script?' I know that my little son Oscar—who was kidnapped from me [in the previous *Ghostbusters*]—I think he has grown up to be a Ghostbuster. I might be in it; I see nothing wrong with being in it, although I don't think I will have a big part. I think Bill Murray has a little more to do with it—he's a ghost."[15]

Reitman remained tight-lipped. "I'm not going to comment on what's in the script and on what Sigourney may or may not have said," he said at the dawn of 2010. "There's some very cool things in the new draft, let's just put it that way."[16] Years later, Reitman confirmed that Eisenberg and Stupnitsky killed Murray's beloved Peter Venkman in the very first scene to set up a unique father-son story with a now twentysomething Oscar.[17]

The highest-grossing movies during this time span were all younger franchises like *Harry Potter*, *Pirates of the Caribbean*, the animated *Ice Age* films, and various superhero adventures.[18] Yet the late 2000s also witnessed a small-scale revival of cinematic champions from the '80s, one that seemed to be setting the stage for another *Ghostbusters*. *Rocky Balboa*, a 2006 addendum to Sylvester Stallone's *Rocky* series, wasn't a number one hit but many were shocked that it cracked the top three the week it was released.[19] The *Die Hard* franchise was dusted off the following year and enjoyed a similar reception with *Live Free or Die Hard*.[20] The most powerful '80s relic was Indiana Jones, whose 2008 return in *Indiana Jones and the Kingdom of the Crystal Skull* became the year's third-highest-grossing film with a tally of $317 million.[21]

Hopes that *Ghostbusters* might be the next revival title were about to be dashed. Though he may have dreaded the workload, Ivan Reitman felt obligated and also entitled to direct *Ghostbusters III*, as he'd been so heavily involved in the first two films.[22] Sony disagreed, according to a March 2010 *New York* magazine report. Word had it the studio was looking to employ a director who could give this long-simmering project more current flavors. Alas, firing Reitman was impossible due to the contractual tontine shared by the primary *Ghostbusters* talent. No major decision could be made without the consent of Dan Aykroyd, Bill Murray, Harold Ramis, and Reitman himself.[23] This agreement was stalling *Ghostbusters III* in another major way. Rumor had it Murray wasn't answering the phone to talk about the script. In fact, he hadn't even read it. That's what the *National Enquirer*'s Mike Walker said when he appeared on the April 1 edition of *The Howard Stern Show*. Walker claimed a livid Aykroyd called Murray to berate him: "Stop acting like a jerk!"[24]

Aykroyd denied the story. "I did not call him and tell him the ultimatum—don't be a jerk. I was quoted as saying, 'You better get on board.' I would never ever talk to Billy like that." Aykroyd added that *Ghostbusters III* afforded Murray "the role of a lifetime" and that "we're going to start work pretty soon." Eisenberg and Stupnitsky were working on the second draft, but when Murray spoke he made it sound like there was no script at all. "It's just a myth," he told the *Tampa Bay Times*. "It's like the white alligator in the sewer, you know? Who's seen it, really?"[25] When a *Chicago Tribune* reporter asked Murray about *Ghostbusters III*, he insisted it was "a horrible rumor . . . like illegitimate children in Antarctica."[26] The *World Entertainment News Network* ran a lengthier diatribe. "It's getting so annoying I might just write the damn thing because everyone is driving me nuts," Murray said. "But then they'll want *Ghostbusters IV* and I won't be in that. I don't know who started this. It was an imaginary thing that there were gonna be some new writers that were gonna write it. Honestly, it's just the studio who wants the movie made."[27]

In July, *GQ* published an in-depth interview with Murray where the actor provided greater color on the *Ghostbusters III* issue. "There was a story—and I gotta be careful here," he began. "I don't want to hurt someone's feelings. When I hurt someone's feelings, I *really* want to hurt them. Harold Ramis said, 'Oh, I've got these guys, they write on *The Office*, and they're really funny. They're going to write the next *Ghostbusters*.' And they had just written this movie he had directed. *Year One*. Well, I never went to see *Year One*, but people who did, including other Ghostbusters, said it was one of the worst things they had ever seen in their lives. So that dream just vaporized. That was gone."[28] Murray was telling no lies about *Year One*. Released in June 2009, the film collapsed under scalding reviews that damned it as a lethargic void that was also lacking taste. "Harold Ramis is one of the nicest people I've met in the movie business, and I'm so sorry *Year One* happened to him," wrote Roger Ebert in his one-star write-up.[29]

Murray also spoke about meeting *Ghostbusters* fans in the *GQ* piece and gleaning motivation from their enthusiasm. "I was down in Austin at South by Southwest . . . [and] I got into it one night with a bunch of younger people who were like, 'Oh, I love Peter Venkman! I grew up with Peter Venkman!' We got to talking, and the more we talked about it, the more I thought, *Oh Christ, I should just do the thing*." Interviewer Dan Fierman brought up the rumor Murray might play a ghost in *Ghostbusters III*. The actor explained that concept was a joke he used to express his disinterest in the sequel, but then it was incorporated into the story by Eisenberg and Stupnitsky. "Kinda clever, really," Murray admitted. Fierman wondered if the ghost bit was too similar to Murray's appearance as one of the undead in 2009's *Zombieland*. "But that was a zombie," the actor replied, expressing legitimate confusion. "Not a ghost."[30]

Murray's bit in *Zombieland* won him the prize for Best Cameo at Spike TV's Scream Awards that October, and the actor turned heads by accepting his award while wearing a *Ghostbusters* flight suit and proton pack. "It doesn't mean anything," Murray told the crowd. "It's just the only thing I had clean."[31] A few more *Ghostbusters III* tidbits were circulating at this point: the filmmakers were aiming for a Christmas 2012 release; Sigourney Weaver and Rick Moranis had reportedly signed on (Weaver refused to confirm); Aykroyd was taking a pass at the script and wanted *Buffy the Vampire Slayer* and *Dollhouse* actress Eliza Dushku to play a part. A month later, Aykroyd announced casting was under way. Fearless comedienne Anna Faris and genial goof Bill Hader were two more "fresh faces" he thought were "strong possibilities."[32] Of course, there remained a mitigating factor to all this pillow talk.

"Without [Bill] Murray, the studio absolutely will *not* make the film," stated a January 2011 report from Deadline. An anonymous Sony rep also confirmed that for a project this big, the company needed something more substantial than Murray's usual verbal agreement. "The studio won't even think about [going] forward on a $150 million film unless Bill has closed a deal and [made] a commitment. It's too huge a risk to do any meaningful prep, hoping he shows up." They might have a script and a cast, but *Ghostbusters III* wouldn't move into preproduction without Murray. With Murray, cameras were expected to roll "as *fast* as possible."[33] Cowriter Lee Eisenberg confirmed shortly after the Deadline story that the filmmakers were still waiting for Murray to read their work. "The studio seems high on it," Eisenberg said of the script in general. "We're very proud of it. We worked really hard on it, and I think it'd be a really fun movie."[34]

"Yeah, I guess I'm the problem," Murray sniffed when he called into *The Howard Stern Show* on February 22. "Before I was an asset, now I'm a problem." The actor confirmed he hadn't read the *Ghostbusters III* script. "Why haven't you read it?" Stern asked. "Because you think it's a bullshit idea? That, in other words, *Ghostbusters* had its time and you did a remarkable job with that and now you've moved on?" Murray conceded that was part of his aversion, as well as the way *Ghostbusters II* turned out. Stern wondered how long the script for *Ghostbusters III* had been sitting on Murray's desk. "Well, it may not be on the desk," the actor joked. "It's not the foremost thing on my mind right now, so I don't think about it. But, you know the studio gets excited about it every ten years or so, it seems like. . . . I remember once upon a time it was gonna be—and the Ghostbusters will be Chris Rock, Chris Farley, and, you know, Chris Crane . . . or Kris Kringle . . . or someone. They had it together."[35]

May 2011 came and went. *Ghostbusters III* did not begin filming.

Harold Ramis was always the first to joke about the ravages of age. "There's a lot more hair dye being used this time," he cracked to the *New York Times* while making *Ghostbusters II*. "When it's face-lift time, we'll have to quit."[36] In the late '90s, Ramis relayed an anecdote about being recognized in a Los Angeles supermarket, long after his famously thin frame expanded. "This woman said to my wife, 'Is that Harold Ramis? What happened to him?'"[37] Ramis remained self-deprecating in 2010. After leading the traditional seventh inning sing-along during an April 18 Chicago Cubs game, the comedian told Cubs announcers Len Kasper and Bob Brenly that *Ghostbusters III* would feature "the original ghostbusters . . . in larger costumes."[38]

The Cubs game would be one of Ramis's final public appearances. A month later, the comedian was hospitalized for an abscess in his colon that was causing tremendous pain. This infection brought on vasculitis, a rare autoimmune condition that leads to blood vessel swelling in the brain. Anticoagulants prescribed to treat the vasculitis ended up triggering a brain hemorrhage. The entire ordeal robbed Ramis of speech and mobility; he gained them back, and while there was hope he could one day put all of this behind him, daughter

Violet Ramis Stiel admitted that her father "never really recovered" from his maladies.

Ramis's wife Erica decided not to go public with her husband's woes. "I think that an unforeseen and unfortunate consequence of that decision was that she didn't get a lot of support," Stiel said, "and, frankly, he didn't get the outpouring of love and good wishes he deserved." While convalescing, Ramis wrote a letter to his children. "I used to think I was one of the luckiest guys in the world, but now I'm not so sure. Still glad to be alive but life sucks in ways I never anticipated. I live in a world described by aches and pains and bodily inconveniences. The lessons are obvious, patience, and the knowledge that I can't take anything for granted."[39]

Contemporaries of Ramis also stayed silent regarding his condition, never mentioning it when discussing the mire that was *Ghostbusters III*. It's interesting to consider in retrospect, however, comments Dan Aykroyd made in October 2011 about specific problems the elder Ghostbusters would be facing in this new movie. "My character, Ray, is now blind in one eye and can't drive the Cadillac," Aykroyd said. "He's got bad knees and can't carry the packs. . . . Egon is too large to get into the harness. . . . [So] we're gonna hand it to a new generation." In the same interview, Aykroyd revealed that *Ghostbusters III* would happen now even if Murray opted out. "What we have to remember is that *Ghostbusters* is bigger than any one component, although Billy was absolutely the lead and contributive to it in a massive way, as was the director and Harold, myself, and Sigourney. The concept is much larger than any individual role."[40]

Had Murray read the *Ghostbusters III* script yet? No one was sure, but one tabloid report suggested he had at least picked it up. According to a *National Enquirer* story in December, Aykroyd and Ramis were enraged after they received a parcel from Murray stuffed with the shredded remains of the *Ghostbusters III* script and a note that read "No one wants to pay money to see fat, old men chasing ghosts!"[41] Once again, Aykroyd went on the defense. "Bill Murray is not capable of such behavior," he told Empire the following February, a laughable statement considering Murray's lengthy history of bullying and abuse. "We have a deep, private personal relationship that transcends business. We communicate frequently and his position on the involvement in *Ghostbusters III* has been made clear and I respect that. But Bill has too much positive estimation of my writing skills to shred the work." In keeping with his previous comments about *Ghostbusters* being bigger than a single actor, Aykroyd went on to suggest Murray's part could be recast.[42]

Ivan Reitman didn't think Murray had made anything clear, and by his account, communication with the actor was far from frequent. The director said Murray was "literally impossible to find" the whole time they were working on the Eisenberg and Stupnitsky script. The conclusion of this saga was just as vague. "When Bill finally . . . well, he never actually said no," Reitman tried to explain, "but he never said yes, so there was no way to make that film."[43] As late as 2020, Eisenberg wasn't sure what happened. "We worked on *Ghostbusters* for four years," he told the *Hollywood Reporter*. "It got very close. At one point I think it was green-lit, contingent on Bill Murray doing it. And then Bill Murray did not do it. Bill Murray I don't think read it."[44] Just a couple years after the fact, however, Murray said he did read Eisenberg and Stupnitsky's work. "It was kinda funny, but not well executed," he remarked.[45]

Etan Cohen was hired to give *Ghostbusters III* a rewrite in July 2012.[46] Cohen's writing credits suggested a fantastic intersection for a *Ghostbusters* film—he'd worked on satirical comedies like *Idiocracy* and *Tropic Thunder* but he also wrote *Men in Black 3*, which bucked the trend of diminishing returns by earning $10 million more worldwide than the original *Men in Black*. In a review for *Entertainment Weekly*, Lisa Schwarzbaum said *Men in Black 3* "ought to serve as a blueprint for other filmmakers faced with the particular challenges of reviving big-ticket and time-dated hunks of pop culture."[47]

By December, Cohen had a *Ghostbusters III* draft that looked good to Aykroyd—one that omitted Murray entirely by Aykroyd's request—but the studio was hesitant. They wanted a second draft, and problems with Murray weren't going away either. The actor still had a controlling stake in *Ghostbusters* and he had to give his okay to make *Ghostbusters III* even if he wasn't going to act in it. In no surprise, Murray wasn't engaging with Sony at all. There was a possibility, however, that Murray had actually abrogated his rights by this point.

As Aykroyd explained to *Esquire* that month, "Two years ago [Murray] said, 'I don't want to be involved,' and the picture company I think had some clause in there that if he actually passed on the third or fourth offer, he no longer had a view of the franchise. So, that's for the lawyers to decide." Aykroyd said regardless of all this, they'd "always leave a hole" for Murray in the script. "He can come back at any time and be rebuilt into it." When asked about the *Ghostbusters III* drafts Eisenberg and Stupnitsky authored, Aykroyd was evasive before saying there would have to be arbitration to try to get the pair credit on Cohen's final product. The actor then seemed to give Sony an ultimatum about *Ghostbusters III*, which he insisted would make nine figures. "We can't wait forever. And now's the time to tell the picture company, and I'd say this quite publicly, it's time now to sit down and make this movie, or you will lose your main principals, and you won't be able to make it without us, because we have the rights."[48]

On December 3, the day before *Esquire*'s interview with Aykroyd was published, a bombshell started circulating through the Internet: Bill Murray had read the latest draft of *Ghostbusters III* and enjoyed it so much that he called Harold Ramis at nearly three o'clock in the morning to say he wanted a part. This scoop came from SuperOfficialNews.com, which quoted previously unheard-of *Ghostbusters III* cowriter Paul Horner.[49] The *Philadelphia Examiner* busted this hoax. "If you believe the SuperOfficialNews front page, Paul Horner also won the Arizona Powerball drawing and is quoted in an article in support of President Obama's decision to declare December National Gay Guy Appreciation Month."[50]

"This script is just so medium funny and not edgy it scares me."

Sony Pictures chairperson Amy Pascal had her concerns with Etan Cohen's *Ghostbusters III* script, titled *Ghostbusters: Alive Again*. It was January 2014 and Cohen had already authored several drafts. *Alive Again* revolved around a group of new Ghostbusters including Chris, a kindhearted scholar; Jeremy, Chris's cynical friend who loves debunking ghost stories; Dean, the son of original Ghostbuster Ray Stantz who now licensed the Ghostbusters name to a theme restaurant; and Anna, who has a romance with Chris that stalls because she doesn't like to date coworkers. The primary antagonist is called Gniewko and there are many instances of "hellions" controlling people and animals. Ray Stantz and Egon Spengler were given cameos—as ghosts. *Alive Again* also had brief appearances from Dana Barrett, Louis Tully and his wife, the Stay Puft Marshmallow Man, and Peter Venkman. The ending battle featured a giant baby.

Pascal found herself getting distracted while reading *Alive Again*. "[I] wonder why we are doing this version and what the actual idea is here," she wrote in an email. A scene in FAO Schwarz where ghosts take control of various toys bothered her, not just because it mirrored a scene in Sony's recent live-action *Smurfs* movie. "Why are the ghosts bringing toys to life? Isn't the idea of the ghosts themselves being characters? Isn't that the whole thing about the original movie?" Pascal also had doubts about the giant baby ending, feeling it had already been done. "I think we need everyone to read this at the studio and finally make the big decision," she wrote. "And I do want some [input] from everyone we trust."

Doug Belgrad, president of Sony Pictures, agreed. "I'm still struggling with whether there is enough of an idea. Some days I think there is, on others I think we get killed." Production president Hannah Minghella thought the characters lacked spark, the story beats were off, and wondered about *Alive Again*'s references to the original *Ghostbusters* ("Can we really bring back the Marshmallow Man?"). Belgrad and Pascal both wanted to forward the script to Seth Rogen and Evan Goldberg. "We've always believed that Seth/Evan producing with Ivan [Reitman] is a game changer," Belgrad wrote. "And I think Seth would be an awesome Chris."[51]

The shaky script didn't stop the studio or the filmmakers from trying to assemble a dream cast for *Alive Again*. Two months earlier, the part of Jeremy was offered to Jonah Hill, who had garnered acclaim costarring in Rogen's *Superbad*; Hill passed. Emma Stone, another *Superbad* alum, was offered the Anna role at the same time but her response wasn't recorded.[52] Ivan Reitman thought either Brie Larson or Anne Hathaway would be right for Anna. "I have met with both," he told Sony, "and both have expressed a strong desire to do it." Adam Pally, Charlie Day, and Jesse Eisenberg were the actors Reitman was considering for Chris. Kaufman-esque funnyman Zach Galifianakis was his choice to play Dean, and there were other parts he thought could go to Rebel Wilson, Aubrey Plaza, and Aziz Ansari. For Gniewko, Reitman pictured *Borat* star Sacha Baron Cohen. Pascal wanted Will Ferrell in that role, but Reitman didn't think Ferrell could play it seriously enough.[53]

There was another issue between Pascal and Reitman. As the rumors from just a few years earlier had suggested, Reitman believed he was entitled to direct *Ghostbusters III* because he'd directed the previous two, and Pascal wanted Reitman to give up the director's chair and simply take a producer credit. "We can't unilaterally force him out as director because [of] the way the original [*Ghostbusters*] deal was set up," confirmed Sony business department head Andrew

Gumpert. "He (and the other guys) have individual functional blocking rights because they have pre-set financial deals that don't work in today's world. So we need him and the others to greatly modify their deals. If we toss him as director, we risk him not [being] willing to modify out of spite."

Gumpert told Pascal she might have to have a "sit down" with Reitman to coax him into "the role of godfather producer" for "the good and welfare" of the *Ghostbusters* franchise.[54]

On February 24, 2014, at 12:53 a.m., Harold Ramis died from complications of autoimmune inflammatory vasculitis. A shocked world mourned the loss of an entertainment legend. "Ramis' comedies were often wild, silly and tilting toward anarchy, but they also were cerebral and iconoclastic," wrote Mark Caro in the *Chicago Tribune*, "with the filmmaker heeding the Second City edict to work at the top of one's intelligence."[55] Tributes poured in from fellow comedians, from mayors and governors, even from the president of the United States.

"Michelle and I were saddened to hear of the passing of Harold Ramis, one of America's great satirists," Barack Obama said on February 25. "When we watched his movies—from *Animal House* and *Caddyshack* to *Ghostbusters* and *Groundhog Day*—we didn't just laugh until it hurt. We questioned authority. We identified with the outsider. We rooted for the underdog. And through it all, we never lost our faith in happy endings. Our thoughts and prayers are with Harold's wife, Erica, his children and grandchildren, and all those who loved him, who quote his work with abandon, and who hope that he received total consciousness."

"May he now get the answers he was always seeking," said a "deeply saddened" Dan Aykroyd. Ivan Reitman praised Ramis as having "the most agile mind I've ever witnessed. He always had the clearest sense of what was funny and how to create something in a new clever way. . . . Harold had an extraordinary impact on my career and I loved him like a brother."[56]

Bill Murray's eulogy was short but sweet: "He earned his keep on this planet. God bless him."[57] The icy waters between Murray and Ramis thawed just before the latter's passing when Murray visited his ailing friend. "In classic Bill fashion, he showed up at the house, unannounced, at 7 a.m., with a police escort and a dozen doughnuts," said Violet Ramis Stiel. "My dad wasn't able to talk much by this point, so they didn't get into the nitty gritty of what happened. . . . but they spent a couple hours together, laughed a little, and made their peace."[58]

One would assume the demise of a linchpin *Ghostbusters* figure would halt *Ghostbusters III* for the foreseeable future. It did not. On February 26, the *Hollywood Reporter* revealed that Reitman was meeting with Sony within the week to "assess how to move forward" on the active development of the new *Ghostbusters* movie. "[Ramis] was poised to appear in a third outing in a cameo role—like Murray and Aykroyd—that set up a baton-passing to a trio of newcomers," the report stated. "A studio source downplayed the impact [of Ramis's death] on the project, however, insisting that Ramis was involved in *Ghostbusters III* only minimally." Ramis's "first dollar gross stake" in *Ghostbusters III* automatically reverted to his estate. The *Reporter* also pointed out that "no deals have been inked yet" and they saw signals that this sequel might be another instance where the actors agree to smaller payouts just to get the film made.[59]

Naturally, there was still one outspoken critic of *Ghostbusters III*. In an interview with Dazed published February 27 but apparently conducted before Ramis's death, Murray reignited his objections. "We made the first *Ghostbusters*—it was one of the great movies, one of the great entertainments of all time. Then we made a second one; it was okay, right? Right? So what are we going to do? Are we going to rush to make a third one? It would be great if you could make one that was as good as the first one. It would probably be good if you could make one that was as good as the second one. But, you know, there was *The Godfather*. Then there was *The Godfather II*. And then there was *The Godfather III*. So if you want *Godfather III* . . ."

What about Murray's friends who wanted to do *Ghostbusters III*? "Well, my friends. Man, *do* they want to do it? They kind of do. But someone with a lot more to gain than my friends wants to do it more than they want to do it. Right? And I understand, it's business. They want to refresh the franchise. The franchise is fantastic. But I find that you don't really lose by saying no in show business. If you say no, sometimes they come back with a better script. Or sometimes it just goes away."

"But I don't know," Murray concluded. "Are you thinking of going back to high school?"[60]

GIRLS TO THE FRONT

Ivan Reitman couldn't help but take stock of his life following Harold Ramis's death. Specifically, he was thinking about *Ghostbusters III*, and after weeks of reflection he decided all he really wanted to do was produce the film. He'd let someone else sit in the director's chair. "It was such an amazing time in my life 30 years ago," Reitman told Deadline for a March 2014 report, "and I felt that way on the second film. With Harold no longer with us I couldn't see it."

"We are determined to retain the spirit of the original film, and I am pleased that all of this seems to have happened organically," he added. "I'm hoping we can get started by the fall, set in New York, but given the logistics and the stuff that happens, the beginning of 2015 seems more likely."[1] Reitman also recognized that the knotty rights situation between the studio, himself, Dan Aykroyd, Bill Murray, and now the estate of Harold Ramis wasn't doing the brand any favors. The other parties agreed. In a deal Reitman boasted would rain money upon the *Ghostbusters* creatives "for the rest of our lives, and for the rest of our children's lives," primary control was sold to Sony Pictures, leaving the future of the franchise in studio hands.[2]

News of a major job opening on a *Ghostbusters* movie set off a feeding frenzy. Directors of all stripes were barraging Sony Pictures chairperson Amy Pascal, falling all over themselves for consideration. "Hopefully I am not being inappropriately aggressive," *Zombieland*'s Ruben Fleischer wrote to Pascal in an email, "but I think you know this is my all time dream project and I will do whatever it takes to make this movie for you." Dominique Adams, a rookie filmmaker from Montreal, also emailed Pascal: "I will cost you pennies [and] I will make you billions (with a B, because people will love my work THAT MUCH). It's an unorthodox way to ask for a job, given the fact that I only have one feature film under my belt, but Montreal's own Denis Villeneuve had only one feature under his belt as well when he directed *Prisoners* with Hugh Jackman and Jake Gyllenhaal which performed well at the box office."[3]

Naturally, Pascal already had directors in mind that she was communicating with, and at the top of her list was the team of Phil Lord and Christopher Miller.[4] Lord and Miller specialized in vibrant layered comedy exemplified by hits like *21 Jump Street* and *The Lego Movie*. Audiences were especially bowled over by the latter; what sounded like a naked excuse for a two-hour toy commercial was ultimately praised for being equally funny and subversive (the *New York Times* called *The Lego Movie* "an allegory about the nature of creativity and the meaning of amusement").[5] Lord and Miller passed on directing *Ghostbusters III* in April. The world was their oyster and evidently they "wanted to keep their options open."[6]

Pascal's number two choice to direct *Ghostbusters III* was Paul Feig. In his early fifties, Feig's career had run the gamut. He'd been a tour guide at Universal Studios, where he was apparently the first guide to fall into the *Jaws* lagoon. As a standup comic in the late '80s, Feig took fourth place in the 3rd Annual San Diego Laugh Off and also opened for Elvis Costello. *LA Weekly* championed his "sublimely goofy" routines, which included a character who taught wood shop. Feig's boyish mug and brown flop of hair were on display in the '90s when he acted in movies like *Heavyweights* and TV shows like *Good Sports* and *Sabrina the Teenage Witch*.[7] *Heavyweights* was cowritten by Judd Apatow, who helped Feig get the ball rolling on an idea he had for a realistic TV show about teenagers in the early 1980s. "From the day I put pen to paper, I saw it as an adult show," Feig said. "The only way to do it, if you do these characters speaking honestly, is to throw out anything that doesn't sound like something a kid would say."[8]

The resulting program, *Freaks and Geeks*, made an indelible mark even though it only ran for a season on NBC at the turn of the century. Critics hailed *Freaks and Geeks* as honest and refreshing, not just for the way it explored teenage frustrations but also, as *USA Today* put it, for "[casting] actors who look like real people instead of magazine covers." As time went on, *Freaks and Geeks* was granted near-legendary status.[9] Meanwhile, Feig continued in television, directing episodes of *Arrested Development*, *Weeds*, and *The Office*. *The Office* provided Feig the most work, making him an executive producer as well. Among Feig's directorial entries for that show was the Lee Eisenberg and Gene Stupnitsky cringe apex "Dinner Party." Feig was blown away when those writers were hired to pen *Ghostbusters III*. "I couldn't believe that," he said. "It was so cool. I was still deep in movie jail at that point but I thought if there was ever a point in my life where I could be asked to direct *Ghostbusters* . . . well, I couldn't even imagine it."[10]

Growing up in Michigan, Feig's closest friends had always been girls or boys he described as "feminized geeks like me." He felt more attuned to women's humor, and that came across when his third directorial feature, *Bridesmaids*, lit up the box office in May 2011. Coproduced by Apatow, *Bridesmaids* was viewed as nothing short of a miracle—it was an uproarious gross-out comedy carried almost entirely by women with a believable nucleus about the complexity of female friendships. The *Los Angeles Times* said *Bridesmaids* was a landmark because it "erased the line between comedy and tragedy with a level of daring that few movies, regardless of their intended demographic, ever attempt anymore." *Bridesmaids* raked in $149 million within a month of release, making it the most lucrative movie to bear the Apatow name (and Apatow himself believed *Bridesmaids* was the funniest movie he'd ever made).[11]

Pascal reached out to Feig several times about *Ghostbusters III*. "Back in 2008, I'd have taken any version of *Ghostbusters*," Feig said, "but now I was like, I don't know . . . I thought [the script] was really good, and by writers that I really like. Etan Cohen, an amazing talent, worked on it too. But the core thing of the sequel was, in all the scripts that I'd read, that there was a new team that had come together. The old team had been forgotten. Then the old team showed up and gave them the stuff and trained the new team up. To me, it felt like it'd been so long since *Ghostbusters II* even. It felt like a big gap. I love *Ghostbusters II*, but even the way they had to start that up with them being disgraced—how would the *Ghostbusters* be disgraced after they saved New York? Because they left it in a mess? Would they be mad at Neil Armstrong for leaving a golf ball on the moon?" Feig couldn't see a plausible way to make this story. He turned down *Ghostbusters III* every time Pascal asked.[12]

Sony's hunt continued. *Old School* director Todd Phillips passed; he was too busy. Discussions with Brad Bird, the multifaceted animation veteran who also helmed *Mission Impossible—Ghost Protocol*, went nowhere.[13] Apatow, *Anchorman* director Adam McKay, *Austin Powers* director Jay Roach, *South Park* creators Matt Stone and Trey Parker, and *Family Guy* creator Seth McFarlane were also on Pascal's list.[14] For all his campaigning, Ruben Fleischer was only a "maybe." Nick Stoller of *Forgetting Sarah Marshall* was in the same category; Sony liked Stoller but there was concern he wasn't up to the task.[15] One of the more left-field considerations was *Arrested Development* star Jason Bateman, who had recently made his directorial debut with the comedy *Bad Words*. Bateman's agency got in touch and although Pascal told them they were "thinking differently at the moment," there was agreement that the studio would like to work with him as a director at some point.[16]

In late July, with no candidates at the ready, an exasperated Pascal circled back to Feig. She asked him why no one wanted to make this movie. Feig responded, "It's this giant thing. It's like redoing *The Godfather*." Pascal was shocked that *Ghostbusters*, this amazing franchise, was collecting dust. The next day, Feig cracked it. "I thought, *If I could put four women in the lead roles, that's exciting to me. That I know how to do, and I know how to make that funny. . . .* Then I thought, *I'd rather do it as a reboot so I'm not tied to the old movies. The old movies are so good, I don't want to mess with them. And I also want to see the beginnings of this group. I want to see people seeing ghosts for the first time, and how they're going to fight them for the first time, how they develop their technology.* So it just got very exciting to me."

Feig called his agent with the idea. Mere seconds after that conversation, Pascal was on Feig's line, asking to hear his concept. "If I could reboot it with women, with the story I wanted to tell, I'd be all into it," Feig said. "Done," Pascal replied.[17]

Feig suggested some names for the cast: Kristen Wiig, cowriter and headlining talent of *Bridesmaids*, dubbed by *Rolling Stone* "an indisputable goddess of comedy"; Melissa McCarthy, a *Bridesmaids* breakout whose bawdy turns in the film were so potent there was talk of pushing for an Oscar nomination; Emma Stone, a funny woman on the rise thanks to her outstanding performance in 2010's *Easy A*; sexually frank standup and sketch comedienne Amy Schumer; *Hunger Games* and *X-Men* megastar Jennifer Lawrence.[18]

"Sounds like a cool idea," said Sony advertising exec Michael Pavlic when Pascal relayed the news. "Obviously worth hearing his pitch."[19]

It's not easy keeping big secrets in Hollywood. On August 2, roughly a week after Paul Feig mapped out his *Ghostbusters* reboot idea to Amy Pascal, the *Hollywood Reporter* leaked the news that Feig "has emerged as the front-runner" for directing *Ghostbusters III*. "Feig has shown interest in taking on the project. Sources caution that no formal negotiations have taken place and a lot must be worked out before the casual discussions turn serious and Feig accepts the job. But he is the studio's first choice, these sources say. Sony declined to comment."[20] A little over an hour after that story ran on *THR*'s website, *Variety* swooped in with more details.

"Paul Feig is being courted to direct a *Ghostbusters* comedy reboot. . . . Feig is not helming *Ghostbusters III* or another sequel, in any sense of the word, as has been incorrectly reported. The movie is a total reboot most likely with female characters played by comedic actresses in ghostbusting roles, according to sources. The script will be written from scratch."[21]

Sony was beside themselves. They couldn't believe the accuracy of these reports.[22] Feig was surprised, but it didn't deter him from moving forward.[23] Meanwhile, it only took one day for the first major criticism of the *Ghostbusters* reboot to be published via Deadline. Mike Fleming Jr., a staple of the *Ghostbusters III* beat, may have been aiming for self-parody when he referred to "knuckle-dragging Neanderthals like me who have little else going for us" outside a perceived ownership of the established *Ghostbusters* universe. The editorial's title was certainly baiting—"Film Chauvinist Asks: Do We Want an Estrogen-Powered 'Ghostbusters'?"—and there's a lot of space wasted on sexist jokes about imagined gender-swapped reboots. However, Fleming was accurately summarizing the way some *Ghostbusters* fans were feeling. They waited so long for *Ghostbusters III* only to have it flushed away for a reset. "I feel slimed," Fleming wrote.[24]

Feig had more pressing issues at that moment. Worried about retaining creative control of his *Ghostbusters*, the director was pushing for a producer credit. Ivan Reitman and Sony pushed back because it wasn't really protocol to add a franchise newcomer to a group of established producers like Reitman, Aykroyd, and Joe Medjuck (Feig got his producer credit in the end, becoming one of eleven on the finished film). Reitman also wanted to try to bring Lee Eisenberg and Gene Stupnitsky back on as writers, something he'd been pushing for even before Feig was Sony's top pick. The studio dissuaded Reitman from this on the stance it was impractical and too expensive.[25] Feig would cowrite the script with *Parks and*

Recreation writer Katie Dippold (Dippold had scripted Feig's 2013 cop comedy *The Heat*).

The *Ghostbusters* deal with Feig was still being worked out when there was, as Sony production president Hannah Minghella put it, "a curious turn of events." *21 Jump Street* hunk Channing Tatum and his friend Chris Pratt had been looking for a project they could work on together. Pratt was one of the supporting comedic players on *Parks and Recreation*, but he'd recently proven his action hero mettle by anchoring the Marvel Studios theatrical hit *Guardians of the Galaxy*. Tatum and Pratt, along with Tatum's production partner Reid Carolin, connected with director brethren Anthony and Joe Russo. The Russos were known for *Captain America: The Winter Soldier*, a crackerjack action-mystery that was also the ninth entry in Marvel's hugely successful experiment in overlapping comic-book-style filmmaking. Tatum, Pratt, Carolin, and the Russos wanted to create a similar cinematic universe for *Ghostbusters*.

In an email, Carolin pitched the founding title in this canon as "a movie that scares the shit out of you like great horror can, makes you laugh your ass off, has real action, real romance, real movie stars. Everything that you want in a blockbuster. *Oceans 11* in the paranormal universe." Tatum chimed in: "Let us show the world the dark side and let us fight it with all the glory and epicness of a HUGE *BATMAN BEGINS* MOVIE. I know we can make this a huge franchise. Fun adventure craziness. COME OONNN!!!"

Pascal was over the moon that Marvel stars were knocking on her door and volunteering to construct a new multi-movie mythology. Could they find a way to make this line up with what Feig was doing? Sony execs thought so, but the Russos and Carolin disagreed. Feig was doing a pure comedy film, and the Russos, et al., clearly envisioned something more akin to *Captain America* or *The Avengers*.[26] In the midst of this, Feig gave a detailed plot breakdown for what he called "the first film" (he was obviously thinking of a multiple-part saga himself).

"It's a reboot of the franchise in a world (our world) that has never actually had any legitimate contact with the ghost world," Feig wrote. "Our villain ghost is an executed murderer, a Ted [Kaczynski] type (think Peter Dinklage) who has left behind a manifesto of how he wants to change and destroy the world. When his electrocution is hit by a supercharged electrical storm, he is turned into a powerful ghost able to rouse other villainous spirits from the ghost world to carry out the ever expanding plans of his manifesto. Our four new female Ghostbusters come together in an origin story that sees them forming a team based on their diverse skills and plays with the invention and trial-and-error of their various Ghostbusting technology and techniques."

Feig didn't want his Ghostbusters to actually launch their business until the end of the movie (in the proposed sequel, these Ghostbusters would become clandestine federal employees helping to save the entire country from ghosts). For the villain, he imagined a figure who could resurrect famous deceased criminals and "ghost aliens" from other planets. The director also envisioned a big set piece where his villain possesses groups of soldiers and police officers and makes them do "a big ridiculous dance number in the middle of Fifth Avenue" just to make them look silly.[27] This sounded good to Sony. They closed their deal with Feig by October 4.[28] Simultaneously, development continued on the Tatum/Pratt *Ghostbusters*.

There was some heated internal debate about the phrasing around Feig's *Ghostbusters* in press releases. Feig wanted it to be clear this movie was a complete reboot and not in any way a sequel to the original films, but Ivan Reitman felt the existing characters and mythology were too important to rule out entirely before a script was written. Reitman's stumping for this new entry to become *Ghostbusters III* had been so persistent over the preceding months that Pascal likened it to Whac-A-Mole. Although some Sony executives thought unifying Feig's movie with the earlier efforts would help to build an entity as powerful as Marvel or Star Wars, the higher-ups felt both Reitman and Aykroyd were acting too big for their britches when it came to "protecting" the *Ghostbusters* franchise.[29] Besides, the entire deal with Feig was predicated on his *Ghostbusters* movie being a clean break from the 1984 and 1989 films.

Reitman was still furious when an October 8 *Hollywood Reporter* story announcing Dippold's involvement described the movie as a reboot.[30] Pascal believed that Feig's movie might connect to the earlier films in nonliteral ways, and Reitman seemed to accept this after meeting with Feig. "He is just looking for nods to the old movie, which Katie has been wanting to do anyway," Feig told Pascal. "Will there be as many nods as Ivan would like? Probably not. But at this point, I just want to see how our first draft shakes out. . . . The bottom line is that we heard Ivan and he made it clear that he wouldn't get in our way, that he would definitely weigh in on things but that in the end, the decisions were ours to make."[31]

While peace was achieved between producer and director, Sony was still trying to maneuver around Reitman. An especially juvenile move on the studio's part came mid-October when Pascal told subordinates not to inform Reitman of a meeting with several key members of Feig's *Ghostbusters* production.[32]

A *Toronto Star* reporter asked Bill Murray that September about the *Ghostbusters* reboot while the actor was promoting his latest film, *St. Vincent*. "I'm fine with it," Murray said. "I would go to that movie, and they'd probably have better outfits, too." Did he have any casting suggestions? Murray said his *St. Vincent* costar Melissa McCarthy would be "spectacular." "And Kristen Wiig is so funny," he added. "God, she's funny. I like this girl Linda Cardellini a lot. And Emma Stone is funny. There are some funny girls out there."[33]

Wiig caught wind of Murray's endorsement during a press junket for her movie *The Skeleton Twins*. "That's very flattering," she responded. "I guess they're making one from what I hear, which is pretty great." Wiig's *Skeleton Twins* costar Bill Hader interrupted: "You should do it . . . and you should have a friend, who's like a guy, who has to carry around your proton pack." A few more jokes followed before Wiig said, "I will do whatever Bill Murray tells me to."

"That will run *everywhere*," said Wiig's very concerned publicist. "I know. That's why I said it."[34]

The concept of comedy as a boys' club had eroded to a degree by 2014. *Saturday Night Live*, then preparing to enter its fortieth year, had spent the prior fifteen shifting away from the testosterone that marked so much of its legacy. Tina Fey became *SNL*'s first female head writer in 1999; a year later, she was co-anchoring the show's staple news parody "Weekend Update" (a woman hadn't been a regular behind that desk since Christine Ebersole in 1982).[35] The Fey era was defined by versatile talents like Maya Rudolph, Amy Poehler, and Rachel Dratch. Wiig joined up just as Fey was exiting in 2005 and quickly became a favorite with a stable of characters who, as Sara Stewart of the *New York Post* put it, were "outrageous versions of people we've all had the misfortune to encounter." The most beloved of these characters included the quiet braggart Penelope, the weird but chipper Target Lady, and a mischievous tyke named Gilly.[36] Paul Feig may have put it best when he said, "[Kristen's] comedic energy is so inner turmoil, and on the razor's edge of holding it together in a funny way."[37]

Wiig's ascension via *Bridesmaids*, which costarred Rudolph, and the film's general popularity seemed like a signal that entertainment's gender disparities were ending. They weren't. "The hope was that *Bridesmaids* would make everyone go, 'Okay, great. Now it's no longer an issue,'" Feig said. "But that wasn't the case. There wasn't a flood of projects starring women—just a few came up."[38] And there was still plenty of sexism reflected in paychecks. Easily the most in-demand star of its cast, Jennifer Lawrence was only granted a 7 percent stake in the gross profits from 2013's Oscar-nominated *American Hustle* compared to the 9 percent given to all her male costars and the film's director.[39] Could Feig's *Ghostbusters* change that?

First the director had to cast the film. Indecision plagued Feig for months. He was glad Wiig was interested; he assumed she wouldn't be, based on recent career choices that reflected more dramatic inclinations. Who else would make a perfect Ghostbuster? Melissa McCarthy had worked with Feig thrice by this point (on *Bridesmaids*, 2013's *The Heat*, and the forthcoming *Spy*) and she seemed like a given. Feig insisted otherwise. "Melissa was never a shoo-in," he said. "She was not, because I was like, 'I got to get four very distinct personalities for this.' And I know so many funny people. . . . If you could see the lists of people, it was crazy, but who complements each other?"[40] This actually liberated Feig and Dippold when it came to writing the script. They could focus on creating characters free of other influence.[41]

Feig started meeting with some of the actresses he initially pitched to Amy Pascal that summer. Emma Stone read a draft of the *Ghostbusters* script and thought it was funny, but after making two *Spider-Man* movies she was not eager to charge headfirst into another potentially years-long, multiple-film commitment. "It just didn't feel like the right time for me," she said.[42] Jennifer Lawrence wanted to get involved, but the *Ghostbusters* filming schedule couldn't be altered to accommodate her work on *X-Men: Apocalypse*.[43] There was certainly no shortage of talent to chose from. "I think every lady in town who fancies herself a jokester wants in," *Girls* creator Lena Dunham said while guesting on an October 20 episode of *The Ellen Degeneres Show*.

McCarthy was on the panel next to Dunham, and while she denied being involved with *Ghostbusters* she did agree that herself, Dunham, and Degeneres should do the movie together at the host's sugges-tion.[44] Around the same time, *X-Files* star Gillian Anderson issued an enthusiastic public appeal. "Paul Feig, cast me now!" she typed when learning about the reboot during a Q&A on Reddit. "Start a Twitter petition! I'm free!!!! I'm free I'm free and I'm funny, goddamnit!"[45] *Cloverfield* actress Lizzy Caplan was more discreet but perhaps no less excited. Caplan was "passionate" about *Ghostbusters*, according to an email sent to Sony by her agent, who previously tried to get her involved with *Ghostbusters: Alive Again* in 2013.[46]

During a December interview on *The Today Show*, Rebel Wilson admitted they wouldn't have to pay her anything to be a Ghostbuster. Wilson was a supporting player in *Bridesmaids* who was better known for her role in the musical *Pitch Perfect*. She met with Feig but, as she remarked in the same interview, "Who knows?"[47] Feig still didn't. The only actress he mentioned by name in his written *Ghostbusters* story pitch to Amy Pascal was Cecily Strong, another *Saturday Night Live* cast member: "There's a funny dynamic we want to play with where the government eventually starts working with the Ghostbusters but has to keep denouncing them publicly, having a Cecily Strong type character always saying terrible things about them in the press conferences and then apologizing to them behind the scenes, even though her public attacks on them get more and more personal."[48]

That's exactly the part Strong was given in the completed film, though rumors suggested she was up for one of the leads. "I was cast in this movie on the Internet way before I was cast in this movie," Strong said later. "The way people will just pick up a story and run with it without ever checking anything is mind-boggling to me. Because of *SNL* I got kind of used to it. I was like, *The day I show up and film then I'll know I'm doing it*. I'm very new to the movie industry but that's how it feels like they all kind of are."[49] *Workaholics* costar Jillian Bell also met with Feig around the same time he began courting Strong, though it's unclear if Bell was in consideration for the same part or another role in the movie.

By January 27, 2015, Feig had his four Ghostbusters. McCarthy and Wiig signed on, to no one's surprise. Rounding out the marquee players were Kate McKinnon and Leslie Jones, two more *Saturday Night Live* comics who still counted the program as their main gig. Since 2012, the Emmy-nominated McKinnon applied her off-the-wall energy to a series of deft impressions that prompted *GQ* to dub her the "first lady of weird" (a nod to McKinnon's widely acclaimed Hillary Clinton impression). Jones was an unconventional *SNL* hire—a comedienne with no improv experience who was a generation older than the average player—but she was recommended by superstar former cast member Chris Rock. Jones's electricity couldn't be denied; Feig was mesmerized within seconds of first seeing her on his television.[50]

"The Aykroyd family is delighted by this inheritance of the *Ghostbusters* torch by these most magnificent women in comedy," Dan Aykroyd said in response to the casting news. "My great grand-father, Dr. Sam Aykroyd, the original Ghostbuster, was a man who empowered women in his day, and this is a beautiful development in the legacy of our family business."[51]

Ernie Hudson also lent his support, saying, "Four fiercely funny, foxy females busting ghosts . . . phenomenal!"[52] This was, how-ever, a major reversal on Hudson's part. The previous October, he expressed serious misgivings about Feig's entry to the *Telegraph*. "If it has nothing to do with the other two movies, and it's all female, then why are you calling it *Ghostbusters*?"

"I love females," Hudson continued. "I hope that if they go that way at least they'll be funny, and if they're not funny at least hopefully it'll be sexy. I love the idea of including women, I think that's great. But all female I think would be a bad idea. I don't think the fans want to see that. Maybe it will come out and be the most amazing thing, but in my opinion I think it would be wrong to do another movie that didn't include the guys. And that didn't include me!"[53]

As far as Dan Aykroyd was concerned, turning *Ghostbusters* into a multi-armed goliath like the Marvel films was a fantastic idea that could easily extend his creation another two decades. He wanted to see, as he put it, "the whole mythology from the beginning of their lives, the end of their lives. Ghostbusters at nine years old, Ghostbusters in high school."[54] The project that got Sony Pictures into this mind-set, the *Ghostbusters* film proposed by Channing Tatum for himself, Chris Pratt, and the Russo brothers, started moving forward in March 2015 in the sense that *Iron Man 3* writer Drew Pearce was hired to write a script. Perhaps because both Tatum and Pratt cultivated laddish everyman personas, the press framed their *Ghostbusters* as "guy-centric" or "male-driven." The suggestion was that this film was put into motion to appease the virulent sexists who had immediately and loudly voiced their delusions on social media that Paul Feig's women *Ghostbusters* was political correctness gone mad.[55]

A report on Badass Digest allegedly sourced from three anonymous Sony employees refuted these claims. The Tatum/Pratt *Ghostbusters* wasn't "guy-centric," though it did revolve around several male char-acters, and it was in fact set in the same universe as Feig's movie.

This would allow for an "*Avengers*-style" crossover between the two Ghostbusting teams in a third movie. A fourth prequel movie was also being planned, it was said; curiously, this prequel was not meant to outline the adventures of the '80s *Ghostbusters* characters.[56] All of this was being developed under a new production company called Ghost Corps headed by Dan Aykroyd and Ivan Reitman.

"We want to expand the *Ghostbusters* universe in ways that will include different films, TV shows, merchandise, all things that are part of modern filmed entertainment," said Reitman. "Paul Feig's film will be the first version of that, shooting in June to come out in July 2016. He's got four of the funniest women in the world, and there will be other surprises to come. The second film has a wonderful idea that builds on that. Drew will start writing and the hope is to be ready for the Russo Brothers' next window next summer to shoot, with the movie coming out the following year. It's just the beginning of what I hope will be a lot of wonderful movies."[57]

It quickly became apparent that no one involved with the Tatum/Pratt *Ghostbusters* was on the same page. Less than a week after Reitman's assertion that the movie would be a part of Feig's universe, Drew Pearce told a reporter the story he was writing took place within the time line of the '80 movies.[58] As far as Pratt was concerned, the entire project was "complete bullshit." "No one has ever spoken to me about that," he said in a May *GQ* profile. "Never. I've even seen Channing a couple times."[59] Tatum admitted a month later that the situation had "gotten messy." When asked about their *Ghostbusters* movie around the same time, Tatum's producing partner Reid Carolin informed Screen Rant, "We're not doing that anymore," citing vague complications and a personal belief that the "brand" was now "over-saturated."[60]

In July, Pearce spoke about his *Ghostbusters* script in a few interviews, saying that he'd completed a draft and hinting that it might include some way to bridge the original movies to the newer productions.[61] Reitman didn't take long to respond. "There has been a lot of excitement recently about what is happening with the *Ghostbusters* franchise," he said. "As the producer of the new *Ghostbusters* film, I feel the need to clarify. There is only one new *Ghostbusters* movie and that is the Paul Feig directed version coming next July, presently filming and going fantastically. The rest is just noise."[62] A year later, he was less tactful.

"The Pratt and Tatum stuff is all bullshit," Reitman told io9. "That was never real. I never met with them. I know Chris Pratt from way back as an actor but I've never had that conversation with him. Never talked to either of those guys about the script. There was no script."[63]

In a 1974 essay for *Literature/Film Quarterly*, Irene Kahn Atkins touched on the history of motion picture remakes in a larger examination of *Great Gatsby* adaptations. Atkins explained that the remake could be traced back to 1903 when illicit shot-for-shot reproductions of *The Great Train Robbery* earned more money than the original. Continuing, she wrote, "A great many modern film remakes, however, have been distinguished more by the technological progress they represented—silents emerging as talkies, talkies metamorphosing into musicals, black-and-white films blooming in glowing Technicolor—than improvements in plot structure, direction, or acting. Today, an announcement of the forthcoming release of a remake is usually greeted with a mixture of a modicum of hope and a great deal of cynicism."[64]

This remained true in the twenty-first century and it certainly pertained to Paul Feig's *Ghostbusters*. There were many who believed in it, like Lizzy Caplan. "I think that there's not a chance that it won't be good," she said, "because that cast is amazing and Paul Feig is amazing."[65] There were devout fans of the original *Ghostbusters* films who felt embittered that a third installment had been tossed aside in favor of a reboot. Some fans subscribed to the "If it ain't broke, don't fix it" mantra—was one of the most entertaining and successful movies of all time crying out for a do-over? And there were, of course, louts and cretins lodging nasty complaints, often directly at the filmmakers via Twitter, that having women play Ghostbusters was offensive for all sorts of stupid reasons (the equipment was too heavy for women to use, excluding men from the lead roles was "gender pandering" to "feminazis," etc.).[66] Of course, a Venn diagram might have shown some overlapping between each of these differing groups.

"I knew it was going to be really hard when the movie was released," said Feig's *Ghostbusters* cowriter Katie Dippold, "but I did not expect that to be the case prior. Like, I didn't think people were going to get upset immediately. That part surprised me."[67] Feig noted that there was an initial wash of "overwhelmingly positive" reaction to his reboot announcement. "Everyone's so happy and you're like, *This is great*," he told *Variety*. "Then comes the second wave and you're like, *Oh my God*. Some of the most vile, misogynistic shit I've ever seen in my life. The biggest thing I've heard for the last four months is, 'Thanks for ruining my childhood.' It's going to be on my tombstone when I die." When Feig received these comments on Twitter, he would often click through to see the sender's profile. "I figure it's some wacked-out teenager. But almost constantly it's someone [whose] bio says, 'Proud father of two!' And [he] has some high-end job. You're raising children and yet you're bashing me about putting women in my movie?"[68]

The cutting language and crude tone that dominated the most heated of Internet debates (over *Ghostbusters* or anything else) was less than a year away from crossing over into mainstream political discourse thanks to the presidential campaign of Donald Trump. In February, Trump, who hadn't yet declared his candidacy, briefly weighed in on Feig's *Ghostbusters* in one of his seconds-long Instagram videos that found him shouting at the viewer from his office chair. The primary topic of this clip was the rumor that *Indiana Jones* might be rebooted with Chris Pratt.

"They're remaking *Indiana Jones* without Harrison Ford, you can't do that!" Trump bellowed as if he was witnessing a crime against humanity. "And now they're making *Ghostbusters* with only women. What's going on?"[69] This was restrained compared to the rhetoric that would mark Trump's political career. Still, it was enough to get his point across, which was something must be wrong with Hollywood if women are getting equal footing.

What of fears that a *Ghostbusters* reboot might accidentally desecrate a cinematic classic? Feig admitted, "If I wasn't doing it, I'd have the same concerns."[70] Ivan Reitman also addressed this shortly after news of the reboot became public; he was refreshingly honest. "Generally, people are always cynical about these things because at their heart they start as financial desires by a studio," he said. "But here are really good creative people behind this that are trying their best. It doesn't mean it will be as great a movie as the first one."

"I hope strangely that it isn't. And strangely I hope that it is."[71]

ANSWER THE CALL

Sony Pictures originally assumed that Paul Feig's *Ghostbusters* reboot wouldn't start filming until the summer of 2016, that Feig and cowriter Katie Dippold would spend a year developing the script as he juggled other projects. Feig surprised the studio by making *Ghostbusters* his priority for a summer 2016 release. "I told Sony we could have a draft for Christmas [2014]," Feig said, "and that's what we did. We got it ready, they loved it, had notes and thoughts, but overall were extremely positive. And suddenly we were going, 'We can actually do this.' Otherwise, they were going into this summer without a giant comedy summer tentpole movie like this."[1]

Dippold understood how high the bar would be for a new *Ghostbusters* movie, but the reboot angle only made her more engaged. As an orthodox fan of the originals, Dippold said, "I don't want someone new to tell me what happened to Venkman or Egon. I always thought Paul's idea of a reboot was protecting that legacy."[2]

Feig and Dippold wrote a story centered on Erin Gilbert and Abby Yates, two friends who fell out after authoring a book about ghostly incidents. Gilbert, now a paranormal skeptic, sees her career as a professor at Columbia University jeopardized when the previously out-of-print book resurfaces. She has a confrontation with true believer Yates in the latter's research lab, which ends with Gilbert agreeing to investigate an alleged museum haunting with Yates and Yates's new partner, the eccentric Jillian Holtzmann. The trio witness an evil spirit and capture it on video; this emboldens the women to set up their own paranormal examination service above a Chinese restaurant. A brash MTA worker named Patty Tolan becomes part of the team after asking them to check out a phantasm in the subway.

Meanwhile, lone disillusioned scientist Rowan North vows revenge on a world he perceives to be unjust by implementing technology that exacerbates New York's growing ghost problem. The Ghostbusters use their newfangled ghost-stopping technology to try to keep the hauntings at bay, but they also have to contend with municipal and federal governments, which secretly retain their services while creating a publicity smokescreen that paints them as charlatans. Rowan commits suicide and ascends to some sort of demigod who possesses the Ghostbusters' dim-witted secretary Kevin so he can rain ghostly hell upon the entire city. A portal is opened to the ghost world and only by turning their tricked-out car into a nuclear bomb can the Ghostbusters close the gateway and save New York. In one of the story's clever meta twists, during the final confrontation Rowan assumes a kaiju form of the ghost featured in the "no ghost" logo.

"The very first draft of the script, there was no cast," Dippold said. "To be honest, for [the Patty] part, Melissa [McCarthy] kept popping in my head because there's something so funny about her up against any sort of snobbery. But Leslie [Jones] has such strong energy and we wanted someone to be that powerful in the role."[3] Jones was given Patty Tolan, while McCarthy would play the more restrained Abby Yates. Kristen Wiig agreed to portray wet blanket Erin Gilbert, and it was perhaps kismet that brought Kate McKinnon to wild-eyed weirdo Jillian Holtzmann. "Yes, this is the closest character to my actual self that I've ever played," said McKinnon, who described Holtzmann as another character in her performing lineage who was "just on the fringes but not aware" of it.[4]

Feig discovered another one of his cast members through *Saturday Night Live* when he watched swaggering *Thor* star Chris Hemsworth host an episode in early 2015. As Hemsworth explained, "[Paul] called me up [afterward] and said: 'That was great. I didn't know you could do that. Do you have a bigger interest in doing more of that?' And I said, 'Yeah, I've always wanted to do some comedy.'" Hemsworth was cast as Kevin, the team's handsome but stupid admin assistant.[5] Writer and comedian Neil Casey, who had a costarring role in Feig's one-season sci-fi TV series spoof *Other Space*, nabbed the part of Rowan. Casey's background as a computer programmer helped him conjure up feelings of isolation and loneliness for Rowan. "I thought that the most interesting thing about him was that he was the dark mirror image of any one of the Ghostbusters," Casey said. "That he was the sort of twisted, sad, angry, nerdy version of . . . well, they're both nerdy, but the twisted, angry version of them."[6]

Of the original *Ghostbusters* actors, Dippold and Feig only knew for sure that Dan Aykroyd wanted to do something on-screen. Aykroyd was also guiding the ship as one of the film's many producers. As the writing was getting under way, Aykroyd gifted Dippold a copy of his father's book *A History of Ghosts* with a personal inscription. "[It] said something like, 'I'm here if you need any help at all, but most importantly, just have fun,'" Dippold said. She was touched by the gesture, which came when the negative outcry surrounding the film was starting to get to her. "Hollywood can be terribly disappointing. It can be a gauntlet of shit and it was one of those rare moments someone you looked up to your whole life does something like that."[7]

"*Ghostbusters* was unlike anything I'd ever done," says production designer Jefferson Sage, who previously worked with Paul Feig on *The Heat*, *Bridesmaids*, and *Freaks and Geeks*. "It was the biggest film I'd been hired to do. My background is mid-level comedy. This was a special effects extravaganza. Managing that workflow is much harder. Normally I work with ten or twelve people. Here I had twenty-eight, all looking for input. . . . All of them were brilliant and it was so challenging to stay ahead of them and get them fed. Juggling all those things and the changes in the script that were ongoing, it was tough."[8] *Ghostbusters* art director Audra Avery was a ten-year veteran of art department work by that point and she echoes Sage. "It was the first time I was on a project that had such a huge history. We really had to pay attention to what already had been established. The caveat is that we're making a modern movie. It's not 1984 anymore."[9]

"This was a big, big discussion," Sage adds. "How much is the movie different from the originals and how much is it the same?" The decision was made to adhere to basic established elements, like the proton packs, the ghost traps, the Ectomobile, and the jumpsuits, and to add or subtract certain embellishments. "Paul wanted this whole arc—he wanted the proton packs to look more primitive, for instance, more 'in development,'" says Sage. "He had this story beat that the Holtzmann character is always tinkering. . . . You see the technology once, but then the next time you see it it's slightly different. There are a few lines in the script that reflect this."[10]

Feig took more liberties with the *Ghostbusters* sound design. Supervising sound editor Andrew DeCristofaro recalls gathering some of the iconic sounds from the first two *Ghostbusters* movies early on only to have Feig veto their use. "I was initially concerned," DeCristofaro admits. "When you work on something that has a prior existence, like when you're doing a *Star Trek*, you don't deviate from those sounds. He wanted it to be his own, but at the same time he didn't want to be disrespectful. So we would use the original [sound] element in the energy streams but it's only one element out of twelve layers. Paul wanted the streams to sound like liquid lava. They looked like that when I saw the first visual effects."[11]

Sage says that although the prep window for *Ghostbusters* was twenty weeks, twice the normal amount on a given film, it still wasn't enough time given the scale of the production. "We didn't have much time to really consider the big questions, like 'What does New York look like in this *Ghostbusters*?' or 'What do the ghosts look like?'" he laments. "I would have given it another three months, maybe four. Who knows?" More time would have been allotted had *Ghostbusters* been cast sooner. "If they don't have the cast yet, they don't want to have anyone working, even a small team," says Sage. Regardless, Sage and his artists, whom he praises as "immensely talented," concocted hundreds of ghosts, many of which weren't used at all.

"We did a whole family of New York ghosts . . . like these real historical New York figures who got lost in the vortex and now they're pissed off and coming out. The New York ghosts come into the film briefly in the end battle. The guy with hatchet was taken from a 1920s guy clearly hired by the government to bust up illegal liquor. He was a federal agent hired to bust up bars, to go in and roll the barrels out and pour the liquor into the streets. The third guy on the left with the hatchet in this historical picture we saw, we said, 'He's a thug.'" Sage also reveals that Feig at one point wanted the ghost vortex to allow any kind of evil creature from our imagination to appear. "So we thought about slimy, slippery reptilian aliens things. We kind of pulled back from that because it didn't feel right."[12]

Being a major Hollywood movie in the twenty-first century, Paul Feig's *Ghostbusters* would include a number of corporate product tie-ins. "When we started, we already knew they had a Lego tie-in and a Papa John's tie-in," says Avery. "So sometimes there was a situation where the thing that's supposed to be in the commercial isn't ready yet, so we need to pull it up."[13] Sage remembers Sony Pictures being "very concerned" about the look of *Ghostbusters* because of those special branding opportunities. "They came in very late, right before we were gonna shoot, because they were thinking they wanted to do a toy set based on the Ghostbusters' lab," he says. "So we put together a presentation, like an exhibit with the proton packs, the ambulance, all that stuff, and the studio would bring in people from toy manufacturers to look at it. You know, it was a way of enticing business interests with Sony."

"When I heard this was all gonna happen, I had a big panic. *If this is where they want to go, they should have been here four months ago.* [They'd say], 'If you had done this with the proton packs, it would have made a better toy.' 'Well, you should have been here before.' . . . So the studio was involved in where things were going, but they also didn't tell us [things like], 'Make sure it's like this' or 'Do this with the ambulance.'" Sage insists that Paul Feig was "the foreman" on *Ghostbusters* and the buck stopped with him regarding every design decision.[14] Editor Brent White, another figure who'd worked with Feig several times prior, disagrees.

"It wasn't all completely Paul's," White says. "He had a lot of input on the design and what have you, but it was a big franchise everyone needed money from. So Amy Pascal came on as a producer and was there with us while we were shooting to help us not stray too far away from what the studio had in mind."[15] Pascal had been forced out at Sony Pictures in February 2015 after the notorious email hack that started four months earlier. The hack revealed that Pascal had made racist jokes about President Barack Obama in private correspondence. Almost immediately, she launched her own production company, one Sony agreed to back, allowing her to have a hand in *Ghostbusters*.[16]

Pascal's replacement in Sony's upper echelon was Tom Rothman, a former 20th Century Fox figurehead who had butted heads with Feig when the latter directed *The Heat* for that studio. Rothman told Feig he wanted to bring the *Ghostbusters* budget down from $169 million to $150 million. Not looking to start a war, Feig revised the script and the pair settled on $154 million. It should be noted that neither Feig's salary, said to be above $10 million, nor Melissa McCarthy's $14 million paycheck could be reduced thanks to the contractual terms set by Pascal.[17]

Ghostbusters began shooting under the code name *Flapjack* in June 2015. Substituting for the Big Apple was one of New York's most bitter rivals—Boston ("New York did not have enough stage space for the square footage we needed," Avery explains).[18] Although it closed in 1997, the South Weymouth Naval Air Station offered a "big free-span area" perfect for the production inside an old aircraft hangar and corresponding runway. A representative from LStar Management, the company in charge of leasing the station, said, "We're enormously proud that our first movie is *Ghostbusters*. We're huge fans of Kristen Wiig and Melissa McCarthy and we're honored to welcome them to the property."[19] *Ghostbusters* also made use of numerous locales around the city familiar to Bostonians. The old Everett High School became home to Abby Yates's lab; Boston University's Castle reception hall was refurbished as the haunted museum at the start of the movie; the Wang Theatre hosted a heavy metal concert interrupted by marauding spirits.[20] Of course, some locations had to be fabricated.

"You know the subway sequence? It's real difficult to shoot inside an actual subway tunnel," says Sage. "It's almost impossible. So we built this enormous set, it was 180 feet long . . . and we had a shipment of subway parts brought in from Philadelphia that we bought off the Philadelphia Transit Authority that they thought was junk. With that stuff, it felt very authentic. And we had a very talented construction crew, as well as very talented electricians and lighting people."[21]

When they weren't shooting, some of the cast members enjoyed Boston's historic trails. "[Kate McKinnon] had me walking everywhere," said Leslie Jones. "All around Boston, looking at old-fashioned doors and shit. I hated it at first, but then I got really into it.[22]

Prior to the release of Paul Feig's *Ghostbusters*, rumors splashed across the Internet that filming was marred by arguments and dissent. Melissa McCarthy raised hell with Feig because she thought the script was weak and she didn't want another unnamed cast member to have more lines than she did. Kate McKinnon and Leslie Jones, bonded from their time together on *Saturday Night Live*, turned on Kristen Wiig after Wiig took a condescending attitude toward nascent movie actor Jones.[23] If there was any serious rancor between the cast and director on the *Ghostbusters* set, the crew members interviewed for this volume didn't see it. Additional second assistant director J. J. Dalton in particular paints a very rosy picture of *Ghostbusters*.

"I really got very, very close with all the actors, really very close," says Dalton. "That was one of the shows where it just seemed more like a family, more so than any other set I'd previously been on.

It was such a great cast and crew to be a part of because of that camaraderie."[24] Special effects supervisor Mark Hawker agrees, saying *Ghostbusters* was the funniest set he's ever been on: "The girls were all hilarious and Paul Feig is awesome."[25] One of Hawker's bigger duties was helping to create the movie's slime. "We spent a couple months of trial and error on the slime," he says. "Paul wasn't happy with the original compound, so we created a new mixture that was more stringy. They thought they'd have to do visual effects on that, but when you see Kristen Wiig getting slimed in the face, that's all real slime."[26]

Wiig's character cannot avoid a few serious slime attacks over the course of the movie. "When I first read the script, I thought, *That's such a funny running joke*," the actress said. But like Ernie Hudson and Peter MacNicol before her, Wiig soon considered the slimings a curse. "It's not something you shower off. In fact, water activates it. So whenever you shower for the next three days, you still kind of feel it." Melissa McCarthy had trouble getting crew members to tell her what was in the slime. "No one would answer that question," she said. "It was always a bunch of people in masks saying, 'Oh, it's perfectly safe.' Well, I didn't even ask if it was safe, I asked what it was. They're in hazmat gear and Kristen's getting it blown in her face."[27]

Feig wanted to utilize practical special effects over computer graphics as much as possible in order to achieve a more organic feel.[28] "I have talked to so many people about it and they are like, 'Oh, what was the tennis ball like?'" McCarthy commented after the fact. "And I am like, 'No, there was, like the ghost in the subway in the beginning, he went though six, seven, eight hours of prosthetics and it was someone named Dave, I have known Dave for years. I was in there talking to, like I was in there watching him. I had no idea who it was, and it wasn't 'til he spoke that I was like, 'Oh my God, I know who you are.'"[29] Computer imaging couldn't be avoided entirely, however. Jefferson Sage spent roughly two months after the film wrapped constructing digital effects for *Ghostbusters* at his home.[30]

To help root the technology in what some referred to as "hard science," MIT particle physicist James Maxwell was hired to punch up the script and some of the props. Maxwell wasn't sure how effective his expertise ended up being; he was "starry-eyed" by the presence of Hollywood. "I was giddy because of where I was—in the middle of an actual movie set," said Maxwell. "I wasn't thinking critically about the science. . . . I was just happy to be there." Fellow MIT professor Lindley Winslow made sure the mathematical equations seen in *Ghostbusters* were accurate. Meanwhile, Kate McKinnon picked Maxwell's brain about string theory. Maxwell was pleased not just to be involved with this production but to have it happening at all. "I think it's really important to have role models in culture that are scientists," he said. "They're not Captain America, but they've got their own superpowers, which is the scientific method and patience and scientific inquiry. And the fact that this movie has female leads—I think it's really important to see more female scientists in general, and particularly in physics to see more female involvement."[31]

Of course, the comedy came first for *Ghostbusters*, and the stars couldn't believe their luck when they started riffing on camera with the actor playing their secretary, Chris Hemsworth. "I knew he was going to be nice," said McCarthy. "Everybody said, 'Oh, he's such a great guy. He's so nice. You're going to love him.' No one mentioned that he was bizarrely funny. He was so funny and he was one of the best improvisors I've ever worked with, and I've been lucky enough to work with a lot of really funny guys. He just kind of blew us all away."[32] Feig captured a plethora of takes on the scene where Kevin is being interviewed because Hemsworth kept delivering.

"He was saying the funniest things I've ever heard in rapid succession for hours," McKinnon attested. "We met in the bathroom and [we] were like, 'Does he have writers?'"[33] This was a relief for Hemsworth, who felt nerves getting the best of him the night before his first day of shooting when he realized he had no concrete dialogue to learn. The actor had been told that specific pages were being written for him; those pages never arrived. They were likely never written. Improvisational comedy was a tenet of Feig's movies and often the director preferred using little more than "an emotional roadmap" while filming certain scenes. This technique allowed the actors to build something unique together.[34, 35]

As Hemsworth remembered, "I said [to Paul], '[The pages aren't] here and we shoot tomorrow.' He said, 'It's fine—This is the way we work.' And everyone around him, like his producers, said, 'This is Paul's thing.' I was like, 'Oh my God, this is going to be a disaster.' [But] it ended up being so much fun. It was so liberating. It was like, 'Okay, if it doesn't work, it's not my fault.' As opposed to, 'Here's the greatest script in the world, don't screw it up.'"[36]

"A lot of that stuff you see from Chris in the final cut is from him," says Dalton. "It's all him. A big reason [Marvel] said okay to *Thor: Ragnarok*, which is more comedic than the other *Thor* films, is because of what Chris did in *Ghostbusters*."[37] Dalton adds that

Wiig and McCarthy both had "a huge part" in script rewrites and that "two or three" alternate writers from *Saturday Night Live* visited the set each day during shooting to pitch jokes. "I asked why and [Paul] said it was because a year from now they wouldn't be sure what was really gonna take."[38]

Invective-laced vitriol continued to blanket online discussion of Paul Feig's *Ghostbusters* as he crafted the film. Actually, it seemed to be ramping up. "It was really difficult," says supervising sound editor Andrew DeCristofaro. "I sat on a soundstage with Paul for months. At one point Paul said, 'I will never ever do another remake again.' He'd slide his laptop over—I'd ask, 'Hey, what's bothering you?'—he'd slide his laptop over and I'd see the hate mail."[39]

Feig received a boost in August 2015 when Bill Murray filmed a small part for the movie as a supernatural skeptic who challenges the Ghostbusters to prove they do what they say. "You know, they were incredibly nice to ask me, and I really enjoyed being there," Murray said. "I like those girls a lot. I mean, I really do. They are tough to say no to. And Paul is a really nice fellow." Murray said he'd spent "a very long time" considering the offer. "I started to feel like if I didn't do this movie, maybe somebody would write a bad review or something, thinking there was some sort of disapproval [on my part]."[40] Murray's appearance was one of several involving original *Ghostbusters* cast members. Dan Aykroyd had a gag as a nervous cabdriver, Ernie Hudson agreed to play the uncle of Jones's character, Sigourney Weaver would play an elder scientist, and Annie Potts was given a cameo as a hotel clerk.[41]

One famous face who couldn't be lured into a cameo was Rick Moranis. "I wish them well," Moranis said in an interview that October. "I hope it's terrific. But it just makes no sense to me. Why would I do just one day of shooting on something I did 30 years ago?" Moranis clarified that he wasn't completely retired from acting—the break he took in 1997 after his wife passed away from brain cancer just sort of stretched out. "I'm interested in anything that I would find interesting. I still get the occasional query about a film or television role and as soon as one comes along that piques my interest, I'll probably do it. [This] didn't appeal to me."[42]

Ghostbusters wrapped principal photography in September, moving into the often complicated process of editing. "We were trying really hard to make the best and funniest movie that we could," says editor Brent White, who notes that specific attention was paid to the friendship between the two main characters. Naturally, White and his editing team had to contend with the special effects. "The way we make comedies, we're constantly adjusting the rhythm to smooth out the pace and make sure there are no dead spots," he explains. "I kept trimming stuff down before we got to the effects to make the movie move and sing, but then I went back and opened the movie up because we got the effects and they were so gangbusters. They had a great energy and oomph to them. That said, a laugh is more valuable than a visual effect." As he had with the other comedies he'd edited, White had the filmmakers record the laughter of test screening audiences so he could lay it over his edit to see what was working and what wasn't.

It was during editing, White says, that "the dissatisfaction of what the filmmaker thought his movie should be and what the studio thought their movie should be" became apparent. "Because of everything online, there was a little bit of second-guessing as to what it could do." As such, Ivan Reitman and his longtime editor Sheldon Kahn stepped in for a handful of weeks to take a crack at some cutting ideas with help from half of White's crew. Both Feig and White welcomed Reitman in this capacity, because he was, as the latter put it, an "amazing technician of comedy." White had previously worked with Reitman on 1992's *Stop! Or My Mom Will Shoot*. "I'd never think to take the second line of a joke and make it the third. Ivan would suggest that to make a joke work, and yeah, then it would work."

Lightning did not strike for Reitman and the editors working under him on Feig's *Ghostbusters*. "The changes they came up with or decided on . . . they didn't move the needle enough," says White. "It didn't make it a better movie, it just made it a different movie."[43]

There was push and pull over the marketing as well. When the first full trailer for Paul Feig's *Ghostbusters* debuted on March 3, 2016, it began with a preamble saying, "Thirty years ago, four scientists saved New York. This summer, a new team will answer the call." Feig explained that this introduction was just an acknowledgment of what came before. "We went through a million different wordings," he said. "I said, 'It can't play as a sequel, because I can't support that, so what's the way to pass the torch?' And Ivan [Reitman], when he saw the trailer, he was really happy about it."[44] Regardless of intent, viewers were confused by the introduction, as it seemed to imply this *Ghostbusters* was, in fact, a sequel. Even some cast members raised doubts. "Believe me, the question was asked," Melissa McCarthy said a few months later. "I was like, 'I think that's very confusing.' But then everyone said, 'We don't care what you think.'"[45]

A number of viewers were also dismayed that this *Ghostbusters* was another iteration featuring three college-educated white characters and a lone black character who was the "regular" person "off the street." As Twitter filled up with complaints about that dynamic, Leslie Jones defended her role on the platform. "Why can't a regular person be a ghostbuster? I'm confused. And why can't I be the one who plays them? I am a performer. Just go see the movie!"[46] Cowriter Katie Dippold said later that "the race thing" didn't enter her mind when Jones was cast. "I'm bummed people feel that way because it all came from a good place."[47]

There was plenty of outcry in a general sense as the *Ghostbusters* trailer became a flash point in the culture war over the reboot's very existence. Positive and even measured responses were drowned out by the hyperbolic screeds of purists and sexists. Negative reaction on the trailer's YouTube page was unrelenting; in just two months, *Ghostbusters* earned 647,600 "dislikes" over 220,800 "likes" to become the most unpopular film trailer in YouTube history. "I signed in under both of my [YouTube] accounts so that I could dislike this twice," wrote a user named Crippled Camel.[48] Many in the industry were stunned.

"I haven't seen this level of hatred by an extremely vocal group before a movie came out or before anyone even saw it," said Alicia Malone, correspondent for movie ticketing website Fandango. "It's unprecedented. There are some who don't want their beloved *Ghostbusters* to be remade. But much of this hatred we've been seeing is toward an all female cast. And it's been really intense."[49] *Ghostbusters*' production designer Jefferson Sage noticeably deflates when discussing "the haters." "It's hard to overstate how hard that hurt the movie," he says. "A fun afternoon at the movies with this new take on *Ghostbusters* was poisoned. It scared the studio, it scared the actors. Paul tried to stoically blank it out. We tried to ignore it. We figured they'd get tired and go away, but it didn't. It got bigger, and as the movie came out, it swelled. It was a big coordinated response . . . and it was baffling."[50]

It was disheartening for the cast as well. Like the majority of the people attacking them, they were fans of the original *Ghostbusters*. For McCarthy, it was a childhood favorite. "It's a classic for a very good reason," said Wiig. "Bill Murray is just so damn funny in it," said Jones. "The way he reacted to the scariness with comedy was brilliant. Sigourney Weaver was great too. She was so innocent-looking and then she turned into this vixen. I was like, 'Whoa, I want to be like her.'" McKinnon was also a fan, but having been born the year *Ghostbusters* was first released, she liked to joke she had trouble seeing it from her mother's womb.

"I don't understand why there's been such a backlash," Jones told the *New Zealand Herald*. "It seems to me it's always that way when women appear in something different but I don't know why. Is it sexist? Maybe, I'm not sure. All I know is, I don't think like that. I pay more attention to what the project is, not who's in it."[51]

The stars of the *Ghostbusters* reboot eventually grew weary of questions about being women. "Are we still talking about that?" McCarthy said after rolling her eyes when gender came up during an interview with the *Sydney Morning Herald*.[52] Wiig cut off *New York Times* writer Dave Itzkoff when he began a query about *Ghostbusters* being a litmus test. "How many litmus tests do we need?" she replied emphatically, generating laughter from her castmates. "I've been hearing this for five years. Sorry, I'm finished."[53]

Two press screenings of Paul Feig's *Ghostbusters* were held in New York on July 7, 2016. The screening *Village Voice* writer Melissa Anderson attended was marked by a "stupefying chaos" and "unprecedented incompetence" that made her wonder if Sony was sabotaging the movie. Per her report: "After the *Lord of the Flies*–level mayhem of the press check-in, *Ghostbusters*, which was supposed to be shown in IMAX 3-D, began in 2-D . . . with the Windows logo glaringly visible in the bottom left of the screen and running a timer tracking each second in the bottom right. At around the fifteen-minute mark, the lights came up, and a Sony rep announced, 'This isn't the way we wanted you to see it' and then told us the film would start over."

The preview got back on track, but Anderson was underwhelmed by what she saw. She found it "too risk-averse" and suffering from "the anxiety of influence." "The main performers rarely get to display their individual idiosyncratic strengths," she wrote. "It's particularly dispiriting to hear [Melissa] McCarthy, one of the most floridly gifted verbal riffers in comedy, have to utter frat-brah catchphrases like, 'Let's do this.' That kind of lifeless, recycled language sounds even worse when [Kristen] Wiig, another performer who has perfected how to do things with words, cries out, 'Say hello to my little friend' before zapping a spook in the film's near-interminable final act, a glut of green beams that suggests nothing more than an f/x trade show."[54]

Other reviews ahead of the movie's July 15 general release were mixed. *Time* magazine's Stephanie Zacharek called the *Ghostbusters* reboot "an affable, inventive riff" on the original that's "presented with a wink" and moments of "visual glory."[55] Jen Yamato of the Daily Beast found the movie "saddled with the trappings of 21st century studio filmmaking: lulls in pacing, kiddie-safe comedy, choppy editing, and the general sense that a sharper, ballsier version exists in an alternate Hollywood universe." At the same time, Yamato praised *Ghostbusters* for having a "crackling sense of purpose and a surplus of reverence for [its] predecessors."[56] In *Rolling Stone*, Peter Travers announced, "No big whup and no big fat flop either, the female reboot of *Ghostbusters* settles for being a fine, fun time at the movies."[57]

"I am not a die-hard fan of the original *Ghostbusters*," Richard Lawson wrote in *Vanity Fair*, "but I can at least appreciate that it's more an admirably offbeat horror-comedy than it is an epic action movie. Feig's *Ghostbusters* tries hard to prove its place in the modern world, and in the summer blockbuster season, by turning itself into an aimless spectacular. That feels like a wrong read of *Ghostbusters*, and it drowns out any wit and charm the movie has managed to create. The wit and charm does exist, mind you. Though it's unfortunate to say about a women-led movie like this, Chris Hemsworth, playing the Ghostbusters' hunky-dumb assistant, is easily the funniest part of the movie, his loopy job interview scene hinting at a better, more discursive, more improv-y film that could have been."[58]

Raves piled up for Hemsworth but the real breakout star was Kate McKinnon, whose fearless and gender-fluid take on Jillian Holtzmann seized countless viewers. Yamato rhapsodized that McKinnon "oozes visceral charisma . . . emanating cocksure confidence even if we learn very little about [her]." *New York Times* scribe Manohla Dargis hailed the actress as "magnificent," comparing her to Jerry Lewis and Amy Poehler. "She's like a figure out of 1980s cyberpunk," countered Jake Wilson in *The Age*, "or Harpo Marx by way of Duckie in *Pretty in Pink*."[59] Holtzmann was a new icon for the pansexual age. Gender studies scholar Bridget Kies had a few other deft observations about the gender dynamics at play in *Ghostbusters*.

"The 1984 film hinged upon the sexual union of two ghosts who inhabited the bodies of a man and a woman—a testament to heterosexual reproduction, even in death," Kies wrote. "By contrast, the new *Ghostbusters* foregrounds women's homosocial bonding. In the film's climax, during which ghosts rampage through New York, there is a touching moment in which Erin risks her life to save Abby. She jumps into a vortex that leads to another dimension, grabs onto Abby and pledges not to lose her again. They manage to escape the vortex and emerge embracing each other. The moment is a celebration of the power of women's friendship as much as it is rife with queer possibilities."[60]

The prerelease hysteria that engulfed *Ghostbusters* did not translate to box office dominance. The movie only rose to number two during its debut weekend, earning $46 million against a $50.6 million take from *The Secret Life of Pets*, which was in its second week of release. Regardless, Sony called *Ghostbusters* a victory, throwing out the qualifier that $46 million was the biggest opening for a live-action comedy in over a year. "We've successfully restarted a very important brand and we're just ecstatic at the results," said marketing and distribution president Josh Greenstein. Rory Bruer, another distribution executive, promised a sequel: "While nothing has been officially announced yet, there's no doubt in my mind it will happen."

Reports suggested that Feig had managed to bring the film's final budget down to $144 million, but even that, coupled with over $100 million spent on marketing, made many wonder if a $46 million opening was anything to crow about. *Ghostbusters* needed to make $300 million just to break even, insiders said, but by early August the worldwide gross hovered near $180 million. This nuked any hopes of franchise building (the cast was allegedly contracted for a minimum of two sequels; zero sequels to Paul Feig's *Ghostbusters* have materialized as of this writing).[61]

"The reaction might have been justified," says Audra Avery, who served as art director for this *Ghostbusters*. "I saw it and thought, *I can see how people aren't into this*. It was super fun to work on, though, and there are parts I'm really proud of."[62] Sound designer Anthony Lamberti concurs. "Is it one of my all-time favorites? Well, it's not really my cup of tea. But it's got a lot of fun stuff. The girls are great in it."[63] Production designer Jefferson Sage says he's "quite pleased with the film overall," though he has minor quibbles here and there. "Maybe what we did with a lot of the design was too subtle," he says. "Maybe we should have hit it harder."[64]

Unfortunately, the abominable online behavior of racist and sexist trolls did not abate once *Ghostbusters* was out. Leslie Jones decided to quit using Twitter less than a week after the movie's release, the victim of relentless offensive attacks. Users sent Jones graphic photos and made bigoted remarks, leaving her with "tears and a very sad heart." This episode also served to underline Twitter's incredibly weak moderation system, which relied on user reports to flag abusive behavior (as opposed to employing an active content moderation team).[65] Jones got the last laugh, as it were, returning to Twitter the following month and receiving adulation for her commentary on that month's Olympic games. "Jones hits the sweet spot between irreverence, carnal patriotism, and straight shooting," said Vox's Alex Abad-Santos. "It's play-by-play in its most honest form. It's jarringly hilarious. And it's also endearing."[66]

As Paul Feig's *Ghostbusters* was being released on DVD and Blu-ray in October 2016, Sony's marketing department began pushing the subtitle the studio insisted the director add to the film to help differentiate it from the 1984 movie in catalogs. Feeling a moniker like *Ghostbusters 2016* would date his work, the director decided to use the subtitle *Answer the Call*. "I just said, 'Don't put it on the front of the movie,'" he recounted. "'If you put it on the end, I don't care.'"[67]

A year after the theatrical bow of *Ghostbusters: Answer the Call*, Dan Aykroyd offered his perspective on the film. "The girls are great in it," he told Britain's Channel 4. "I was really happy with the movie, but it cost too much. . . . It made a lot of money around the world but just cost too much, making it economically not feasible to do another one. So that's too bad. The director, he spent too much on it. He didn't shoot scenes we suggested to him and several scenes that were going to be needed and he said, 'Nah, we don't need them.' Then we tested the movie and they needed them and he had to go back. About $30 to $40 million in reshoots. So he will not be back on the Sony lot any time soon."

Sony issued a rebuttal that day, saying *Ghostbusters: Answer the Call* reshoots had only cost between $3 and $4 million. Within forty-eight hours, Aykroyd himself posted a clarification on Facebook that suggested his comments had more to do with bruised feelings: "Paul Feig made a good movie and had a superb cast and plenty of money to do it. We just wish he had been more inclusive to the originators. It cost everyone as it is unlikely Kristen, Leslie, Melissa and Kate will ever reprise their roles as Ghostbusters, which is sad."[68]

Feig's postmortem touched more on the fact that *Answer the Call* blossomed into a serious social cause. "I think for some of the audience, they were like, 'What the fuck? We don't wanna go to a cause. We just wanna watch a fuckin' movie,'" he remarked that November. "It was a great regret in my life that the movie didn't do better, 'cause I really loved it. It's not a perfect movie. None of my movies are perfect. I liked what we were doing with it. It was only supposed to be there to entertain people."[69]

Ghostbusters: Answer the Call has its indelible moments outside the Looney Tunes anarchy of Kate McKinnon and the absurd stupidity of Chris Hemsworth. A scene where the famous "no ghost" logo is revealed in graffiti on a grimy subway wall is a brilliant way to recontextualize this emblem as a part of New York City. Cecily Strong, Andy Garcia, Michael K. Williams, and Matt Walsh are perfect as condescending authoritarians trying to corral the Ghostbusters on behalf of the government. The cinematography is crisp and the colors pop, evoking memories of *The Real Ghostbusters* cartoon (many thought McKinnon's puffy hairstyle was a tribute to Egon's pompadour in *Real Ghostbusters* but the likeness was unintentional).

The film is otherwise burdened by its insistence on repeating the 1984 original. Forming the business, tan jumpsuits, a red and white car, pushback from bureaucrats, a giant entity near the end—it's like a cover version of a classic song that reaches adequacy but isn't daring enough for major reinvention. Of course, the same accusation has been leveled at *Ghostbusters II*. Some argue that *Ghostbusters: Answer the Call*'s extended cut, released on home media, creates a superior movie by adding fifteen minutes that were cut from the theatrical release.[70] Editor Brent White says those fifteen minutes had been excised to appease the movie's distributors. "They'd say, 'If *Ghostbusters* is that long, we have to cut one [theatrical] showing a day. Which of course means that much less money is coming in. Paul was trying to accomplish things for the studio and that made some of the jokes go away, until this extended cut."[71]

Paul Feig's reboot was probably always destined for controversy. It re-created an artifact many held sacred and gave equal opportunity to a gender still considered secondary by the scores of backwards thinkers who make up too much of our populace. Perhaps everything surrounding the movie was heightened by the overlapping of that year's US presidential election. Republican candidate Donald Trump, unabashed in his nationalist policies and chauvinism, got in on the ground floor of complaining about the *Ghostbusters* reboot in February 2015. Democrat Hillary Clinton, the first woman in our nation's history to receive a presidential nomination from a reigning political party, had an avatar in Kate McKinnon, whose impression of Clinton was her best known on *Saturday Night Live*.

Clinton's loss could be seen as going hand in hand with *Answer the Call*'s failure to best or even match its predecessors. Then again, Clinton only lost because of our country's archaic and profoundly flawed electoral college system, which canceled out her clear victory in the popular vote. And *Ghostbusters: Answer the Call* succeeded in ways that can't be measured in integers. It spoke to a new generation of young women in need of heroes.

Nine-year-old Marissa Soto and ten-year-old Natalie Lopez were part of a young dance troupe hired to perform at the premiere of *Ghostbusters: Answer the Call* on July 9, 2016. At one point, Soto and Lopez, still wearing their jumpsuits and inflatable proton packs from the performance, exchanged high fives with a clearly appreciative Kristen Wiig. Photos of the two girls beaming up at Wiig with gleeful adoration soon went viral.

"After shaking hands with or high-fiving every one of the female ghostbusters, she said she was never washing her hands," said Soto's mother, Alma Garcia. "The cast was so nice and beautiful, and my daughter loved that in the movie they are so tough. She said she wants to be just like Kristen Wiig."

Teenager Anna Spiess, who posted the photos on Twitter with the caption "this is important," told BuzzFeed News, "It *is* important for young girls to realize that they, after all, are a valid part of this society and can be anyone they want to be, even a GHOSTBUSTER!"[72]

HAVE YOU MISSED US?

"Any chance of a real, honest *Ghostbusters III?*"

Storied newscaster Dan Rather posed this question to Dan Aykroyd during a November 2018 conversation on *The Big Interview*.[1] The plan for a multipronged *Ghostbusters* cinematic universe had not yet come to pass. *Ghostbusters: Answer the Call* stopped at one movie; an animated *Ghostbusters* film told from the perspective of a ghost hadn't made much progress since being announced in 2015; a new TV cartoon set in the year 2050 called *Ghostbusters: Ecto Force* was put on hold in 2017 after a year of development.[2]

That left many, like Rather, wondering about the third chapter of the original continuity. Rather's question seemed loaded against *Answer the Call*, so Aykroyd reiterated his support and affection for that film before telling Rather yes, a *Ghostbusters III* was once again in the cards. "There's a possibility of a reunion with the remaining three Ghostbusters. . . . I think we got a story that's gonna work and it's being written now by a really, really good filmmaker." Aykroyd declined to name the filmmaker or their writing partner, but he assured everyone watching that this team was striving to "bring back all the emotion and spirit of the first two movies and then take it into the twenty-first century with the vernacular that's needed today to get across to audiences."[3]

Ivan Reitman made passing mention of another live-action film when discussing projects like the animated feature and *Ecto Force* in previous years, but until Aykroyd's chat with Rather no one understood this project was *Ghostbusters III*.[4] The Ghost Corps heads were

229

remaining tight-lipped about the identity of the director involved probably for a variety of reasons, one of which may have been to retain maximum impact for the official reveal.

On January 15, 2019, *Entertainment Weekly* ignited a frenzy when they reported that Jason Reitman, Ivan's son and an established director in his own right, was cowriting and helming "the next chapter in the original [*Ghostbusters*] franchise." "It is not a reboot," Jason declared. "What happened in the '80s happened in the '80s, and this is set in the present day." Gil Kenan, director of *Monster House* and *City of Ember*, was Jason's cowriter.

"I've always thought of myself as the first *Ghostbusters* fan, when I was a 6-year-old visiting the set [of the first movie]," Jason said. "I wanted to make a movie for all the other fans. This is very early, and I want the film to unwrap like a present. We have a lot of wonderful surprises and new characters for the audience to meet." He added that he had "so much respect" for *Ghostbusters: Answer the Call* and hoped there would be future adventures with "those brilliant actresses."

The next day *Entertainment Weekly* debuted a teaser trailer for this *Ghostbusters* movie, as if to prove it was really happening. The clip opens with a cloudy night hanging over a barn. The soft chirping of crickets is interrupted by what sounds like a figure inside the barn trying to use a proton pack. The camera pushes across a leaf-strewn field to the barn's interior, where the wind is disturbing a covered vehicle. As a sting from Elmer Bernstein's original *Ghostbusters* score swells, the "no ghost" logo on the back door of the Ectomobile is revealed.

Jason Reitman's *Ghostbusters* was slated for a summer 2020 release.[5]

He wasn't born on a movie set, but Jason Reitman was visiting them before he could talk; his parents brought him to the set of *National Lampoon's Animal House* a mere ten days after his birth in 1977.[6] So it's no surprise that the calling to make movies always lived inside the younger Reitman. For years, however, he avoided exploring his passion because he feared being compared to his father. Reitman tried going premed at Skidmore College after high school, but that only convinced him he had to give filmmaking a shot. He transferred to the University of Southern California, where he worked on an English degree while selling advertising for a campus coupon calendar to finance his first short film.

With $8,000 from sales (which his parents matched once they found out their son was pursuing his dream), the twenty-one-year-old Reitman made a twenty-minute comedy about organ trafficking called *Operation. Operation* premiered at the 1998 Sundance Film Festival and set the stage for a six-year run of short films. Some were clever; 2000's *In God We Trust* follows a trucker who dies and learns entry to Heaven works on a point system. Others were derivative; *Consent*, from 2004, is just a variation on the 1989 *Kids in the Hall* sketch where two lawyers negotiate the terms of a sexual encounter between their clients.[7]

Reitman began receiving offers to direct features around the time of *Operation*, but the vacant teen comedies up for grabs were of no interest (he turned down the opportunity to direct *Dude, Where's My Car?* twice).[8] What Reitman actually wanted to do for his first feature was a movie based on Christopher Buckley's satirical 1994 novel *Thank You for Smoking*, which skewered lobbyists for the tobacco industry. Reitman's agent warned him this project would be a very tough sell. Reitman met with the rights holders anyway. "I told them the kind of movie I wanted to make," he explained. "They loved it. They hired me. A few months later, I turned in a screenplay. They loved that. They had no notes. They literally did not change a word. They said, 'Let's go out with it,' and I thought, *Wow, this is going to be so easy, my agent's an idiot!*"

Thank You for Smoking hit a wall when Reitman couldn't get any studio interest. His screenplay languished for years, leaving him heartbroken. Everything changed after millionaire and aspiring Hollywood mogul David O. Sacks read the script. Sacks loved it. He called Reitman and said, "I have a checkbook. I want to make your movie."[9]

Jason Reitman's *Thank You for Smoking* became a critical darling upon release in 2006. "Here is a satire both savage and elegant," wrote Roger Ebert, "a dagger instead of a shotgun."[10] *Rolling Stone* called it "easily the best and wickedest comedy of the new year."[11] *Thank You for Smoking* was read as anti-tobacco but Reitman, a Libertarian, insisted it was about independent thought. "We have to prepare the next generation not to hate cigarettes, but to make decisions for themselves," he told *Los Angeles* magazine. "If they are empowered to make decisions for themselves, they won't be fooled by spins and we won't have to worry about them making a decision as stupid as starting to smoke cigarettes."[12]

Reitman's next film, 2007's *Juno*, was his breakout. An unorthodox yet poignant story of teen pregnancy written by Diablo Cody that only cost $7 million to make, *Juno* had a resonance that translated to over $100 million at the box office and four Academy Award nominations (Reitman lost Best Director but Cody won for Best Original Screenplay).[13] *Juno* had its detractors, like *Chicago Sun-Times* writer Jim DeRogatis, who hated the film partly because the weirdo slang Cody wrote for the main character struck him as ridiculous. "The notion that kids—even smart and sarcastic ones—talk like Juno is a lie only thirty-something filmmakers and fifty-something movie critics could buy," DeRogatis said. "You want accurate wisecracking high-school dialog? Go back to MTV's animated 'Daria' or Sara Gilbert's Darlene on 'Roseanne.'" He also felt both sides of the abortion debate "deserve more complex, nuanced and thoughtful portraits than the simplistic and insulting caricatures drawn by Cody."[14]

While promoting *Juno* that December, MTV asked Reitman if he'd ever thought about making a *Ghostbusters*. "It would be the most boring *Ghostbusters* movie of all time," he said. "There would be no ghostbusting. . . . My [*Ghostbusters*] would just be guys talking about ghosts, really. 'You hear about that ghost? Spooky stuff!' And then the other guy would be like, 'Yeah.' It's like, if I was Michael Jordan's son, I would probably never slam dunk. It would be irony. I'd be a perimeter shooter."[15] During his interview earlier in the year with *Los Angeles* magazine that was actually a roundtable with screenwriter Michael Arndt, Reitman talked about applying his sensibilities to big-budget filmmaking. "Right now I have no interest in doing that," he said. "I'm excited about making my kind of movies. . . . I'm young enough where I have plenty of time to sell out. And when I sell out, I'm going to sell out—"

"Huge!" Arndt interrupted.

"Like you've never seen!" joked Reitman. "Being the son of a filmmaker gives you perspective. You look at a lot of directing and writing careers, and you see the transitions from when people seemed to care and have something to say to the moment where they don't anymore." And when that happened to him? "I'm going to blow it all out on *Top Gun 2* or something!"[16]

In 2009, Jason Reitman released what he called "the most personal film I've ever made," an adaptation of Walter Kim's 2001 novel *Up in the Air* that explores the nomadic lifestyle of a commitment-averse business consultant. With George Clooney in the lead role, *Up in the Air* had critics comparing Reitman to Frank Capra and Billy Wilder; it also earned six Academy Award nominations.[17] Another character study, *Young Adult*, came in 2011. "[*Young Adult*] challenges the dreary conventional wisdom that a movie protagonist must be likable," *New York Times* writer A. O. Scott said of the film's embittered former prom queen, played by Charlize Theron. "The established codes of modern movie comedy are scrambled and subverted [by *Young Adult*] in ways that are puzzling, amusing, horrifying and ultimately astonishing."[18]

Reitman had dipped his toe into blockbuster moviemaking by this point. He couldn't resist the opportunity to work as a script doctor for Michael Bay's $195 million sequel *Transformers: Dark of the Moon.* "It's very easy to look at a director and their work and think this is the sum total of that human being," Reitman explained years later. "The truth is I love horror films. I love big box office movies. To play in that *Transformers* world was like, I used to play *with* Transformers [and] now I get to play *in Transformers.*" *Dark of the Moon* was released in June 2011, six months before *Young Adult* and light years away figuratively. *Transformers* was critic-proof, of course, making over $1 billion in the wake of absolutely dismal reviews.[19]

Transformers were toys that kept Reitman entertained as a child, but *Ghostbusters* shaped his world. He cherished memories of visiting the original movie's set in 1983 when he was six (a hard, foamy chunk of the Stay Puft Marshmallow Man came home with him after they filmed the character's death).[20] The following year for Halloween, his father let him use one of the neutrona wand props with his costume.[21] Reitman was immortalized in *Ghostbusters II* as the smart-mouthed kid who accosts Ray Stantz at the start of the film: "My dad says you guys are full of crap." Like any other child of the '80s, he was a fan of *Ghostbusters*, but as an adult filmmaker he never wanted to make one. Until he had a vision.

Around the time of *Young Adult*, Reitman started thinking about a young girl in a cornfield firing up a proton pack. A piece of popcorn would appear, which the girl grabbed and ate. The vision floated through his head for a while with no embellishment until Harold Ramis died in 2014. A narrative about Egon Spengler's granddaughter came into focus. Reitman hashed it out with Gil Kenan, and the pair brought it to Ghost Corps in 2016. Reitman's father got choked up hearing the pitch; the film was green-lit but shrouded in secrecy. "I really didn't want it out there that we were writing this movie," Reitman said. "Particularly after years of me saying I didn't want to make a *Ghostbusters* movie." Code-named *Rust City*, only three Sony executives knew the project even existed.[22]

Reitman's growing interest in making a *Ghostbusters* coincided with what many saw as a major quality decrease in his own style of filmmaking. *Labor Day*, a 2013 escaped con drama from the director, was knocked for being sluggish and campy. Critics lambasted 2014's *Men, Women & Children* as a trite morality play about the dangers of common technology.[23] "Reitman's career seems to be developing a worrying trend," David Sims wrote in *The Atlantic*. "He's taking his material far too seriously and has lost sight of the humor and humanity of his earlier works."[24]

"You're always trying," Reitman told ScreenCrush. "I can imagine someone looking at *Labor Day* and going, 'Remember when he fucking gave up?'" This quote was part of a larger conversation about *Men, Women & Children* costar Adam Sandler; the interviewer felt Sandler had "stopped caring about doing work that was a little more important." "I guess so," Reitman responded. "But the question becomes what is important?"[25] In a different chat with *Interview* magazine, Reitman touched on the uncertainty that can plague the cinematic process. "There's a moment where you're reading a book and you're like, 'I should make this into a movie,'" he said. "Then there's a moment where you're on set and it's either working or not working. And then there's the edit and it's like, 'Is this movie actually coming together?'" Reitman offered a philosophical view about a film's life after editing: "That's when ownership of the movie changes. It stops belonging to me and it starts belonging to the audience."[26]

Jason Reitman's perceived bankruptcy of ideas wasn't the reason Leslie Jones was upset about the director's *Ghostbusters* project. As one of the stars of 2016's *Ghostbusters: Answer the Call*, Jones felt she and her female castmates were being disrespected by taking the franchise back to the established male characters. "So insulting. Like fuck us," she tweeted a week after Reitman's *Ghostbusters* was announced. "We didn't count. It's like something Trump would do. (Trump) voice 'Gonna redo ghostbusteeeeers, better with men, will be huge. Those women ain't ghostbusteeeeers.' Ugh so annoying. Such a dick move. And I don't give a fuck I'm saying something!"[27] *Answer the Call* director Paul Feig chimed in later: "Leslie spoke her truth and I support her. I am very open to Jason's new version of GB but am also sad that our 2016 team may not get to bust again. We all are. We're forever proud of our movie."[28]

Reitman was forced to respond after catching heat for comments he made about his *Ghostbusters* while guesting on a February 2019 episode of comedian Bill Burr's podcast. "This is going to be a love letter to *Ghostbusters*," he told Burr. "I love this franchise. I grew up watching it. . . . We are in every way trying to go back to the original technique and hand the movie back to the fans." The implication being that Feig's movie snatched *Ghostbusters* away from the dedicated.

"That came out wrong!" Reitman tweeted the next day. "I have nothing but admiration for Paul and Leslie and Kate and Melissa and Kristen and the bravery with which they made Ghostbusters 2016. They expanded the universe and made an amazing movie!"[29]

The story Jason Reitman and Gil Kenan conceived for their *Ghostbusters* film centered on the adolescent Phoebe, a shy science-obsessed kid who is always tinkering. Phoebe and her older brother Trevor are uprooted from Chicago to rural Summerville, Oklahoma, when their estranged grandfather dies and leaves a decaying farm to their cash-strapped single mother, Callie. A friendly unseen spirit inhabits the residence, leading Phoebe to discover a ghost trap. She has no idea what it is because a disillusioned Callie has kept her father's career as a Ghostbuster hidden from her children. Phoebe and her new pal Podcast, an enthusiastic boy with a penchant for ghosts, are examining the trap at school when their teacher Gary Grooberson recognizes it.

Teaching is only Grooberson's day job. He's also a seismologist who's investigating a series of unnatural earthquakes occurring in the area. More immediate problems are at hand after Phoebe lets Grooberson fiddle with the ghost trap—an angry, destructive entity is unleashed that makes a beeline for the town's abandoned mine. A more benign metal-chewing ghost is discovered a short time later when Phoebe and Podcast experiment with an old proton pack. The kids chase this blue spirit around Summerville's downtown area with help from Trevor, who has discovered the old Ectomobile and taken it for a joyride. Euphoria surrounding the bust of this ghost is short-lived as the children are arrested and their paranormal tools seized. Desperate, Phoebe telephones Ray Stantz. Stantz explains that he too was estranged from her grandfather, Egon Spengler. When ghost activity dwindled due to the Ghostbusters' continued success, Spengler absconded to Oklahoma with his equipment to monitor an apocalyptic event he was foreseeing.

It's revealed that the abandoned mine contains a monument to Gozer, the supernatural despot the Ghostbusters fought in 1984, and that Egon moved to Summerville to prevent Gozer from returning. Unfortunately, the trap Grooberson opened earlier released one of Gozer's sentinels. He and Callie both become possessed, which allows Gozer to materialize. The kids, now being aided by the sheriff's daughter (and Trevor's crush) Lucky, steal back the equipment and confront Gozer. They lure the demigod to the farm, where Egon set up an elaborate multi-trap containment system years ago. The climactic battle is in doubt until all three surviving original Ghostbusters and the hazy visage of Egon show up to lend a hand.[30]

The first draft of this script was completed while Reitman was putting the finishing touches on his 2018 Gary Hart drama *The Front Runner*. "We turned it in in December," Reitman said. "And I have to admit my presumption was it was going to be [like] any other studio film I heard about where there's years of rewrites and they grind it into the ground and it never happens. I was kind of fully prepared for this year to be a little taking time off and doing rewrites. . . . Instead the studio read the first draft and said, 'Yeah, go make it.'"[31]

And so they did. Twelve-year-old McKenna Grace was cast as Phoebe. Despite her youth, Grace had an impressive résumé that included roles in *The Angry Birds Movie*; *I, Tonya*; and *Captain Marvel*.[32] Grace was also a self-described *Ghostbusters* "mega-fan," a passion she shared with one of her friends. "Whenever we were little, we would sit and we'd go watch *Ghostbusters*," she recalled. "And we had *Ghostbusters* t-shirts that we'd wear. Our moms would go and buy extra large men's shirts that had *Ghostbusters* on them and they'd turn them into dresses for us. And we used to have *Ghostbusters* stuffed animals. It's really, really weird." According to Reitman, Grace wept with joy when she got to wear a real proton pack.[33]

Finn Wolfhard, sixteen-year-old star from the Netflix series *Stranger Things*, was cast as Trevor. Set in the 1980s, there'd been an episode of *Stranger Things* where Wolfhard and his castmates dressed up as Ghostbusters for Halloween. "For that exact reason, I thought, 'Jason Reitman is probably not even going to look at my tape because I've already done it,'" Wolfhard said. "I guess he just identified a lot with my tape, and it ended up working out for the best."[34]

Due to the secretive nature of the project, many of the other actors had no idea what they were actually auditioning for when Reitman first came calling. Logan Kim, the tween actor hired to play Phoebe's new pal Podcast, remembered the script he was given containing no names. "'Boy' and 'girl' were on the script," he said, "so I was like, 'Okay, that's a little weird.' I read through it, and I was like, 'This is super good. It's very mysterious.' And I liked it." The truth wasn't bestowed until the teaser trailer was released. "My mom and dad were all screaming, 'Aahh, this is insane!' My dad especially really loved it."[35] A newcomer to movie acting, Kim was praised by Reitman for his talent and conviction. "Logan feels like he would have been cast on *Saturday Night Live* in 1975," the director remarked.[36]

Gone Girl and *Avengers: Infinity War* actress Carrie Coon had reservations about accepting the role of Callie. Would this typecast her as a mom? "That was certainly one of the things I was afraid of when I first was approached about it," she said. "I think of Dee Wallace in *E.T.* who is a wonderful actress who then sort of became—well, she actually went on, had a really interesting life, but, you know, she became sort of the franchise mom. And I thought about that, but Jason is smarter than that. Jason is the next generation, and he wrote a lot of fun for all of us, and it was one of the reasons I said yes to it. You know, [Callie] actually has a personality, a sense of humor, and she does get in on the action, and that was really fun for me!"[37]

Paul Rudd agreed to play Gary Grooberson. Rudd often subverted his leading man looks and charm by acting in silly comedies like *Wet Hot American Summer* and *Anchorman: The Legend of Ron Burgundy*. (Years earlier, his name was one of many to be proposed for *Ghostbusters III*.) Another massive *Ghostbusters* fan, Rudd had trouble adjusting to actually being cast in this sequel. "I never quite got used to it," he said after filming wrapped. "It was always exciting. Every day, there'd be something else. . . . There are certain props and things in the film where I immediately step out of the actor role and fall into the fan role of just thinking it's pretty cool seeing it in real life. And then there's the other side of that, where I'm looking at it, and then I turn my head and I'm looking over and seeing Jason Reitman behind the monitor sitting next to Ivan Reitman. Then Dan Aykroyd's walking around, and there's this thing that makes it, in a way, too overwhelming to think about. Because there's a job at hand, and we have to do it."[38]

"I remember being really scared of [the *Ghostbusters* movies]," said twenty-one-year-old Celeste O'Connor, who was cast as Lucky, "but when I got this part, I watched the films again and they were hilarious. I was like, 'This isn't scary. This is a funny movie, right?'"[39]

Given Jason Reitman's oeuvre and his self-deprecating remarks regarding what he'd do if given the opportunity to make a *Ghostbusters*, it is no surprise to learn that when this moment came to pass the director coauthored a character-driven adventure. "Jason didn't want to make a big visual effects movie per se," visual effects supervisor Alessandro Ongaro told Digital Trends. "It's about the story and the family. The movie ends with a big hug, not a big explosion."[40]

Of course, the special effects in 1984's *Ghostbusters* remain a massive part of its appeal. Reitman had to replicate them if he was authoring a sincere love letter to his father's most beloved work. And that was certainly his intent. "Jason told every department, 'This is not about your voice,'" recalled composer Rob Simonsen, a frequent Reitman collaborator who wound up scoring this *Ghostbusters*. "It was about the voice of everyone contributing to the original."[41]

"It's funny," Ongaro said, "because to the untrained eyes it might look like [we took] a simplistic approach to the visual effects—but it was actually more challenging because it's tricky to give something that nostalgic look without looking cheap or cheesy, too." Optical printing techniques used thirty-five years earlier were too dated to incorporate into a twenty-first-century production; the artists on the new movie had to stay mindful of their digital hazes and textures.[42]

Ongaro spoke more about this in another interview, using the metal-chomping ghost named Muncher as a specific example. "Well, it could have gone two ways. You can go for the glowy, super transparent and very fancy look, or the other way—which is what we did—where we literally studied how Slimer was done optically in the '84 film, to try to give Muncher somehow the same feeling. If you notice, there's not much glow around Muncher. We kept it very minimal and we kept some of the skin details, but not too much."[43] Sheena Duggal, another visual effects supervisor, convinced Reitman to base Muncher's appearance on a tardigrade, though personality-wise the ghost was inspired by Chris Farley. Reitman was still trying to figure out who could provide the anguished shrieks and groans Muncher elicits when he bumped into *Frozen* actor Josh Gad on the Sony lot. Gad expressed interest in the part and was immediately ushered into a recording booth.[44]

Some techniques from the mid-'80s were happily repeated for Jason Reitman's *Ghostbusters*. Forgoing faster processes with computers, creature designer Arjen Tuiten and his coworkers sculpted new terror dog puppets by hand over the course of two or three weeks. An effect where Gozer cultist Ivo Shandor is sliced in half was created with a life-size dummy and a mechanism that tore it apart on command.[45] The tiny havoc-wreaking marshmallow men known as the Mini-Pufts that Grooberson encounters at a Walmart just before his possession were all animated traditionally; that way, Mini-Pufts could have distinct personality traits as if they were just another group of actors on set.[46] Though time-consuming, these old-school techniques appear to have saved the production money. The final budget for this *Ghostbusters* was $75 million, nearly $100 million less than the average budget of a Marvel movie.[47]

Beyond practical effects, this farmhouse *Ghostbusters* incorporated real farming. Reitman's team visited their Alberta, Canada, filming locations half a year before the summer 2019 shoot to scope out a plot of land where they could grow the barley field that Trevor was scripted to tear through in the Ectomobile.[48] The rusted-out jalopy the kids start driving in the movie is supposed to be Ecto-1 from the 1984 *Ghostbusters*, but the filmmakers couldn't use that specific vehicle. Ecto-1 had been restored to pristine condition in 2009 to promote *Ghostbusters: The Video Game*. Instead, Reitman's team stripped down the gaudier Ecto-1a from *Ghostbusters II*, already in disrepair on the Sony lot, to use with two other Cadillacs purchased for filming.[49]

Reitman knew that *Ghostbusters* fans who spent all their spare time crafting meticulous replicas of the proton packs, particle throwers, and ecto goggles would pore over his movie's gadgets to spot inconsistencies, so he invited local fan club the Alberta Ghostbusters to help prop master Ben Eadie maintain accuracy.[50] One correction was made to the proton packs that satisfied a long-standing complaint—Jason Reitman's *Ghostbusters* made visible the famous "on/off" switch that is never actually seen on the packs in the original movie despite factoring into the classic sequence in the hotel elevator.[51] When it came time to add sound effects, Reitman went for authenticity by excavating tapes containing proton pack noises from three decades ago.[52]

Much of this was child's play compared to fashioning Egon Spengler's ghost out of thin air for the movie's surprise ending and emotional climax. Ongaro called this the biggest challenge the effects team faced. "You can do it wrong so easily," he said. "It was such an important moment for the film." Duggal added, "We had to approach Egon with a great deal of sensitivity, because not only is Harold Ramis like a family member [to Jason], but Jason knew that if we weren't able to capture the essence and emotion in the CG character, his scenes would never work."[53] A scenario like this played out with *Rogue One*, the 2016 *Star Wars* movie that was hammered for dubious reconstructions of a long-dead Peter Cushing and a 1977 version of Carrie Fisher.[54]

"We didn't have any body scans [of Harold Ramis] or anything like that," explained Ongaro, "so we had to start completely from scratch. MPC was the VFX vendor on it, and we just took some frames from the '84 film and started building a digital version of Egon Spengler. I didn't show anything to Jason, Ivan, or anybody else until we had a realistic copy of the '84 Egon. We took a scene from the [original] movie with Dan Aykroyd and replaced that Egon with our version. We put it in black and white and I called Jason and Ivan into the office, and played the shot. They looked at it and then looked at me like, 'Why are you showing us the '84 film?' That's when I said, 'This is a digital Egon.' They were blown away."

Actor Bob Gunton was hired as the body stand-in to mimic Ramis's gait and body language on set (though Ivan Reitman stood in as Egon for a couple of brief shots). From there, the effects artists used materials supplied to them by the Ramis family as well as outtakes from the original *Ghostbusters* films to digitally create a face and facial expressions. "Usually, when you build a digital character, you create a library of expressions," Ongaro said. "There are 40-something faces and shapes you create that get you the whole range of emotions. You usually have an actor perform them, but in this case, a lot of it was done by the animators themselves. It was a lot of manual work, and it was really, really well done."[55]

Initially, Ramis's daughter Violet Ramis Stiel thought a CGI version of her father sounded "weird," but she was allowed to sit in on the process and felt the end result was very satisfying. "They could have done him as this jolly Santa-type, but that wouldn't have been true to his character," she said. "He was in great shape, nice and trim. My dad would have loved that."[56]

Paternal themes were reinforced as Jason Reitman worked side by side with his father, Ivan, every day on his *Ghostbusters*. "Sometimes it got complicated, as you can imagine with your father coming to work with you every day and weighing in on all your decisions," the younger Reitman admitted to Insider. "It tries on your patience, but at the same time we got to have a father-son experience unlike anything."[57] When asked by Screen Rant to name their biggest dispute, Jason said, "I know people are gonna totally take my father's side on this: more slime, less slime."

"I wanted more slime," said Ivan. "I think slime was an important iconographic idea to the movie, and I thought Jason had a more delicate approach to it than I would have."[58]

"The script is good. It's got lots of emotion in it. It's got lots of family in it, with through lines that are really interesting. It's gonna work."

That was Bill Murray's summation of Jason Reitman's *Ghostbusters*. He read the script because he had fond memories of working with its cowriter Gil Kenan on 2008's *City of Ember*.[59] Lo and behold, Murray liked it, so he signed up to briefly appear in the film alongside Dan Aykroyd, Ernie Hudson, Annie Potts, and Sigourney Weaver.

Aykroyd was also impressed with the story. "Jason Reitman wrote a beautiful heartfelt script that takes the real DNA from the first two movies and transfers that directly to the next generation," he said. "It's a great story, a great setting. It's gonna be scary. Thought-provoking."[60] There were challenges, though, with going once more unto the breach. "Jason says, 'Okay, you guys, hop up now,'" Aykroyd recalled of one take. "Yeah, there will be no 'hopping up' here. There will be a slow climb to one knee, a hefting of the pack, both hands grasping the automobile as a leverage point, and pulling myself up to my feet. That's the 'hop' that you're going to get."[61]

Murray still hated wearing his equipment. To illustrate just how taxing it was, he made a *Vanity Fair* writer visiting the set wear a proton pack for an hour. The writer, Anthony Breznican, remarked that the first thirty seconds weren't too bad. Murray snorted and told him, "It's that *last* 30. And the dismount." Breznican admitted that the human spine probably wasn't built for long-term proton pack use. "Murray is right about the pack getting heavier as time goes on, partly because it extends back so far and gravity exploits the leverage. The width and depth also make it easy to accidentally knock into a script supervisor or sweep a tabletop clear."[62]

As for Ernie Hudson, he described playing Ghostbuster again with Murray and Aykroyd as an "almost spiritual" experience. "I didn't cry, but some of those emotions welled up in me," he said. "To see Jason, who was running around the set at six years old and now he is at the helm of it; I was so proud of him. I am so appreciative that he established himself as a wonderful director-producer before stepping into *Ghostbusters*. I had heard, although he never told me this, that Bill did not want to do another one. So I wrapped it all up as this will never happen. . . . *Ghostbusters* altered my life in a weird way. When you make a movie and it is successful, that has an impact, but *Ghostbusters*—it was a shift. And the way people responded to it and continue to respond to it—it crosses generations. I see little kids who just love the movie."[63]

There were plenty of laughs when the three surviving original Ghostbusters reunited. "Danny and Ernie and I together, not in separate scenes, but together—there's a force," Murray said. "It's like Mick Jagger and Keith Richards have done their solo albums, but when they're all on the stage, it's a whole different thing." In their scene, they confront Gozer, whose physical portrayal was now split between dancer Emma Portner and *Tron: Legacy* actress Olivia Wilde (Gozer's voice in *Afterlife* was dubbed by *House of Sand and Fog's* Shohreh Aghashloo). Wilde was in the costume that day and she broke character with peals of laughter during one take because Murray's improvised insults were overwhelming. "Too far, TOO FAR!" she cried.

Murray couldn't help ribbing his old friends either. When he noticed Hudson had a safety pad in front of him under the dirt, Murray feigned disgust. "Have you got a *pad* here?! You're *soft*."

"Nah," Hudson replied. "That was for the stunt man!"[64] [65]

Filming for Jason Reitman's *Ghostbusters* wrapped in mid-October 2019. On December 6, the movie's title was officially revealed—*Ghostbusters: Afterlife*. A theatrical poster was unveiled at the same time that depicted an ominous seafoam sky hanging over an Oklahoma barley field as the Ecto-1 raced across the frame, kicking up dust as its lights flashed. Four days later, Sony Pictures uploaded the first trailer to YouTube, which expanded on idyllic countryside vistas juxtaposed with strange supernatural activity. "COMING SOON" a title card flashed at the trailer's end. Those words were quickly disproven thanks to unprecedented circumstances.[66]

The exact genesis of the deadly COVID-19 respiratory syndrome remains contested, but the very first cases were beginning to be reported around this time in the Chinese metropolis of Wuhan. Lax government response allowed the disease to spread across the country rapidly; by January 29, one hundred people were dead and over four thousand were infected.[67] The World Health Organization declared COVID-19 a pandemic on March 11 after the disease was recorded on nearly every continent.[68] People were gripped with fear as global infections rose to ninety thousand. In the United States, grocery stores were quickly decimated by panic buyers who didn't plan to leave their houses again for the foreseeable future.[69]

There were roughly 4,500 positive COVID-19 cases in the United States by March 16.[70] That week, Regal Cinemas and AMC Theatres both announced the closure of all their nationwide locations to stave off further infection (Regal indefinitely, AMC for six to twelve weeks). "The health and wellbeing of AMC guests and employees, and of all Americans, takes precedence above all else," said the company's chief executive Adam Aron.[71] With so much uncertainty, Hollywood began rescheduling their summer tentpole movies. *Ghostbusters: Afterlife* was among them. Sony pushed it back from July 10, 2020, to March 5 of the following year.[72]

COVID-19 also exacerbated tensions between industry figures who wanted to keep traditional (and traditionally lucrative) theatrical release cycles in place and those who supported the emerging convenience of at-home video on demand, or streaming. In a gesture of goodwill that April, Universal Pictures released their animated film *Trolls: World Tour* on streaming the same day it started playing in whatever theaters were still open.[73] It was a huge hit on streaming, prompting NBC/Universal CEO Jeff Shell to talk about using this business model in the future. AMC's Aron was incensed by Shell's comments. Universal films were immediately banned from AMC Theatres (even though none were open) and Aron threatened the same fate for any other studio that dared to "abandon current windowing practices absent good faith negotiations."[74] Universal blinked in July, cutting AMC into their streaming revenues and agreeing to a seventeen-day window between cinema and home debuts.[75]

AMC reopened their theaters that month, following the lead of numerous businesses across the United States after municipal restrictions were lifted. COVID-19 wasn't flagging, but politicians were getting antsy about the economy and Republicans specifically were turning the basic public safety protocol of wearing a face mask into an issue of personal liberty. By October, 8.1 million COVID-19 infections were reported in the United States and over 219,000 deaths.[76] Sony bumped the release of *Ghostbusters: Afterlife* again that month to June 11, 2021.[77] It was one of many films becoming a chess piece in a ludicrous game with no obvious ending.[78] Experts couldn't predict what would happen with COVID-19 because it wasn't following any established pandemic pattern and there wasn't enough data about the disease. That said, most scenarios suggested COVID-19 would be in our lives through 2025.[79]

At the beginning of 2021, *Ghostbusters: Afterlife* was moved for a third time, to November 11 of that year.[80] Simpatico relationships with theater owners aside, one may guess as to why Sony Pictures did not simply sell *Afterlife* to the highest-bidding streaming service. Some of the actors may have had salary points on the theatrical gross. That was the heart of Scarlett Johansson's complaint when she sued Disney in July over her movie *Black Widow*'s streaming release simultaneous to theatrical; home viewing ate into box office receipts, shrinking her bonus (Johansson and the studio settled a few months later).[81] There may have been similar contracts for marketing tie-ins with *Afterlife*. Eddie Murphy's *Coming to America* sequel could only go to Amazon after deals with McDonald's and Crown Royal had been fine-tuned.[82]

Besides, people were still going to theaters despite the public danger. Hollywood simply decided to try to adjust to a new normal of much lower box office grosses. *Tenet*, a spy movie from visionary Christopher Nolan that cost $200 million to make and was delayed several times because of COVID-19, was hailed as a champion when its August theatrical debut earned $53 million (a laughable figure in pre-pandemic times). Warner Bros. chair Toby Emmerich trumpeted, "We are off to a fantastic start internationally and we couldn't be more pleased. Christopher Nolan has once again delivered an event worthy motion picture that demands to be seen on the big screen, and we are thrilled that audiences across the globe are getting the opportunity to see *Tenet*." Nolan has been described as "a champion of the theatrical experience" who shuddered at the idea that his movie might debut on the small screen.[83]

In that regard, Jason Reitman was a kindred soul. Addressing a crowd of theater owners at the annual CinemaCon gathering on August 23, Reitman said, "I am honored to be here tonight on behalf of Sony because they are the only studio that is completely dedicated to theatrical distribution." The director then treated attendees to a surprise screening of *Ghostbusters: Afterlife*. "Please, no spoilers," he asked. "We've kept the ending secret so that people who come to your movie theaters [can discover it]."[84] Sony remained unsure when the film would see release; the most recent trailer advertised no firm date, just "this Thanksgiving."[85]

The following month, Sony pushed *Ghostbusters: Afterlife* back to November 19, 2021.[86]

The pandemic delays allowed Jason Reitman to add a handful of accentuations to *Ghostbusters: Afterlife*. One was an extra ghost, the ocular nightmare Bug-Eye, a fan favorite from *The Real Ghostbusters* cartoon.[87] Reitman also decided to expand the film's soundtrack to include a pop song by *Afterlife* star McKenna Grace appropriately titled "Haunted House." Grace wasn't angling for her song to be in the movie. "I just asked [Jason] if he would direct my music video," she said, "and he was like, 'Can I put it in the end credits?'"[88] "It's so funny because there's two secret hidden scenes in the credits and to get to the other one, everybody has to sit through my song." Grace told Nylon. "So, let's go everybody! All these people who wouldn't usually listen to my song have to go and sit and listen to it. I'm like, *Yes, this is great for me.*"[89]

Ghostbusters: Afterlife screened again as a surprise on October 8 at New York Comic-Con.[90] Sitting with his father Ivan, cowriter Gil Kenan, and most of the cast on a panel beforehand, Jason Reitman reiterated his dedication to the theatrical experience. Yes, he appreciated streaming and he himself had relied on it during the pandemic, but *Ghostbusters: Afterlife* was meant "to be enjoyed with a huge audience with popcorn on a big screen, with incredible sound, where you're experiencing it the way you experienced the movie in '84." Though the filmmakers and stars all walked onto the Comic-Con dais wearing *Ghostbusters: Afterlife* face masks, they removed their protections while addressing the crowd, most of whom remained masked.[91]

The first professional reviews started popping up the next day. "It's taken 36 years and six presidencies, but with *Ghostbusters: Afterlife* fans finally have an unembarrassing sequel to love," Johnny Oleksinski declared in the *New York Post*. "[Reitman] finds the perfect tone here, especially in how he uses composer Elmer Bernstein's original music while Phoebe and Trevor tinker with Egon's gadgets. He's also skilled at getting genuine performance out of young actors, as he proved in *Juno*, and balancing humor with stakes—essential for comedy-horror like *Ghostbusters*. The jokes are very funny and Wolfhard and Grace make life-threatening peril look like a ball. The ending will be divisive, but I found it tastefully done. And throughout the movie, fans will be thrilled to be reunited with many familiar, hilarious faces."[92]

Entertainment Weekly's Christian Holub was less impressed. "There are some jokes here—Paul Rudd brings a little lightness to the proceedings as the kids' science teacher, Mr. Grooberson—but it's hard to escape the overall sensation of, well, a corpse being exhumed. The tone is overall rather dour; Callie is constantly lashing out at her absent father in what comes off like [Jason Reitman] trying to imagine what a broken family would feel like, and not quite getting the tone right. Intentional or not, *Ghostbusters: Afterlife* is a stark reminder of how much of modern American culture consists of excavating the ruins of past glories."[93]

"In some ways, [*Ghostbusters: Afterlife* is] a harmless night out for the faithful," surmised Jesse Hassenger for the AV Club, "the equivalent of a quote-along/egg hunt at a local rep house, with some likable new performances thrown in. Yet seeing [Jason] Reitman inherit this particular mantle is still discomfiting. His hit-and-miss filmography of comedies and dramas includes a couple of incisive ones about the pleasures and perils of nostalgia. Now he's made a franchise-starter about how great his wealthy father's movie is. That movie is also framed as a tribute to someone who often seemed like he could take or leave the prospect of another *Ghostbusters* sequel, reducing Harold Ramis to an absence from a franchise without paying any attention to his comic sensibility. *Afterlife* wants desperately to summon the spirit of watching the first movie back in 1984. It winds up ghoulish in the wrong way."[94]

An especially negative review came from Charles Bramesco in *The Guardian*. "It's pandering all the way down, the shocking part being the variety of Reitman's ploys. It's not all groaners like a cop offering a jailed-for-the-night Trevor the phone and asking, 'Who you gonna call?' There's the set piece with cutesy, nattering mini-Stay-Pufts scratching the itch for cloying mischief-makers planted by the Minions. Consider the casual cowardice of a script that uses its own mythology to subtly erase 2016's all-gals reboot from the canon, giving the rage-choked trolls carpet-bombing IMDb with zero-star ratings the vindication they've always craved. Even the championing of scientific expertise comes off as overreaching and aggrieved, from Grooberson's declaration that science is 'punk' to the smug superiority of the pint-sized Phoebe. The message is clear, as are its intended recipients: there's nothing more powerful, important or cool than being a nerd." Bramesco also felt *Afterlife* crossed a line with its "digitally reanimated corpse" of Harold Ramis that's used for the "movie's most nauseating cornball moment."

"There's a disturbing sense of ownership over the past in Reitman's continuity-building," Bramesco concluded, "as if he's the heir apparent entrusted with sacred texts rather than a guy running roughshod over the memory of a movie still a staple of middle-school sleepovers for its laugh quotient. Perhaps it's appropriate and telling that the 2021 incarnation of an 80s artifact would be imbued with all the issues most endemic to the current studio release. Here, we can find a damning summary of modern Hollywood's default mode—a nostalgia object, drained of personality and fitted into a dully palatable mold, custom-made for a fandom that worships everything and respects nothing."[95]

The *New York Times* published a critique from Manohla Dargis on November 19, the day of *Afterlife*'s release, that was positive yet dismissive, both of the film and franchise fever in general. "There's a story, sure, though you don't care and neither do I. What matters are the jokes, energy, boos and characters, who are appealing mostly because the performers playing them are too. . . . Franchise sequels bank on dependability and giving the audience exactly what it expects. *Ghostbusters: Afterlife* certainly makes good on that contractual promise: There are ghosts, and they are busted. By design, there isn't a single genuine surprise in the movie."[96]

Ghostbusters: Afterlife debuted with a $44 million weekend, a strong pandemic-era opening that put the film at number one. What this meant for *Ghostbusters* at large felt difficult to parse. $44 million was a victory, but it still wasn't superhero numbers. In October, Sony's Spider-Man spin-off *Venom: Let There Be Carnage* clinched a $90 million opening.[97] The next proper Spider-Man movie, *Spider-Man: No Way Home*, arrived on December 17 and pulled a stunning $260 million out of the gate.[98] It was as if COVID-19 didn't exist anymore. It did, of course. The virus had killed 800,000-plus in the United States by mid-December and over a thousand people died every day the week *No Way Home* was released. Vaccines rolled out, but there were breakthrough infections thanks to aggressive variants like Delta and Omicron (and many "patriots" refused the vaccine, again citing personal liberty). Simultaneously, there was "long COVID," cases where debilitating symptoms lingered in patients for months after the basic ailments vanished.[99]

In week two of release, *Ghostbusters: Afterlife* doubled its take. This must have pleased Sony Pictures, for the company soon announced Jason Reitman and Gil Kenan would be launching a new production company under their corporate umbrella.[100] It was auspicious news, but Reitman's metric for success revolved more around his father's approval. "My father and I talk almost every day," he said. "We talk almost always about movies. Our relationship with the world goes through movies. And the most intimidating thing I've ever done is pick up my father's franchise and attempt to make a film in it. And he sat next to me the whole way through. God knows I wanted to make him proud. And last night at Comic Con, I watched crowds cheer for him. And he cried. And it made me feel like a good son."[101]

In 2011, director J. J. Abrams released *Super 8*, an otherworldly mystery-adventure centered on a group of small-town kids that offers a retro Spielbergian flourish—partly because Steven Spielberg was one of its producers. "*Super 8* is a wonderful film," Roger Ebert raved, "nostalgia not for a time but for a style of filmmaking, when shell-shocked young audiences were told a story and not pounded over the head with aggressive action. Abrams treats early adolescence with tenderness and affection. He uses his camera to accumulate emotion."[102] A decade later, *Super 8* is largely forgotten, a pebble between the 2009 *Star Trek* reboot Abrams helmed and his 2015 *Star Wars* sequel, *The Force Awakens*.[103]

Cynics harrumphed that Jason Reitman applied too much emotional weight to *Ghostbusters: Afterlife* or that he was marring an otherwise entertaining family dramedy by dressing it up as his father's biggest hit, but the truth is a compelling story has to be attached to an established marketable property in the twenty-first century if the creators want people to actually see it. Movies like *Juno* and *Young Adult* are going extinct and have been for years. Reitman knows this; Jason Guerrasio, a writer who interviewed the director about *Afterlife* for Insider, said the director sidestepped the question when asked, "Can you still make your kind of movies?"[104] This is not to say Reitman wasn't genuinely inspired to make a *Ghostbusters* movie. This is to say we all know a mid-budget film about a family that inherits a haunted farmhouse from a nameless deadbeat would not be able to compete against Spider-Man, the Joker, or Darth Vader.

The strength of *Ghostbusters: Afterlife* is indeed its character work. It's a joy to watch friendship blossom between Phoebe and Podcast, two outsiders who need each other. It's also a relief to watch this unfold without extraneous romantic underpinnings. Gary Grooberson is the perfect upbeat antidote to Callie's poisoned heart. As Trevor's crush, Lucky prompts some bumbling on his part but they settle into real human interactions instead of becoming "movie teenagers." All four kids are so naturally funny and fun to keep up with that *Afterlife* doesn't need the original Ghostbusters. They show up anyway, and it plays like a Super Bowl commercial when Aykroyd, Murray, and Hudson mysteriously appear from out of nowhere, fully decked out in their famous costumes. Later, there are mid- and post-credits sequences with the old characters that feel out of place, as if they were cut from earlier in the movie (or a different movie entirely).

At first blush, Egon Spengler's estrangement from the other Ghostbusters in *Afterlife* feels implausible, but consider Bill Murray and Harold Ramis in real life. They had a two-decade falling-out over a movie about a time-traveling weatherman (and who would have guessed Murray was the one pushing for it to be brainier?). Truth is stranger than fiction, and fiction is boring if we ignore certain truths. And there is certainly something potent in the movie's other substantial assertion about Egon, that he had a daughter he was keeping out of bounds during the events of the first two *Ghostbusters* movies. In retrospect, Callie's embitterment was justified. Would you feel positively about your father if he was a Ghostbuster who never brought you to the firehouse to spend time with the other Ghostbusters?

Changing the tenor of *Ghostbusters* to family drama may have been the only way Jason Reitman could give *Afterlife* a fighting chance against the "been there, done that" dismissals that both *Ghostbusters II* and Paul Feig's *Ghostbusters* suffered. Reitman saw no other choice, apparently, as he was trying to exorcise his own demons. Actually, that's not one of the metaphors he used. "I always felt [*Ghostbusters*] was the dragon that was waiting for me, and that the longer I didn't make it, the more I was simply ignoring what was at the gate," Reitman said. "I always felt the proton pack would be too heavy, but it turns out once you put it on it feels kind of light."[105]

That leaves the moral question of digitally reconstructing a version of Harold Ramis to appear as Egon Spengler's ghost. No can say with 100 percent certainty how Ramis would have felt about this endeavor. That might be the perfect argument against raising the dead in this manner. Surely there was a more inventive way to bring Egon back outside of what stands here in the literal. At least *Afterlife's* end result is impressive, more plausible and visually rich than the cosplayer rendition of Gozer or the film's division of the Marshmallow Man into cut-rate Gremlins.

A huge reason Egon's ghost works is because a lot of its detail is obscured in an otherworldly haze. Jason Reitman also made a wise decision not to have the apparition speak. That's usually where this technology's inability to convey the human intricacy is revealed. Writing about the computer-generated rendering of a thirty-two-year-old Mark Hamill used in 2020 *Star Wars* TV show *The Mandalorian*, *GQ's* Jack King said, "It's passable until his face is revealed, he starts talking . . . and it feels terribly off." Viewer complaints prompted a redesign when the CGI Hamill was brought back for 2022's *The Book of Boba Fett*, but the character remained janky at best.

King had a salient point about this type of recreation in general. "The longer we're stuck in the past, seeking out shallow facsimiles of the joys from our youth, the less impetus filmmakers have to create novel works from which we can build new culture memories. And that is painfully sad."[106]

"*Ghostbusters* is, of course, the greatest film ever made. What is the secret of its success?"

This question was posed to Ivan Reitman in 2014 by *Guardian* interviewer Hadley Freeman. Reitman, who was promoting his latest directorial effort, *Draft Day*, gave a thoughtful response.

"Just on a most general level, these are all really smart guys and even when they do silly things they're still the smartest guys in the room. They're the kind of guys most of us would want to be friends with—there's that quality. You know, I'm a refugee from communist Czechoslovakia, my parents escaped the Nazis. The desire to entertain and to make people feel better as a result of spending a few hours with me has always been an important goal, and my movies with Bill [Murray]—they make you feel happy! There's a kind of joy in watching *Singin' in the Rain* that is rarer and rarer in your experience as an audience. But that was always my benchmark."[107]

Ivan Reitman died in his sleep on February 12, 2022, having achieved his benchmark through an array of films over the course of four decades. Jason Reitman and his sisters Catherine and Caroline referenced this in a joint statement on Ivan's passing: "Our family is grieving the unexpected loss of a husband, father, and grandfather who taught us to always seek the magic in life. We take comfort that his work as a filmmaker brought laughter and happiness to countless others around the world. While we mourn privately, we hope those who knew him through his films will remember him always." [108]

Jason Reitman has said there are ideas in play for a sequel to *Ghostbusters: Afterlife*, but nothing has been set in stone.[109] To wit: an announcement from Sony Pictures just as this book was going to press in April 2022 that a fifth *Ghostbusters* movie was on their production slate did not specify which continuity it would follow.[110, 111] Whatever the future holds for Jason Reitman and for *Ghostbusters*, one might assume he will follow some of his father's advice.

"You will be surprised by your greatest success and your greatest failure," Ivan Reitman once told his son. "You can't decide them in advance."

"Your only regret will be not making more movies, so just keep telling stories."[112]

Acknowledgments

Television shows in my youth would often end with the tag, "If you'd like to learn more, visit your local library." This saying grew into sort of a kitsch joke, but now more than ever libraries are vital to our larger understanding of the world and each other. Their books, databases, and special collections house chasms of information that make Google look like a lemonade stand. To help everyone during COVID-19, many libraries have opened online portals so you can access their treasures from home.

I'm taking the long way to give special thanks and praise to the Los Angeles Public Library, the New York Public Library, the Beinecke Rare Book & Manuscript Library, the Margaret Herrick Library, and the UCLA Library. *A Convenient Parallel Dimension* wouldn't exist without them.

I must also give recognition to the following people who went out of their way to help shape this book: Rollie Hatch, Derek Osborn, Anthony Bueno, Rick Rinehart, Alex Newborn, and of course my mother, Teddi Greene.

This book is dedicated to my wife Amy and our kids Lola and Jason, but I must thank them again here for all their love and support. I will also thank our guinea pigs, Nutmeg and Popcorn.

If you enjoyed this book and want to do something nice for me, please consider donating to the Friedreich's Ataxia Research Alliance (curefa.org), the National Center for Transgender Equality (transequality .org), or the American Friends Service Committee (afsc.org).

Notes

CHAPTER 1: RUBBER SOULS

1. Joy Horowitz, "From Slapstick to Yuppie Fantasy," *New York Times*, June 15, 1986, A30; Albion Ross, "Czech Reds Seizing Power, Occupy Some Ministries; Socialist Party Taken Over," *New York Times*, February 25, 1948, 1, 7; "The Czechoslovakia Coup," Cold War Museum website, accessed September 14, 2019, http://www.coldwar.org/articles/40s/czech_coup.asp.
2. Kim Masters, "Who's That Guy with the Ghostbusters?," *Premiere*, July 1989, 78; Doug Foley, "Mac Grad's Reit Stuff; Ivan Reitman's Rise to Movie Mogul Profiled on CBC Life & Times," *The Spectator*, February 26, 2002, D11; "Starting Over: The Legacy of Leslie and Clara Reitman," directed by Nobu Adilman, Shibui, 2010, accessed September 9, 2019, https://vimeo.com/17419515.
3. Stephen Broomer, *Hamilton Babylon: A History of the McMaster Film Board* (University of Toronto Press, 2016), 88–94.
4. John Hofesse, "The Magic and Decidedly 'Ungroovy' Garden of Film-maker Ivan Reitman," *Macleans*, November 1, 1970, 93–95.
5. Foley, "Mac Grad's Reit Stuff."
6. Broomer, *Hamilton Babylon*, 111.
7. Broomer, *Hamilton Babylon*, 3, 7.
8. Broomer, *Hamilton Babylon*, 122, 123, 120.
9. Charles Legge, "Trouble with Playing God: Answers to Correspondents [Scot Region]," *Daily Mail*, December 9, 2019, 62.
10. Walter, *My Secret Life*, vol. 1, chap. 3 (originally published 1888; Kindle edition March 16, 2017), 31.
11. Broomer, *Hamilton Babylon*, 125; "Judge: 'I Know Porno When I See It': McMasters U. Vexed about Invasion," *Variety* 258, no. 7 (April 1, 1970), 20.
12. "Film Review: Columbus of Sex," *Variety* 258, no. 13 (May 13, 1970), 14.
13. Broomer, *Hamilton Babylon*, 125–27; "Ontario Burg Holds 'Columbus of Sex,'" *Variety* 256, no. 2 (August 27, 1969), 32.
14. Broomer, *Hamilton Babylon*, 155–56, 164–65, 166, 173.
15. Broomer, *Hamilton Babylon*, 188.
16. Broomer, *Hamilton Babylon*, 188–89.

253

17. Foley, "Mac Grad's Reit Stuff."

18. Sid Adilman, "Foxy Lady's Budding Canadian Cinemogul," *Toronto Daily Star*, November 18, 1971, 46; Masters, "Who's That Guy?," 78.

19. Masters, "Who's That Guy?," 78.

20. *Foxy Lady*, directed by Ivan Reitman, Cinépix Film Properties, 1971; Broomer, *Hamilton Babylon*, 6.

21. *Cannibal Girls*, directed by Ivan Reitman, Cinépix Film Properties, 1973.

22. Ivor Davis, "How to Get There from Here," *Maclean's* 92, no. 13 (March 26, 1979), 54.

23. John Harrison, *Spellbound: The Wonder-Filled Life of Doug Henning* (New York: BoxOffice Books, 2009), 47–48; Masters, "Who's That Guy?," 78.

24. Neil McNally, "Spellbound Pamphlet!" *The Doug Henning Project*, June 27, 2017, accessed September 4, 2019, https://doughenningproject.com/2017/06/27/spellbound-pamphlet.

25. Kenneth Jones, "Tony-Nominated Magician Doug Henning Is Dead at 52," *Playbill*, February 8, 2000, http://www.playbill.com/article/tony-nominated-magician-doug-henning-is-dead-at-52-com-86982.

26. Masters, "Who's That Guy?," 78.

27. Chris Nashawaty, *Caddyshack: The Making of a Hollywood Cinderella Story* (New York: Flat Iron Books, 2018), 27–28, 36–40,41.

28. Masters, "Who's That Guy?," 78.

29. Judith Belushi Pisano and Tanner Colby, *Belushi: A Biography* (New York: Rugged Land, 2005), 92.

30. Nashawaty, *Caddyshack*, 51–52; Robert Davis, "News Briefs," *Chicago Tribune*, September 22, 1970, 3.

31. Gene Triplett, "'Ghostbuster' Bill Ready for Recess," *The Oklahoman*, June 10, 1984.

32. "Bill Murray," Second City website, accessed September 6, 2019, https://www.secondcity.com/people/other/bill-murray; Nashawaty, *Caddyshack*, 51–52.

33. Megh Wright, "Saturday Night's Children: Brian Doyle-Murray (1979–1980; 1981–1982)," *Splitsider*, February 6, 2013, archived on Vulture, https://www.vulture.com/2013/02/saturday-nights-children-brian-doyle-murray-1979-1980-1981-1982.html; Pisano and Colby, *Belushi*, 80.

34. "Bill Murray," Second City website.

35. William Leonard, "Variety: Always Poking Fun, Second City's at It Again . . .," *Chicago Tribune*, February 1, 1974, B3.

36. Nashawaty, *Caddyshack*, 52.

37. Nashawaty, *Caddyshack*, 49, 52.

38. Pisano and Colby, *Belushi*, 80.

39. Pisano and Colby, *Belushi*, 79; Nashawaty, *Caddyshack*, 52.

40. Douglas Martin, "Harold Ramis, Director, Actor and Alchemist of Comedy, Dies at 69," *New York Times*, February 24, 2014, https://www.nytimes.com/2014/02/25/movies/harold-ramis-who-helped-redefine-what-makes-us-laugh-on-screen-dies-at-69.html.

41. Dave Thomas, Robert Crane, and Susan Carney, *SCTV: Behind the Scenes* (Toronto: McClelland & Stewart, 1996), 26; Violet Ramis Stiel, *Ghostbuster's Daughter: Life with My Dad, Harold Ramis* (New York: Blue Rider Press, 2018), 80.

42. Nashawaty, *Caddyshack*, 50–51.

43. Mel Gussov, "Stage: A New 'Lampoon': Audiences Still Hurrying to be Insulted," *New York Times*, March 3, 1975, 34.

44. Pisano and Colby, *Belushi*, 132.

45. Tom Shales and James Andrew Miller, *Live from New York: An Uncensored History of Saturday Night Live* (New York: Little, Brown & Company, 2002), 69.

46. Mark Ribowsky, *Howard Cosell: The Man, the Myth, and the Transformation of American Sports* (New York: W. W. Norton, 2012), 335–43.

47. Gary Deeb, "ABC Executioners Ready Cosell for 'Hit' Parade," *Chicago Tribune*, October 9, 1975, B9; Ribowsky, *Howard Cosell*, 343.

48. John J. O'Conner, "Sprightly Mix Brightens NBC's 'Saturday Night,'" *New York Times*, November 30, 1975, D31.

49. Shales and Miller, *Live From New York*, 52.

50. Shales and Miller, *Live From New York*, 32.

51. Dan Aykroyd, "Did I want to be a priest?," Facebook, March 6, 2012, https://www.facebook.com/DanAykroyd/posts/did-i-want-to-be-a-priest-sureyeah-i-wanted-to-for-about-9-seconds-this-is-not-t/292123190853845.

52. Joe Baltake, "Dan Aykroyd," *Philadelphia Daily News*, May 6, 1983, 71; Lynn Saxberg, "Aykroyd Rides the Blues Away," *Ottawa Citizen*, June 15, 2007, https://www.pressreader.com/canada/ottawa-citizen/20070615/282016142908076; Dan Aykroyd, "The Art of Motorcycle," *Crawdaddy*, January 1978.

53. Tony Atherton, "Fact, Fiction or Fable Has Come a Long Way," *Ottawa Citizen*, November 19, 1994, E6; David Sheff, "Dan Aykroyd: The Playboy Interview," *Playboy*, August 1993, archived at http://www.angelfire.com/celeb2/elwood3/daplay.html.

54. Shales and Miller, *Live from New York*, 32, 33.

55. Pisano and Colby, *Belushi*, 132.

56. Tad Friend, "Comedy First," *New Yorker*, April 11, 2004, https://www.newyorker.com/magazine/2004/04/19/comedy-first.

57. Advertisement, *Screen International*, no. 52 (September 4, 1976), 20.

58. Adil, "Film Review: Death Weekend," *Variety* 284, no. 9 (October 6, 1976), 21.

59. "Films," Cinépix, accessed December 4, 2019, cinepix.ca/films; "From Cinépix to Cineplex: The Studios That Dropped Maple Syrup," Canuxploitation! Your Complete Guide to Canadian B-Film, accessed December 4, 2019, http://www.canuxploitation.com/article/studio.html.

60. "Ilsa the Tigress of Siberia: Full Cast & Crew," IMDb, accessed December 4, 2019, https://www.imdb.com/title/tt0078398/companycredits.

61. "Universal, Nat'l Lampoon Plan Joint Film Venture," *BoxOffice* 110, no. 10 (December 13, 1976), 10.

62. Richard Christiansen, "Movies: Harold Ramis—Second City Alum Pens a Hit 'House,'" *Chicago Tribune*, August 27, 1978, 10.

63. Thomas, Crane, and Carney, *SCTV*, 26, 28.

64. Thomas, Crane, and Carney, *SCTV*, 55–56.

65. Stiel, *Ghostbuster's Daughter*, 33–34.

66. Pisano and Colby, *Belushi*, 133.

67. Roger Ebert, "Animal House," accessed October 21, 2019, https://www.rogerebert.com/reviews/national-lampoons-animal-house-1978.

68. Nashawaty, *Caddyshack*, 90.

69. Masters, "Who's That Guy?," 78.

70. "Reitman Moving from Ca. to U Lot; $1-Mil Cut on Pic," *Variety* 293, no. 3 (November 22, 1978), 33.

71. Lenny Blum, "Cooking Up Meatballs," *Globe and Mail*, June 23, 1979, 12–16; "Pictures: Canada's 'Meatballs' and Par's Got Them," *Variety* 294, no. 11 (April 18, 1979), 37.

72. Eric Spitznagel, "Meatballs: An Oral History," *Vanity Fair*, July 6, 2017, https://www.vanityfair.com/hollywood/2017/07/meatballs-movie-an-oral-history.

73. Spitznagel, "Meatballs: An Oral History."

74. "The Summer of Bill Murray," Fox Sports, February 16, 2015, https://www.foxsports.com/mlb/just-a-bit-outside/story/bill-murray-snl-40th-anniversary-grays-harbor-loggers-1978-021515; Masters, "Who's That Guy?," 80.

75. Spitznagel, "Meatballs: An Oral History."

Notes

76. William K. Knoedelseder, "The No Longer Interested in Prime Time Players," *Los Angeles Times*, November 18, 1979, L1; *Next Stop, Greenwich Village*, directed by Paul Mazursky, 20th Century Fox, 1976; Spitznagel, "Meatballs: An Oral History."

77. Nashawaty, *Caddyshack*, 99.

78. Masters, "Who's That Guy?," 80.

79. Stephen Klain, "Reitman, 'Meatballs' and Canadian Success, Maker," *Variety* 296, no. 2 (August 15, 1979), 6.

80. "Meatballs," *Variety* 295, no. 8 (June 27, 1979), 18.

81. Pauline Kael, "The Current Cinema," *New Yorker*, July 13, 1981, 82.

82. Sid Adilman, "Pictures: Of 9 Nominations, 8 Categories Win Genies for 'Changeling'; Pique at Canadian Awards," *Variety* 298, no. 8 (March 26, 1980), 5, 40.

83. Noel Taylor, "Insensitive Film Bad Joke on Blind," *Ottawa Citizen*, July 10, 1978, 52; Debra Sharp, "Mary Ann McDonald: From Song and Dance Artist to Girl Next Door and Now She's an Easy-Going Punker," *Globe and Mail*, November 3, 1979, F10.

84. Dennis Perrin, *Mr. Mike: The Life & Work of Michael O'Donoghue* (New York: Avon Books, 1998), 362–64.

85. Bob Woodward, *Wired: The Short Life & Fast Times of John Belushi* (New York: Pocket Books, 1984), 162–63; David Ansen, "Spielberg's Misguided Missile," *Newsweek* 94, no. 25 (December 17, 1979), 111.

86. Pisano and Colby, *Belushi*, 173–74.

87. Dale Pollack, "Pictures: Spielberg Cuts '1941' 17 Min," *Variety* 297, no. 7 (December 19, 1979).

88. J. W. Rinzler, *The Making of Star Wars: The Empire Strikes Back* (New York: el Ray, 2010), 206.

89. Ivor Davis, "Star Trek: The $50 Million Countdown Begins," *Globe and Mail*, November 17, 1979, E13.

90. Vincent Canby, "Film: California Goes to War in '1941': Pearl Harbor Plus 6," *New York Times*, December 14, 1979, C10, https://www.nytimes.com/1979/12/14/archives/film-california-goes-to-war-in-1941pearl-harbor-plus-6.html.

91. Gary Arnold, "Daze of the Year," *Washington Post*, December 15, 1979, C1.

92. Pisano and Colby, *Belushi*, 148–51, 152, 182.

93. "Pictures: Landis to Direct 'Blues Brothers' for Universal," *Variety* 294, no. 6 (March 14,1979), 5.

94. John Rockwell, "Soul: The Blues Brothers," *New York Times*, July 3, 1980, 50.

95. Knoedelseder, "No Longer Interested"; Pisano and Colby, *Belushi*, 178.

96. Nashawaty, *Caddyshack*, 104–7.

97. Nashawaty, *Caddyshack*, 154.

98. "Pictures: 'Caddyshack' for Orion via Jon Peters Outfit," *Variety* 295, no. 8 (June 27, 1979), 5; "Pictures: Bill Murray's Orion Pic with Script Co-Written by Brother; Others Cast," *Variety* 296, no. 2 (August 15, 1979), 5.

99. Nashawaty, *Caddyshack*, 138–39.

100. Kate Meyers, "A Bill Murray Filmography," *Entertainment Weekly*, March 19, 1993, https://ew.com/article/1993/03/19/bill-murray-filmography; Janet Maslin, "Screen: Bill Murray Is Star of 'Where the Buffalo Roam,'" *New York Times*, April 26, 1980, 18; "ffolkes, Nothing Personal, Where the Buffalo Roam," *Sneak Previews*, May 8, 1980, archived on IMDb, https://www.imdb.com/title/tt0081748/videoplayer/vi3749362457.

101. Pam Lambert, "Film: Busting Loose: Success for a Shy Comedian," *Wall Street Journal*, June 19, 1984, 1.

102. Linda Gross, "'Caddyshack': Old Gags on the Links," *Los Angeles Times*, July 25, 1980, G11.

103. Vincent Canby, "Film View: The Golden Age of Junk," *New York Times*, August 17, 1980, A13.

104. Nashawaty, *Caddyshack*, 236–37.

105. Nashawaty, *Caddyshack*, 244–48.

106. Nashawaty, *Caddyshack*, 251.

107. Michael Ovitz, *Who Is Michael Ovitz?* (New York: Portfolio/Penguin, 2018), 115–16.

108. Michael Gillis, "Stars and Stripes," *Stripes* Special Edition DVD, Columbia Pictures, 2006.

109. Masters, "Who's That Guy?," 80; Jeffrey Wells, "Ivan Reitman Earns His 'Stripes,'" *Film Journal* 84, no. 11 (June 22, 1981), 8.

110. Author interview with Frank Price, June 24, 2020, and September 8, 2020.

111. Wells, "Ivan Reitman Earns His 'Stripes,'" 8; Michael Blowen, "The One and Only Bill Murray," *Boston Globe*, June 20, 1981, 1.

112. Adrian Mack, "The Hangover Part II Producer Dan Goldberg Talks about Cronenberg, Will Ferrell, and the Late, Great Warren Oates," *The Georgia Straight*, May 25, 2011, https://www.straight.com/blogra/hangover-part-ii-producer -dan-goldberg-talks-about-cronenberg-will-ferrell-and-late-great-warren-oates.

113. "Columbia Pictures," *Variety* 304, no. 7 (September 16, 1981), 18–19; Bernard F. Dick, *Columbia Pictures: Portrait of a Studio* (Lexington: University of Kentucky Press, 1992), 36.

114. Pauline Kael, "The Current Cinema," *New Yorker*, July 13, 1981, 82.

115. Blowen, "One and Only Bill Murray"; Michael Blowen, "'Stripes' Is Devilishly Inconsistent; Bill Murray's Anarchic Humor Provides Film's Best Moments," *Boston Globe*, May 30, 1982, 1.

116. Dane Lanken, "Ivan Reitman Aims to Strike Gold with Heavy Metal," *Globe and Mail*, April 4, 1981, E7.

117. *Imagining Heavy Metal*, directed by Jeffrey Schwarz, Columbia Tri-Star Home Video, 1999.

118. Lanken, "Ivan Reitman Aims to Strike Gold," E7.

119. *Imagining Heavy Metal*, directed by Jeffrey Schwarz.

120. Pisano and Colby, *Belushi*, 232–33.

121. Pisano and Colby, *Belushi*, 231, 235.

122. Pisano and Colby, *Belushi*, 248; Robert Kaus, "Cosmo Talks To: Frank Price," *Cosmopolitan* 199, no. 4 (November 1985), 166.

123. Woodward, *Wired*, 272–73; Pisano and Colby, *Belushi*, 248; Michael Blowen, "Breakfast with Belushi and Aykroyd: Meet the Me Generation's Laurel and Hardy," *Boston Globe*, January 7, 1982, A1.

124. Pisano and Colby, *Belushi*, 236, 248

125. Woodward, *Wired*, 432, 437–38.

126. Pisano and Colby, *Belushi*, 257.

127. Woodward, *Wired*, 464–65.

128. Thomas Quinn, "Oh Brother, He's Back—Dan Aykroyd Tells Thomas," *Daily Mirror*, May 22, 1998, 4.

129. Joe Baltake, "Dan Aykroyd," *Philadelphia Daily News*, May 6, 1983, 71.

130. Michael Janusons, "Aykroyd Hits His Stride after Belushi's Death," *Providence Journal*, May 1, 1983, H11.

131. Peter H. Aykroyd, with Angela Narth, *A History of Ghosts: The True Story of Séances, Mediums, Ghosts, and Ghostbusters* (New York: Rodale, 2009), ix, 187–88.

132. Don Shay, *Making Ghostbusters* (New York: Zoetrope, 1985), 6.

133. Lesley M. M. Blume, "The Making of Ghostbusters: How Dan Aykroyd, Harold Ramis, and 'The Murricane' Built 'The Perfect Comedy,'" *Vanity Fair*, June 4, 2014, https://www.vanityfair.com/hollywood/2014/06/ghostbusters-making-of; Jason

Matloff, "An Oral History of Ghostbusters," *Esquire*, February 24, 2014, https://www.esquire.com/entertainment/movies/news/a27498/ghostbusters-oral-history.

134. Rick Lyman, "Getting Us Ready for 'Ghostbusters,'" *Philadelphia Inquirer*, June 8, 1984, D1.

135. Matloff, "Oral History of Ghostbusters"; Shales and Miller, *Live from New York*, 230–33.

136. Army Archerd, "Just for Variety," *Variety* 195, no. 40, April 30, 1982, 3; John Stuart, "NY CLIPS: Malkovich Duels Hoffman for Spotlight," *Globe and Mail*, June 8, 1984, E1.

137. Ethan Anderton, "Chevy Chase Talks Comedy Sitcom Woes & Regrets Not Doing 'Ghostbusters,'" Screen Rant, September 27, 2012, https://screenrant.com/chevy-chase-sitcom-comments-louis-ck-ghostbusters; author interview with Thom Enriquez, February 25, 2020.

138. Shay, *Making Ghostbusters*, 7; Matloff, "Oral History of Ghostbusters"; Blume, "Making of Ghostbusters.'"

139. Rita Zekas, "'A Great Bag Is a Miracle' and Other Truths," *Toronto Star*, February 10, 2010, https://www.thestar.com/life/fashion_style/2010/02/20/a_great_bag_is_a_miracle_and_other_truths.html; "TO175: Toronto Timeline Part 3: The City Comes of Age." CityNews, March 6, 2009, https://toronto.citynews.ca/2009/03/06/to175-toronto-timeline-part-3-the-city-comes-of-age; "A Triple Blow His Producer Ivan Reitman," *Toronto Star*, April 26, 1973, 34; Beverly Slopen, "Dini Petty: She's CITY-TV's Sweet City Woman," *Toronto Star*, August 25, 1973, 4, 6; Jack Miller, "Veterans Said It Was Too Far Out but CITY-TV's Proving Them Wrong," *Toronto Star*, December 20, 1972, 64.

140. Matloff, "Oral History of Ghostbusters."

141. Shay, *Making Ghostbusters*, 7.

CHAPTER 2: THIS IS A PIECE OF CAKE

1. Army Archerd, "Just for Variety," *Daily Variety*, December 9, 1982, 3.

2. *Ghost Buster*, directed by Hal Yates, RKO Radio Pictures, 1952.

3. Lee Marguiles, "Kids' Television Shows Get Some Grownup Talent," *Chicago Tribune*, August 26, 1975, B8; "CBS Will Institute Tripartite Plan for Children's Programs," *Broadcasting* 90, no. 10 (March 8, 1976), 26.

4. Author interview with Erika Scheimer, June 25, 2019, and March 24, 2020.

5. Author interview with Anthony Bueno, March 10, 2022.

6. Author interview with Erika Scheimer, June 25, 2019.

7. Author interview with Thom Enriquez, February 25, 2020, and March 11, 2020.

8. "TV Commercial Outtakes," Special Features, *Ghostbusters* SteelBook Blu-ray set, Sony, 2019.

9. Don Shay, *Making Ghostbusters* (New York: Zoetrope, 1985), 15.

10. Shay, *Making Ghostbusters*, 125, 152, 170.

11. Shay, *Making Ghostbusters*, 197.

12. Shay, *Making Ghostbusters*, 67.

13. Shay, *Making Ghostbusters*, 102, 165

14. Drew McWeeny, "Our Epic Interview with Ivan Reitman Looks to the Past and the Future for 'Ghostbusters,'" HitFix, July 17, 2016, archived at https://web.archive.org/web/20160721085130/http://www.hitfix.com/motion-captured/our-epic-interview-with-ivan-reitman-looks-to-the-past-and-the-future-for-ghostbusters.

15. Michael Sragow, "Ghostwriters," *Film Comment* 19, no. 2 (March/April 1983), 15.

16. David Elliott, "'Ghostbusters' . . . At Times, Monstrous Overkill," *San Diego Union*, June 8, 1984, A31

17. Marc Weinberg, "The Battle Over Billing," *Orange Coast*, February 1989, 168.

18. Joe Baltake, "Doctor Detroit," *Philadelphia Daily News*, May 6, 1983, 71.

19. Brillstein, "Vet Packager, Mulls Budgetary Effect of 'Bankables.'" *Variety* 311, no. 2, May 11, 1983, 44.

20. Bill Cosford, "'Doctor,' Heal Thy Jokes," *Miami Herald*, May 10, 1983, 5B; Michael Janusonis, "Doctor Detroit Needs a Transfusion," *Providence Journal*, May 6, 1983, W06.

21. Baltake, "Doctor Detroit."

22. Mike Bygrave, "Dan Aykroyd, Funny Man with a Serious Message," *South China Morning Post*, January 5, 1985, 15.

23. Shay, *Making Ghostbusters*, 7–8; Jason Matloff, "An Oral History of Ghostbusters," *Esquire*, February 24, 2014, https://www.esquire.com/entertainment/movies/news/a27498/ghostbusters-oral-history; Kim Masters, "Who's That Guy with the Ghostbusters?," *Premiere*, July 1989, 80.

24. Daniel Wallace, *Ghostbusters: The Ultimate Visual History* (San Rafael, CA: Insight Editions, 2015), 16.

25. Patrick Goldstein, "He's the Mild-Mannered Gremlin of Gross-Outs," *Los Angeles Times*, April 23, 1983, E1; Pam Lambert, "Film: Busting Loose: Success for a Shy Comedian," *Wall Street Journal*, June 19, 1984, 1.

26. Shay, *Making Ghostbusters*, 8.

27. "Jumpin' at the Genies," *Variety* 310, no. 9. (March 30, 1983), 20.

28. Matloff, "Oral History of Ghostbusters"; Columbia Pictures, Letter to Harold Ramis Enterprises, Inc., May 10, 1983, Larry Jones Papers, Special Collections, Margaret Herrick Library, AMPAS; Columbia Pictures, Letter to Basket Weaving Productions, Inc., May 10, 1983, Larry Jones Papers, Special Collections, Margaret Herrick Library, AMPAS.

29. Shay, *Making Ghostbusters*, 8–9; Jean-Marc and Randy Lofficier, "Ghostbusters Associate Producer: Michael Gross," *Enterprise Incidents*, November 1984, 46; Dale Pollack, "Murray Walks a Razor's Edge in Hollywood," *Los Angeles Times*, October 12, 1984, AD3.

30. Wallace, *Ghostbusters*, 16.

31. Michael Ovitz, *Who Is Michael Ovitz?* (New York: Portfolio/Penguin, 2018), 115–16.

32. Shay, *Making Ghostbusters*, 9; Matloff, "Oral History of Ghostbusters"; Lofficier, "Ghostbusters Associate Producer," 46.

33. Philip Wuntch, "Murray: A Guy Who Can't Stop Mugging," *Dallas Morning News*, June 16, 1989, 1C; Pollack, "Murray Walks a Razor's Edge," AD3.

34. Roger Ebert, "Watch Out for Comical Trio of 'Ghostbusters,'" *Herald News*, January 29, 1984, E3.

35. Wendy Weinstein, "John Byrum Traverses 'The Razor's Edge,'" *Film Journal* 87, no. 9 (September 1, 1984), 8, 82.

36. Timothy Crouse, "Bill Murray: The Rolling Stone Interview," *Rolling Stone*, August 16, 1984, https://www.rollingstone.com/movies/movie-news/bill-murray-the-rolling-stone-interview-39596.

37. Crouse, "Bill Murray Interview"; Michael London, "Remake of 'Razor's Edge' is Getting on a Few Nirvanas," *Los Angeles Times*, October 12, 1984, K1.

38. Columbia Pictures, Letter to Basket Weaving Productions, Inc., May 10, 1983, Larry Jones Papers, Special Collections, Margaret Herrick Library, AMPAS; Columbia Pictures, Letter to Black Rhino Enterprises, Ltd., May 10, 1983, Larry Jones Papers, Special Collections, Margaret Herrick Library, AMPAS.

39. Author interview with Frank Price, June 24, 2020.

40. Lesley M. M. Blume, "The Making of *Ghostbusters*: How Dan Aykroyd, Harold Ramis, and 'The Murricane' Built 'The Perfect Comedy,'" *Vanity Fair*, June 4, 2014, https://www.vanityfair.com/hollywood/2014/06/ghostbusters-making-of.

41. Matloff, "Oral History of Ghostbusters"; Blume, "Making of *Ghostbusters*."

42. Harry Harris, "Chatter: Philadelphia," *Variety* 309, no. 8 (December 22, 1982), 61; Rob Will, "It's the 30-Year Anniversary of the Greatest Wall Street Movie Ever Made: Here's the Story Behind It," *Business Insider*, June 27, 2013, https://www.businessinsider.com/an-oral-history-of-trading-places-2013-6.

43. Gary Arnold, "Walter Hill on Sequels, Buddy Pics," *Washington Times*, June 11, 1990, E1.

44. "Pictures: Murphy's 'Unique' Deal with Par: Big Salary (Upfront), Prod. Role," *Variety* 309, no. 7 (December 15, 1982), 40.

45. Harris, "Chatter: Philadelphia," 61.

46. Wallace, *Ghostbusters*, 24.

47. "Eddie Murphy Confirms Rumors and Stories about Prince, Ghostbusters and More," *The Tonight Show Starring Jimmy Fallon*, YouTube, December 20, 2019, https://www.youtube.com/watch?v=CABVnXoe9gw.

48. "US News: Briefly—Murphy Signed for 'Beverly Hills,'" *Screen International*, no. 442 (April 21, 1984), 6; Lindsey Gruson, "Exit Stallone, Enter Eddie Murphy," *New York Times*, December 16, 1984, Section 2, 21.

49. Vincent Canby, "Film View: 'Trading Places' Brings 30's Comedy into the 80's," *New York Times*, June 19, 1983, https://www.nytimes.com/1983/06/19/movies/film-view-trading-places-brings-30-s-comedy-into-the-80-s.html.

50. Jeff Labrecque, "Ghostbusters: Ivan Reitman and Dan Aykroyd Examine Past and Future of Ghostbusters," *Entertainment Weekly*, October 28, 2015, https://ew.com/article/2015/10/28/ghostbusters-book-ivan-reitman-dan-aykroyd.

51. Shay, *Making Ghostbusters*, 9–10, 15.

52. Shay, *Making Ghostbusters*, 11–12.

53. Nick De Semlyen, *Wild and Crazy Guys* (New York: Crown Archetype, 2019), 99–100.

54. Author interview with Thom Enriquez, February 25, 2020.

55. Kathleen A. Hughes, "Enough Already: The Producer Glut Is a Hollywood Joke—Selznick and Goldwyn Made Movies; Now, Credits Go to a Legion of Egotists," *Wall Street Journal*, December 7, 1989, 1.

56. Dan Aykroyd and Harold Ramis, *Ghostbusters* script, September 30, 1983, transcribed by Paul Rudoff, pp. 1–135, archived at https://www.theraffon.net/~spookcentral/gb1_script_1983-09-30.pdf.

57. Shay, *Making Ghostbusters*, 97; Guy Lyon Playfair, *This House Is Haunted* (New York: Stein and Day, 1980), 12–34, 65.

58. Duffy, Mike. "The Ghoul Returns for an Ova-dae Encore." *The Detroit Free Press*. June 12, 1992. Pg 1C, 5C.

59. "Ultra Ghoul vs The Abominable Doughman." *YouTube*. Uploaded by hack editor. December 5, 2008. https://www.youtube.com/watch?v=KhxwMdSz8cA&t=118s.

60. Avildsen, John. 1982. *Neighbors*. Columbia Pictures.

61. Adam Eisenberg, "*Ghostbusters*," *Cinefex*, no. 17 (June 1984), 6; Shay, *Making Ghostbusters*, 69.

62. "Ghostbusters," *Daily Sentinel*, Entertainer section, June 8, 1984, 18.

63. Wallace, *Ghostbusters*, 15; author interview with Thom Enriquez, February 25, 2020, and March 11, 2020.

64. McWeeny, "Epic Interview with Ivan Reitman"; Ebert, "Watch Out for Comical Trio.'"

65. Don Lechman, "'Ghostbusters' Quartet Shines," *Daily Breeze*, June 1, 1984, E6.

66. Dan Aykroyd and Harold Ramis, *Ghostbusters* script, August 5, 1983, transcribed by Paul Rudoff, p. 23, archived at https://www.theraffon.net/~spookcentral/gb1_script_1983-08-05.pdf.

67. Author interview with Anna Maria Monticello, May 22, 2020.

68. Author interview with Merete Van Kamp, June 18, 2020.

69. "Ghostbusters" Dana Audition List, August 23–September 6, 1983.

70. Author interview with Ronnie Carol, May 26, 2020.
71. Author interview with Melanie Mayron, November 27, 2020; "Ghostbusters" Dana Audition List, August 23–September 6, 1983.
72. Frank Swertlow, "Wham! Puts the Lid on Film of China Tour," *San Francisco Chronicle*, December 20, 1985, 86; Malcolm J. Barach, "Names & Faces," *Boston Globe*, June 1, 1983, 1.
73. Shay, *Making Ghostbusters*, 44.
74. Bob Campbell, "Harold Ramis Gets Serious about Comedy," *Star-Ledger*, July 20, 1996, 23.
75. Frank Bruni, "'Death' and the Actress: Sigourney Weaver Grows into Role of Front-Rank Performer," *Chicago Tribune*, January 15, 1995, M8.
76. Charles Champlin, "The Horror of 'Alien:' Scare-City of Another Kind," *Los Angeles Times*, May 20, 1979, N1; Vincent Canby, "Screen: 'Alien' Brings Chills from the Far Galaxy: A Gothic Set in Space," *New York Times*, May 25, 1979, C16.
77. Vincent Canby, "Screen: 'Year of Living Dangerously,'" *New York Times*, January 21, 1983, C4.
78. Philip Wuntch, "The Lighter Side of Sigourney," *Dallas Morning News*, June 18, 1989, 1C.
79. Joe Baltake, "Sigourney Weaver—She's Formidable, but in a Friendly Way," *Philadelphia Daily News*, June 25, 1984, 33.
80. Stephen Farber, "Sigourney, Weaver of Spells," *Cosmopolitan* 197, no. 6 (June 1984), 92.
81. Gene Triplett, "Sigourney's Charm No Ghostly Illusion," *The Oklahoman*, June 17, 1984; Wuntch, "Lighter Side of Sigourney"; "Sigourney Weaver," Internet Off-Broadway Database, accessed October 21, 2019, http://iobdb .com/CreditableEntity/9406.
82. Bill Brownstein, "The 'Has-Been' Who Hung In," *The Gazette*, March 7, 1986, C1.
83. "Sigourney Weaver 'Ghostbusters' 5/26/84," YouTube, posted by the Bobbie Wygant Archive on May 31, 2020, https://www.youtube.com/watch?v=wH _HuRFJ_Rc; "Ghostbusters Co-Star Doesn't Mind Height," *Calgary Herald*, June 8, 1984, C5.
84. David T. Friendly, "'Aliens': Diary of a Film That Almost Wasn't Made," *Palm Beach Post/ Evening Times*, August 1, 1986, 18; Stephen Galloway, "'Aliens' Books Ordered Open," *Hollywood Reporter* 331, no. 37 (April 8, 1994), 6.
85. Marilyn Beck, "Barr Autobiography Will Omit Adoption," *Daily News of Los Angeles*, June 15, 1989, L21; Liz Smith, "Bruce Willis as Young Frank Sinatra? Producer Hopes So," *Baltimore Sun*, 2B; Rita Zekas, "Sigourney's Calling Her Accountant This Time," *Toronto Star*, June 20, 1989, G1.
86. Aykroyd and Ramis, *Ghostbusters* script, August 5, 1983, pp. 29, 51, 128–29
87. Shay, *Making Ghostbusters*, 99.
88. Author interview with Yaphet Kotto, November 6, 2019, and November 15, 2019.
89. Rick Selvin, "Frank Might Write His Own Story," *Philadelphia Daily News*, October 3, 1983, 30.
90. Ryan Parker, "'Family Matters' Actor Reginald VelJohnson Says Everyone Still Thinks He's a Cop," *Hollywood Reporter*, November 16, 2015, https://www.hollywood reporter.com/tv/tv-news/reginald-veljohnson-talks-comedy-action-840152.
91. Karen Cherry, "Busting Loose: Ghostbuster Role Is Just One of Many for Ernie Hudson," *St. Petersburg Times*, June 24, 1989, 1D.
92. "To Be Here for BH Queen Contest," *Herald-Palladium*, February 18, 1988, 5.
93. Rohan Preston, "Burnsville Resident and 'Ghostbusters' Star Ernie Hudson Returns to Twin Cities Stage," *Star Tribune*, January 9, 2019, https://www .startribune.com/ghostbusters-star-ernie-hudson-calls-himself-the-lucky-one-as

-he-returns-to-twin-cities-stage/504108542; "To Be Here for BH Queen Contest," *Herald-Palladium*, February 18, 1988, 5.

94. Ed Zdrojewski, "Actor Visits Friends in BH," *Herald-Palladium*, July 10, 1982, 3; Preston, "Burnsville Resident and 'Ghostbusters' Star."

95. Mark Dawidziak, "'Ghostbusters' Made a Star of Him," *Philadelphia Inquirer*, August 5, 1984, I3; "BH Native Wins Acting Award," *Herald-Palladium*, February 8, 1978, 3.

96. Dawidziak, "'Ghostbusters' Made a Star."

97. Vincent Canby, "Movies: In 'Penitentiary II,' Too Sweet Gordon Gets Out," *New York Times*, April 2, 1982, 30; Peter Stack, "An Actor Craves the Spotlight—Ernest Hudson Plays Wesley Snipes' Rival in the Gritty 'Sugar Hill,'" *San Francisco Chronicle*, February 16, 1994, F1.

98. Shay, *Making Ghostbusters*, 44.

99. Gene Siskel, "Movies: Sour Movies Keep Candy Just Short of Sweet Success," *Chicago Tribune*, March 30, 1986, K5

100. Dave Thomas, Robert Crane, and Susan Carney, *SCTV: Behind the Scenes* (Toronto: McClelland & Stewart, 1996), 153.

101. "Michael McKean #120," *The Kevin Pollack Chat Show*, July 25, 2011, YouTube, https://www.youtube.com/watch?v=H5gDae126xw; Thomas, Crane, and Carney, *SCTV*, 114–22.

102. Thomas, Crane, and Carney, *SCTV*, 192.

103. "Jumpin' at the Genies," *Variety* 310, no. 9 (March 30, 1983), 20; David McDonnell and John Sayers, "Rick Moranis: Nebbish, Nerd & Famous Hoser," *Starlog*, no. 86 (September 1984), 66; Gene Siskel, "Movies: Bob & Doug Film 'A Foot in the Door' for Moranis & Thomas," *Chicago Tribune*, August 28, 1983, K11; Rick Von Sickle, "Dan Goes North Looking for Gold in a Comic Vein," *Globe and Mail*, September 25, 1981, 17.

104. Von Sickle, "Dan Goes North," 17; McDonnell and Sayers, "Rick Moranis," 66.

105. Hank Gallo, "Acting Just Helps Feed His Philosophy," *New York Daily News*, June 5, 1984, 63.

106. Aykroyd and Ramis, *Ghostbusters* script, August 5, 1983, pp. 122–23.

107. Shay, *Making Ghostbusters*, 170

108. Author interview with Anne Carlisle, January 28, 2020.

109. "Ghostbusters," *Monthly Film Bulletin* 51, no. 600 (January 1, 1984), 379.

110. "Kosa od pre 40 godina," See Cult, January 1, 2010, http://www.seecult.org/vest/kosa-od-pre-40-godina; Slavitza Jovan résumé, undated.

111. *Mlad i zdrav kao ruža*, directed by Jovan Jovanović, Dunav Film, 1971.

112. V. Milivojević, "Vizija kriminalne budućnosti," *Glas javnosti*, March 3, 2006, archived at http://arhiva.glas-javnosti.rs/arhiva/2006/03/03/srpski/K06030106.shtml; Daniel J. Goulding, *Liberated Cinema: The Yugoslav Experience, 1945–2001* (Bloomington: Indiana University Press, 1985), 78–81.

113. "Prison Dossier Lazar Stojanović," Courage Connecting Collections, accessed July 12, 2020, http://cultural-opposition.eu/registry/?uri=http://courage.btk.mta.hu/courage/individual/n9242&type=masterpieces.

114. Nancy Lane, "Ask Us," *Philadelphia Inquirer*, January 28, 1976, D19.

115. "Bride 1970–79," California Marriage Index, p. 15,550; "Bride 1970–79," California Marriage Index, p. 2,159.

116. *El Norte*, directed by Gregory Nava, American Playhouse / Channel Four Films / Independent Productions / Island Alive / PBS, 1983; "Listen: LISTEN," *Los Angeles Times*, July 13, 1984, F12.

117. Harris M. Lentz, "Other Obituaries," *Science Fiction Chronicle* 21, no. 2: 46; Joy Horowitz, "From Slapstick to Yuppie Fantasy," *New York Times Magazine*, June 15, 1986, 32–35.

118. Nora Sayre, "Film: Goldie Hawn on 'The Sugarland Express,'" *New York Times*, March 30, 1974, 20; Tom Buckley, "'The Day of the Locust': Hollywood, by West, by Hollywood," *New York Times Magazine*, June 2, 1974, 58.

119. David Friedman, "The Mouth That Roars," *Newsday*, March 27, 1988, 3; Bill Zehme, "Who's Afraid of Sandra Bernhard?," *Rolling Stone*, no. 538 (November 3, 1988), 80.

120. Linda Gross, "Boy, Girl, Car in 'Corvette Summer,'" *Los Angeles Times*, August 30, 1978, K13; Lee Margulies, "TV Review: 'Ladies' Worth Waiting For," *Los Angeles Times*, January 8, 1979, E14.

121. Lydia Lane, "Beauty: Annie Diets, Exercises for Stamina," *Los Angeles Times*, April 16, 1979, F4; James Brown, "The Dramatic Debut of the First Brother," *Los Angeles Times*, November 9, 1978, H1.

122. Weinstein, "John Byrum Traverses," 82.

123. Jamie Reno, "Bill Murray Wants More than Laughs," *Baltimore Sun*, November 20, 1988, 1N

124. *Ghostbusters* Daily Production Report, Wednesday, October 12, 1983, p. 1; "Pictures: New York Sound Track," *Variety* 312, no. 1 (August 3, 1983), 28; Crouse, "Bill Murray Interview."

125. Shay, *Making Ghostbusters*, 12

126. "Pictures: Film Production," *Variety* 313, no. 4 (November 23, 1983), 24; "International: Film Production," *Variety* 312, no. 13 (October 26, 1983), 173; Shay, *Making Ghostbusters*, 12; Crouse, "Bill Murray Interview"; Gene Triplett, "'Ghostbuster' Bill Ready for Success," *Oklahoman*, June 10, 1984.

127. *Ghostbusters* Daily Production Report, Tuesday, October 11, 1983, p. 2; author interview with Peter Giuliano, January 14, 2020.

128. Randy Lofficier, "Laszlo Kovacs, ASC, and Ghost Busters," *American Cinematographer* 65, no. 6 (June 1984), 62–66.

129. Shay, *Making Ghostbusters*, 12.

130. Eisenberg, "*Ghostbusters*," 13–14, 21.

131. Shay, *Making Ghostbusters*, 41.

132. Author interview with Peter Giuliano, January 14, 2020.

133. Author interview with Peter Giuliano, January 14, 2020.

134. Matloff, "Oral History of Ghostbusters."

135. Amy Friedman, "Kick the Dog: Movie-Set Madness," *Kingston Whig-Standard*, April 9, 1988.

136. David Spade, "Calling Doctor Detroit," *SPIN* 8, no. 11 (February 1, 1993), 44.

137. Friedman, "Kick the Dog."

138. Michael London, "Seems Like Old Times on New 'Ghostbusters' Set," *Los Angeles Times*, November 30, 1983, H1, H4; Graham Yost, "Belushi of the Spirits," *New York* 20, no. 3 (May/June 1984), 4.

139. *Ghostbusters* Daily Production Report, Tuesday, January 3, 1984, p. 2; Eisenberg, "*Ghostbusters*," 21.

140. Cherry, "Busting Loose."

141. Hadley Freeman, "Ernie Hudson on Being the Squeezed Ghostbuster: 'If I Blame Racism There's Nothing I Can Learn From It,'" *The Guardian*, October 16, 2014, https://www.theguardian.com/film/2014/oct/16/ernie-hudson-ghostbusters-winston.

142. Shay, *Making Ghostbusters*, 54.

143. Freeman, "Ernie Hudson on Being the Squeezed Ghostbuster."

144. Shay, *Making Ghostbusters*, 184.

145. Shay, *Making Ghostbusters*, 11.

146. Lofficier, "Ghostbusters Associate Producer," 46; Eisenberg, "*Ghostbusters*," 9.

147. J. W. Rinzler, *The Making of the Empire Strikes Back* (New York: Del Ray, 2010), 2.

148. Eisenberg, "*Ghostbusters*," 18.

149. Shay, *Making Ghostbusters*, 78.

150. Steve Johnson, *Rubberhead* (Montauk, NY: Montauk Publishing, 2017), 39–48.

151. Shay, *Making Ghostbusters*, 75.

152. Michael London, "A Movie Maker Who Tamed High-Tech in 'Ghostbusters,'" *Los Angeles Times*, June 13, 1984, G6.

153. Shay, *Making Ghostbusters*, 189.

154. Matloff, "Oral History of Ghostbusters."

155. Shay, *Making Ghostbusters* 194.

156. Joseph Viskocil, "Simon Stay-Puft," *Los Angeles Times*, July 29, 1984, 83.

157. Randy Lofficier, "Visual Effects for Ghostbusters," *American Cinematographer* 65, no. 6 (June 1984), 76; Eisenberg, "*Ghostbusters*," 41–42.

158. Shay, *Making Ghostbusters*, 72; Eisenberg, "*Ghostbusters*," 10

159. Author interview with Thom Enriquez, February 25, 2020, and March 11, 2020.

160. Eisenberg, "*Ghostbusters*," 18; Shay, *Making Ghostbusters*, 112, 169.

161. Author interview with Saul Saladow, March 25, 2019.

162. Gabrilella Oldham, *First Cut: Conversations with Film Editors* (Berkeley: University of California Press, 1991), 17–18.

163. London, "Movie Maker Who Tamed High-Tech"; author interview with Saul Saladow, March 25, 2019.

164. Shay, *Making Ghostbusters*, 63.

165. Shay, *Making Ghostbusters*, 112, 135, 137.

166. Shay, *Making Ghostbusters*, 121; Feature: "Ghostbusters," New York Breakdown, undated, p. 1, Larry Jones Papers, Special Collections, Margaret Herrick Library, AMPAS; "Joe Schmieg," BFI, accessed October 24, 2021, https://www2.bfi.org .uk/films-tv-people/4ce2bb360b0bc; C. M. Crockford, "How Freddy Krueger Led to Mark Hamill's Star Wars Role," Looper, October 19, 2021, https://www .looper.com/637734/how-freddy-krueger-led-to-mark-hamills-star-wars-role.

167. "Col, Filmation Settle Over 'Ghost' Title," *Variety* 315, no. 9 (June 27, 1984), 4; Aljean Harmetz, "Where Movie Ticket Income Goes," *New York Times*, January 28, 1987, C19; "Michael C. Gross Talks Ghostbusters (1984)," Filminutiae, archived at http://filminutiae.com/take-03-ghostbusters-1984-michael-c-gross -interview; "Columbia's Ghost Is a Smash, Too," *New York Times*, September 29, 1984, 31; "Pictures: 'Ghostbusters' Overcomes Short Prod. Sked to Smash Results," *Variety* 315, no. 9 (June 27, 1984), 30; B. J. Carter, "Interview: Lou Scheimer: A Candid Conversation with Filmation's Founder," The Trades, June 11, 2007, archived at https://web.archive.org/web/20080423051330/http:// www.the-trades.com/article.php?id=5561.

168. Stuart Cohn, "Cynthia Millar Goes from Classical to 'Heavy Metal' with Her Pre-Synth Sonic Wonder, the Ondes Martenot," *Los Angeles Times*, March 31, 1996, archived at https://www.latimes.com/archives/la-xpm-1996-03-31-ca -53172-story.html.

169. Aykroyd and Ramis, *Ghostbusters* script, August 5, 1983, p. 61; Aykroyd, and Ramis, *Ghostbusters* script, September 30, 1983, p. 29; Shay, *Making Ghostbusters*, 47.

170. Shay, *Making Ghostbusters*, 47; Matloff, "Oral History of Ghostbusters"; "Behind the Music: Huey Lewis & The News," originally aired February 4, 2001, VH-1.

171. Author interview with the Alessi Brothers, August 26, 2019; Mike Ryan, "Who You Gonna Call? The Inside Story of the 'Ghostbusters' Music Video," Screen Crush, June 5, 2014, https://screencrush.com/ghostbusters-music-video.

172. Author interview with Patrick Thrall, February 28, 2019, and March 3, 2019.

173. Dennis Hunt, "Faces: Ray Parker Jr. Going Like Ghostbusters," *Los Angeles Times*, August 19, 1984, T72.

174. Scott Lapatine, "Lindsey Buckingham Reveals Stories Behind His Solo Songs and Whether He'll Ever Rejoin Fleetwood Mac," Stereogum, December 10, 2018, https://www.stereogum.com/2025688/lindsey-buckingham-interview-fleetwood-mac/franchises/interview.

175. Hunt, "Faces: Ray Parker Jr."; Dale Kawashima, "Special Interview with Ray Parker Jr., Renowned Artist/Writer/Producer of 'Ghostbusters' and Many Other Classic Hit Songs," Song Writer Universe, December 18, 2016, https://www.songwriteruniverse.com/ray-parker-jr-interview-2016.htm.

176. Dennis Hunt, "Pop News: Parker Pens Own Tunes for Raydio," *Los Angeles Times*, February 19, 1978, 75.

177. Susan Toepper, "Top of Pop," *Daily News*, March 19, 1978, 23.

178. R. D. Heldenfels, "Ray Parker, a Positive Performer," *Daily Press*, February 12, 1978, E4; Kawashima, "Special Interview with Ray Parker Jr."; Mary Campbell, "Parker Striving for More Creative Ideas," *Daily Advertiser*, October 2, 1982, 26.

179. Dennis Hunt, "Faces: Raydio's Parker: Home Is Studio," *Los Angeles Times*, May 10, 1981, O74.

180. Clive Davis, with Anthony DeCurtis, *The Soundtrack of My Life* (New York: Simon & Schuster, 2013), 187–89, 260.

181. Hunt, "Faces: Raydio's Parker"; Hunt, "Pop News: Parker Pens Own Tunes."

182. Kawashima, "Special Interview With Ray Parker Jr."

183. "Ghostbusters by Ray Parker, Jr.," Professor of Rock, accessed October 12, 2019, https://www.professorofrock.com/ghostbusters-by-ray-parker-jr.

184. Author interview with Martin Page, December 12, 2019.

185. Kawashima, "Special Interview with Ray Parker Jr."

186. Blair Jackson, "Classic Tracks: Ray Parker Jr.'s 'Ghostbusters,'" Mix, September 1, 2006, https://web.archive.org/web/20070930015711/http://mixonline.com/recording/interviews/audio_ray_parker_jrs.

187. "Ghostbusters by Ray Parker, Jr.," Professor of Rock.

188. Kawashima, "Special Interview with Ray Parker Jr."

189. Ellie Gibson, "Eurogamer Meets Ray Parker Jr.," Eurogamer, March 12, 2009, https://www.eurogamer.net/articles/eurogamer-meets-ray-parker-jr-interview; Bud Wilkinson, "Loquacious Barfly Norm Spills Beans about Plot of 'Cheers,'" *Arizona Republic*, August 3, 1984, D7; Ryan, "Who Ya Gonna Call?"

190. Laurie Deans, "LA Clips: Moranis Hopes to Ride Hill Fame to Europe," *Globe and Mail*, June 1, 1984, E4.

191. Kawashima, "Special Interview with Ray Parker Jr."; Jackson, "Classic Tracks: Ray Parker Jr.'s 'Ghostbusters.'"

192. Author interview with Patrick Thrall, February 28, 2019, and March 3, 2019.

193. Author interview with the Alessi Brothers, August 26, 2019.

194. Richard Christiansen, "'Groundhog Day' Director at Forefront of Comedy for 20 Years," *Las Vegas Review*, February 12, 1993, 15E.

195. Violet Ramis Stiel, *Ghostbuster's Daughter: Life with My Dad, Harold Ramis* (New York: Blue Rider Press), 120.

196. Gavin Edwards, "Being Bill Murray," *Rolling Stone*, October 29, 2014.

CHAPTER 3: BIBLICAL PROPORTIONS

1. John Huey and Stephen J. Sansweet, "Coca-Cola to Pay Over $820 Million for Movie Firm," *Wall Street Journal*, January 20, 1982, 2; Tim Metz, "Cost of Acquiring Columbia Pictures Is Slippery Subject," *Wall Street Journal*, January 21, 1982, 37; George Anders, "Coke's Bid for Film Concern Goes Down Poorly with Beverage Firm's Holders as Shares Drop," *Wall Street Journal*, January 21, 1982, 49; Laura Landro, "Columbia Pictures, HBO and CBS Plan to Form Venture for a New Movie Studio," *Wall Street Journal*, December 1, 1982, 10.

2. Huey and Sansweet, "Coca-Cola to Pay."
3. Julie Salamon, "Film: Coke Gets 'Double' Exposure at the Movies," *Wall Street Journal*, October 25, 1984, 1.
4. Dale Pollock, "Movie Moguls Predict Big Summer Box Office," *Los Angeles Times*, May 7, 1984, G1.
5. Stephen J. Sansweet, "'Annie' Is a Costly Disappointment So Far, Hurt by Bad Reviews, Blockbuster Rivals," *Wall Street Journal*, July 13, 1982, 35; Stephen J. Sansweet, "Columbia Hoping Big 'Annie' Promotion Will Turn Costly Film Into a Phenomenon," *Wall Street Journal*, May 12, 1982, 29; Syd Silverman, "Lotsa Slow Biz for Showbiz in '82," Variety 309, no. 11 (January 12, 1983), 70.
6. Author interview with Frank Price, June 24, 2020.
7. Liz Smith, "Aykroyd, Murray of 'Ghostbusters' Have Studio Spooked," *Baltimore Sun*, May 30, 1984, B2.
8. Lou Cedrone, "Aykroyd Calls Belushi Book 'Stale, Trashy,'" *San Diego Union-Tribune*, June 2, 1984, B6.
9. "Bumps in the Night," *Variety* 315, no. 9 (June 27, 1984), 24.
10. Michael London, "Film Clips: Hollywood's Wired Up for Belushi Story," *Los Angeles Times*, June 6, 1984, I1; Michael Ovitz, *Who Is Michael Ovitz?* (New York: Portfolio/Penguin, 2018), 131.
11. Anne Bogart, "Eye: Ghost Appeal," *Women's Wear Daily* 147, no. 116 (June 14, 1984), 3.
12. London, "Film Clips: Hollywood's Wired Up"; Ovitz, *Who Is Michael Ovitz?*, 131
13. London, "Film Clips: Hollywood's Wired Up."
14. David Chute, "Dante's Inferno," *Film Comment*, May/June 1984, 22.
15. Janet Maslin, "At the Movies," *New York Times*, April 13, 1984, C8.
16. Aljean Harmetz, "'Indiana Jones' Stirs Ratings Debate," *New York Times*, May 21, 1984, C12.
17. Vincent Canby, "As a Rating, PG Says Less Than Meets the Eye," *New York Times*, June 10, 1984, H1; "LA Clips: Ratings System and Its Gremlins Come Under Fire," *Globe and Mail*, June 8, 1984, E1
18. Desmond Ryan, "PG-13 Fails to Silence Critics," *Philadelphia Inquirer*, June 29, 1984, E1.
19. Peter H. Brown, "'Ghostbusters' and the Exorcists of the Raunch," *Los Angeles Times*, January 24, 1985, J7.
20. Dan Aykroyd and Ramis, Harold, *Ghostbusters* script, August 5, 1983, transcribed by Paul Rudoff, pp. 9, 14, 103–4, archived at https://www.theraffon.net/~spookcentral/gb1_script_1983-08-05.pdf.
21. Jean-Marc and Randy Lofficier, "Ghostbusters Associate Producer: Michael Gross," *Enterprise Incidents*, November 1984, 47.
22. Aykroyd and Ramis, *Ghostbusters* script, August 5, 1983, pp. 63–64; Jason Matloff, "An Oral History of Ghostbusters," *Esquire*, February 24, 2014, https://www.esquire.com/entertainment/movies/news/a27498/ghostbusters-oral-history; Chuck Conconi, "Personalities," *Washington Post*, September 19, 1983, B3.
23. Janet Maslin, "Film: 'Ghostbusters,' with Murray and Aykroyd," *New York Times*, June 8, 1984, C5, https://www.nytimes.com/1984/06/08/movies/film-ghostbusters-with-murray-and-aykroyd.html.
24. Maslin, "Film: 'Ghostbusters.'"
25. Vincent Canby, "Cynicism Is Souring Today's Comedies," *New York Times*, March 24, 1986, https://www.nytimes.com/1985/03/24/movies/film-view-cynicism-is-souring-today-s-comedies.html.
26. Lor, "Film Review: Ghostbusters," *Variety* 315, no. 6 (June 6, 1984), 20.
27. Jay Scott, "Ghostbusters, a Pale Imitation of TV Sketches," *Globe and Mail*, June 9, 1984, E5.

28. Jay Carr, "Review Movie: A Ghost of a Comedy," *Boston Globe*, June 9, 1984, 1.

29. Leonard Buder, "1980 Called Worst Year of Crime in City History," *New York Times*, February 25, 1981, B3.

30. "Ravitch Keeps His Son Off Subways at Night," *New York Times*, January 21, 1982, B7.

31. Damon Stetson, "City Is Termed Youth Jobless 'Capital,'" *New York Times*, January 7, 1982, B3.

32. Suzanne Daley, "Crime Rises and Ridership Drops for New York City Subway System," *New York Times*, May 8, 1984, A1; William G. Blair, "Unemployment Drops in Jersey; Holds in New York City and State," *New York Times*, June 2, 1984, 29.

33. Sneed & Lavin Inc., "INC.lings . . .," *Chicago Tribune*, June 12, 1984, 16.

34. "'Ghostbusters' Cruise in Lincoln," *Omaha World Herald*, July 11, 1984, 1.

35. Sean McCormally, "Reporter's Notebook: At the Dallas Convention," UPI, August 19, 1984; George Boosey, "Mondale Hints at Comeback in the U.S. Senate," UPI, November 5, 1980.

36. Special to the New York Times, "Variations of 'No Ghost' Are Coming on Like Gangbusters," *New York Times*, October 12, 1984, A12, https://www.nytimes.com/1984/10/12/us/variations-of-no-ghost-are-coming-on-like-gangbusters.html; John O'Brien, "Swept Up in Rage Over Ghostbusters," *Philadelphia Inquirer*, October 4, 1984, B18.

37. Albert Parisi, "New Jersey Journal," *New York Times*, July 8, 1984, A3.

38. Roger Ebert, "Ghostbusters," archived at https://www.rogerebert.com/reviews/ghostbusters-1984.

39. David Denby, "'Oh, Zuul, You Nut!'" *New York*, June 11, 1984, 66–67.

40. "'Ghostbusters' Made No. 1 Box-Office Spot in Its First Three Days," *Baltimore Sun*, June 15, 1984, B9; "Biggest Ever US Box Office Weekend," *Screen International*, no. 450 (June 16, 1984), 2.

41. "Pictures: Ghosts Scare Up Robust Followup B.O.," *Variety* 315, no. 8 (June 20, 1984), 3, 28.

42. Lenny Litman, "'Gremlins Playful 109G, Pitt.; 'Ghost' Tall 108G," *Variety* 315, no. 7 (June 13, 1984), 10; Richard Klein, "L.A. 'Gremlins' 510G Keep Pace with the Joneses' 515G; 'Ghost' Boff; 'Spock' Out-of-This-World," *Variety* 315, no. 7 (June 13, 1984), 8; Andrew Kirtzman, "'Gremlins' Raid N.Y., $1.8-Mil; 'Ghost' $1.6-Mil; 'Indiana' Pow $1.4-Mil; 'Spock' Sparks 925G," *Variety* 315, no. 7 (June 13, 1984), 8.

43. Richard Gold, "N.Y. 'Ghost' Exorcises $1.5-Mil; 'Gremlins' Voracious; 'Indiana,' 'Kid' Tough; 'Man' Eyeing 48G," *Variety* 315, no. 11 (July 11, 1984), 8; "'Purple Rain' Ousts 'Ghostbusters' as No. 1," *New York Times*, August 1, 1984, C22.

44. From the *Los Angeles Times*, "Studio Postpones Release of Film from 'Airplane' Creators," *Atlanta Constitution*, June 3, 1984, 3G.

45. Chris Nashawaty, *Caddyshack: The Making of a Hollywood Cinderella Story* (New York: Flatiron Books, 2018), 236–37.

46. From the *Los Angeles Times*, "Studio Postpones Release."

47. "Big Rental Films of 1984," *Variety* 317, no. 12 (January 16, 1985), 16; Tasha Robinson, "'Weird Al' Yankovic's Vote for Funniest Movie Ever: *Top Secret!*" The Dissolve, September 23, 2013, http://thedissolve.com/features/compulsory-viewing/173-weird-al-yankovics-vote-for-funniest-movie-ever-to.

48. "'Purple Rain' Ousts 'Ghostbusters,'" *New York Times*.

49. "'Ghostbusters' Regains Top Spot at Box Office," *New York Times*, August 8, 1984, C15; James Greenberg, "Pictures: New Pics Hot, Cold at Nat'l. B.O.; 'Ghostbusters' Takes 1984 Lead," *Variety* 316, no. 3 (August 15, 1984), 28.

50. Michael London, "A Record-Busting Summer," *Los Angeles Times*, September 7, 1984, OC_D1.

51. "Movie Box Office: The Moneymakers," *Philadelphia Daily News*, January 10, 1985, 43.

52. "'Ghostbusters' Off to Scary Int'l Start." *The Hollywood Reporter* 285, no. 4 (December 26, 1984), 2; Jim Robbins, "Col's 'Ghostbusters' A Grossbuster in First Foreign Dates," *Variety* 317, no. 5 (November 28, 1984), 4; "'Ghostbusters' Is Australian Hit," *Screen International*, no. 474 (December 1, 1984), 82; Tina McFarling, "Box Office Set for Christmas Bonanza," *Screen International*, no. 476 (December 15–22, 1984), 1; "'Ghostbusters' Best Yet for Col Overseas," *Variety* 317, no. 8 (December 19, 1984), 33.

53. Jim Robbins, "'Ghostbusters' Pulls $1.5-Mil in Germany During First 3 Days," *Variety* 318, no. 1 (January 30, 1985), 42.

54. "Japanese Rush to See 'Ghostbusters,'" *Screen International*, no. 478 (January 5, 1985), 37.

55. "'Ghostbusters' Sets a New Precedent," *Screen International*, no. 499, June 1, 1985, 42.

56. "After 54 Years in Comics, Joe Palooka Has Thrown His Last Punch," *Philadelphia Inquirer*, November 25, 1984, A3.

57. "'Ghostbusters' Best Yet," *Variety*; "Pictures: Coke to Inaugurate $15-Mil Tie-In with 'Ghostbusters' O'seas Break," *Variety* 316, no. 11 (October 10, 1984), 5.

58. "'Belt' at Home in Norway," *Screen International*, no. 485, February 23, 1985, 33; "Berlin Round-Up: International Demand for 'Belt,'" *Screen International*, no. 488 (March 16, 1985), 20.

59. "Big Draws in Italy," *Baltimore Sun*, September 23, 1985, 2B.

60. David Robinson, "Expensive Toys for Grown-Up Infants," *The Times*, December 7, 1984, 9.

61. David Elliott, "'Ghostbusters' . . . At Times, Monstrous Overkill," *San Diego Union*, June 8, 1984, A31.

62. Richard Schickel, "Cinema: Exercise for Exorcists," *Time*, June 11, 1984, http://content.time.com/time/subscriber/article/0,33009,926579-1,00.html.

63. Denby, "'Oh, Zuul, You Nut!'"

64. David Ansen, "Got a Demon in Your Icebox?" *Newsweek* 103, no. 24 (June 11, 1984), 80.

65. Pauline Kael, "The Current Cinema," *New Yorker*, June 25, 1984, 104–5.

66. Gene Siskel, "Bill Murray Busts Loose with Ghosts," *Chicago Tribune*, June 8, 1984, S3.

67. Dale Pollack, "Murray Walks a Razor's Edge in Hollywood," *Los Angeles Times*, October 12, 1984, AD3.

68. Rick Lyman, "Murray Goes over the Top to Superfame," *Philadelphia Inquirer*, October 21, 1984, I1.

69. Ovitz, *Who Is Michael Ovitz?*, 132; Columbia Pictures, Letter to Harold Ramis Enterprises, Inc., May 10, 1983, Larry Jones Papers, Special Collections, Margaret Herrick Library, AMPAS; Columbia Pictures, Letter to Basket Weaving Productions, Inc., May 10, 1983, Larry Jones Papers, Special Collections, Margaret Herrick Library, AMPAS.

70. "Briefly," *Globe and Mail*, October 1, 1984, E8.

71. Joe Baltake, "Movies: Comedian Bill Murray Edges into Drama," *Philadelphia Daily News*, October 5, 1984, 55.

72. Pollack, "Murray Walks a Razor's Edge."

73. Julie Salamon, "A 'Ghostbuster' in Maugham Country," *Wall Street Journal*, October 18, 1984, 28; Janet Maslin, "Movies: Bill Murray in 'Razor,'" *New York Times*, October 19, 1984, C14, https://www.nytimes.com/1984/10/19/movies/movies-bill-murray-in-razor.html; Jay Carr, "Murray Can't Save 'Razor's Edge'

Remake," *Boston Globe*, October 19, 1984, 36; Patrick Goldstein, "A Fool for Love—and Wisdom," *Los Angeles Times*, October 19, 1984, J1.

74. Allen Young, "Pictures: 16 Sellouts Mark Denver Film Fest," *Variety* 317, no. 1 (October 31, 1984), 34.

75. Joann Rhetts, "The Boys Are Back in Town," *Charlotte Observer*, June 3, 1984, 1F.

76. Kate Meyers, "A Bill Murray Filmography," *Entertainment Weekly*, March 19, 1993, archived at https://ew.com/article/1993/03/19/bill-murray-filmography.

77. Lynda Rose Obst, "Movie Business/Monkey Business," *Vogue* 174, no. 12 (December 1, 1984), 404.

78. Deborah Caulfield, "Meet John Murray—Yes, He Does Resemble Bill," *Los Angeles Times*, April 16, 1985, H1.

79. Roger Ebert, "In a Violent Cinema Summer, Bill Murray Hopes Filmgoers Will Enjoy a Comic 'Change,'" *Chicago Sun-Times*, July 8, 1990, 1.

80. Bob Thomas, "Bill Murray: Off the Wall," *St. Louis Post-Dispatch*, January 25, 1989, 1; Jamie Portman, "The Enigma of Bill Murray: Outrageous as . . .," *Southam News / CanWest News*, November 9, 1988, 1; Jamie Reno, "Bill Murray Wants More than Laughs," *Baltimore Sun*, November 20, 1988, 1N; Charles Taylor, "Murray's All Scrooged-Up for the Holidays," *San Francisco Examiner*, November 25, 1988, C3; Gannett News Service, "Murray, Like Scrooge, Was Changed by Revelation," *Santa Fe New Mexican*, December 4, 1988, D6; Frank Walker, "Comic Comeback," *Sydney Morning Herald*, April 11, 1993, 95.

81. "Pictures: Col Claims Major Win with Piracy Settlement of 'Ghostbusters' Items," *Variety* 317, no. 1 (October 31, 1984), 4.

82. Michael London, "Film Clips: Toying Around with Success," *Los Angeles Times*, July 4, 1984, F1.

83. Author interview with Thom Enriquez, February 25, 2020, and March 11, 2020; United Press International, "Columbia Sued on Ghost," *New York Times*, November 20, 1984, C22, https://www.nytimes.com/1984/11/20/movies/columbia-sued-on-ghost.html; "Casper's Creators Aren't So Friendly," UPI, November 16, 1984, archived at https://www.upi.com/Archives/1984/11/16/Caspers-creators-arent-so-friendly/1331469429200.

84. *Harvey Cartoons v. Columbia Pictures Industries*, 645 F. Supp. 1564 - Dist. Court, SD New York 1986, https://scholar.google.com/scholar_case?-case=1984718000534919691&q=645+f+supp+1564&hl=en&as_sdt=6,47.

85. "Ghostly Dispute Settled in Earthly Manner," *New York Times*, October 30, 1986, B3, https://www.nytimes.com/1986/10/30/nyregion/ghostly-dispute-settled-in-earthly-manner.html.

86. Linda Renaud, "LA Clips: Victories, Casualties Mark Ongoing Battle for Summer Box Office," special to the *Globe and Mail*, August 25, 1989, C3.

87. *Harvey Cartoons v. Columbia Pictures Industries*.

88. Rob Tannenbaum, "Soundtracks Thrived in Summer of '85," *Rolling Stone*, no. 461 (November 21, 1985), 16.

89. "Hot 100," *Billboard* 96, no. 28 (July 14, 1984), 68; Paul Grien, "News: Chartbeat," *Billboard* 96, no. 32 (August 11, 1984), 10; "Retailing: Video—Video Music Programming," *Billboard* 96, no. 23 (June 23, 1984), 33.

90. *Ray Parker, Jr. v. Hugh Cregg*, Superior Court of the State of California, County of Los Angeles, Case No. BC247313, Dismissed—Other 12/19/2001, p. 2.

91. "Huey Lewis 'Drug' Hit 'Ghostbusters' Root, Sez Fed Suit in L.A.," *Variety* 316, no. 11 (October 9, 1984), 152.

92. Michael Goldber, "Parker Doesn't Have Ghost of a Chance in Shedding Image," *Daily Breeze*, October 5, 1984, E12.

93. Weinger, Harry. "Paranormal Success For Parker." *Billboard*. Vol. 96, Iss. 34. August 25, 198, 58.

94. *Ray Parker, Jr. v. Hugh Cregg*, Notice of Motion and Motion to Strike Certain Allegations in Complaint, Memorandum of Points and Authorities in Support Thereof, filed May 11, 2001, p. 7.

95. Water Berry, "For Huey Lewis, It's Still Hip to be Hip," *Daily Breeze*, January 30, 1987, E3.

96. Matloff, " Oral History of Ghostbusters."

97. Ron Base, "When Ghostbusters Director Needs a Hit, Who's He Gonna Call?," *Toronto Star*, February 22, 1986, F3.

98. Tannenbaum, "Soundtracks Thrived," 15–16; Robert Palmer, "Prince Creates a Winner with 'Purple Rain,'" *New York Times*, July 22, 1984, H19.

99. James Lochner, James. Liner Notes, *Ghostbusters: Original Motion Picture Score*. Varèse Sarabande, 2006.

100. Various artists, *Ghostbusters: Original Soundtrack*, Arista Records, 1984.

101. James Lochner, Liner Notes, *Ghostbusters: Original Motion Picture Score*, Varèse Sarabande, 2006.

102. Ophelia D. Johnson, "'Hand That Rocks' Role a Stretch for Hudson," *Richmond Times-Dispatch*, January 12, 1992, K12.

103. Maslin, "Film: 'Ghostbusters'"; Carr, "Movie Review: Ghost of a Comedy"; Sheila Benson, "'Ghostbusters' Stays in a State of Pure Silliness," *Los Angeles Times*, June 8, 1984, H1; Julie Salamon, "Film: Movies That Go Bump in the Night," *Wall Street Journal*, June 14, 1984, 1.

104. Siskel, "Bill Murray Busts Loose"; Ansen, "Got a Demon?"

105. Michael Cader, ed., *Saturday Night Live: The First Twenty Years* (Boston and New York: Houghton Mifflin, 1994), 152; Dick Ebersol, producer, *Saturday Night Live*, November 10, 1984, NBC.

106. Mark Dawidziak, "'Ghostbusters' Made a Star of Him," *Philadelphia Inquirer*, August 5, 1984, I3.

107. Gail Shister [Mart Ann Norbom], "A Journalist's Son Shuns Hollywood Games," *Philadelphia Inquirer*, December 12, 1984, F7; "Gertrude Gipson's Candid Comments," *Los Angeles Sentinel*, November 29, 1984, B7.

108. Dawidziak, "'Ghostbusters' Made a Star."

109. Anthony Breznican, "*Ghostbusters* at 35: Ernie Hudson on Winston Zeddemore's Proud Legacy as a Black Movie Hero," *Entertainment Weekly*, June 6, 2019, archived at https://web.archive.org/web/20190615023917/https://ew.com/movies/2019/06/06/ghostbusters-at-35-ernie-hudson-on-winston-zeddemore-legacy.

110. "NAACP Image Awards Nominations," *Los Angeles Times*, November 2, 1984, OC_E12; "Rock Star Prince Dominates NAACP's Annual Image Awards," *Boston Globe*, December 6, 1984, 81.

111. "NAACP Image Awards Nominations," *Los Angeles Times*; "Films in 1985," BAFTA, accessed July 17, 2020, http://awards.bafta.org/award/1985/film; Michael London, "'Amadeus,' 'Fields' Top Golden Globe Choices," *Los Angeles Times*, January 8, 1985, G3; "Here's a List of the Main Contenders for Grammy Awards," *Gazette*, January 12, 1985, C12; Michael Blowen, "Academy Goes for Art Over Commerce," *Boston Globe*, February 7, 1985, 64.

112. Terrence O'Flaherty, "Did the Chinese Fall Asleep?," *San Francisco Chronicle*, March 27, 1985, 56.

113. "Ray Parker Jr.: Awards," IMDb, accessed February 18, 2021, https://www.imdb.com/name/nm0662018/awards; "Films in 1985," BAFTA; London, "'Amadeus,' 'Fields' Top Golden Globe"; Blowen, "Academy Goes for Art."

114. Ellie Gibson, "Eurogamer Meets Ray Parker, Jr.," Eurogamer, March 12, 2009, https://www.eurogamer.net/articles/eurogamer-meets-ray-parker-jr-interview.

115. Clive Davis, with Anthony DeCurtis, *The Soundtrack of My Life* (New York: Simon & Schuster, 2013), 262; Robert Hilburn, "When You Wish Upon a Star," *Los Angeles Times*, April 7, 1985, Calendar section, 55; Frank Rizzo, "Sound Check: Other Notes," *Hartford Courant*, June 6, 1985, Calendar section, 5.

116. Dennis Hunt, "Faces: Ray Parker Jr. Going Like Ghostbusters," *Los Angeles Times*, August 19, 1984, T72.

117. Lee Marguiles, "Update," *Los Angeles Times*, October 21, 1984, AB5; "Circus Celebrates Centennial," *Los Angeles Sentinel*, September 13, 1984, B7; "Class Explores Black Hollywood," *Los Angeles Sentinel*, October 11, 1984, B5.

118. Desmond Ryan, "Racial Violence Underpins Tale of Handicapped Vet," *Philadelphia Inquirer*, October 26, 1987, E3; Walter Goodman, "Film: Teen-Age Gang in 'Enemy Territory,'" *New York Times*, May 22, 1987, C7.

119. David Browne, "Making Waves: Looking Through the Single File," *New York Daily News*, October 5, 1987, 35; Eric Snider, "Parker's Calculations Just Don't Add Up," *Tampa Bay Times*, September 27, 1987, 2F.

120. Jim Harwood, "Michael J. Fox Rules Natl. B.O.; 'Sign' Shaky, 'Ghostbusters' Pale," *Variety* 320, no. 5 (August 28, 1985), 3; Brown, "'Ghostbusters' and the Exorcists."

121. Michael London, "Eddie Murphy Gets Jump on Clint, Burt and Hal," *Los Angeles Times*, December 12, 1984, OC_E1.

122. London, "Eddie Murphy Gets Jump"; Thomas C. Hayes, "Disappointments for Some Studios," special to the *New York Times*, December 27, 1984, D19; Michael London, "'Beverly Hills Cop' Laps the Field at the Box Office," *Los Angeles Times*, December 12, 1984, H1.

123. Associated Press, "'Cop' Breaks Its Own Box-Office Record," *Boston Globe*, January 4, 1985, 22.

124. Aljean Harmetz, "'Beverly Hills Cop' Wins at Christmas Box Office," *New York Times*, December 29, 1984, 9.

125. Harwood, "Michael J. Fox Rules."

126. "Domestic Box Office for 1985," Box Office Mojo, accessed June 30, 2020, https://www.boxofficemojo.com/year/1985; Aljean Harmetz, "At the Movies," special to the *New York Times*, November 1, 1985, C10; Harwood, "Michael J. Fox Rules."

127. Stephen Advokat, "Video's Profits: Selling the Soul of Cinema?," KNT News Service for *Orlando Sentinel*, December 29, 1985, D1; Tony Seidman, "Paramount Home Video Sets $29.95 'Beverly Hills Cop,'" *Billboard* 97, no. 38 (September 21, 1985), 1.

128. Aljean Harmetz, "At the Movies," *New York Times*, December 31, 1985, C10, https://www.nytimes.com/1985/12/13/movies/at-the-movies.html; Aljean Harmetz, "Studios Woo Cassette Mass Market," *New York Times*, January 27, 1986, C26, https://www.nytimes.com/1986/01/27/movies/studios-woo-cassette -mass-market.html.

129. "'Ghostbusters' Sneak on HBO Riles Distribs," *Variety*, Vol. 322, Iss. 1. January 1, 1986, 1, 145; John Carmody, "The TV Column," *Washington Post*, December 24, 1985, C6; "Tonight on TV," *Los Angeles Times*, December 24, 1985, part IV, 10.

130. "HBO Touts Holiday Premieres," *Variety* 321, no. 10 (January 1, 1986), 30, 116.

131. George Mair, *Inside HBO* (New York: Dodd, Mead, 1988), 160; Laura Landro, "Columbia Pictures, HBO and CBS Plan to Form Venture for a New Movie Studio," *Wall Street Journal*, December 1, 1982, 10; Stephen J. Sansweet, "Columbia Pictures Forms Joint Venture to Provide $160 Million for Movies Unit," *Wall Street Journal*, February 9, 1982, 4; Andrew Yule, *Fast Fade: David Puttnam,*

Columbia Pictures, and the Battle for Hollywood (New York: Delacorte Press, 1989), 184–186.

132. *Evening Sun* Television Listings, November 1, 1985, 20.

133. "ABC Gobbles Up 'Ghostbusters' for $15-Million after HBO Play," *Variety* 316, no. 8 (September 19, 1984), 47.

134. Lisa Belkin, "On the Trail of Pirated Video Cassettes," *New York Times*, May 18, 1987, C13.

135. "Venezuela Achieves Legit Video Market," *Variety* 318, no. 8 (March 20, 1985), 92; "Television and Video: Pirate Imports—Still a Mystery," *Screen International*, no. 485 (February 23, 1985), 25.

136. "Home Video: 7,000 Pirated Cassettes Seized in Buenos Aires," *Variety* 316, no. 6 (September 5, 1984), 44.

137. Nick Roertshaw, "International: 'Pirate Proof' Vid Box Bows," *Billboard* 96, no. 47 (November 24, 1984), 9.

138. Jay Stuart, "Italian Pirates Crank Out 'Dune,' 'Cotton Club' at Breakneck Speed," *Variety* 317, no. 10 (January 2, 1985), 21.

139. Kim Masters, "Who's That Guy with the Ghostbusters?," *Premiere*, July 1989, 80.

140. Sneed & Lavin Inc., "Reel News . . .," *Chicago Tribune*, December 21, 1984, 32.

141. Michael Sneed and Cheryl Lavin, "Back to Normal . . .," *Chicago Tribune*, January 23, 1985, 20.

142. Desmond Ryan, "More Hitchcock Titles to Reach the Big Screen," *Philadelphia Inquirer*, December 2, 1984, H2; David Bianculli, "'Hitchhiker' Heads in a New Direction," *Philadelphia Inquirer*, December 26, 1984, C1.

143. "Pictures: Hollywood Soundtrack," *Variety* 317, no. 8 (December 19, 1984), 28; "Pictures: New York Sound Track," *Variety* 312, no. 5 (August 31, 1983), 9; "Film Review: Club Paradise," *Variety* 323, no. 11 (July 9, 1986), 18.

144. "Pictures: Hollywood Soundtrack," *Variety* 318, no. 2 (February 6, 1985), 28; "Local Newsfront: Columbia," *Film Journal* 88, no. 3 (March 1, 1985), 34.

145. "Pictures: Hollywood Soundtrack," *Variety* 316, no. 7 (September 12, 1984), 36; Aljean Harmetz, N.Y. Times News Service, "Brian Grazer: A 10-Year 'Overnight Success,'" *Daily Breeze*, March 29, 1985, E5; Elizabeth Gordon, "Actor James Keach Launched Career as 'Creative Producer,'" *Film Journal* 88, no. 5 (May 1, 1985), 8; Glenn Lovell, "Summer's Starting Lineup," *Mercury News*, June 23, 1985, 18.

146. "Calendar of Feature Releases," *Film Journal* 87, no. 11 (November 1, 1984), 59; Michael Fleming, "Buzz: WB Gets 'X'-Cited Over Spike's Pic," *Variety* 347, no. 4 (May 11, 1992), 144; "Home Video: Around the Homevideo Track," *Variety* 311, no. 4 (May 25, 1983), 40; Todd McCarthy, "Pictures: Diverse Orion Slate Readied, with 23 Releases through 1984," *Variety* 311, no. 8 (June 22, 1983), 3.

147. "Pictures: U Slates 'Dragnet' Feature Penned By & Starring Aykroyd," *Variety* 318, no. 10 (April 3, 1985), 4.

148. Marilyn Beck, "No More 'Vacations,' No More 'Fletch' for Chevy Chase," *Chicago Tribune*, December 20, 1985, O; "Calendar of Feature Releases," *Film Journal* 88, no. 4 (April 1, 1985), 38.

149. "People," *Philadelphia Daily News*, June 5, 1985, 54; "People," *Philadelphia Daily News*, December 9, 1985, 49.

150. Laura Landro, "Too Many Movies and Too Few Successes Result in Poor Summer for Film Industry," *Wall Street Journal*, August 2, 1985, 15.

151. Geraldine Fabrikant, "Columbia Cuts Back Production; Things Not Going Well with Coke," *Houston Chronicle*, November 13, 1985, 1.

152. Laura Landro, "New Team at Columbia Movie Division Is Attempting to Revive Coca-Cola Unit," *Wall Street Journal*, November 12, 1985, 45.

153. Laura Landro, "Columbia Names Puttnam to Head Its Movie Division," *Wall Street Journal*, June 27, 1986, 10; Laura Landro, "David Puttnam Stirs Controversy as Chief of Columbia Pictures," *Wall Street Journal*, February 20, 1987, 1; Kim Masters, "Kim Masters Reveals How the Notorious Firing of Columbia CEO David Puttnam Launched Her Own Career," *Hollywood Reporter*, June 27, 2016, https://www.hollywoodreporter.com/news/kim-masters-reveals-how-notorious-905218.

CHAPTER 4: THE TYRANNY OF THE BOX OFFICE

1. Andrew Yule, *Fast Fade: David Puttnam, Columbia Pictures, and the Battle for Hollywood* (New York: Delacorte Press, 1989), 13–20.

2. Yule, *Fast Fade*, 28–31.

3. Yule, *Fast Fade*, 35–38; Derek Malcolm, "City Light Show," *Guardian*, November 10, 1973, 10; Derek Malcolm, "Not-So-Cheapskate," *Guardian*, December 6, 1973, 14.

4. Yule, *Fast Fade*, 41, 45–46.

5. Yule, *Fast Fade*, 58–59, 61–62.

6. Yule, *Fast Fade*, 66–67, 79–83, 87.

7. Yule, *Fast Fade*, 66.

8. Yule, *Fast Fade*, 88–89, 109.

9. Yule, *Fast Fade*, 109–10.

10. Sheila Benson, "Movies: 'Chariots of Fire' Bursts from the Screen," *Los Angeles Times*, September 20, 1981, K28; Vincent Canby, "Screen: Olympic Glory in 'Chariots of Fire,'" *New York Times*, September 25, 1981, C14.

11. Jay Scott, "Hank, Kate Win Oscars, Chariots Named Best Film," *Globe and Mail*, March 30, 1983, 15.

12. Marilyn Beck, "'Chariots' Oscar Bittersweet," *Battle Creek Enquirer*, April 2, 1983, B5; "The 54th Academy Awards: 1982," Academy of Motion Picture Arts and Sciences, accessed July 31, 2020, https://www.oscars.org/oscars/ceremonies/1982; Yule, *Fast Fade*, 204.

13. Associated Press, "'Amadeus' Is Oscar Leader," *Boston Globe*, March 26, 1985, 21; "Films in 1985," BAFTA, accessed July 31, 2020, http://awards.bafta.org/award/1985/film; Michael Sneed, Cheryl Lavin, and Kathy O'Malley, "The Parking Plot . . . ," *Chicago Tribune*, March 26, 1985, 16.

14. Yule, *Fast Fade*, 137–38.

15. "Quebec Film Wins Cannes Critics' Prize; British Entry Grabs Golden Palm," *The Gazette*, May 20, 1986, C10; Yule, *Fast Fade*, 168–69.

16. Laura Landro, "Columbia Names Puttnam to Head Its Movie Division," *Wall Street Journal*, June 27, 1986, 10.

17. Yule, *Fast Fade*, 170.

18. David Friendly, "People: Guy McElwaine Quits Top Post at Columbia," *Los Angeles Times*, April 10, 1986, OC_C3; Katherine Gilday, "Midnight Express's Hayes: Truth Stranger Than Fiction," *Globe and Mail*, September 22, 1978, 17.

19. Yule, *Fast Fade*, 168–71.

20. Yule, *Fast Fade*, 217–18.

21. Yule, *Fast Fade*, 190–91.

22. Vincent Canby, "Film: John Landis's 'Into the Night,'" *New York Times*, February 22, 1985, C8.

23. Stephen Farber and Marc Green, *Outrageous Conduct: Art, Ego, and the Twilight Zone Case* (New York: Arbor House Morrow, 1988), 228–29; Jay Matthews, "Landis Pleads Not Guilty," *Washington Post*, June 25,1983, archived at https://www.washingtonpost.com/archive/lifestyle/1983/06/25/landis-pleads-not-guilty/392a48fd-c9e4-46df-b451-e1d3e9b45ece.

24. "Witnesses to the Helicopter Crash That Killed Actor Vic . . .," UPI Archives, December 1, 1982, https://www.upi.com/Archives/1982/12/01/Witnesses-to -the-helicopter-crash-that-killed-actor-Vic/2748407566800; Ted Rohrlich, "Hearing Opens in 'Twilight Zone' Manslaughter Case," *Los Angeles Times*, January 10, 1984, C1; Ted Rohrlich, "'Twilight Zone' Trial Ordered," *Los Angeles Times*, April 23, 1984, A1.

25. Farber and Green, *Outrageous Conduct*, 241; Julie Salamon, "At the Movies: Los Angelinos, Miami Vice," *Wall Street Journal*, February 21, 1985, 1.

26. Tim Whitaker, "Inklings," *Philadelphia Inquirer*, June 5, 1983, 4; Farber and Green, *Outrageous Conduct*, 202.

27. Farber and Green, *Outrageous Conduct*, 216; Peter Stack, "'Spies Like Us'—A String of Skits That Falls Flat," *San Francisco Chronicle*, December 6, 1985, 90; Noel Taylor, "Spies Like Us Just Isn't Likable," *Citizen*, December 7, 1985, C5; "Rocky Wins Another Round," *Citizen*, December 11, 1985, F4; Douglas Durden, "Punch Line Eludes 'Spies Like Us,'" *Richmond Times-Dispatch*, December 7, 1985, B11; Lloyd Sachs, "Far from Great, 'Spies' Bails Out with Warmth," *Chicago Sun-Times*, December 9, 1985, 54; Janet Maslin, "Screen: 'Spies Like Us,'" *New York Times*, December 6, 1985, C14; Michael Wilmington, "'Spies' Is Like Saturday Night Dead," *Los Angeles Times*, December 6, 1985, SD_D8.

28. Jonathan Dee, "David Cronenberg's Body Language," *New York Times Magazine*, September 18, 2005, 78.

29. Carrie Rickey, "Film: Starpower Reigns in 'Legal Eagles,'" *Philadelphia Inquirer*, June 20, 1986, E24; Vincent Canby, "Film: Ivan Reitman's 'Legal Eagles,'" *New York Times*, June 18, 1986, C17; Scott Myers, "Go Into The Story Interview (Part 3): Jack Epps," *Go Into The Story*. October 11, 2017, https://gointothestory .blcklst.com/go-into-the-story-interview-part-3-jack-epps-981808f172fb.

30. Ron Base, "When Ghostbusters Director Needs a Hit, Who's He Gonna Call?," *Toronto Star*, February 22, 1986, F3; Bart Mills, "Bill Murray Dying to Take Comedic Risks," *Rocky Mountain News*, July 14, 1990, 72; "Romantic Comedy Next for Reitman," *Variety* 320, no. 12 (October 16, 1985), 20.

31. Joy Horowitz, "From Slapstick to Yuppie Fantasy," *New York Times*, June 15, 1986, A30.

32. Michael Ovitz, *Who Is Michael Ovitz?* (New York: Portfolio/Penguin, 2018), 204–5; Michele Willens, "Still on Her Terms," *Los Angeles Times*, March 3, 2002, F3.

33. Ovitz, *Who Is Michael Ovitz?*, 204–5.

34. Jack Mathews, "De Laurentiis' Epic Plan for Embassy," *Los Angeles Times*, October 9, 1985, 1.

35. Kevin Thomas, "Movie Review: 'Legal Eagles' Loses Its Entertainment Case," *Los Angeles Times*, June 18, 1986, 1; Gene Siskel, "The Crime Story Is the Real Crime in 'Legal Eagles,'" *Chicago Tribune*, June 20, 1986, 29; Canby, "Film: Ivan Reitman's 'Legal Eagles'"; Tod McCarthy, "Pictures: Smash 'Kid II,' Strong 'Eagles' Put Summer Natl. B.O. into Gear," *Variety* 323, no. 9 (June 25, 1986), 3; Tina McFarling, "International Box Office: Karate Kid II Chops Away Opponents," *Screen International*, no. 554 (June 28, 1986), 26.

36. Stephen Farber, "Where There's Smoke, There's a Fiery Actress Named Debra Winger," *New York Times*, July 6, 1986, Section 2, 15.

37. Lynn Snowden, "Raising 'Twins,'" *Rolling Stone*, no. 544 (January 26, 1989), 20.

38. Fiona Hughes, "Back to School Topples Top Gun," *Screen International*, no. 553 (June 21, 1986), 18; Jack Matthews, "Some New Flickers on the Big Screen," *Los Angeles Times*, August 22, 1986, SD_D1; Jack Matthews, "Checkbook Count on Summer Films: Hit Time," *Los Angeles Times*, September 3, 1986, Calendar section, 6.

39. Scott Cain, "'Club Paradise' Is a Lethargic, Nebulous Time at the Big Beach," *Atlanta Journal-Constitution*, July 11, 1986, P/1; Gina Mallet, "Club Paradise Is Tiresome," *Toronto* 59, no. 9 (September 1986), 12; Scott Cain, "Moranis' Career Is Blooming," *Atlanta Journal-Constitution*, December 18, 1986, E1; Joshua Klein, "Interview: Harold Ramis," AV Club, March 3, 1999, https://www.avclub.com/harold-ramis-1798207996.

40. "News in Brief," *Screen International*, no. 325 (January 9, 1982), 6; Vernon Scott, United Press International, "The Candy Man of Comedy Is One Shy Guy," *Chicago Tribune*, August 23, 1986, archived at https://www.chicagotribune.com/news/ct-xpm-1986-08-23-8603030435-story.html.

41. Steve Swires, "Terror Tales from Tinseltown," *Starlog*, no. 115 (February 1987), 53–54.

42. "Pictures: Hollywood Soundtrack," *Variety* 319, no. 9 (June 26, 1985), 24.

43. Swires, "Terror Tales from Tinseltown."

44. Scott, "Candy Man of Comedy"; "Pictures: Hollywood Soundtrack," *Variety*; Klein, "Interview: Harold Ramis."

45. Marilyn Beck, "No More 'Vacations,' No More 'Fletch' for Chevy Chase," *Chicago Tribune*, December 20, 1985, O; "Calendar of Feature Releases," *Film Journal* 88, no. 4, April 1, 1985, 38; Michael Fleming, "Buzz: WB Gets 'X'-Cited Over Spike's Pic," *Variety* 347, no. 4 (May 11, 1992), 144; "Home Video: Around the Homevideo Track," *Variety* 311, no. 4 (May 25, 1983), 40; Todd McCarthy, "Pictures: Diverse Orion Slate Readied, with 23 Releases through 1984," *Variety* 311, no. 8 (June 22, 1983), 3.

46. "Summer Film Roundup," *BoxOffice* 122, no. 5 (May 1, 1986), 23; Brit, "Film Reviews: One More Saturday Night," *Variety* 324, no. 4 (August 20, 1986), 14; Paul Willistein, "Big Stars and Directors to Light Up the Screen," *Morning Call*, September 12, 1986, D1.

47. Dave Kehr, "'One More' Too Many," *Chicago Tribune*, September 30, 1986, 8.

48. "Pictures: New Film Starts," *Variety* 325, no. 1 (October 29, 1986), 42; Associated Press, "'Dragnet' in First Place in Holiday Ticket Sales," special to the *New York Times*, July 9, 1987, C14, https://www.nytimes.com/1987/07/09/movies/dragnet-in-first-place-in-holiday-ticket-sales.html.

49. Jack Matthews, "Newman Gets 7th Chance; Will He Finally Get Oscar?" *Los Angeles Times*, February 11, 1987, 1.

50. "Une femme ou deux (One Woman or Two)," *Monthly Film Bulletin* 53, no. 624 (January 1, 1986), 169; "Holdovers Pace Paris Biz," *Variety* 321, no. 4 (November 20, 1985), 122; Roger Ebert, "One Woman or Two," *Chicago Sun-Times*, March 2, 1987, 35.

51. Peter Stack, "No Logic on 'Half Moon Street,'" *San Francisco Chronicle*, September 29, 1986, 52; Sheila Benson, "Weaver Shows Her Best Stuff in 'Half Moon,'" *Los Angeles Times*, September 26, 1986, I1; Todd McCarthy, "Aussie 'Croc' Gobbles Up U.S. Box Office," *Variety* 324, no. 10 (October 1, 1986), 3, 20.

52. Cain, "Moranis' Career Is Blooming"; John Hartl, "Blockbusters Arrive at Theaters," *Seattle Times*, May 22, 1985, E1.

53. Laurie Deans, "LA Clips: Moranis Hopes to Ride Hill Fame to Europe," *Globe and Mail*, June 1, 1984, E4.

54. Cain, "Moranis' Career Is Blooming."

55. Roger Ebert, "Little Shop of Horrors," *Chicago Sun-Times*, December 19, 1986, archived at https://www.rogerebert.com/reviews/little-shop-of-horrors-1986; Janet Maslin, "The Screen: 'Little Shop of Horrors,'" *New York Times*, December 19, 1986, C5; Bob Thomas, "Oscar Nominees: 'Platoon,' 'Room with a View' Lead Race," *Philadelphia Daily News*, February 11, 1987, 3.

56. Joan E. Vadeboncouer, "Murray's Gift," *Syracuse Herald American*, November 20, 1988, 21; Philip Wutch, "There's Trouble in 'Paradise,'" *Dallas Morning News*, July 16, 1986, 1F.

57. Roger Ebert, "In a Violent Cinema Summer, Bill Murray Hopes Filmgoers Will Enjoy a Comic 'Change,'" *Chicago Sun-Times*, July 8, 1990, 1.

58. Ovitz, *Who Is Michael Ovitz?* 4–5; Will Lerner, "Bill Murray Could Have Starred in 'Rain Man,' and 4 Other Things You Didn't Know as Classic Film Turns 30," Yahoo! Entertainment, December 12, 2018, https://www.yahoo.com/entertainment/bill-murray-starred-rain-man-4-things-didnt-know-classic-film-130106808.html.

59. "Zemeckis to Direct Amblin', Disney Tie-Up Roger Rabbit," *Screen International*, no. 571 (October 25, 1986), 384; Audio Commentary by Robert Zemeckis, Frank Marshall, Jeffrey Price, Peter Seaman, Steve Starkey, and Ken Ralston, *Who Framed Roger Rabbit 25th Anniversary DVD & Blu-ray Combo Pack*, 2013.

60. Louis B. Parks, "Director Is Mad to the Max About Nicholson," *Houston Chronicle*, June 18, 1987, 8.

61. Laurie Deans, "Pollack to Direct Murray's New Film," *Globe and Mail*, September 25, 1987, D3.

62. Marilyn Beck, "Davis Plans Big-Screen Return in 'Chrome,'" *Reno Gazette-Journal*, June 9, 1986, 3D; "Turner Stars in Remake of The Front Page," *Leader-Post*, May 15, 1987, C16.

63. Jamie Reno, "Bill Murray Wants More than Laughs," *Baltimore Sun*, November 20, 1988, 1N; "New Film Sarts," *Variety* 329, no. 7 (December 9, 1987), 26; Lynda Rose Obst, "Movie Business/Monkey Business," *Vogue* 174, no. 12 (December 1, 1984), 404; Timothy White, "The Rumpled Anarchy of Bill Murray," *New York Times Magazine*, November 20, 1988, Section 6, 38, https://www.nytimes.com/1988/11/20/magazine/the-rumpled-anarchy-of-bill-murray.html.

64. Kathy O'Malley and Hanke Gratteau, "Celebrities Inc.," *St. Louis Post-Dispatch*, March 2, 1988, Magazine section, 2.

65. Dennis Perrin, *Mr. Mike: The Life and Work of Michael O'Donoghue* (New York: Avon Books, 1998), 409; Kate Meyers, "A Bill Murray Filmography," *Entertainment Weekly*, March 19, 1993, archived at https://ew.com/article/1993/03/19/bill-murray-filmography; Roger Ebert, "Bill Murray, 'Quick Change' Artist," *Daily Breeze*, July 13, 1990, E3.

66. Author interview with Erika Scheimer, June 25, 2019, and March 24, 2020

67. Lee Margulies, "TV Series Promoted: Fat Albert to Teach in Schools," *Los Angeles Times*, June 9, 1976, F16; Joseph Blake, "He-Man: A Hot Toy with Cash Register Muscle," *Philadelphia Daily News*, June 12, 1984, 53; Charles Solomon, "Animation Goes Down the Tube," *Los Angeles Times*, June 21, 1981, N31.

68. Author interview with Erika Scheimer, June 25, 2019, and March 24, 2020.

69. John Dempsey, "Hey! That's My Ghost, Buster," *Variety* 320, no. 5 (August 28, 1985), 65; Bill King, "Tuning In: TV Programmers Hitting the Syndication Mills," *Atlanta Journal-Constitution*, February 5, 1986, B11.

70. Bill Daniels, "Col TV on a Syndie Sales High as Revenues Hit $200-Mil Mark," *Variety* 322, no. 7 (March 12, 1986), 63; Charles Solomon, "A Brace of 'Ghostbusters' Shows," *Los Angeles Times*, September 18, 1986, G12.

71. "The Real Ghostbusters," *Broadcasting* 110, no. 4 (January 27, 1986), 1.

72. "Ghosts R Us," *The Real Ghostbusters*, ABC, September 13, 1986; Dempsey, "Hey! That's My Ghost, Buster."

73. Rick Bentley, "'Who Ya Gonna Watch?,'" *Town Talk*, August 16, 1986, 43, 54.

74. Ken Plume, "Interview: Maurice LaMarche," Fred (website), August 14, 2006, http://asitecalledfred.com/2006/08/14/quick-stop-interview-maurice-lamarche/2.

75. Bentley, "'Who Ya Gonna Watch?,'" 54; Ethan Alter, "'Scooby-Doo' at 50: Original Cartoon Voice Talks Spinoffs, Pot Jokes and Who's the Gang's Stealth MVP,"

Yahoo! September 13, 2019, https://www.yahoo.com/now/scooby-doo-frank
-welker-interview-50th-anniversary-130048355.html; Myrna Oliver, "Lorenzo
Music: Voice of Garfield the Cat," *Los Angeles Times*, August 8, 2001, archived
at https://www.latimes.com/archives/la-xpm-2001-aug-08-me-31716-story.html.

76. Will Harris, "Ernie Hudson Talks Oz and Losing Out on the
    Ghostbusters Cartoon," AV Club, June 13, 2012, https://tv.avclub.com/
    ernie-hudson-talks-oz-and-losing-out-on-the-ghostbuster-1798231857.

77. Author interview with Marsha Goodman, June 3, 2021.

78. Ron Miller, for Knight-Ridder, "How TV Got Two Ghostbusters Cartoons,"
    Ottawa Citizen, August 14, 1986, D13.

79. Proquest Annual Reports, *Coca-Cola Co Annual Report -- 1986*, 22; author
    interview with Pat Fraley, August 6, 2020.

80. Solomon, "Animation Goes Down the Tube."

81. J. Michael Straczynski, *Becoming Superman: My Journey from Poverty to
    Hollywood* (New York: Harper Voyager, 2019), e-book, 236, 244, 246; Daniel
    Akst, "Studio City Firm Changing Saturday Mornings," *Los Angeles Times*,
    May 28, 1985, D2.

82. Kenneth Plume, "Interview with J. Michael Straczynski (Part 2 of 4)," IGN,
    September 6, 2000, archived at https://web.archive.org/web/20100720195734/
    http://uk.movies.ign.com/articles/035/035905p1.html.

83. Plume, "Interview with J. Michael Straczynski"; Diane Haithman, "How
    Image Makers Shape Kids' TV," *Los Angeles Times*, September 3, 1987, H1;
    Straczynski, *Becoming Superman*, 236, 263–67; Charles S. Kaufman, Len
    Janson, and Chuck Menville, "Slimer! Series Bible," revised final 3/9/88, p. 16;
    Kari Granville, "The Fight for Young Viewers Lends Variety to Fall Season,"
    Newsday, September 4, 1988, 82.

84. Eileen Ogintz, "Ghostbusting a Fad That No One Seems to Object To," *Chicago
    Tribune*, May 25, 1988, 1.

85. "A Ghost-Zapping Device Is the Season's Stunner," special to the *New York
    Times*, December 25, 1987, D1, https://www.nytimes.com/1987/12/25/business/
    a-ghost-zapping-device-is-the-season-s-stunner.html.

86. Dana Jackson, "A Stand-Up Comic Actor," *Detroit Free Press*, January 1, 1988,
    6C; Plume, "Interview: Maurice LaMarche."

87. "Episode 90 Dave Coulier (Live Ustream)," *Ron Paulsen Live*, posted June
    14, 2013, archived at https://web.archive.org/web/20141020173747/http://
    robpaulsenlive.com/episode-90-dave-coulier-live-ustream; author interview
    with Marsha Goodman, June 3, 2021.

88. Yule, *Fast Fade*, 196–97, 202.

89. "Special Feature: Yes, I'm Turning . . . All That Matters," *Screen International*,
    no. 571 (October 25, 1986), 404–5; Kate Bales, "Power Kvetching," *American
    Film* 12, no. 10 (September 1, 1987), 40.

90. Morgan Gendel, "Sequel Materializes," *Los Angeles Times*, August 24, 1986,
    https://www.latimes.com/archives/la-xpm-1986-08-24-ca-17145-story.html;
    Alan Mirabella, "Truth, Justice and Pink Slime; Ghostbusters Crew Returns
    'For Fun of It,'" *Ottawa Citizen*, June 15, 1989, D15.

91. Tom Davis, *39 Years of Short-Term Memory Loss: The Early Days of SNL from
    Someone Who Was There* (New York: Grove Press, 2009), 167, 256–57; Tom
    Davis and Jerry Garcia, *Sirens of Titan*, second draft, June 1987, 1–116.

92. Dan Aykroyd, Tom Davis, Susan Beaver, Stuart Kreisman, and Chris Cluess,
    "Mars: Base One," Kreisman/Cluess revision, November 23, 1988.

93. Scott Cain, "Directing Clownish Robin Williams is 'Paradise,'" *Atlanta Journal-
    Constitution*, July 14, 1986, B2.

94. Yule, *Fast Fade*, 261–62; David Friendly, "Lee Rich Recasts MGM/UA's Image," *Los Angeles Times*, February 19, 1987, 1; L. J. Davis, "Hollywood's Most Secret Agent," *New York Times*, July 9, 1989, SM24.

95. Cyndi Lauper, with Jancee Dunn, *Cyndi Lauper: A Memoir* (New York: Atria Paperback, 2012), 178–79; Yule, *Fast Fade*, 254–58; Kim Masters, "Who's That Guy with the Ghostbusters?," *Premiere*, July 1989, 80–81.

96. "Pictures: Weekend Box Office Report," *Variety* 332, no. 3 (August 10, 1988), 4; Rick Groen, "Film Review: Vibes," *Globe and Mail*, August 5, 1988, C4.

97. Yule, *Fast Fade*, 258–59.

98. Simon Baner, "Haunted by Success—Bill Murray," *The Times*, November 21, 1988, 20.

99. Yule, *Fast Fade*, 259–61.

100. Ovitz, *Who Is Michael Ovitz?*, 134–35.

101. "School of Hard Knocks: Ken Wiederhorn," The Flashback Files, 2013, archived at https://www.flashbackfiles.com/ken-wiederhorn-interview.

102. "Grandad Coppola Stops Work to Welcome Late Son's Daughter," *Orlando Sentinel*, January 11, 1987, 23; Klein, "Harold Ramis."

103. Yule, *Fast Fade*, 215–17.

104. Yule, *Fast Fade*, 221–22.

105. Charles Kipps, "The Rise & Fall of the Coca-Cola Kid," *Variety* 331, no. 4 (May 18, 1988), 9.

106. Yule, *Fast Fade*, 282–83.

107. Will Tusher, "Col Sets $270-Mil Package of In-House Pics, Acquisitions as David Puttnam's Initial Program," *Variety* 326, no. 11 (April 8, 1987), 3, 26; Liz Smith, "Paper Parody Wows Washington," *New York Daily News*, September 22, 1986, 8.

108. Yule, *Fast Fade*, 72–75, 204–5, 287

109. Yule, *Fast Fade*, 204–5, 287.

110. Aljean Harmetz, "Elaine May's 'Ishtar': A $51 Million Film in Trouble," special to the *New York Times*, May 19, 1987, C17; Janet Maslin, "Film: Hoffman and Beatty in Elaine May's 'Ishtar,'" *New York Times*, May 15, 1987, C3; David Ansen, "The $40 Million Movie Souffle," *Newsweek* 109, no. 20 (May 18, 1987), 76; Yule, *Fast Fade*, 287.

111. Yule, *Fast Fade*, 270–73; Simon Hattenstone, "Through Slick and Thin," *Guardian*, September 22, 1994, A9.

112. Yule, *Fast Fade*, 332–33; Tusher, "Col Sets $270-Mil Package"; Laura Landro, "Fans of Bill Cosby Like His New Film Less than He Does," *Wall Street Journal*, December 22, 1987, 1.

113. "Weekend Film Box Office Reports," *Variety* 329, no. 9 (December 23, 1987), 4; Landro, "Fans of Bill Cosby."

114. Landro, "Fans of Bill Cosby"; John Voland and Deborah Caulfield, "Movies," *Los Angeles Times*, November 16, 1987, G2; Yule, *Fast Fade*, 320.

115. Yule, *Fast Fade*, 293, 295–96.

116. Smith, "Paper Parody Wows Washington"; Roger Ebert, "Housekeeping," *Chicago Sun-Times*, January 22, 1988, archived at https://www.rogerebert .com/reviews/housekeeping-1988.

117. "Puttnam Firms Pack for Soviet Filming of Columbia Pair," *Variety* 327, no. 12 (July 15, 1987), 7; Aljean Harmetz, "In Re: Columbia Pictures and Puttnam's Orphans," special to the *New York Times*, February 2, 1989, C17; "Cannes Prizes—1989," *Screen International*, no. 204 (May 10, 1990), 22; Ross Johnson, "Stairway to Heaven," *Hollywood Reporter* 347, no. 17 (May 2, 1997), 204.

118. "1987 Distribution Guide," *Film Journal* 90, no. 9 (September 1, 1987), 40; Yule, *Fast Fade*, 289; Dave Kehr, "'Emperor,' Cher, Douglas Get Oscars," *Chicago Tribune*, April 12, 1988, 1.

119. Dawn Steel, *They Can Kill You but They Can't Eat You* (New York: Pocket Books, 1994), 238–40, 242–44; Bernard Weinraub, "Dawn Steel, Studio Chief and Producer, Dies at 51," *New York Times*, December 22, 1997, B6.

120. Ellen Farley, "Hollywood's Hottest Comedy Director Takes a Break: Movies: After 'Twins' and 'Ghostbusters II,' Producer-Director Ivan Reitman Decides There's More to Film Than Laughs," *Los Angeles Times*, December 5, 1989, https://www.latimes.com/archives/la-xpm-1989-12-05-ca-313-story.html.

121. "Pictures: New Film Starts," *Variety* 329, no. 4 (November 18, 1987), 6; Jane Galbraith, "Universal Finds Out 'Great Outdoors' Is a Troublesome Title," *Variety* 331, no. 8 (June 15, 1988), 28; "Production: New Film Starts in the U.S.," *Screen International*, no. 638 (February 6, 1988), 80; "Calendar of Feature Releases," *Film Journal* 90, no. 10 (October 1, 1987), 49; "Pictures: Film Starts," *Variety* 332, no. 1 (July 27, 1988), 6.

122. AP, Georg Szalai, "Ivan and Jason Reitman Draw Laughs," *Hollywood Reporter*, July 17, 2008, https://www.hollywoodreporter.com/business/business-news/ivan-jason-reitman-draw-laughs-115890; Warren Adler, "Film: How My Novel Was Almost 'Developed' Into Oblivion," *New York Times*, October 3, 1999, Section 2, 11; Leonard Klady, "Random Harts?," *Los Angeles Times*, May 10, 1987, 22; Marilyn Beck, Tribune Media Services Inc., "'Ghostbusters II' Filming Is to Begin Next Autumn for an '89 Release," *Chicago Tribune*, November 5, 1987, 10; Snowden, "Raising 'Twins,'" 20.

123. Peter Noble, "News: In Confidence," *Screen International*, no. 627 (November 21, 1987), 6; "Pictures: Hollywood Soundtrack," *Variety* 329, no. 8 (December 16, 1987), 17; "Pictures: New Film Starts," *Variety* 329, no. 7 (December 9, 1987), 26.

124. Robert Slater, *Ovitz: The Inside Story of Hollywood's Most Controversial Power Broker* (New York: McGraw-Hill, 1997), 145–46.

125. Perrin, *Mr. Mike*, 409; Meyers, "Bill Murray Filmography."

126. Ebert, "Bill Murray, 'Quick Change' Artist."

127. Clarke Taylor, "A Scrooge for the '80s," *Chicago Tribune*, November 20, 1988, 4.

128. Perrin, *Mr. Mike*, 408.

129. Taylor, "Scrooge for the '80s."

130. Thomas, "Bill Murray: Off the Wall."

131. Marianne Costantinou, "A Murray Christmas," *Philadelphia Daily News*, November 28, 1988, 48; Aljean Harmetz, "Willis Becomes $5 Million Man," *Globe and Mail*, February 19, 1988, D11; Richard Natale, "The Price Club," *American Film* 14, no. 8 (June 1, 1989), 42.

132. Patrick Goldstein, "'Ghostbusters II': Return of the Money-Making Slime," *Rolling Stone*, no. 553 (June 1, 1989), 56.

133. "Comedy Legend Bill Murray in 1984 Talks with Jimmy Carter," YouTube, posted by Jimmy Carter on May 2, 2020, https://www.youtube.com/watch?v=jP9JE9fjBgw.

134. Vadeboncouer, "Murray's Gift."

135. Goldstein, "'Ghostbusters II.'"

136. Natale, "Price Club"; Richard Natale, "The Return of the Hollywood Star System," *St. Louis Post-Dispatch*, August 30, 1989, 6; Mitchell Fink, "Page Two," *San Francisco Examiner*, June 29, 1989, B2

137. Ovitz, *Who Is Michael Ovitz?*, 135.

138. "FW: 'Ghostbusters'—Merchandising Revenues," Wikileaks, accessed November 23, 2020, https://wikileaks.org/sony/emails/emailid/26538.

139. "007 in the Keys Series: Headliners," *St. Petersburg Times*, May 30, 1988, 3D.

CHAPTER 5: SOMEWHERE IN BETWEEN

1. Morgan Gendel, "Sequel Materializes," *Los Angeles Times*, August 24, 1986, https://www.latimes.com/archives/la-xpm-1986-08-24-ca-17145-story.html; David Ehrenstein, "Ghostbusters Serious Silliness, Writer Says," *San Francisco Examiner*, June 16, 1989, C3; Adam Eisenberg, "Ghostbusters Revisited," *Cinefex*, no. 40 (November 1989), 5–6; Jim Emerson, "Harold Ramis: The Egghead Is the Reluctant 'Buster," *Orange County Register*, June 16, 1989, P08.

2. "Police Hiring Trails Crime Rise, Report Says," *New York Times*, August 28, 1989, A15; "Rise in Drug Arrests Is Reported in New York," *New York Times*, November 12, 1989, 46; David W. Dunlap, "In Enclave, Mayor's Race Hinges on Crime," *New York Times*, August 5, 1989, 27.

3. Harold Ramis and Dan Aykroyd, *Ghostbusters II* script, August 5, 1988, transcribed by Paul Rudoff, pp. 64, 79–80, 85, 87,100, archived at https://www.theraffon.net/~spookcentral/files/gb2_script_1988-08-05.pdf; Eisenberg, "Ghostbusters Revisited," 5–6; Emerson, "Harold Ramis"; James Boatwright, "A Shrink at Work: Couch Trip," *New York Times Book Review*, September 13, 1970, 59, 60; "The Couch Trip," AFI Catalog, accessed August 20, 2021, https://catalog.afi.com/Catalog/moviedetails/58631.

4. Tom Green, "Weaver, a Natural Out in the Wild," *USA Today*, September 20, 1988, 6D; Ian Spelling, "Bill Murray Ain't Afraid of No Ghosts!," *Starlog*, no. 140 (March 1989), 29–32.

5. Terry Kelleher, "Poltergeist-Popping Psychics Getting Slimed by 'Ghostbusters II,'" *Newsday*, June 14, 1989, 02; Spelling, "Bill Murray Ain't Afraid"; Green, "Weaver, a Natural."

6. Frank Sanello, "Weaver Combines Toughness and Class," *Chicago Sun-Times*, May 29, 1992, Weekend Plus section, 68; Stephen Prince, *A New Pot of Gold: Hollywood Under the Electronic Rainbow, 1980–1989* (Berkeley and Los Angeles: University of California Press, 2000), 22; Frank Sanello, "Heroic Stature," *Starlog Platinum* 2 (1994), 13; Michael Ovitz, *Who Is Michael Ovitz?* (New York: Portfolio/Penguin, 2018), 132; Liz Smith, "Bruce Willis as Young Frank Sinatra? Producer Hopes So," *Baltimore Sun*, April 27, 1987, 2B; Marilyn Beck, "Barr Autobiography Will Omit Adoption," *Daily News of Los Angeles*, June 15, 1989, L21; Rita Zekas, "Sigourney's Calling Her Accountant This Time," *Toronto Star*, June 20, 1989, G1; Peter H. Brown, "'Ghostbusters' and the Exorcists of Raunch," *Los Angeles Times*, January 24, 1985, 7; author interview with Frank Price, June 24, 2020; Linda Winer, "Beauty and the Beasts," *Newsday*, September 18, 1988, 28.

7. David Foil, "High-Grossing Movie 'Batman' May Not Turn a Profit," *The Advocate*, June 30, 1989, 1C; Arnold H. Lubasch, "Caine and Connery Sue Allied on Fee: 'Skimming' Alleged," *New York Times*, March 2, 1978, C16; Dale Pollock, "007 Zeroes In with a $225-Million Lawsuit," *Los Angeles Times*, August 31, 1984, OC_D1; "Sir Sean Connery: Obituaries," *Times*, November 2, 2020, 28.

8. Carol Blue and Al Delugach, "'Superman': Rare Look at Film Finances," *Los Angeles Times*, April 3, 1980, B1; "Brando Says Pact Was Broken, Sues 'Superman' Producers," *Los Angeles Times*, December 15, 1978, E5.

9. Sanello, "Weaver Combines"; Sanello, "Heroic Stature."

10. Ramis and Aykroyd, *Ghostbusters II* script, August 5, 1988, pp. 6–10, 24.

11. Ramis and Aykroyd, *Ghostbusters II* script, August 5, 1988, pp. 20–21; Kelleher, "Poltergeist-Popping Psychics."

12. Ramis and Aykroyd, *Ghostbusters II* script, August 5, 1988, pp. 3–5, 16, 20.

13. Ramis and Aykroyd, *Ghostbusters II* script, August 5, 1988, pp. 1–3, 92–93.

14. Ramis and Aykroyd, *Ghostbusters II* script, August 5, 1988, pp. 6–88.

15. Ramis and Aykroyd, *Ghostbusters II* script, August 5, 1988, pp. 54–56, 88–89.

16. Ramis and Aykroyd, *Ghostbusters II* script, August 5, 1988, pp. 30–34, 44–45, 94, 98.

17. Ramis and Aykroyd, *Ghostbusters II* script, August 5, 1988, pp. 34–35.

18. Ramis and Aykroyd, *Ghostbusters II* script, August 5, 1988, pp. 101–12.

19. Ehrenstein, "Ghostbusters Serious Silliness"; Kelleher, "Poltergeist-Popping Psychics."

20. Ramis and Aykroyd, *Ghostbusters II* script August 5, 1988; Walter Belcher, "A New Cartoon Lineup Is Scheduled for Saturday," *Tampa Tribune-Times*, September 4, 1988, 61; Kari Granville, "The Fight for Young Viewers Lends Variety to Fall Season," *Newsday*, September 4, 1988, 91; Harold Ramis and Dan Aykroyd, *Ghostbusters II* script, September 29, 1988, pp. 95–96.

21. Ramis and Aykroyd, *Ghostbusters II* script, September 29, 1988, pp. 75–78.

22. Lewis Beale, "Weaver's 'Mist'-ique: 'Gorillas' Star Brings Her Blend of Skill, Research to Latest Role," *Daily News of Los Angeles*, September 23, 1988, L11.

23. Harold Ramis and Dan Aykroyd, *Ghostbusters II* script, October 20, 1988, revision, pp. 82–86.

24. Marilyn Beck, "Mazursky Finds Home for 'Enemies' Project," *Daily News of Los Angeles*, August 5, 1988, L4; Liz Smith, "'Ghostbuster' Script Due for Reworking," *San Francisco Chronicle*, November 18, 1988, E1.

25. Aljean Harmetz, "How Studio Maneuvered 'Temptation' Into a Hit," *New York Times*, August 24, 1988, C19.

26. Lynn Snowden, "Raising 'Twins,'" *Rolling Stone*, no. 544 (January 26, 1989), 20.

27. Jay Carr, "The Scrooge of the '80s," *Boston Globe*, November 23, 1988, 21.

28. Roger Ebert, "Murray Christmas? Humbug!," *Daily News*, November 23, 1988, 39.

29. Marsha McCreadle, "A Dickens of a Film for Murray," *USA Today*, November 1, 1988, 2D.

30. Spelling, "Bill Murray Ain't Afraid," 32; Bruce Westbrook, "A Mean Murray—'Scrooged': Comedian Has Fun in Humdinger of an Updated Humbug Part," *Houston Chronicle*, November 27, 1988, 8.

31. Stephen Galloway, "Hollywood Freeway—Sean Penn by Any Other Name . . .," *Daily News of Los Angeles*, November 29, 1988, L15.

32. Sanello, "Weaver Combines"; Sanello, "Heroic Stature"; Liz Smith, "Weaver Will Do 'Ghostbusters II,'" *San Francisco Chronicle*, November 2, 1988, E1.

33. Kim Masters, "Who's That Guy with the Ghostbusters?," *Premiere*, July 1989, 80.

34. Roger Ebert, "'Gorillas in Mist' Buries Character of Dian Fossey," *Chicago Sun-Times*, September 23, 1988, 25; Jay Carr, "Oshima to be Honored at Dartmouth," *Boston Globe*, March 23, 1987, 10; Christopher Durang, "Sigourney's Gorilla War," special to the *Gazette*, July 31, 1988, D7; Julie Salamon, "Film: The Loves of a Primatologist," *Wall Street Journal*, September 22, 1988, 1; Jay Carr, "Gorillas Steal the Show," *Boston Globe*, September 23, 1988, 51; Kevin Thomas, "The Glories of 'Gorillas in the Mist,'" *Los Angeles Times*, September 23, 1988, 1.

35. Michael Sragow, "*Tootsie*: One Great Dame," The Criterion Collection, December 17, 2014, https://www.criterion.com/current/posts/3404-tootsie-one-great-dame; Author interview with Derek Osborn, January 6, 2022; Liz Smith, "'Ghostbuster' Script"; Charles Taylor, "Murray's All Scrooged-Up for the Holidays," *San Francisco Examiner*, November 25, 1988, C3.

36. Ehrenstein, "Ghostbusters Serious Silliness."

37. Joan E. Vadeboncouer, "Murray's Gift," *Syracuse Herald American*, November 20, 1988, 21.

38. Philip Wuntch, "The Lighter Side of Sigourney," *Dallas Morning News*, June 18, 1989, 1C.

39. Dennis Muren and Mark Vargo, "Ghostbusters II Update Report," November 16/17, 1988, 1–3.

40. Author interview with Ira Rosenstein, January 11, 2020; Tom Green, "Will the Limelight Follow the Slimelight?," *USA Today*, July 6, 1989, 2D; Bill Warren, "Ha-Ha-Horror Star," *Fangoria*, no. 150 (March 1996), 77–78.

41. Leslie Bennetts, "He Gets Wrapped Up in Other People's Lives," *New York Times*, December 17, 1982, C3.

42. Jan Benzel, "A Young American Dons Richard II's Crown," *New York Times*, June 28, 1987, H5; "MacNicol Faces the Dragon of Stardom," *Windsor Star*, June 26, 1981, 21; Leo Seligsohn, "Papp's Richard II Reigns in Central Park," *Newsday*, July 10, 1987, 9; Salem Alaton, "Unlikely Actor Brings Astonishing Wit to Shakespeare's Elusive King," *Globe and Mail*, July 11, 1987, C9; Bennetts, "He Gets Wrapped Up."

43. "Meryl's Choice: The Role of Sophie," *Globe and Mail*, December 10, 1982, E1; Benzel, "Young American Dons Richard II's Crown."

44. Associated Press, "Supporting Actors Steal the Show in 2 of the Summer's Biggest Hits," *Orlando Sentinel*, August 30, 1989, E4; Warren, "Ha-Ha-Horror Star"; Harold Ramis and Dan Aykroyd, *Ghostbusters II* script, November 27, 1988. Transcribed by Paul Rudoff. Archived at https://www.theraffon.net/spookcentral/media/sclib/files/gb2_script_1988-11-27.pdf.

45. Eisenberg, "Ghostbusters Revisited," 9.

46. John Hall, "Neutral Corner: Homburg Adds Spark to Vegas Title Card," *Los Angeles Times*, May 26, 1963, I8; Sid Ziff, "Beatnik of Ring," *Los Angeles Times*, September 19, 1963, B3.

47. Shaun Raviv, "The Hateful Life and Spiteful Death of the Man Who Was Vigo the Carpathian," Deadspin, October 27, 2015, https://deadspin.com/the-hateful-life-and-spiteful-death-of-the-man-who-was-1737376537; Tom Buckley, "At the Movies: Von Sydow, from Classics to the Comics," *New York Times*, December 19, 1980, C12; "Wilhelm von Homburg," *Times*, April 13, 2004, 25; *The Devil's Brigade*, directed by Andrew V. McLaglen, United Artists, 1968.

48. Harold Ramis and Dan Aykroyd, *Ghostbusters II* script, September 14, 1988, pp. 61–64; "YHS Ep. 84: Ghostbusters 2 Talk with Kurt Fuller!," *Yes Have Some* podcast, January 24, 2018, https://anchor.fm/yhspodcast/episodes/YHS-Ep--84-Ghostbusters-2-talk-with-Kurt-Fuller-eib4uv; Sylvie Drake, "Stage Review: A 'Kvetch' Worth Listening To," *Los Angeles Times*, March 18, 1986, L1; Don Shirley, "Stage Watch: Aerobics Injury Puts Lily, 'Life' on Hold; Berkoff's 'Kvetch' to Test the New York Jinx," *Los Angeles Times*, February 12, 1987, H3; Will Harris, "Kurt Fuller on Manhattan Love Story, Psych, and a Check from Hulk Hogan," AV Club, September 30, 2014, https://www.avclub.com/kurt-fuller-on-manhattan-love-story-psych-and-a-check-1798273565.

49. Emerson, "Harold Ramis."

50. "November 1988 Ghostbusters II Plate Schedule," first draft, October 17, 1988.

51. Ramis and Aykroyd, *Ghostbusters II* script, November 27, 1988, pp. 4–8, 29.

52. Ramis and Aykroyd, *Ghostbusters II* script, November 27, 1988, pp. 1–4.

53. Ramis and Aykroyd, *Ghostbusters II* script, November 27, 1988, pp. 34–36, 38–50.

54. Ramis and Aykroyd, *Ghostbusters II* script, November 27, 1988, pp. 13–14, 28–29, 65–67, 94, 103–4.

55. Ramis and Aykroyd, *Ghostbusters II* script, November 27, 1988, pp. 107–11, 115–16, 118–19, 124–25.

56. Author interview with Ned Gorman, February 3, 2021.

57. Ron Magid, "Busting Ghosts—Job That Keeps Returning," *American Cinematographer* 70, no. 12 (December 1989), 82; Eisenberg, "Ghostbusters Revisited," 25.

58. Author interview with Ned Gorman, February 3, 2021.

59. Magid, "Busting Ghosts," 82; Ramis and Aykroyd, *Ghostbusters II* script, September 14, 1988, pp. 89–90.
60. Author interview with Thom Enriquez, February 25, 2020.
61. Author interview with Ned Gorman, February 3, 2021.
62. Eisenberg, "Ghostbusters Revisited," 21.
63. Eisenberg, "Ghostbusters Revisited," 21.
64. Tim Lawrence, "There were a lot more scenes . . .," Facebook, February 28, 2016, https://www.facebook.com/photo/?fbid=10154254041480228&set=a.10151174877630228&comment_id=10156592076910228; Tim Lawrence, "Ghostbusters 2 (1989) Original Studio Copies—Storyboards: Slimer & Louis," WorthPoint, https://www.worthpoint.com/worthopedia/ghostbusters-1989-original-studio-1801041934; Ned Gorman, "Ghostbusters II Meeting Notes/Updates," January 6, 1989, p. 1; "Ghostbusters II (1989): Louis Tully Raw Footage of Slimer Scenes," YouTube, posted by Ghostbusters fan 64513 on July 15, 2020, https://www.youtube.com/watch?v=lNf6U6_eBwI.
65. Eisenberg, "Ghostbusters Revisited," 7–9; Andrew Turner, "Rolston Rolls Up Magic in 'Art People: The Pageant Portraits,'" *TCA Regional News*, July 3, 2021; "Laguna's Art Festival Will Be Opened Today," *Los Angeles Times*, June 29, 1935, 11; "'Last Supper' Offered in Living Picture as Laguna Opens Festival of Arts," *Los Angeles Times*, July 30, 1936, 8.
66. Erin McCarthy, "Creating Vigo the Carpathian, and the *Ghostbusters II* Ending Fans Never Saw," Mental Floss, July 11, 2016, https://www.mentalfloss.com/article/71284/creating-vigo-carpathian-and-ghostbusters-ii-ending-you-never-saw.
67. Eisenberg, "Ghostbusters Revisited," 9. McCarthy, "Creating Vigo the Carpathian"; author interview with Ned Gorman, February 3, 2021.
68. Author interview with Ned Gorman, February 3, 2021.
69. Author interview with Christine Larson-Nitzsche, November 18, 2019.
70. "Pictures: New Film Starts," *Variety* 330, no. 7 (March 9, 1988), 22; Benjamin Bergery, "Reflections 5: Laszlo Kovacs, ASC," *American Cinematographer* 69, no. 11 (November 1988), 58; Adam Eisenberg, "Ghostbusters II for Laughs & Liberty," *American Cinematographer* 70, no. 8 (August 1989), 58–68.
71. Magid, "Busting Ghosts," 86, 88.
72. Eisenberg, "Ghostbusters Revisited," 42.
73. Eisenberg, "Ghostbusters Revisited," 34, 37.
74. Magid, "Busting Ghosts," 84, 86.
75. Author interview with Christine Larson-Nitzsche, November 18, 2019.
76. Author interview with Kim Masters, May 8, 2019.
77. Masters, "Who's That Guy?," 75.
78. Author interview with Kim Masters, May 8, 2019.
79. Masters, "Who's That Guy?," 80.
80. Author interview with Peter Giuliano, April 22, 2020; *Ghostbusters II* Call Sheet, Monday, December 12, 1988, p. 2; *Ghostbusters II* Call Sheet, Tuesday, December 13, 1988, p. 2; *Ghostbusters II* Call Sheet, Wednesday, December 14, 1988, p. 2.
81. "Bill MacSems." Internet Movie Database. Accessed March 20, 2021. https://www.imdb.com/name/nm0534356/?ref_=fn_al_nm_1.
82. Hope Parrish, email to author, March 25, 2021.
83. Eisenberg, "Ghostbusters Revisited," 6–7.
84. Eisenberg, "Ghostbusters Revisited," 37.
85. Jim Slotek, "Frowning and Clowning," *Toronto Sun*, July 8, 1990, S6.
86. Christina Radish, "Bill Murray Gets Candid on 'Ghostbusters' Sequels, 'Groundhog Day,' Working with Wes Anderson & Sofia Coppola and

More," Collider, April 5, 2021, https://collider.com/bill-murray-interview-ghostbusters-groundhog-day-wes-anderson.

87. Author interview with Christine Larson-Nitzsche, November 18, 2019.
88. Author interview with Rebecca Baehler, June 30, 2021.
89. Glen Ade Brown, "*Scrooged*: Meeting Bill Murray / Michael Chapman: Filmmaker," Web of Stories, recorded May 2004, https://www.webofstories.com/play/michael.chapman/66; Glen Ade Brown, "Bill Murray and *Quick Change* / Michael Chapman: Film-maker," Web of Stories, recorded May 2004, https://www.webofstories.com/play/michael.chapman/67.
90. Lou Cedrone, "Sigourney Weaver—Actress Was Reluctant to Take Role in 'Working Girl,'" *Tulsa World*, January 5, 1989, C8.
91. Gene Triplett, "Sigourney's Charm No Ghostly Illusion," *The Oklahoman*, June 17, 1984; Jack Matthews, "Newman Gets 7th Chance; Will He Finally Get Oscar?," *Los Angeles Times*, February 11, 1987, 1; Michael Cieply, "'Rain Main' Given 8 Oscar Nominations; Sigourney 2," *Los Angeles Times*, February 15, 1989, G1.
92. Charles Champlin, "Does Weaver Have a Shot at Oscar History?," *Los Angeles Times*, March 16, 1989, 4; Patrick Goldstein, "'Ghostbusters II': Return of the Money-Making Slime," *Rolling Stone*, no. 553 (June 1, 1989), 54.
93. Susan Stark, "'I Think of This as the Boys' Movie,' Sigourney Weaver Says Airily," *USA Today*, June 20, 1989.
94. Masters, "Who's That Guy?," 81; Goldstein, "'Ghostbusters II,'" 64.
95. Masters, "Who's That Guy?," 78, 81.
96. Snowden, "Raising 'Twins,'" 20.
97. Masters, "Who's That Guy?," 78.
98. Masters, "Who's That Guy?," 81.
99. Eisenberg, "Ghostbusters Revisited," 6–7.
100. "Not Necessarily a Nerd, Rick Moranis Insists," *Deseret News*, June 23, 1989, W1.
101. Ernest Tucker, "Fellow Ghostbusters Make Ernie Hudson Feel at Home—Finally," *Chicago Sun-Times*, June 18, 1989, 3.
102. Jim Sullivan, "Bill, Dan, Harold and . . . Ernie?," *Boston Globe*, June 14, 1989, 81.
103. Eisenberg, "Ghostbusters Revisited," 28.
104. Sullivan, "Bill, Dan, Harold"
105. Green, "Will the Limelight Follow?"
106. Tucker, "Fellow Ghostbusters."
107. "Growing Up Helps Brown Soar Up Record Charts," *Jet* 75, no. 10 (December 5, 1988), 58; Jim Miller, "Scifi Street Sounds," *Newsweek* 101, no. 25 (June 20, 1983), 80; Deborah Wilker, "Bobby Brown Continues His Surprising Chart Run," *Sun Sentinel*, December 9, 1988, 19; Steve Morse, "Brown Breaks Out with 'Monster' Album," *Boston Globe*, October 7, 1988, 49; Rob Tannenbaum, "Bobby Brown's Uneasy Passage," *Rolling Stone*, no. 560 (September 7, 1989), 68, 71.
108. Brett Milano, "Bobby Brown's Garden Party," *Boston Globe*, April 27, 1989, 77, 79.
109. "Band Enjoys Reunion at Junos," *Calgary Herald*, April 30, 1989, D12.
110. Kevin C. Johnson, "Listen to This Group 'After 7,'" *USA Today*, January 12, 1990.
111. Ronin Ro, *Raising Hell: The Reign, Ruin, and Redemption of Run-D.M.C.* (New York: Amistad, 2005), 222–23.
112. Darcy MacDonald, "We Interviewed DMC of Run DMC," Cult MTL, February 17, 2016, https://cultmtl.com/2016/02/run-dmc-darryl-mcdaniels.
113. Ellie Gibson, "Eurogamer Meets Ray Parker Jr.," Eurogamer, March 12, 2009, https://www.eurogamer.net/articles/eurogamer-meets-ray-parker-jr-interview.
114. Mike Boehm, "Getting Darker: Oingo Boingo's a Bit More Serious, but Still Up for Halloween," *Los Angeles Times*, October 25, 1990, OC6.

115. Marcus Mabry and Rhonda Adams, "How to Sell a Soundtrack: First, Ignore the Movie," *Newsweek* 114, no. 9 (August 28, 1989), 47.

116. John McDonough, "'Funny Music' Maestro Gets Serious," *Wall Street Journal*, November 8, 1990, A22.

117. Robert Palmer, "Pop: Randy Edelman," *New York Times*, January 26, 1978, C19; Evonne Coutros, "The Guy Who Knows the Score," *Record*, May 18, 1994, 13; Hannah Brown, "Randy Edelman Knows the Score," *Jerusalem Post*, June 28, 2010, 24.

118. "Pictures: New Film Starts," *Variety* 333, no. 6 (November 30, 1988), 6; "Film Production," *Variety* 333, no. 13 (January 18, 1989), 30; Spelling, "Bill Murray Ain't Afraid."

119. Richard Gold, "Armed with Pricey Sequels and High-Stakes Originals, Studios Enter Seasonal Fray," *Variety* 335, no. 6 (May 24, 1989), 13.

120. Goldstein, "'Ghostbusters II,'" 54.

121. "Film: 1989 U.S. Film Releases," *Variety* 334, no. 5 (February 22, 1989), 92; Eisenberg, "Ghostbusters Revisited," 25.

122. "BOF Interview with Michael Uslan: Getting the Rights to Batman on Film," YouTube, posted on December 12, 2018, by by Batman on Film, https://www .youtube.com/watch?v=3oOCd57ULmA&t=295s.

123. Nancy Griffin and Kim Masters, *Hit & Run: How Jon Peters and Peter Guber Took Sony for a Ride in Hollywood* (New York: Simon & Schuster, 1996), 107, 114, 165.

124. Sal Manna, "Ivan Reitman: Magic, Meatballs and Making Movies," *Starlog*, no. 85 (August 1984), 51, 65.

125. "A Watershed of Surreal Moments," *The Statesman*, June 28, 2014.

126. Griffin and Masters, *Hit & Run*, 165–66.

127. Steven Rea, "Keaton as Batman? Great Scott! They Say," *Philadelphia Inquirer*, July 24, 1988, I3.

128. Frank DeCaro, "Holy Trend Setting, Batman!," *Newsday*, August 31, 1988, 5.

129. Jill Young Miller, "Comic Hero Banished to Bat Grave," *Sun Sentinel*, October 22, 1988, 1A.

130. Joe Morgenstern, "Tim Burton, Batman and the Joker," *New York Times Magazine*, April 9, 1989, 46, 50, 53, https://www.nytimes.com/1989/04/09/ magazine/tim-burton-batman-and-the-joker.html; Griffin and Masters, *Hit & Run*, 171; Susan Spillman, "Fans Batty for Glimpse of 'Batman,'" *USA Today*, February 24, 1989, 1A.

131. Eisenberg, "Ghostbusters Revisited," 25.

132. Marilyn Beck, "Spring Release Date Forces Haste in Filming of 'Ghostbusters II,'" *Austin American Statesman*, February 13, 1989, D7; *Ghostbusters II* Call Sheet, Tuesday, April 4, 1989, p. 1; *Ghostbusters II* Call Sheet, Thursday, April 27, 1989, p. 1.

133. Michael Walker, "High Atop Mt. Goofiness," *Los Angeles Times*, November 20, 1994, 86; Joseph McCabe, "Set 'Em Up Joe," *The Complete SFX Guide to Ghostbusters*, 2016, 74–75; "Ghostbusters II; Buzz," *Sunday Times*, June 18, 1989.

134. Eisenberg, "Ghostbusters Revisited," 22, 25.

135. Beck, "Spring Release Date"; Jody *Oliver v. Columbia Pictures Industries et al.*, Supreme Court of the State of New York, Case No. 011618-1991, Verified Complaint, filed May 23, 1991, p. 4; author interview with Peter Giuliano, January 14, 2020.

136. John Stanley, "Slime-Time Slayers—'Ghostbusters II': Bustin'," *San Francisco Chronicle*, June 11, 1989, 19; Stacy Jenel Smith, "Second Time Around," *Los Angeles Times*, May 21, 1989, M24.

137. Daniel Cerone, "A High Profile for a Hero of the Masses," *Los Angeles Times*, June 18, 1989, https://www.latimes.com/archives/la-xpm-1989-06-18-ca-3771-story.html.
138. Barbara Beck, "A Batload of Bataphernalia," *Philadelphia Daily News*, May 2, 1989, 37.
139. Cerone, "High Profile for a Hero."
140. Nikki Finke, "Industry Gossip Takes Over as Star-Hungry ShoWest Winds Down," *Los Angeles Times*, February 18, 1989, J5.
141. Aljean Harmetz, "Boom Summer for Film Sequels," *New York Times*, May 3, 1989, C19; Paul Fahri, "Hollywood's Hit Formula: Sequels," *Washington Post*, May 9, 1989, B01.
142. Tom Matthews, "It's Slime Time Again," *BoxOffice* 124, no. 7 (July 1, 1989), 13.
143. Goldstein, "'Ghostbusters II,'" 56.
144. David Giammarco, "Get Ready for Prime Slime," *Toronto Sun*, May 28, 1989, S14.

CHAPTER 6: I HATE THAT PAINTING

1. Joe Leydon, *Houston Post*. "They're Back—And Badder Than Ever!" *St. Petersburg Times*. June 16, 1989, 16.
2. Jack Garner, Gannett News Service. "The Ghostbusters Take a Reality Break." *Tucson Citizen*. June 13, 1989, 3C.
3. Blackadar, Bruce. "Ghostbusters II." *Toronto Star*. June 17, 1989, H1, H10.
4. Blackadar, Bruce. "Ghostbusters II." *Toronto Star*. June 17, 1989, H1, H10.
5. Leydon, Joe. "They're Back—And Badder Than Ever!" *St. Petersburg Times*. June 16, 1989, 16.
6. Garner, Jack. "Ghostbusters II: Why'd the Gang Decide to Do a Sequel? For Fun, They Say." *The Journal News*. June 14, 198, C3.
7. Kobel, Peter. "Slime Time II: 'Ghostbusters' Jumps Laughs-First into a Sequel-Squeezed Sweepstakes." *Chicago Tribune*. June 18, 198, 10.
8. Garner, Jack. "Ghostbusters II: Why'd the Gang Decide to Do a Sequel? For Fun, They Say." *The Journal News*. June 14, 198, C3.
9. Gail Shister, "Aykroyd Joins Critics of Book on Belushi," *Philadelphia Inquirer*, May 30, 1984, C7; Stephanie Mansfield, "The Hollywood Funny Business," *Washington Post*, January 19, 1988, D01.
10. Nina J. Easton and Jack Matthews, "Another Chapter in the Strange Odyssey of 'Wired,'" *Los Angeles Times*, April 13, 1989, J1E.
11. Garner, Jack. "Ghostbusters II: Why'd The Gang Decide to Do a Sequel? For Fun, They Say." *The Journal News*. June 14, 19, C3.
12. Garner, "Ghostbusters II."
13. Lou Cedrone, "'Ghostbusters' Star Makes His Way in Good Humor," *Evening Sun*, June 6, 1984, B4.
14. Stephen Hunter, "Ghost Busters II: Flaccid-thed Murray and His Friends Try to Explain Movie's Philosophy," *Baltimore Sun*, June 16, 1989, F4; Garner, "Ghostbusters II"; Philip Wuntch, "Bill Murray Finally Speaks; Between Jokes, Actor Has Some Things to Say About New Movie," *Ottawa Citizen*, June 19, 1989, A17; Vincent Canby, "Comedy That Smirks at Itself," *New York Times*, April 16, 1989, H1; Sigourney Weaver, "Movie Comedians: The Virtues of Standing Apart," *New York Times*, May 7, 1989, H3.
15. Kobel, "Slime Time II"; Garner, "Ghostbusters II."
16. Joanna Connors, "Ghostbusters Slimes Movie Reviewers," *Plain Dealer*, June 17, 1989.
17. Nina J. Easton, "A Smashing Opening Day for 'Indiana,'" *Los Angeles Times*, May 26, 1989, E1, E30.

18. Nina Easton, "'Indiana Jones' Box-Office Champ," *Asbury Park Press*, June 1, 1989, D10.

19. Easton, "Smashing Opening Day"; Susan Spillman, "'Indiana' Whips the $100M Box Office Record," *USA Today*, June 9, 1989, 1D.

20. Nina J. Easton, "Paramount Scales Box-Office Heights," *Los Angeles Times*, June 13, 1989, E1; Jefferson Graham, "'Star Trek V' Voyages to No. 1," *USA Today*, June 13, 1989, 1D.

21. Mike McGrady, "Movie Reviews: It's Worse Than That: He's Dead, Jim," *Newsday*, June 9, 1989, 3; Roger Ebert, "'Star Trek' Crew Bombs with Slow Fifth Chapter," *Chicago Sun-Times*, June 9, 1989, 33; Mike Clark, "'Trek V': A Low Warp Factor," *USA Today*, June 9, 1989, 4D; "'Kids from Any Planet Would Love It,' Young Star-Gazers Say," *Gazette*, June 10, 1989, H1; Aaron Curtiss, "Beam Them Aboard, Scotty: 'Trekkors' Already in Line for 'Star Trek V: The Final Frontier,'" *Fresno Bee*, June 7, 1989, A10; Troy Moon, "Full-Blooded Trekkies Make Tracks for 'Final Frontier,'" *Pensacola News Journal*, June 10, 1989, D1.

22. Bob Quick, "Even in Santa Fe, They're Getting in Line for the Blockbuster Movies This Summer," *Santa Fe New Mexican*, June 21, 1989, A3; Pat Berman, "Some Towns Won't Show Disney Movies," *State*, August 18, 1989, 4D.

23. John Griffin, "Comic Sequel Set to be a Gross-Buster," *The Gazette*, June 16, 1989, C1; Bob Strauss, "Boom, Bust at Box Office," *Daily News of Los Angeles*, August 31, 1989, L19.

24. Ian Spelling, "Bill Murray Ain't Afraid of No Ghosts!," *Starlog*, no. 140 (March 1989), 29–32.

25. Richard De Atley, Associated Press, "'Ghostbusters II' Delivers Best Opening Gate," *Tyler Courier-Times*, June 20, 1989, 12; Claudia Puig, "Record-Busting Opening for 'Ghostbusters II,'" *Los Angeles Times*, June 20, 1989, https://www .latimes.com/archives/la-xpm-1989-06-20-ca-2613-story.html.

26. David Kehr, "'Ghostbusters' Sequel Missing Original's Charm," *Chicago Tribune*, June 16, 1989, 28.

27. David Ansen, "Who's Sliming Who?," *Newsweek* 113, no. 26 (June 26, 1989), 68.

28. Joanna Connors, "This Time, Don't Call on Ghostbusters," *Plain Dealer*, June 17, 1989, C1.

29. Jay Carr, "Murray's Back in the Slime," *Boston Globe*, June 16, 1989, 33.

30. Mick LaSalle, "Too Much Fluff, Not Enough Slime," *San Francisco Chronicle*, June 16, 1989, E1.

31. Perry Clark, "Give Up the Ghost, Busters," *St. Petersburg Times*, June 19, 1989, 1D.

32. "Pics and Pans Review: Ghostbusters II," *People*, July 3, 1989, https://people .com/archive/picks-and-pans-review-ghostbusters-ii-vol-32-no-1.

33. "Batman/Honey, I Shrunk the Kids/Tummy Trouble/Ghostbusters II/Kung-Fu Master," *Siskel & Ebert*, produced by Buena Vista Television, June 24, 1989.

34. Hal Hinson, "Ghostbusters Again: Murray & Co. in a Spirited Sequel," *Washington Post*, June 16, 1989, B01.

35. Jay Boyar, "Ghostbusters II Brings the Charm Back to Life," *Orlando Sentinel*, June 17, 1989, F1.

36. Vincent Canby, "Review/Film: Citywide Bad Temper: Better Call In Ghostbusters!," *New York Times*, June 16, 1989, C5, https://www.nytimes.com/1989/06/16/ movies/review-film-citywide-bad-temper-better-call-in-ghostbusters.html.

37. Lou Lumenick, "The Hits Are Limited Success Stories," *The Record*, June 29, 1989, C13.

38. "'Batman' Breaks Box-Office Records," *Santa Cruz Sentinel*, June 27, 1989, D6; Matt Spetalnick, Reuters, "Holy Box Office, Batman! Caped Crusader Movie Sequel Sets Record for Opening Weekend," *Philadelphia Daily News*, June 22,

1992, 6; Aljean Harmetz, N.Y. Times News Service, "'Batman' Dominates for Second Weekend," *Town Talk*, July 7, 1989, C6.

39. United Press International, "'Batman' Surpasses $100 Million at Box Office," July 3, 1989; Bob Strauss, "While 'Batman Passes $200 Million in Record Time, 'Turner' Is Top Dog," *Daily News of Los Angeles*, August 1, 1989, L19.

40. Roger Ebert, "'Batman' Looks Great but Lacks Substance," *Chicago Sun-Times*, June 23, 1989, 37.

41. Jack Mathews, "Batman, the Gamble: Warner Bros. Is Betting Big Money That a 50-Year-Old Comic Book Vigilante Will Be a 'Hero for Our Times,'" *Los Angeles Times*, June 18, 1989, https://www.latimes.com/archives/la-xpm-1989-06-18-ca-3768-story.html.

42. Mathews, "Batman, the Gamble."

43. Tom Green, "Weaver, a Natural Out in the Wild," *USA Today*, September 20, 1988, 6D; David Ehrenstein, *Los Angeles Herald Examiner*, "'Ghostbusters' Serious Silliness, Writer Says," *San Francisco Examiner*, June 16, 1989, C3; Terry Kelleher, "Poltergeist-Popping Psychics Getting Slimed by 'Ghostbusters II,'" *Newsday*, June 14, 1989, 02.

44. Harold Ramis and Dan Aykroyd, *Ghostbusters II* script, September 29, 1988, pp. 110–11.

45. Matt Paprocki, "How the Director of Ghostbusters Crossed the Streams of Politics and Comedy," Polygon, June 18, 2019, https://www.polygon.com/2019/6/18/18682991/ghostbusters-original-reboot-sequel-director-ivan-reitman-interview.

46. Ellen Farley, "Hollywood's Hottest Comedy Director Takes a Break: Movies: After 'Twins' and 'Ghostbusters II,' Producer-Director Ivan Reitman Decides There's More to Film Than Laughs," *Los Angeles Times*, December 5, 1989, https://www.latimes.com/archives/la-xpm-1989-12-05-ca-313-story.html.

47. Marc Shapiro, "Fantasymaker," *Starlog*, no. 164 (March 1991), 40.

48. Author interview with Thom Enriquez, February 25, 2020.

49. Roger Ebert, "Watch Out for Comical Trio of 'Ghostbusters,'" *The Record*, January 29, 1984, E3.

50. Joe Baltake, "Give Up the Ghost, Busters," *Sacramento Bee*, June 17, 1989, Scene section, 1; Ansen, "Who's Sliming Who?"; Canby, "Citywide Bad Temper."

51. Bill O'Conner, "Sequel Way Off the Slime Mark," *Akron Beacon Journal*, June 17, 1989, B4.

52. Rene Jordan, "*Ghostbusters II* a Gooey Good Time," *Miami Herald*, June 16, 1989, 5H.

53. PKH/SH, "Reviews: Ghostbusters II," *Screen International*, no. 710 (June 24, 1989), 26–27.

54. Pauline Kael, "The Current Cinema," *New Yorker*, July 10, 1989, 85.

55. Kory Grow, "Big Black on 'Songs About F-king' at 30: 'We Wanted to Make Filthy Music,'" *Rolling Stone*, September 8, 2017, https://www.rollingstone.com/music/music-features/big-black-on-songs-about-f-king-at-30-we-wanted-to-make-filthy-music-197265.

56. "'Batman' Breaks Box-Office Records," *Santa Cruz Sentinel*.

57. Jack Mathews, "Honey, They've Enlarged the Field," *Los Angeles Times*, June 28, 1989, 1.

58. Daniel Cerone, "Can Roger Rabbit Sweeten 'Honey?,'" *Los Angeles Times*, June 17, 1989, E1, E9.

59. "The Oprah Winfrey Show: Cast of Ghostbusters II—June 1989," YouTube, posted by Blu-ray Extras on August 14, 2020, https://www.youtube.com/watch?v=t_3nZBwsKqE.

60. "Rick Moranis @ David Letterman #2, SCTV, 1989," YouTube, posted by fivealex2010 (n.d.), https://www.youtube.com/watch?v=sKs-m-ac53w&t=364s.

61. Castewar, "Interview: Rick Moranis," Proton Charging, May 27, 2006, http://protoncharging.com/2006/05/27/interview-rick-moranis.

62. Roger Ebert, "In a Violent Cinema Summer, Bill Murray Hopes Filmgoers Will Enjoy a Comic 'Change,'" *Chicago Sun-Times*, July 8, 1990, 1.

63. Philip Wuntch, "Bill Murray's Detour to Sanity," *Dallas Morning News*, July 9, 1990, 1C; Christina Radish, "Bill Murray Gets Candid on 'Ghostbusters' Sequels, 'Groundhog Day,' Working with Wes Anderson & Sofia Coppola and More," Collider, April 5, 2021, https://collider.com/bill-murray-interview-ghostbusters-groundhog-day-wes-anderson; Hal Hinson, "Prince of the Put-On," *Washington Post*, July 13, 1990, C01.

64. Richard Christiansen, "Harold Ramis: The New King of Comedy," *Dallas Morning News*, February 6, 1993, 5C.

65. "Single Reviews," *Billboard* 101, no. 22 (June 3, 1989), 75; "Prince's 'Bat' LP Goes Multi-Plat," *Variety* 336, no. 8 (September 6, 1989), 80.

66. "Bobby Brown—On Our Own (Ghostbusters 2 Soundtrack)," YouTube, posted by Mostly Simpsons on July 26, 2016, https://www.youtube.com/watch?v=e2sLeruRZio.

67. *Moore v. Columbia Pictures Industries, Inc.*, 972 F. 2d 939, Court of Appeals, 8th Circuit 1992, https://scholar.google.com/scholar_case?-case=3465844067806940715; Associated Press, "Minneapolis Man Sues Over Song in 'Ghostbusters II,'" *St. Cloud Times*, October 3, 1989, 10.

68. Jon Bream, "Exotic Storm Will Release Debut Album," *Star Tribune*, August 15, 1986, 6C.

69. "Reviews: Recommended: Exotic Storm," *Billboard*, October 18, 1986, 94; Jon Bream, "Premature Precipitation," *Star Tribune*, October 24, 1986, 6C.

70. "Minneapolis: Copyright Lawsuit Dismissed," *Star Tribune*, June 29, 1991, 3B.

71. "Court Affirms Dismissal of Song Lawsuit," *Star Tribune*, August 15, 1992, 3B.

72. *Moore v. Columbia Pictures Industries, Inc.*

73. "Court Affirms Dismissal," *Star Tribune*.

74. *Moore v. Columbia Pictures Industries, Inc.*

75. "Court Rejects Copyright Infringement Claim Against Writers of 'On Our Own' Due to Lack of Substantial Similarity," *Entertainment Law Reporter*, edited by Lionel S. Sobel, vol. 14, no. 9 (February 1993).

76. *Jody Oliver v. Columbia Pictures Industries et al.*, Supreme Court of the State of New York, Case No. 011618-1991, Verified Complaint, filed May 23, 1991, pp. 4–7; *Jody Oliver v. Columbia Pictures Industries et al.*, Verified Bill of Particulars, undated, pp. 1–4.

77. *Jody Oliver v. Columbia Pictures Industries et al.*, Verified Answer, undated, p. 2.

78. "Motion Details," The Supreme Court Records On-Line Library, Index No. 108329-1993, accessed November 27, 2021, https://iapps.courts.state.ny.us/iscroll/MotionDetails.jsp?IndexNo=108329-1993&CID=004.

79. Rhonda Y. Williams, "Hardee's Says Kids Gulp Toy Batteries," *Charlotte Observer*, July 11, 1989, 1C.

80. "Hardee's Recalling 2.8 Million Toys It Sold," *Patriot-News*, July 25, 1989, A9; Rhonda Y. Williams, "Swallowed Batteries Lead Hardee's to Recall Toys," *Charlotte Observer*, July 15, 1989, 1B; Pat Butler, "Few People Requesting Refunds for Ghostblasters," *The State*, July 28, 1989, 2B.

81. Roger Ebert, "The Unkindest Cut—Unjust System Stamps Out 'Wild Bunch,'" *Chicago Sun-Times*, April 11, 1993, Show section, 3; Leslie Doolittle "Really Most Sincerely, Still a Munchkin," *Orlando Sentinel*, October 29, 1996, A2.

82. Tawanda Williams, "It Was '3 Men, a Baby & a Ghost,'" *Pittsburgh Post-Gazette*, August 24, 1990, D1.

83. Mike Spohr, "17 Shocking Urban Legends About Famous Movies—And Whether They Were True," Buzzfeed, October 2, 2021, https://www.buzzfeed.com/mikespohr/17-shocking-urban-legends-about-famous-movies-and-whether.

84. "GB II Slimer Ending Myth," GBFans message board, posted by GuyX on October 21, 2014, https://www.gbfans.com/forum/viewtopic.php?t=38330; Paul Rudoff, "Paul's Ghostbusters II Alternate Scenes Theory," Spook Central, December 4, 2016, https://www.theraffon.net/spookcentral/2016/12/04/ghostbusters-ii-alternate-scenes-theory.

85. Harold Ramis and Dan Aykroyd, *Ghostbusters II* script, revised November 27, 1988, line 136. Transcribed by Paul Rudoff. Archived at https://www.theraffon.net/spookcentral/media/sclib/files/gb2_script_1988-11-27.pdf; Rudoff, "Paul's Ghostbusters II."

86. *Ghostbusters II* Call Sheet, Monday, December 5, 1988, p. 1; *Ghostbusters II* Shooting Calendar: December.

87. Author interview with Ned Gorman, December 7, 2021.

88. Author interview with Robin Shelby, December 13, 2021.

89. Rudoff, "Paul's Ghostbusters II"; "GB II Slimer Ending," GBFans; author interview with Alex Newborn, December 4, 2021.

90. Michael Walker, "High Atop Mt. Goofiness," *Los Angeles Times*, November 20, 1994, 86; Joseph McCabe, "Set 'Em Up Joe," *The Complete SFX Guide to Ghostbusters*, 2016, 74–75; "Ghostbusters II; Buzz," *Sunday Times*, June 18, 1989.

91. Author interview with Ned Gorman, February 3, 2021.

92. Steve Pennells, "Cinema's Holy Grail," *Sunday Star Times*, February 14, 2005, C5; "Muestran en Buenos Aires las escenas perdidas del 'Metrópolis' de Lang," EFE News Service, July 3, 2008; "Un des premiers films de Georges Méliès a été retrouvé," *Le Monde*, March 26, 2004, 26.

93. Rob Salem, "Dreaming of Genie," *Toronto Star*, March 19, 2005, 10; Alex Strachan, "Saying Yes to Hosting the Genies Was a 'No-Brainer,' Says Canuck Comedienne Andrea Martin," *CanWest News*, March 16, 2005, 1.

94. Beverly Phillips, "This Year's Rage Is Video Game Called Nintendo," *The State*, November 20, 1988, Business section, 1G; "Mutant Ninja Turtles Rare as Hen's Teeth," *New Hampshire Union Leader*, December 17, 1989, 1A.

95. Harry F. Waters, "Bill Targets National Disgrace: Brain-Rotting 'Kidvid' Borders on Child Abuse," *Rocky Mountain News*, January 4, 1990, 4; James J. Kilpatrick, "Congress Has No Business in Children's TV," *Buffalo News*, January 2, 1990, B3; Associated Press, "Bill Limiting Ads on Children's TV Will Become Law," *Sun Sentinel*, October 18, 1990, 3A.

96. "Movie Rape Scene Airs on Children's TV Show," *News-Pilot*, September 14, 1989, C10.

97. "State Sides," *Houston Chronicle*, September 17, 1989, State section, 2.

98. "Jail Inspector Blames Illness on Crowding," *Austin American-Statesman*, September 14, 1989, B3.

99. Grey Hall, "Top Ten Irritable Cartoon Characters," *Entertainment Examiner*, November 3, 2013; Bloomberg Business News, "Coca-Cola Energizing Hi-C Brand," *Plain Dealer*, February 7, 1995, 2C.

100. Knight-Ridder News Service, "People, Etc.," *Baltimore Sun*, June 18, 1989, 4H; Bloomberg Business News, "Coca-Cola Energizing"; Catherine Newton, "An American Family Breakfast," *Fort Worth Star-Telegram*, May 16, 2000, Life & Arts section, 1.

101. Bonnie Tandy and Carolyn Wyman, "Hi-C Ecto Cooler Lacks a Distinctive Flavor," *New Haven Register*, July 19, 1989, 27.

102. Phil Rosenthal, "Dateline: 'Saturday Night,'" *Daily News of Los Angeles*, September 21, 1989, L12; "Saturday Night LIVES!," *Newsweek* 114, no. 13 (September 25, 1989), 40–45.

103. Lynn Geller and Laila Nabulsi, "Mr. Mike," *SPIN* 5, no. 2 (May 1, 1989), 69.

104. Gary Mullinax, "Now That Mary Gross . . .," *USA Today*, March 21, 1989.

105. Celia Rivenbark Rich, "Aykroyd Knows the ABC's of Movies," *Daily Breeze*, September 24, 1988, E5.

106. Carole Kass, "'Caddyshack II' Shanks," *Richmond Times-Dispatch*, July 23, 1988, B8; Mick LaSalle, "Country Club Spoof Is Way Under Par," *San Francisco Chronicle*, July 23, 1988, C3; Rita Kempley, "'Caddyshack II': Double Bogey," *Washington Post*, July 22, 1988, D7.

107. Rich, "Aykroyd Knows the ABC's."

108. Celia Brady, "Rolling Heads," *Spy*, March 1988, 122; Celia Brady, "Does Oscar Have a Naughty Little Secret?," *Spy*, June 1991, 20.

109. Mike Cidoni, "Stretching 'Daisy' to Fit Dan," *USA Today*, January 15, 1990; John Jarvis, "Some Questions About Oscars," *Marion Star*, February 19, 1990, 4.

110. Associated Press, "Oscar Wild—'Daisy' Drives Home a Winner," *Austin American-Statesman*, March 27, 1990, A1.

111. Barry Koltnow, "Conehead's Revenge," *Orange County Register*, July 22, 1993, F04.

112. "1989 Top Grossers," *Variety* 338, no. 1 (January 10, 1990), 13; Stephen Prince, *A New Pot of Gold: Hollywood Under the Electronic Rainbow, 1980–1989* (Berkeley and Los Angeles: University of California Press, 2000), 448.

113. Patricia Dobson, "Ghostbusters Bites Back," *Screen International*, no. 734 (December 9, 1989), 52; "Caped Crusader Out-Foxed in Tokyo," *Globe and Mail*, December 28, 1989, C7; Don Groves, "Oz, U.K. Ponder Potential of Minogue's 'Delinquents'; 'Future II' Still Steaming," *Variety* 337, no. 13 (January 3, 1990), 11.

114. Don Groves, "State Grip on Films Eases in the East," *Variety* 339, no. 4 (May 2, 1990), 36.

115. "'Ghostbusters II' a Thrilla in Manila Also a Theater-Filla," *Variety* 336, no. 2 (July 26, 1989), 24.

116. Patrick Goldstein, "Return of the Money-Making Slime," *Rolling Stone*, no. 553 (June 1, 1989), 54; Knight-Ridder News Service, "People, Etc."; Dave Mawson, "The Summer Sequels Are Here; There Are Eight, Count 'Em, Eight, and They Run From II to VIII," *Telegram & Gazette*, May 28, 1989, 12; "Who You Gonna Call?," *The Economist* 312, no. 7622 (September 30, 1989), 110; "A Star Is Bought," *The Economist* 313, no. 7634 (December 23, 1989), 15; Bob Strauss, "Boom, Bust at Box Office," *Daily News of Los Angeles*, August 31, 1989, L19.

117. Lou Lumenick, "Movie Talk: Sequels Have a Difficult Act to Follow," *The Record*, August 3, 1989, E8.

118. Farley, "Hollywood's Hottest Comedy Director ."

119. "Film: $100-Million-Club Members to Receive EDI Awards," *Variety* 337, no. 10 (December 13, 1989), 12; Lynn Snowden, "Raising 'Twins,'" *Rolling Stone*, no. 544 (January 26, 1989), 20; Brian D. Johnson, "Having His Baby," *Maclean's* 107, no. 49 (December 5, 1994), 81.

120. Joshua Hammer, "The Blockbuster Game," *Newsweek* 115, no. 26 (June 25, 1990), 51.

121. Todd Camp, "Faces, Places: Bill Murray," *Fort Worth Star-Telegram*, May 28, 1991, G7.

122. Wuntch, "Bill Murray's Detour."

CHAPTER 7: THE LONG WINTER

1. Steve Murray, "In Orlando, It's Lights, Camera, a New Attraction!," *Atlanta Journal-Constitution*, June 7, 1990, E1; Louis B. Parks, "Florida Studio Aims for Universal Appeal," *Houston Chronicle*, May 17, 1989, 4.

2. Jerald Hyche, "Attraction's Opening Gets Mixed Reviews," *Tampa Tribune*, June 8, 1990, 1A, 10A.

3. William Arnold, "Hitchcock Show at Universal Is Terrific," *Seattle Post-Intelligencer*, July 19, 1990, G4; Craig Wilson, "Universal's Appeal; Park Wins Fans Despite Glitches," *USA Today*, July 12, 1990, 1D; Ron Hayes, "At Universal Studios, It'll Be a Very Long Wait for Rides," *Palm Beach Post*, August 29, 1990, 1D.

4. Ron Hayes, "Long Wait for Rides at Universal," *Austin American-Statesman*, September 1, 1990, D9.

5. Mal Vincent, "Bill Murray Send in the Clown the Master," *Virginia-Pilot*, July 11, 1990, B1; Pat H. Broeske, "'Die Hard 2' Has a Life of Its Own," *Los Angeles Times*, July 16, 1990, P8.

6. Kate Meyers, "A Bill Murray Filmography," *Entertainment Weekly*, March 19, 1993, archived at https://ew.com/article/1993/03/19/bill-murray-filmography.

7. "Celebs Tell Holiday Tales," *USA Today*, December 16, 1990; David Giammarco, "Madcap Aykroyd: Running Full Tilt Into Nothing but Trouble," *Toronto Sun*, February 10, 1991, S3.

8. Nick de Semlyen, *Wild and Crazy Guys: How the Comedy Mavericks of the '80s Changed Hollywood Forever* (New York: Crown Archetype, 2019), 258–61.

9. "Aykroyd's Toil and 'Trouble,'" *USA Today*, December 17, 1990, 2D; Michael MacCambridge, "Movies in the Making for '91," *Austin American-Statesman*, January 4, 1991, Weekend section, 5; Robert Denerstein, "Here Comes Trouble: Aykroyd's Latest Movie Offers Nothing But," *Rocky Mountain News*, February 16, 1991, 70.

10. Michael Janusonis, "The Trouble Is, It's Just Not Funny," *Providence Journal*, February 16, 1991, B08; Jim Slotek, "Plenty of Nothing/Smarm without Charm," *Toronto Sun*, February 18, 1991, 40; Peter Stack, "Chevy Chase in Aykroyd Bomb," *San Francisco Chronicle*, February 16, 1991, C3; Daniel Neman, "Script Causes Terrible 'Trouble.'" *Richmond Times-Dispatch*, February 16, 1991, A46.

11. "Movie Nudity No Big Deal to Sharon Stone," *Toronto Star*, February 11, 1991, D5; Aleene MacMinn, "Morning Report," *Los Angeles Times*, February 19, 1991, F2.

12. Ryan Parker, "Dan Aykroyd Supports Hurtful Comedy Getting the Cancel-Culture Ax," *Hollywood Reporter*, November 2, 2021, https://www.hollywoodreporter.com/movies/movie-features/dan-aykroyd-ghostbusters-afterlife-snl-cancel-culture-1235036791.

13. Duane Byrge, "L.A. Boxoffice: 'Kindergarten' Gets an A," *Hollywood Reporter* 315, no. 32 (December 27, 1990), 28; "Uni's 'Cop' Busts Out Big Overseas," *Hollywood Reporter* 316, no. 11 (February 8, 1991), 14.

14. Marilyn Beck and Stacy Jenel Smith, "Who Ya Gonna Call to Make 'Ghostbusters III'?," *Daily News of Los Angeles*, January 30, 1992, L22.

15. Alan Citron, "She Holds Torch for Sony Pictures Entertainment," *Los Angeles Times*, August 8, 1991, https://www.latimes.com/archives/la-xpm-1991-08-08-fi-464-story.html.

16. Kevin Maney, "3 Ms in Sony-Columbia Deal," *USA Today*, September 27, 1989; Charles Kipps, "Col's Future Is Sony-Side-Up," *Variety* 336, no. 11 (September 27, 1989), 1.

17. Laura Landro, "Hollywood Ending: Columbia Pictures, Racked by Losses, Is a Valuable Asset Now," *Wall Street Journal*, September 26, 1989, A1, A18.

18. Nancy Griffin and Kim Masters, *Hit & Run: How Jon Peters and Peter Guber Took Sony for a Ride in Hollywood* (New York: Simon & Schuster, 1996), 237–38.

19. Kevin Goldman, "Sitcom Syndicators Are Laughing Less," *Wall Street Journal*, January 24, 1992, B1, B8; Thomas King, "Movies: Another Sequel; For Hollywood: Box Office Blues," *Wall Street Journal*, January 6, 1992, B1, B6; Randall Smith, "Japanese Purchases of U.S. Firms Plunged in 1991 as Caution Grew," *Wall Street*

Journal, January 15, 1992, C1; Griffin and Masters, *Hit & Run*, 328–29; Laura Landro and Kathleen A. Hughes, "Sony Agrees to Purchase Guber-Peters in Bid to Get New Team for Columbia," *Wall Street Journal*, September 29, 1989, A4.

20. Griffin and Masters, *Hit & Run*, 8–9, 168, 252–57.
21. Todd Camp, "What About Bill? The Real Bill Murray Finally Speaks Up, and He's a Total Lunatic Just Like Most of His Movie Characters," *Fort Worth Star-Telegram*, May 21, 1991, 1.
22. Cindy Pearlman, "What About Bill? Murray Doesn't Find Fame Entirely to His Liking," *Waterloo Region Record*, February 10, 1993, F1.
23. Tad Friend, "Comedy First," *New Yorker*, April 11, 2004, https://www.new yorker.com/magazine/2004/04/19/comedy-first.
24. Stephen Schafer, "Double Bill: Murray Returns with Two Movies," *Boston Herald*, February 7, 1993, 031.
25. de Semlyen, *Wild and Crazy Guys*, 265–71.
26. Violet Ramis Stiel, *Ghostbuster's Daughter: Life with My Dad, Harold Ramis* (New York: Blue Rider Press, 2018), 174–76.
27. Michael Blowen, "The One and Only Bill Murray," *Boston Globe*, June 20, 1981, 1; Michael Blowen, "'Stripes' Is Devilishly Inconsistent; Bill Murray's Anarchic Humor Provides Film's Best Moments," *Boston Globe*, May 30, 1982, 1.
28. Author interview with Peter Giuliano. April 22, 2020.
29. Patrick Goldstein and John Horn, "Film Sets Loose, but Barbarian Behavior Rare, Insiders Say," *Baltimore Sun*, October 3, 2003, https://www.baltimore sun.com/news/bal-sets1003-story.html; Kevin Polowy, "Role Recall: Richard Dreyfuss on Doubting 'Jaws,' Coping with an Abusive Bill Murray on 'What About Bob?' and More," Yahoo! Entertainment, June 26, 2019, https://www .yahoo.com/entertainment/richard-dreyfuss-best-movies-roles-stories-interview -jaws-bill-murray-130000701.html.
30. Pearlman, "What About Bill?"
31. Ryan Murphy, "Bill Murray and the Beast: Filming 'Groundhog Day' Turned Out to Be a Nightmare for the Actor," *Philadelphia Inquirer*, February 7, 1993, G1.
32. Hal Hinson, "'Groundhog Day,'" *Washington Post*, February 12, 1993, archived at https://www.washingtonpost.com/wp-srv/style/longterm/movies/videos/ groundhogdaypghinson_a0a7e9.htm.
33. Roger Ebert, "The Shadow of His Smile." RogerEbert.com, January 30, 2005, https://www.rogerebert.com/reviews/great-movie-groundhog-day-1993.
34. Alex Kuczynski, "Groundhog Almighty," *New York Times*, December 7, 2003, https://www.nytimes.com/2003/12/07/style/groundhog-almighty.html.
35. Friend, "Comedy First"; Stiel, *Ghostbuster's Daughter*, 174–76.
36. Lois Romano, "The Reliable Source," *Washington Post*, February 16, 1993, D03.
37. Bob Polunsky, "Bill Murray's Versatility Emerging on Film," *San Antonio Express-News*, February 13, 1993, 5G.
38. Brian D. Johnson, "Resident Alien," *Maclean's* 106, no. 33 (July 26, 1993), 36; Barry Koltnow, "Dan Aykroyd Plans to Have the Last Laugh," *Orlando Sentinel*, August 4, 1993, E1.
39. David Sheff, "Dan Aykroyd: The Playboy Interview," *Playboy*, August 1993, archived at http://www.angelfire.com/celeb2/elwood3/daplay.html.
40. Jamie Portman, "True Blues: Dan Aykroyd Rekindles His Musical Interests with a Sequel to His Blues Brothers Hit," *Waterloo Region Record*, February 5, 1998, C1.
41. Jeffrey Jolson-Colburn, "'HOB Has Tours, TV Show on Tap," *Hollywood Reporter* 341, no. 49 (April 17, 1996), 17; Marilyn Beck and Stacy Janel Smith, "Aykroyd Looking for a Few Good Ghostbusters," *Daily News*, September 10, 1996, L2.
42. Bob Thompson, "Buzz: What's Going On in Showbiz," *Toronto Star*, July 3, 1996, 59; M. E. Russell, "Ramis on 'Ice,'" *In Focus*, November 2005, archived

at https://web.archive.org/web/20051103012401/http://www.infocusmag
.com/05november/ramisuncut.htm.

43. Beck and Smith, "Aykroyd Looking"; Michael B. Dougherty, "Q&A: Dan Aykroyd
Is Keeping *Ghostbusters 3* Alive," *Esquire*, December 4, 2012, https://www.esquire
.com/entertainment/movies/interviews/a17104/dan-aykroyd-interview-14813380;
Dan Aykroyd, *Ghostbusters III* story treatment, February 6, 1997, Tom Davis
Papers, Beinecke Rare Book and Manuscript Library, Yale University.

44. Author interview with Jeff Kline, October 5, 2021; Steve Brennan, "Schwartz
Bringing CTT to Kids TV Playing Field," *Hollywood Reporter* 339, no. 27 (October
24, 1995), 1, 111; author interview with Audu Paden, October 30, 2021.

45. "Advertisement: Columbia TriStar," *Hollywood Reporter* 340, no. 38 (January
23, 1996), S19.

46. Rosey Collins, "Fil Barlow Interview," Jake! + EGB Fan's EGB Fans, May 2015,
https://egbfans.weebly.com/fil-barlow-interview.html.

47. Author interview with Jeff Kline, October 5, 2021.

48. Author interview with Audu Paden, October 30, 2021.

49. Susy Schultz, "Assessing the New Shows: What's Good, What's Not," *Chicago
Sun-Times*, September 7, 1997, 7.

50. Author interview with Jeff Kline, October 5, 2021.

51. Stephen Harber, "Extreme Ghostbusters Is a Lot Better Than You Remember," Den
of Geek, October 19, 2019, https://www.denofgeek.com/tv/extreme-ghostbusters
-is-a-lot-better-than-you-remember; Noel Ransome, "The Surprising and Forgotten
Diversity of 'Extreme Ghostbusters,'" Vice, May 8, 2017, https://www.vice.com/en/
article/mgmgpa/extreme-ghostbusters-when-the-franchise-gave-a-shit-about-me.

52. Collins, "Fil Barlow Interview."

53. Eric Harrison, "Go to the Movies and Pick Whichever Future You Like," *Dallas
Morning News*, April 11, 1999, 10C; Associated Press, "Highest Grossing Films of
1997," January 4, 1998; Corie Brown, "Hollywood's New Math," *Newsweek* 131,
no. 3 (January 19, 1988), 65; Alex Ben Block and Lucy Autrey Wilson, *George
Lucas's Blockbusting* (New York: HarperCollins Publishers, 2010), 788–89.

54. Brian D. Johnson, "A Frolic in the Alien Fun House," *Maclean's* 110, no. 28
(July 14, 1997), 63.

55. David Ansen, "Odd Squad," *Newsweek* 130, no. 1 (July 7, 1997), 60.

56. Aykroyd, *Ghostbusters III* story treatment, February 6, 1997, pp. 1–5.

57. Aykroyd, *Ghostbusters III* story treatment, February 6, 1997, pp. 5–7.

58. Aykroyd, *Ghostbusters III* story treatment, February 6, 1997, pp. 7–11; Russell,
"Ramis on 'Ice.'"

59. Aykroyd, *Ghostbusters III* story treatment, February 6, 1997, pp. 10–13.

60. Aykroyd, *Ghostbusters III* story treatment, February 6, 1997, pp. 15–18.

61. Dave McNary, "New 'Star Wars' Not Far, Far Away," *Daily News of Los Angeles*,
November 10, 1997, N6.

62. "Comic Chris Farley Dies," *Akron Beacon Journal*, December 19, 1997, A1;
Kirk Honeycutt, "Farley in Accidental OD from Cocaine, Morphine," *Hollywood
Reporter* 350, no. 35 (January 5, 1998), 6.

63. Corie Brown, "Hollywood's New Math—'MiB' Made a Fortune; The Sequel
Will Cost One," *Newsweek*, January 19, 1998, 65.

64. "Filmbuzz Reel Talk," *Sun Sentinel*, January 2, 1998, 4; Bob Low, "The Net—
Sites for Sore Eyes, 1998," *Daily Record*, January 1, 1999, 37.

65. "Ghostbusters 3," Corona's Coming Attractions, April 5, 2001, archived at http://
web.archive.org/web/20010405012150/http://www.corona.bc.ca/films/details/
ghostbusters3.html; Funnyontv@aol.com, email to Andrew Shaw, July 17, 1998;
"FUNNYONTV," alt.fan.conan-obrien, July 14, 2000, archived at https://groups
.google.com/g/alt.fan.conan-obrien/c/_V-6yYZhQFo?pli=1.

66. "Ghostbusters 3," Corona's Coming Attractions; Ron Hofmann, email to author, January 5, 2022.

67. "Ghostbusters 3 & 4 News!!!," Ain't It Cool News, March 10, 1998, archived at http://web.archive.org/web/19991117115957/http://www.aint-it-cool-news .com/display.cgi?id=742; "Ghostbusters 3," Proton Charging, April 29, 1999, archived at http://web.archive.org/web/19990429111804if_/http://www.proton charging.com:80.

68. "GB3 Information!," The Ghostbusters Homepage, August 26, 1998, archived at http://web.archive.org/web/19990128231248/http://www.okemosweb .com/ghostbusters/gb3.html; "GB Message Board!," The Ghostbusters Homepage, accessed February 21, 2022, archived at http://web.archive.org/ web/19991118202422/http://okemosweb.com/ghostbusters/board.html; author interview with Bill Emkow, January 20, 2022.

69. Cindy Pearlman, "Teen Batman Could Be Next," *Chicago Sun-Times*, February 16, 1999, 26.

70. Quint, "Quint Chats with Harold Ramis about Ice Harvest, Ghostbusters and Much More!!!," Ain't It Cool News, November 17, 2005, archived at https:// www.theraffon.net/spookcentral/gb3_news.htm.

71. Louis B. Hobson, "Guess Hugh's Turning 40—Actor Is 'Half in Denial and in Complete Misery,'" *Calgary Sun*, May 8, 2000, Entertainment section, 36.

72. Dougherty, "Q&A: Dan Aykroyd"; Undated *Ghostbusters III* script, Tom Davis Papers, Beinecke Rare Book and Manuscript Library, Yale University, pp. 1–6.

73. Undated *Ghostbusters III* script, p. 8.

74. Undated *Ghostbusters III* script, pp. 11–16.

75. Undated *Ghostbusters III* script, pp. 17–19.

76. Undated *Ghostbusters III* script, pp. 25, 29–36.

77. Undated *Ghostbusters III* script, pp. 45–47.

78. Undated *Ghostbusters III* script, pp. 56–67, 76.

79. Undated *Ghostbusters III* script, pp. 68–69.

80. Undated *Ghostbusters III* script, pp. 91–92, 95–102.

81. Undated *Ghostbusters III* script, pp. 110–12.

82. Undated *Ghostbusters III* script, pp. 117–22.

83. Dan Aykroyd, *Ghostbusters III: Hellbent*, First Draft, March 10, 1999.

84. Undated *Ghostbusters III* script, pp. 9–10.

85. Undated *Ghostbusters III* script, p. 120.

86. Aykroyd, *Ghostbusters III: Hellbent*, First Draft, March 10, 1999, p. 120.

87. Dave McNary, "Rumored Sequels Include Everything but 'Ishtar 2,'" *Daily News*, August 7, 1999, N1.

88. Kim Masters, "Sony's Blockbusters Sequel," *Time* 150, no. 21 (November 17, 1997), archived at http://web.archive.org/web/20010619024237/http://www .time.com/time/magazine/1997/dom/971117/business.sonys_blockbu.html; John Lippman, "Sony Hopes This Mouse Can Roar," *Wall Street Journal*, December 16, 1999, B1, B2.

89. Scott Mendelson, "15 Years Ago, 'Godzilla' Was a Flop; By Today's Standards, It Would Be a Hit," *Forbes*, May 20, 2013, https://www.forbes.com/sites/ scottmendelson/2013/05/20/15-years-ago-godzilla-was-a-flop-by-todays -standards-it-would-be-a-hit.

90. "Ghostbusters 3 Access Hollywood Interview with Dan Aykroyd," YouTube, posted by Ghostbusters.net on April 6, 2014, https://www.youtube.com/ watch?v=lKhAc2D6Mf0; Castewar, "Aykroyd Interview Sez GB3 in Jeopardy," Proton Charging, November 12, 1999, http://protoncharging.com/1999/11/12/ aykroyd-interview-bad-news; Stephen Galloway, "What Is the Most Profitable

Movie Ever?," *Hollywood Reporter*, January 18, 2020, https://www.hollywood reporter.com/movies/movie-news/what-is-profitable-movie-ever-1269879.

91. Hobson, "Guess Hugh's Turning 40."

92. Quint, "Quint Chats with Harold Ramis."

93. Dan Aykroyd, *Ghostbusters III: Hellbent*, Limited Revision, June 23, 2006, pp. 21–25; Caramie Schnell, "A Ghostbuster Visits the Vail Valley," *Vail Daily*, March 30, 2007; "Dan Aykroyd Confirms Ghostbusters III?!," *Mike's Blog*, CISN Country 103.9 FM, February 2, 2007, archived at http://web.archive.org/web/20070206015619/http://www.cisnfm.com/station/blog_mike_mcguire.cfm?bid=7500.

CHAPTER 8: I'LL TELL MY BROTHER

1. Jim Sullivan, "Nothing Sly About This Gun-Toting Comedy," *Boston Globe*, February 21, 1992, 29; Gene Siskel, "Best Movies of the Year," *Chicago Tribune*, December 20, 1992, 5; Mike Clark, "In a Sea of Films, the Top Were Easy to Spot," *USA Today*, December 28, 1992, 6D; John Horn, Associated Press, "'Wayne's World' Tops Box Office," *Town Talk*, February 28, 1992, C7; Shane O'Neill, "The '90s Movie Sylvester Stallone Regrets Making," Looper, April 30, 2021, https://www.looper.com/397842/the-90s-movie-sylvester-stallone-regrets-making.

2. Kenneth Turan, "Arnold's Mommy Syndrome," *Los Angeles Times*, November 23, 1994, 1; Roger Ebert, "Pregnant with Comic Possibility," *The Record*, November 23, 1994, D13; Yardena Arar, "'Santa' Claws Its Way to Top," *South Florida Sun Sentinel*, November 30, 1994, 3E.

3. Janet Maslin, "Icons Meet: Bugs, Daffy and Jordan," *New York Times*, November 15, 1996, C18.

4. Liane Bonin, "How *Evolution*'s Stars Forced the Script to Evolve," *Entertainment Weekly*, June 11, 2001, https://ew.com/article/2001/06/11/how-evolutions-stars-forced-script-evolve.

5. John Anderson, "An Original Idea Is Alien to *Evolution*," *Los Angeles Times*, June 8, 2001, F4.

6. Marshall Fine, "'Evolution' Is a Bomb Out of the Stone Age School of Sci-Fi Comedy," *Journal News*, June 7, 2001, G8.

7. Gloria Goodale, "A Science Guy's Don Jakoby Wrote a Science-Based Thriller but Hollywood Had Another Idea," *Christian Science Monitor*, June 8, 2001, 19; author interview with David Diamond and David Weissman, April 4, 2019.

8. Roger Ebert, "Small-Brained Movie Drags Its Knuckles," *Calgary Herald*, June 8, 2001, F5.

9. Bonin, "How *Evolution*'s Stars."

10. Brian Fuson, "'Swordfish' Downloads No. 1 Spot for Warners," *Hollywood Reporter* 368, no. 33 (June 11, 2001), 3, 51.

11. Neil Vitale, "Classic GBHQ: Interview with Michael C. Gross," Ghostbusters HQ, March 12, 2015, http://www.ghostbustershq.net/home/2015/3/12/classic-gbhq-interview-with-michael-c-gross.

12. Louis Hobson, "Blues, Not Movies, Focus for Aykroyd," *London Free Press*, June 10, 2001, C3.

13. Christopher Allan Smith and Scott Collura, "Ghostbusters III News from Dan Aykroyd." Cinescape, June 26, 2001, archived at https://web.archive.org/web/20010627184511/http://www.cinescape.com.

14. *Ray Parker, Jr. v. Hugh Cregg*, Superior Court of the State of California, County of Los Angeles, Case No. BC247313, Complaint for Damages for: Breach of Contract and Public Disclosure of Private Facts, filed March 22, 2001, pp. 3, 4, Exhibit A; "Sunday Highlights February 4, 2001," *Tampa Tribune*, February 4, 2001, Trib TV section, 14.

15. *Ray Parker, Jr. v Hugh Cregg*, Dismissed—Other 12/19/2001, Notice of Motion and Motion to Strike Certain Allegations in Complaint; Memorandum of Points and Authorities in Support Thereof, filed May 11, 2001, pp. 7–8.

16. *Ray Parker, Jr. v Hugh Cregg*, Dismissal, Case Number BC247313, filed December 19, 2001.

17. Stefanie Frith, "Recording Artists Push Labor Law Change," *Modesto Bee*, January 24, 2002, A4.

18. Annie Zaleski, "The Rhymes and Reasons Behind Re-Recording Your Own Classics," NPR, April 12, 2021, https://www.npr.org/2021/04/12/986430235/the-rhymes-and-reasons-behind-re-recording-your-own-classics; Ellie Gibson, "Eurogamer Meets Ray Parker Jr.," Eurogamer, March 12, 2009, https://www.eurogamer.net/articles/eurogamer-meets-ray-parker-jr-interview.

19. Josh Tyrangiel, "The Many Faces of Bill," *Time*, January 3, 2005, http://content.time.com/time/subscriber/article/0,33009,1013228-1,00.html.

20. Tod Friend, "Comedy First," *New Yorker*, April 11, 2004, https://www.newyorker.com/magazine/2004/04/19/comedy-first.

21. Tyrangiel, "Many Faces of Bill."

22. Evgenia Peretz, "Something About Sophia," *Vanity Fair*, September 2006, https://archive.vanityfair.com/article/2006/9/something-about-sofia; Tyrangiel, "Many Faces of Bill"; Bill Brownstein, "Bill Murray's Comic Genius Spelled Out," *Montreal Gazette*, September 5, 2015, F4.

23. Elaine Lipworth, "Million Dollar Bill," *Mail on Sunday*, January 30, 2005, 14.

24. Tyrangiel, "Many Faces of Bill"; Zorianna Kit, "Liu Makes It a Threesome in Col's 'Angels,'" *Hollywood Reporter* 360, no. 28 (November 22, 1999), 3, 22; Zorianna Kit, "Murray Back on Phone with Col for 'Angels' Role," *Hollywood Reporter* 360, no. 34 (November 30, 1999), 7–8; Alisha Davis, "Lucy Liu Lands a Role as a Heavenly Creature," *Newsweek* 134, no. 23 (December 6, 1999), 53.

25. Matt Grobar, "Lucy Liu Opens Up About Altercation with Bill Murray on Set of 'Charlie's Angels': 'I Stood Up for Myself, and I Don't Regret It,'" Deadline, July 27, 2021, https://deadline.com/2021/07/lucy-liu-addresses-clash-with-bill-murray-on-set-of-charlies-angels.

26. Katey Rich, "Bill Murray Thinks McG Deserves to Die," Cinema Blend, October 19, 2009, https://www.cinemablend.com/new/Bill-Murray-Thinks-McG-Deserves-Die-15291.html.

27. Dan Fierman, "Bill Murray Is Ready to See You Now," *GQ*, July 18, 2010, https://www.gq.com/story/bill-murray-dan-fierman-gq-interview; "Bill Murray Here: OK, I'll TALK! I'll TALK!," Reddit, January 17, 2014, https://www.reddit.com/r/IAmA/comments/1vhjag/bill_murray_here_ok_ill_talk_ill_talk/cesy4xm/?context=8&depth=9; Peter Hewitt, *Garfield: The Movie*, 20th Century Fox, 2004; Tim Hill, *Garfield: A Tale of Two Kitties*, 20th Century Fox, 2006.

28. Phil Villarreal, "'Hit & Run' Borderline Brilliant," *Arizona Daily Star*, October 3, 2003, F20; Pete Metzger, "Springfield's in Peril? D'oh!," *Los Angeles Times*, October 16, 2003, E26; "Vivendi Games Unit Signs Deal with Radical," *Los Angeles Times*, February 11, 2004, C3.

29. Matt Paprocki interview with John Melchior, April 16, 2016; author interview with John Melchior, February 17, 2020.

30. Author interview with John Zurr Platten, May 24, 2021.

31. Stephen Totilo, "Sigourney Weaver Appalled by Offer to Be in 'Aliens' Game, Not Slated for 'Ghostbusters,'" MTV News, December 5, 2008. https://www.mtv.com/news/2458234/sigourney-weaver-appalled-by-offer-to-be-in-aliens-game-not-slated-for-ghostbusters; R. Mitchell, "Sigourney Weaver Missed Her Shot at Ghostbusters Game Role," Engadget, March 6, 2009, https://www.engadget.com/2009-03-06-sigourney-weaver-missed-her-shot-at-ghostbusters-game-role

.html; Derrik J. Lang, "Alyssa Milano to Co-Star in 'Ghostbusters' Game," *NBC News*, March 20, 2009, https://www.nbcnews.com/id/wbna29801049.

32. Author interview with John Zurr Platten, May 24, 2021.
33. Author interview with John Melchior, February 17, 2020; Matt Paprocki interview with John Melchior. April 16, 2016.
34. Author interview with John Zurr Platten, May 24, 2021.
35. Matt Paprocki interview with John Melchior, April 16, 2016.
36. Matt Paprocki interview with Drew Haworth, April 20, 2016.
37. Author interview with John Zurr Platten, May 24, 2021.
38. Matt Paprocki interview with John Melchior, April 16, 2016.
39. Author interview with John Melchior, February 17, 2020.
40. Matt Paprocki interview with John Melchior, April 16, 2016.
41. Author interview with John Melchior, February 17, 2020.
42. Matt Paprocki interview with John Melchior, April 16, 2016.
43. Author interview with John Zurr Platten, May 24, 2021.
44. Matt Paprocki interview with Drew Haworth, April 20, 2016.
45. Matt Paprocki interview with John Melchior, April 16, 2016.
46. Lee Alexander, "Sierra Announces *Ghostbusters the Video Game*," Game Developer, November 16, 2007, https://www.gamedeveloper.com/pc/sierra-announces-i-ghostbusters-the-video-game-i-.
47. "Ghostbusters: The Video Game," YouTube, posted by *Time* on April 23, 2009, https://www.youtube.com/watch?v=IoJFJ_4u-8Y; Matt Paprocki interview with John Melchior, April 16, 2016; author interview with John Melchior, February 17, 2020.
48. "Ghostbusters: The Video Game," YouTube; "Press Release Details: Vivendi and Activision Create Activision Blizzard," Activision Blizzard, December 2, 2007, https://investor.activision.com/news-releases/news-release-details/vivendi-and-activision-create-activision-blizzard-worlds-largest; Matt Paprocki interview with John Melchior, April 16, 2016.
49. Matt Paprocki interview with John Melchior, April 16, 2016.
50. Nancy Dillon, "Bill Murray's Wife Files for Divorce, Accuses Actor of Sex Addiction, Abuse," *New York Daily News*, May 29, 2008, https://www.nydailynews.com/entertainment/gossip/bill-murray-wife-files-divorce-accuses-actor-sex-addiction-abuse-article-1.326688.
51. Matt Paprocki interview with John Melchior, April 16, 2016; Rawson Stovall, "Ghostbusters Program Challenging, Lots of Fun," *Odessa American*, November 25, 1984, 2BB.
52. "Press Release Details," Activision Blizzard; Tor Thorsen, "Vivendi Merges with Activision in $18.9B Deal," Gamespot, December 2, 2007, archived at https://web.archive.org/web/20090207091330/http://gamespot.com/news/6183557.html.
53. Brendon Sinclair, "Activision Blizzard 'Streamlining' Vivendi," GameSpot, July 28, 2008, archived at https://web.archive.org/web/20090206141549/http://www.gamespot.com/news/6195105.html.
54. Matt Paprocki interview with John Melchior, April 16, 2016.
55. Michael McWhertor, "Ghostbusters: The Video Game Hands-On," Kotaku, July 26, 2008, https://kotaku.com/ghostbusters-the-video-game-hands-on-5029586.
56. Matt Paprocki interview with John Melchior, April 16, 2016; Stovall, "Ghostbusters Program Challenging."
57. Earnest Cavalli, "Atari Officially Confirms Ghostbusters Game," *Wired*, November 7, 2008, https://www.wired.com/2008/11/atari-officiall.
58. Matt Paprocki interview with John O'Keefe, April 16, 2016.
59. Matt Paprocki interview with John Melchior, April 16, 2016.
60. Matt Paprocki interview with John Melchior, April 16, 2016.

61. Gibson, "Eurogamer Meets Ray Parker Jr."
62. Andrew Marton, "Telekinetic Activity," *Fort Worth Star-Telegram*, July 18, 2009, 1E; Tom Magrino, "Ghostbusters Spooks 1 Million," GameSpot, July 21, 2009, archived at https://web.archive.org/web/20090826023143/http://www.gamespot .com/news/6213739.html; Matthew Peters, "ChartSopt: June 2009," GameSpot, July 17, 2009, archived at https://web.archive.org/web/20090720012855/http:// www.gamespot.com/news/6213540.html.
63. Greg Miller, "Ghostbusters: The Video Game Review," IGN, June 15, 2009, https:// www.ign.com/articles/2009/06/15/ghostbusters-the-video-game-review-3.
64. Ryan Davis, "Ghostbusters: The Video Game Review," Giant Bomb, June 19, 2009, https://www.giantbomb.com/reviews/ghostbusters-the-video-game -review/1900-168.
65. Matt Paprocki interview with John Melchior, April 16, 2016.

CHAPTER 9: ALIVE AGAIN

1. Phoebe Flowers, "A Muscle-Bound Comedy for Young Males," *Sun Sentinel*, June 18, 2004, 6; Cindy Pearlman, "With $30 Million, 'Dodgeball' Tale Bounces Vaughn to Top of Box Office," *Chicago Sun-Times*, June 21, 2004, 51; Laura Randall, "Unlikely Heroes of the Box Office: The Frat Pack," *Christian Science Monitor*, July 9, 2004, 11.
2. Adam Laukhuf, "Big Man on Campus," *WWD* 187, no. 45 (March 4, 2004), 20.
3. Elvis Mitchell, "Film Review: Never Too Late to Have an Adolescence," *New York Times*, February 21, 2003, https://www.nytimes.com/2003/02/21/movies/ film-review-never-too-late-to-have-an-adolescence.html.
4. "Who Ya Gonna Call? Not Seth," *Toronto Sun*, October 23, 2008, 87; Borys Kit and Leslie Simmons, "'Ghostbusters' Scares Up Scribes," *Hollywood Reporter* 406, no. 21 (September 5, 2008), 8; Briana Rodrigues, "The 30 Best Episodes of 'The Office' Ranked," *Variety*, April 15, 2021, https://variety.com/lists/ the-office-best-episodes-ranked; Michael Swaim, "The 25 Best Episodes of The Office of All Time," IGN, January 7, 2021, https://www.ign.com/articles/ best-episodes-of-the-office.
5. "He Makes Dumb Smart," *Boston Globe*, June 20, 2009, G4; Steph Spera, "Q&A with Harold Ramis," *Student Life*, September 10, 2009; Paulington James Christensen III, "Exclusive: Harold Ramis Talks *Ghostbusters 3* and *Meatballs* Remake," MovieWeb, September 30, 2009, archived at https://web.archive.org/ web/20091126014318/http://www.movieweb.com/news/NEy4zEAESl6sBG; David Ansen, "Geek Love, Full Frontal," *Newsweek* 151, no. 16 (April 21, 2008), 56; Tara Brady, "'When People Talk About Being Horrible, It's Always Hilarious,'" *Irish Times*, June 11, 2020, 9.
6. "Longtime Columbia Pictures Chiefs Matt Tolmach and Doug Belgrad Transition into New Roles," *PR Newswire*, October 29, 2010.
7. Will Pfeifer, "Good News for Fans of Ghostbusters . . .," *Rockford Register Star: Blogs*, September 8, 2008, Movie Man section.
8. "Fantastic Fest Day 8—Bill Murray and the City of Ember," YouTube, posted by fantasticfest2008 on September 26, 2008, https://www.youtube.com/ watch?v=IN9alsyOlwE&t=300s.
9. Shereen Low, "Lure of the Dark Side," *Birmingham Mail*, October 10, 2008, 61.
10. Dan Fierman, "Bill Murray Is Ready to See You Now," *GQ*, July 19, 2010, https://www.gq.com/story/bill-murray-dan-fierman-gq-interview; Shawn Adler, "Bill Murray Longs for a More Heated Presidential Race . . . and a Girl Ghostbuster," MTV.com, October 9, 2008, archived at https://web.archive .org/web/20081013031719/http://www.mtv.com/movies/news/articles/ 1596656/story.jhtml.

11. Eric Ditzian, "Original 'Ghostbusters' Cast Onboard for Reboot, Says Harold Ramis," MTV News, March 27, 2009, http://www.mtv.com/news/1607995/original-ghostbusters-cast-onboard-for-reboot-harold-ramis-says.

12. Philip Brown, "Who Ya Gonna Call for Comedy? Try Ramis—Writer/Director/Actor Ponders the Evolution of His Crafts, from 1984's Ghostbusters to the Upcoming Year One," *Toronto Star*, June 13, 2009, E08.

13. Christensen, "Exclusive: Harold Ramis."

14. Kevin Williamson, "Ghostbusters Back to Haunt Us?—Director Ivan Reitman Chatting Up the Idea of a Possible Third Film in the Franchise," *Toronto Sun*, September 19, 2009, 49; Jessica Leo, "Sexiest Man Alive," *The Advertiser*, November 5, 2009, D20.

15. Scott Wampler, "Bill Murray's Going to Be a Ghost in 'Ghostbusters 3' What?!," *Entertainment Examiner*, December 11, 2009.

16. Michael Lee, "Ivan Reitman Confirms He Is Directing 'Ghostbusters 3,'" *Los Angeles Examiner*, January 13, 2010.

17. Jada Yuan, "Ivan Reitman on Bill Murray, Internet Trolls, and Why He Fought for the *Ghostbusters* Reboot," Vulture, July 14, 2016, https://www.vulture.com/2016/07/ivan-reitman-ghostbusters-bill-murray-qa.html.

18. "All-Time Box Office Hits (Domestic Gross) by Decade and Year," Filmsite, accessed February 1, 2022, https://www.filmsite.org/boxoffice2.html.

19. David Colker, "Many Filmgoers Spend 'A Night at the Museum," *Los Angeles Times*, December 24, 2006, Financial section; Associated Press, "Weekend Box Office: It's Good Days for 'Night at the Museum,'" *Daily Herald*, December 25, 2006, 20.

20. Associated Press, "'Ratatouille' Rules Weekend Box Office with $47.2 Million Debut," *Pittsburgh Tribune-Review*, July 1, 2007.

21. Tom Long, "Tops at the Box Office in 2008," *Detroit News*, December 26, 2008, 1C.

22. Williamson, "Ghostbusters Back?"

23. Kristal Cooper, "Is Ghostbusters 3 in Trouble?," *Toronto Examiner*, March 19, 2010.

24. Brad Miska, "Dan Aykroyd Tells Bill Murray to 'Stop Acting Like a Jerk' in Regards to 'Ghostbusters 3,'" Bloody Disgusting, April 2, 2010, https://bloody-disgusting.com/news/19681/dan-aykroyd-tells-bill-murray-to-stop-acting-like-a-jerk-in-regards-to-ghostbusters-3.

25. Williamson, "Ghostbusters Back?"; Joshua Gillin, "Tito, Jenna Made It All Up," *Tampa Bay Times*, April 30, 2010, 82.

26. "Deja Boo: Horror Classics Always Scare Up Remakes," *Chicago Tribune*, May 3, 2010, 21.

27. World Entertainment News Network, "Murray Considering Writing Ghostbusters 3 Himself," April 29, 2010.

28. Fierman, "Bill Murray Is Ready."

29. Jim Slotek, Sun Media, "A Sloppy, Joke-Poor Prehistorical Mess," *Brockville Recorder and Times*, June 19, 2009, Entertainment section, B7; Lynn Venhaus, "Oh Please, Blow Up the Time Machine," *Belleville News-Democrat*, June 19, 2009, Lifestyle section, 5C; Roger Ebert, "Not Historical; Not Hysterical," *Corvallis Gazette-Times*, June 19, 2009, Entertainer section, 12.

30. Fierman, "Bill Murray Is Ready."

31. "Bill Murray in Full Ghostbusters Uniform at the Spike Scream Awards!," *The Ghostbusters III Blog*, posted by the Destructor, October 17, 2010, http://ghostbustersiii.blogspot.com/2010/10/bill-murray-in-full-ghostbustersers.html; "Scream 2010 Winners," Spike, October 22, 2010, archived at https://web.archive.org/web/20101026223749/http://www.spike.com/blog/scream-2010-winners/101031.

32. Aaron W. Tellock, "'Ghostbusters 3' Confirmed by Harold Ramis," *Milwaukee Examiner*, May 12, 2010; Angie Rentmeester, "Rick Moranis, Sigourney Weaver

Reuniting for 'Ghostbusters 3,'" *Chicago Examiner*, September 8, 2010; Kevin Williamson, "Weaver's Spirit Willing—Sigourney Open to Another Ghostbusters Sequel, but First Up Is Comedy, You Again," *Calgary Sun*, September 21, 2010, 29; Lizzie Catt, Lisa Higgins, and Dana Gloger, "The Express: Aykroyd Gets the Call," *The Express*, October 11, 2010; McClatchy-Tribune News, "Boston Herald Inside Track Column," October 25, 2010; Andrew Weymes, "Bill Hader, Anna Faris and Eliza Dushku Possibilities for 'Ghostbusters 3,'" *Ottawa Examiner*, November 30, 2010.

33. Mike Fleming Jr., "The Challenge of Sequelizing Ghostbusters," Deadline, January 11, 2011, https://deadline.com/2011/01/the-challenge-of-sequelizing-ghostbusters-95180.

34. Kristina Dorsey, "Conn College Grad Has 'The Office' Behind Him and Movies Ahead," McClatchy-Tribune Business News, January 25, 2011.

35. Anthony Ocasio, "Bill Murray Gives 'Ghostbusters 3' Update; HAS NOT Read the Script," Screen Rant, February 22, 2011, https://screenrant.com/bill-murray-ghostbusters-3-howard-stern; "Ghostbusters 3 Selected News Archive: 2010s," Spook Central, accessed January 30, 2022, https://www.theraffon.net/spook central/gb3_news.htm.

36. Jeannie Park, "Blast from the Past: 'Ghostbusters II' Is Under Way," *Seattle Post-Intelligencer*, December 23, 1988, 9.

37. "Fast Track," *The Expositor*, August 7, 1999, D8.

38. Carrie Holtz, "Harold Ramis Talks 'Ghostbusters 3,'" *Chicago Examiner*, April 18, 2010.

39. Violet Ramis Stiel, *Ghostbusters Daughter: Life with My Dad Harold Ramis* (New York: Penguin Random House, 2018), 338–41.

40. Virginia Rohan, "'Who Ya Gonna Call?,'" *The Record*, October 12, 2011, F3.

41. dsiegel, "Who Ya Gonna Call? Not Bill Murray!," *National Enquirer*, December 16, 2011, https://www.nationalenquirer.com/mike-walker/who-ya-gonna-call-not-bill-murray.

42. Ali Plumb, "Dan Aykroyd on Ghostbusters 3 Rumors," Empire, February 13, 2012, https://www.empireonline.com/movies/news/dan-aykroyd-ghostbusters-3-rumours; Oliver Lyttelton, "Dan Aykroyd Says Bill Murray Won't Do 'Ghostbusters 3,' Says Project in 'Suspended Animation,' Although Sony Still Interested," Indiewire, February 29, 2012, https://www.indiewire.com/2012/02/dan-aykroyd-says-bill-murray-wont-do-ghostbusters-3-says-project-is-in-suspended-animation-although-sony-still-interested-253660.

43. Mike Fleming Jr., "Third Installment of 'Ghostbusters' a Go for Early 2015; Death of Pal Harold Ramis Prompts Ivan Reitman to Turn Over Directing Reins," Deadline, March 18, 2014, https://deadline.com/2014/03/ghostbusters-movie-going-forward-without-ivan-reitman-sony-701057.

44. Lacey Rose, "How 'Little America' Showrunner Lee Eisenberg Cast International Actors Under Trump's Travel Ban," *Hollywood Reporter*, January 16, 2020, https://www.hollywoodreporter.com/news/general-news/how-little-america-showrunner-cast-international-actors-under-trumps-travel-ban-1269563.

45. Ramin Setoodeh, "'Ghostbusters' Reboot: ll Bill Murray Return in Smaller Role?," *Variety*, October 14, 2014, https://variety.com/2014/film/news/ghostbusters-reboot-will-bill-murray-return-in-smaller-role-1201330132.

46. Evan Dickson, "Bill Murray Officially Out of 'Ghostbusters 3,' Peter Venkman Not in the Script," Bloody Disgusting, August 2, 2012, https://bloody-disgusting.com/news/3157224/bill-murray-officially-out-of-ghostbusters-3-peter-venkman-not-in-the-script.

47. "'Ghostbusters 3' Being Revived," *Bradenton Herald*, July 10, 2012, Buzz Worthy section; Pamela McClintock, "Box Office Report: 'Men in Black 3'

Becomes Highest-Grossing Title in Franchise," *Hollywood Reporter*, July 1, 2012, https://www.hollywoodreporter.com/movies/movie-news/box-office-report-men-black-mib3-will-smith-tommy-lee-jones-josh-brolin-sony-343957; Lisa Schwarzbaum, "Men in Black 3," *Entertainment Weekly*, June 2, 2012, https://ew.com/article/2012/06/02/men-black-3-2.

48. Dickson, "Bill Murray Officially Out"; Kim Masters, "Sony Chief: Film Studio Not for Sale," *Hollywood Reporter*, October 30, 2012, https://www.hollywoodreporter.com/news/sony-chief-kaz-hirai-film-384605; Michael B. Dougherty, "Q&A: Dan Aykroyd Is Keeping *Ghostbusters 3* Alive," *Esquire*, December 4, 2012, https://www.esquire.com/entertainment/movies/interviews/a17104/dan-aykroyd-interview-14813380.

49. World Entertainment News Network, "Ghostbusters 3 Is a Go as Billy Murray Signs On—Report," December 3, 2012.

50. "Bill Murray Has Not Agreed to Do 'Ghostbusters 3,'" *Philadelphia Examiner*, December 5, 2012.

51. Amy Pascal, email to Amy Pascal, January 4, 2014; Hanna Minghella, email to Amy Pascal, January 4, 2014; Doug Belgrad, email to Amy Pascal, January 4, 2014; Jonathan Kadin, email to Amy Pascal, Doug Belgrad, Hannah Minghella, Adam North, Kelsey McCarthy, Alegre Rodriquez, and Anna Kelly, December 19, 2013; Adam North, email to Amy Pascal, December 19, 2013.

52. Mark Reilly, "Jonah Hill and Emma Stone Ain't Afraid of No Ghosts! Ghostbusters 3 Developments!" Schmoesknow, November 7, 2013, http://schmoesknow.com/jonah-hill-and-emma-stone-aint-afraid-of-no-ghosts-ghostbusters-3-developments; Doug Belgrad, email to Amy Pascal, November 7, 2013.

53. Eric Reich, email to Amy Pascal, Doug Belgrad, Jonathan Kadin, Hannah Minghella, Etan Cohen, Ali Bell, Joe Medjuck, and Tom Pollack, December 19, 2013.

54. Andrew Gumpert, email to Amy Pascal, February 22, 2014.

55. Mark Caro, "Harold Ramis, Chicago Actor, Writer and Director, Dead at 69," *Chicago Tribune*, February 24, 2014, https://web.archive.org/web/20140225003701/http://www.chicagotribune.com/entertainment/chi-harold-ramis-dead-20140224,0,4983189,full.story.

56. "Dan Aykroyd Leads Tributes to Harold Ramis," BANG Showbiz, February 24, 2014; "Quinn: Ramis 'Made the World a Better Place,'" Associated Press State Wire: Illinois, February 24, 2014; "Chicago Mayor Calls Harold Ramis 'Legend,'" Associated Press State Wire: Illinois, February 24, 2014; Barack Obama, "Statement from the President on the Passing of Harold Ramis," February 25, 2014, archived at https://obamawhitehouse.archives.gov/the-press-office/2014/02/25/statement-president-passing-harold-ramis.

57. Maria Vultaggio, "Bill Murray Reacts to 'Ghostbusters' Star Harold Ramis' Death: 'God Bless Him,'" *International Business Times*, February 24, 2014, Media & Culture section.

58. Stiel, *Ghostbusters Daughter*, 176–77.

59. Tatiana Siegel and Borys Kit, "*Ghostbusters III* to Move Forward without Ramis," *Hollywood Reporter*, February 26, 2014, 7.

60. Stephen Applebaum, "Popping Bubbly with Bill Murray," Dazed, February 27, 2014, http://www.dazeddigital.com/artsandculture/article/19003/1/bill-murray-hollywoods-last-eccentric.

CHAPTER 10: GIRLS TO THE FRONT

1. Mike Fleming Jr., "Third Installment of 'Ghostbusters' a Go for Early 2015; Death of Pal Harold Ramis Prompts Ivan Reitman to Turn Over Directing Reins," Deadline, March 18, 2014. https://deadline.com/2014/03/ghostbusters-movie-going-forward-without-ivan-reitman-sony-701057.

2. Jennifer Wood, "Ivan Reitman: Why We're Still Talking About 'Ghostbusters' 30 Years Later," *Rolling Stone*, July 6, 2016, https://www.rollingstone.com/movies/movie-news/ivan-reitman-why-were-still-talking-about-ghostbusters-30-years-later-226806; Jada Yuan, "Ivan Reitman on Bill Murray, Internet Trolls, and Why He Fought for the *Ghostbusters* Reboot," Vulture, July 14, 2016, https://www.vulture.com/2016/07/ivan-reitman-ghostbusters-bill-murray-qa.html.

3. Dominique Adams, email to Amy Pascal, March 20, 2014.

4. Ruben Fleischer, email to Amy Pascal, March 19, 2014; Philip Bache, email to Amy Pascal, March 19, 2014; Dominique Adams, email to Amy Pascal, March 19, 2014; Amy Pascal, email to Ivan Reitman, March 20, 2014.

5. "'21 Jump Street' Leaps to No. 1 with $35M Debut," *Cordele Dispatch*, March 20, 2012; Michael O'Sullivan, "'The Lego Movie' Review: Toy-Themed Adventure Celebrates Creativity," *Washington Post*, February 6, 2014, https://www.washingtonpost.com/goingoutguide/movies/the-lego-movie-review-toy-themed-adventure-celebrates-creativity/2014/02/05/ba3d6b26-8cff-11e3-95dd-36ff657a4dae_story.html; A. O. Scott, "Toying with Ideas Outside the Manual," *New York Times*, February 6, 2014, https://web.archive.org/web/20140309041306/http://www.nytimes.com/2014/02/07/movies/the-lego-movie-toys-with-thinking-outside-the-manual.html; Ray Subers, "Weekend Report: Everything Is Awesome for 'The Lego Movie,'" Box Office Mojo, February 9, 2014, https://www.boxofficemojo.com/article/ed545129476.

6. Angie Han, "'Ghostbusters 3': Phil Lord and Chris Miller May Not Direct [Updated]," Slash Film, April 7, 2014, https://www.slashfilm.com/530921/ghostbusters-3-phil-lord-chris-miller-eyed-direct.

7. Mark Petix, "Nailz Crowned San Diego's Comedy King," *Times-Advocate*, April 30, 1987, 18; Judy Brown, "Comedy Pick of the Week," *LA Weekly*, July 16, 1987, 132; Susan Pierce, "'Heavyweights' Loaded Down with Sweet Predictability," *Arkansas Democrat-Gazette*, February 17, 1995, 12; Howard Schindler, "Fawcett, O'Neal to Debut as Sports Anchors in 'Good Sports,'" *Salt Lake Tribune*, January 10, 1991, D7; "The Best in TV This Week," *Miami Herald TV*, November 29, 1992, 4.

8. David Kronke, "Breaking Out All Over; Creators of New Teen Shows Make Their Bid for Credibility," *Daily News*, August 15, 1999, L3.

9. Jeanne Jakle, "Local TV Lineup Targets Teens," *San Antonio Express-News*, August 12, 1999, 4F; Steve Johnson, "TV's Fall Preview Hype-Apalooza an Excuse to Escape Chicago's Heat," *Chicago Tribune*, August 9, 1999, 1; Robert Blanco, "The World According to TV: Everybody Is White, Sex-Crazed, Beautiful and Young—Just Like in Reality, Right?," *USA Today*, August 6, 1999, 01E; Sonia Rao, "How 'Freaks and Geeks' Went from Misfit Dramedy to Cult Classic, as Told by Its Cast and Creators," *Washington Post*, January 27, 2021, https://www.washingtonpost.com/arts-entertainment/2021/01/27/freaks-and-geeks-streaming-hulu-cast-creators-interview.

10. Simon Brew, "Paul Feig Interview: Ghostbusters, the Web, Sony," Den of Geek, July 4, 2016, https://www.denofgeek.com/movies/paul-feig-interview-ghostbusters-the-web-sony.

11. Andrea Hubert, "Paul Feig: Hollywood's Accidental Feminist," *The Guardian*, July 20, 2013, https://www.theguardian.com/film/2013/jul/20/paul-feig-the-heat; Dana Stevens, "Bridesmaids," Slate, May 12, 2011, http://www.slate.com/articles/arts/movies/2011/05/bridesmaids.html; Justin Chang, "Movie Review; Film Critic; A Bit Deja Boo; Brilliant Women Are Haunted by Nostalgia," *Los Angeles Times*, July 14, 2016, E1; "Bridesmaids Officially the Biggest Judd Apatow Film Ever," Movieline, July 1, 2011, http://movieline.com/2011/07/01/bridesmaids-becomes-the-biggest-judd-apatow-film-ever; Meghan Lewit, "Judd

Apatow Is Not Sexist," *The Atlantic*, May 11, 2011, https://www.theatlantic .com/entertainment/archive/2011/05/judd-apatow-is-not-sexist/238621.

12. Brew, "Paul Feig Interview"; Ethan Anderton, "Paul Feig Turned Down 'Ghostbusters 3' in Favor of the Female-Led Reboot," Slash Film, May 31, 2015, https://www.slashfilm.com/537987/paul-feig-turned-down-ghostbusters-3.

13. Tracey Jacobs, email to Amy Pascal, March 21, 2014.

14. Amy Pascal, email to Amy Pascal, Doug Belgrad, Michael Deluca, and Hannah Minghella, March 19, 2014.

15. Doug Belgrad, email to Hannah Minghella, Amy Pascal, and Michael Deluca, March 20, 2014.

16. Doug Belgrad, email to Amy Pascal and Risa Gertner, April 2, 2014.

17. Brew, "Paul Feig Interview"; Anderton, "Paul Feig Turned Down."

18. Amy Pascal, email to Michael Pavlic, July 28, 2014; Peter Travers, "Bridesmaids," *Rolling Stone*, no. 1131 (May 26, 2011), 91; Rose Lacey, "Melissa Is Having Her Moment," *Hollywood Reporter* 417, no. 35 (October 7, 2011), 34–39; Richard Corliss, "The Top 10 Everything of 2010: Emma Stone as Olive in *Easy A*," *Time*, December 9, 2010, https://web.archive.org/web/20101213001150/http://www .time.com/time/specials/packages/article/0,28804,2035319_2035307_2032774,00 .html; Roger Ebert, "Don't Sleep with Anybody, but Say You Did," RogerEbert. com, September 15, 2010, https://www.rogerebert.com/reviews/easy-a-2010; "Naughty but Nice," *Emmy* 35, no. 3 (January 2013), 8; Janice Somosot, "'X-Men: Days of Future Past' Costars Jennifer Lawrence and Nicholas Hoult Spotted on a Date in Hampshire," *International Business Times: Australian Edition*, Entertainment section.

19. Michael Pavlic. email to Amy Pascal. July 28, 2014.

20. Borys Kit, "'Ghostbusters 3' Targets Paul Feig as Director," *Hollywood Reporter*, August 2, 2014, https://www.hollywoodreporter.com/heat-vision/ ghostbusters-3-targets-paul-feig-as-director-723028.

21. Maane Khatchatourian, "Paul Feig in Talks to Direct 'Ghostbusters' Reboot with Women," *Variety*, August 2, 2014, https://variety.com/2014/film/news/ paul-feig-ghostbusters-comedy-reboot-1201274332.

22. Amy Pascal, email to Jean Guerin, August 2, 2014; Doug Belgrad, email to Hannah Minghella, August 2, 2014.

23. Paul Feig, email to Amy Pascal, August 4, 2014.

24. Mike Fleming Jr., "Film Chauvinist Asks: Do We Want an Estrogen-Powered 'Ghostbusters'?," Deadline, August 3, 2014, https://deadline.com/2014/08/ film-chauvinist-asks-do-we-want-an-estrogen-powered-ghostbusters.

25. Amy Pascal, email to Mark Wyman, Doug Belgrad, Michael Deluca, Andrew Gumpert, and Jonathan Kadin, August 8, 2014; Michael Deluca, email to Mark Wyman, Doug Belgrad, Amy Pascal, Andrew Gumpert, and Jonathan Kadin, August 8, 2014; Michael Deluca, email to Jonathan Kadin, Hannah Minghella, Amy Pascal, and Doug Belgrad, June 24, 2014.

26. Rachel O'Connor, email to Hannah Minghella, Amy Pascal, Doug Belgrad, and Michael Deluca, October 12, 2014; Michael Deluca, email to Hannah Minghella, Amy Pascal, and Doug Belgrad, August 22, 2014; Reid Carolin, email to Amy Pascal, August 22, 2014; Channing Tatum, email to Amy Pascal, August 22, 2014; Michael Deluca, email to Doug Belgrad and Amy Pascal, August 28, 2014; Doug Belgrad, email to Amy Pascal, Michael Deluca, and Hannah Minghella, August 31, 2014.

27. Paul Feig, email to Amy Pascal, September 7, 2014.

28. Doug Belgrad, email to Amy Pascal, Hannah Minghella, and Michael Deluca, October 4, 2014.

29. Doug Belgrad, email to Michael Deluca and Amy Pascal, October 8, 2014; Amy Pascal, email to Doug Belgrad and Michael Deluca, September 14, 2014.

30. Ivan Reitman, email to Amy Pascal, Doug Belgrad, and Michael Deluca, October 8, 2014.

31. Amy Pascal, email to Ivan Reitman, Michael Deluca, and Doug Belgrad, October 8, 2014; Paul Feig, email to Amy Pascal, October 21, 2014.

32. Michael Deluca, email to Amy Pascal, Doug Belgrad, and Jonathan Kadin, October 13, 2014.

33. Peter Howell, "TIFF: Bill Murray Scares Up Female Ghostbusters Cast Suggestions," *Toronto Star*, September 7, 2014, https://www.thestar.com/entertainment/tiff/2014/09/07/tiff_bill_murray_scares_up_female_ghostbusters_cast_suggestions.html.

34. Kevin Polowy, "Kristen Wiig Reacts to Bill Murray's 'Ghostbusters 3' Endorsement," Yahoo! News, September 10, 2014, https://www.yahoo.com/news/kristen-wiig-ghostbusters-3-bill-murray-97172198627.html.

35. "'SNL' Picks Fallon & Fey to Do 'News,'" *New York Daily News*, October 6, 2000, Television section, 154.

36. Sara Stewart, "Kristen Wiig—'SNL' Funny Lady Gets Knocked Up to Rock Out in New Comedy," *New York Post*, December 16, 2007, 65; Gary Levin, "'SNL' Has a Tough Act to Follow," *USA Today*, September 25, 2009, 3D.

37. Alison Ashton, "Who You Gonna Call: The All-Female *Ghostbusters*," *Parade*, July 1, 2016, https://parade.com/487240/alison-ashton/who-you-gonna-call-the-all-female-ghostbusters.

38. "33 Defining Moments of the Past Five Years," *Hollywood Reporter* 421, no. 39 (November 27, 2015), 96–97.

39. William Boot, "Exclusive: Sony Hack Reveals Jennifer Lawrence Is Paid Less Than Her Male Co-Stars," *Daily Beast*, December 12, 2014, https://www.thedailybeast.com/exclusive-sony-hack-reveals-jennifer-lawrence-is-paid-less-than-her-male-co-stars.

40. "#210B—Bonus: Ghost Corps Trailer Event Q&A—March 5, 2016," *The Ghostbusters Interdimensional Crossrip Podcast*, March 5, 2016, archived at http://www.ghostbustershq.net/the-ghostbusters-interdimensional-crossrip/2016/3/4/210b-bonus-ghost-corps-trailer-event-qa-march-5-2016.

41. Anna Klassen, "'Ghostbusters' Writer Talks Paul Feig & Horror," Bustle, July 14, 2016, bustle.com/articles/172383-ghostbusters-katie-dippold-talks-horror-influences-upcoming-amy-schumer-project; Ashton, "Who You Gonna Call."

42. Ryan Gajewski, "Emma Stone: I Turned Down 'Ghostbusters' Because 'It's a Whole Thing,'" *Hollywood Reporter*, June 17, 2015, https://www.hollywoodreporter.com/movies/movie-features/emma-stone-ghostbusters-i-turned-803358.

43. "Ghostbusters 3 Cast: Jennifer Lawrence, Shailene Woodley, Christian Bale + More!," YouTube, posted by MTV UK on December 10, 2014, https://www.youtube.com/watch?list=UUuwUfM8E79h2sqp34Fut6kw&time_continue=137&v=skGgbGiiEdo; Kevin Polowy, "Paul Feig Explains Why Jennifer Lawrence Couldn't Join 'Ghostbusters,'" Yahoo! Entertainment, March 9, 2016, https://www.yahoo.com/entertainment/paul-feig-explains-why-jennifer-lawrence-couldnt-194905400.html.

44. Greg Gilman, "Lena Dunham and Melissa McCarthy Talk 'Ghostbusters' on 'Ellen,'" Yahoo! Entertainment, October 20, 2014, https://www.yahoo.com/entertainment/news/lena-dunham-melissa-mccarthy-talk-ghostbusters-ellen-video-145500130.html.

45. Seth Abramovitch, "Yes, I Did Say That!," *Hollywood Reporter* 420, no. 38 (October 31, 2014), 16.

46. Warren Zavala, email to Amy Pascal, November 19, 2013; Amy Pascal, email to Ivan Reitman, Michael Deluca, and Doug Belgrad, October 8, 2014.

47. Randee Dawn, "'Night at the Museum' Star Rebel Wilson Could Be Ghostbusting Soon: 'I'd Do That for Free,'" *Today*, December 10, 2014. https://www.today.com/popculture/night-museum-star-rebel-wilson-could-be-ghostbusting-soon-id-1D80349128.

48. Paul Feig, email to Amy Pascal, September 7, 2014.

49. Esther Zuckerman, "Cecily Strong on *Staten Island Summer*, *Ghostbusters* & Chris Hemsworth," Refinery29, July 22, 2015, https://www.refinery29.com/en-us/2015/07/91098/cecily-strong-ghostbusters-staten-island-summer.

50. Margaret Lange, "Kate Fancy," *GQ* 85, no. 8 (August 2015), https://www.gq.com/story/kate-mckinnon-hillary-impression-snl; Borys Kit, "New All-Female 'Ghostbusters' Cast Chosen," *Hollywood Reporter*, January 27, 2015, https://www.hollywoodreporter.com/movies/movie-news/new-all-female-ghostbusters-cast-767610; "'SNL' Adds Two Black Writers, LaKendra Tookes and Leslie Jones, After Hiring Black Cast Member," *Huffington Post*, January 23, 2014, https://www.huffpost.com/entry/snl-lakendra-tookes-leslie-jones-writing-team_n_4563358; "The 40 Most Hilarious, Surprising Defining Moments from SNL," *Hollywood Reporter* 421, no. 5 (February 13, 2015), 89; Director's & Writers' Commentary, *Ghostbuster* DVD, Columbia Pictures, 2016.

51. Emmet McDermott, "Dan Aykroyd: New 'Ghostbusters' Cast Is 'Magnificent,'" *Hollywood Reporter*, January 28, 2015, https://www.hollywoodreporter.com/news/general-news/dan-aykroyd-new-ghostbusters-cast-767943.

52. Emmet McDermott, "Ernie Hudson Changes Mind About All-Female 'Ghostbusters': 'Phenomenal!,'" *Hollywood Reporter*, January 29, 2015, https://www.hollywoodreporter.com/news/general-news/ernie-hudson-changes-mind-all-768310.

53. Anita Singh, "Female Ghostbusters? Fans Don't Want It, Says Ernie Hudson," *Daily Telegraph*, October 9, 2014, Culture section.

54. Rebecca Hawkes, "Dan Aykroyd: I Want Jason Statham for Ghostbusters," *The Telegraph*, September 18, 2014, https://www.telegraph.co.uk/culture/film/film-news/11103725/Dan-Aykroyd-I-want-Jason-Statham-for-Ghostbusters.html.

55. Mike Fleming Jr., "Guy-Themed 'Ghostbusters' Film with Channing Tatum in the Works," March 8, 2015, Yahoo! Entertainment, https://www.yahoo.com/entertainment/guy-themed-ghostbusters-film-with-channing-tatum-113199869717.html; Sean O'Neal, "Sony Is Also Making Another *Ghostbusters* for Men," AV Club, March 9, 2015, https://www.avclub.com/sony-is-also-making-another-ghostbusters-for-men-1798277338; Daniel Kibblesmith, "Some Men Are Pretty Mad About Female 'Ghostbusters,'" BuzzFeed, January 27, 2015, https://www.buzzfeed.com/danielkibblesmith/who-you-gonna-call-misandry-busters.

56. Devin Faraci, "Chris Pratt Could Join the Ghostbusters Expanded Universe," Badass Digest, March 9, 2015, archived at https://web.archive.org/web/20150315143615/http://badassdigest.com/2015/03/09/chris-pratt-could-join-the-ghostbusters-expanded-universe.

57. Mike Fleming Jr., "Sony Plans New 'Ghostbusters' Film with Russo Brothers, Channing Tatum & 'IM3' Scribe Drew Pearce," Deadline, March 9, 2015, https://deadline.com/2015/03/ghostbusters-channing-tatum-joe-and-anthony-russo-drew-pearce-ivan-reitman-dan-aykroyd-1201388917.

58. "EG's Drew Pearce, Hollywood Writer and Director," East Grinstead Online, March 14, 2015, archived at https://web.archive.org/web/20150521013113/https://www.bluebelldigital.co.uk/eastgrinsteadonline/2015/03/14/drew-pearce-hollywood-writer-and-director.

59. Chris Heath, "Jurassic Pratt," *GQ*, May 17, 2015, https://www.gq.com/story/chris-pratt-cover-story.

60. Russ Fischer, "Channing Tatum Version of 'Ghostbusters' May Be Dead for Now [Updated]," SlashFilm, June 26, 2015, https://www.slashfilm.com/538417/channing-tatum-ghostbusters; Sandy Schaefer, "'Ghostbusters': Channing

Tatum Spinoff Not Happening for Now," Screen Rant, June 25, 2015, https://screenrant.com/ghostbusters-channing-tatum-reboot.

61. Anne T. Donahue, "There's Something Strange in This Neighbourhood," *Globe and Mail*, July 31, 2015, R4; Fred Topel, "Ghostbusters Spinoff Could Connect New and Original Ghostbusters," Nerd Report, July 24, 2015, http://www.nerdreport.com/2015/07/24/ghostbusters-spinoff-could-connect-new-and-original-ghostbusters.

62. Tracy Brown, "Ivan Reitman Says 'There Is Only One New Ghostbusters Movie,'" *Los Angeles Times*, July 30, 2015, https://www.latimes.com/entertainment/herocomplex/la-et-hc-ivan-reitman-ghostbusters-movie-statement-20150730-story.html.

63. Germain Lussier, "The *Ghostbusters* Franchise May Be 'Endless,' but It's All Still Very Much in Flux," io9, July 11, 2016, https://gizmodo.com/the-ghostbusters-franchise-may-be-endless-but-its-all-1783449170.

64. Irene Kahn Atkins, "In Search of The Greatest Gatsby," *Literature/Film Quarterly* 2, no. 3 (Summer 1974), 216–28.

65. Elizabeth Kiefer, "Lizzy Caplan Has a Bag of Tricks in Her Arsenal & They Aren't All Magic," Refinery29, July 1, 2016, https://www.refinery29.com/en-gb/2016/06/113219/lizzy-caplan-now-you-see-me-2.

66. Fleming, "Film Chauvinist Asks"; Brian Raftery, "A Ghostbuster and a Gentleman," *Wired* 24, no. 7 (July 2016). Archived at https://www.wired.com/2016/07/paul-feig-ghostbusters-qa/; Kibblesmith, "Some Men Are Pretty Mad"; Marcy Cook, "Why All Those Sexist Complaints About the New *Ghostbusters* Are Garbage," The Mary Sue, January 31, 2015, https://www.themarysue.com/ghostbusters-sexist-complaints-garbage.

67. Kayleigh Roberts, "The Woman Who Wrote the 'Ghostbusters' Reboot on Being Trolled and Pressing On," *Marie Claire*, May 15, 2017, https://www.marieclaire.com/celebrity/news/a27118/katie-dippold-snatched-interview.

68. Jenelle Riley, "'Spy' Director Paul Feig on Backlash to Female 'Ghostbusters,'" *Variety*, March 15, 2015, https://variety.com/2015/film/news/sxsw-spy-director-paul-feig-on-response-to-female-ghostbusters-1201451451.

69. Sara C. Nelson, "Donald Trump Is Confused About the All-Woman Ghostbusters Film," *Huffington Post*, February 2, 2015, https://www.huffingtonpost.co.uk/2015/02/02/donald-trump-confused-about-all-woman-ghostbusters-film_n_6593046.html; Mike Fleming Jr., "Disney Eyeing Chris Pratt for Indiana Jones Revival," Deadline, January 27, 2015, https://deadline.com/2015/01/chris-pratt-indiana-jones-guardians-of-the-galaxy-disney-1201360637.

70. Raftery, "A Ghostbuster."

71. Megh Wright, "Ivan Reitman on How 'Ghostbusters III' Will Compare to the Original," Vulture, April 11, 2014, https://www.vulture.com/2014/04/ivan-reitman-on-how-ghostbusters-iii-will-compare-to-the-original.html.

CHAPTER 11: ANSWER THE CALL

1. Simon Brew, "Paul Feig Interview: Ghostbusters, the Web, Sony," Den of Geek, July 4, 2016, https://www.denofgeek.com/movies/paul-feig-interview-ghostbusters-the-web-sony.

2. Emma Brown, "Katie Dippold, the Superfan Behind Ghostbusters," *Interview*, July 14, 2016, https://www.interviewmagazine.com/culture/katie-dippold-ghostbusters.

3. Elizabeth Day, "Haunted by Expectation but Defiantly Undaunted," *The Australian*, July 6, 2016, 15.

4. Mark Byrne, "The Punch List: Love in the Time of Slime," *GQ* 86, no. 7 (July 2016), 37; "Crossing the Streams," *Nottingham Evening Post*, July 8, 2016, 2; Claudia Eller, "How

Kate McKinnon Uses Comedy to Cope with Her Social Anxiety," *Variety*, October 2021, https://variety.com/2021/tv/features/kate-mckinnon-saturday-night-live-ghostbusters-1234965601.

5. James Mottram, "Chris Hemsworth Says a Role in the Ghostbusters Remake Was Too Good to Pass Up," *The National*, July 13, 2016.

6. William Bibbiani, "Interview: 'Ghostbusters' Villain Neil Casey on Playing an Evil Ghostbuster," Mandatory, July 15, 2016, https://www.mandatory.com/culture/1010251-interview-ghostbusters-villain-neil-casey-playing-evil-ghostbuster.

7. Day, "Haunted by Expectation."

8. Author interview with Jefferson Sage, June 4, 2019.

9. Author interview with Audra Avery, March 9, 2021.

10. Author interview with Jefferson Sage, June 4, 2019.

11. Author interview with Andrew DeCristofaro, July 30, 2020.

12. Author interview with Jefferson Sage, June 4, 2019.

13. Author interview with Audra Avery, March 9, 2021.

14. Author interview with Jefferson Sage, June 4, 2019.

15. Author interview with Brent White, January 25, 2021.

16. Dave McNary, "Amy Pascal Talks Getting 'Fired,' Sony Hack and Angelina Jolie Emails in Candid Interview," *Variety*, February 11, 2015, https://variety.com/2015/film/news/amy-pascal-sony-angelina-jolie-obama-hack-the-interview-1201431167; Dominic Rushe, "Amy Pascal Steps Down from Sony Pictures in Wake of Damaging Email Hack," *The Guardian*, February 5, 2015, https://www.theguardian.com/film/2015/feb/05/amy-pascal-leaving-sony-pictures-email-leak.

17. Kim Masters and Tatiana Siegel, "'Ghostbusters' Budget Cut, Fox Execs Courted: Tom Rothman Puts His Stamp on Sony," *Hollywood Reporter*, April 20, 2015, https://www.hollywoodreporter.com/news/ghostbusters-budget-cut-fox-execs-789896.

18. "'Ghostbusters' Remake Begins Filming in Everett," *Boston Globe*, June 19, 2015, B16; Meredith Goldstein, "Casting 'Flapjack'—or 'Ghostbusters'?," *Boston Globe*, June 23, 2015, B12; Author interview with Audra Avery, March 9, 2021.

19. Christian Schiavone, "'Ghostbusters' Reboot to Begin Filming at SouthField," Wicked Local Rockland, August 7, 2015, https://rockland.wickedlocal.com/article/20150807/NEWS/150807355.

20. "'Ghostbusters' Remake," *Boston Globe*; Megan Turchi, "Has 'Ghostbusters' Made Its Way to Boston University?," Boston.com, August 17, 2015, https://www.boston.com/culture/movies/2015/08/17/has-ghostbusters-made-its-way-to-boston-university; "Movie/Film Location," Boch Center, accessed February 15, 2022, https://www.bochcenter.org/host-an-event/moviefilm-location.

21. Author interview with Jefferson Sage, June 4, 2019.

22. Meredith Goldstein, "Leslie Jones Talks Boston in The New Yorker," *Boston Globe*, December 28, 2015.

23. Luke Owen, "14 Rumours About the Troubled Ghostbusters Reboot Production," Flickering Myth, July 7, 2016, https://www.flickeringmyth.com/2016/07/14-rumours-about-the-troubled-ghostbusters-reboot-production; Genevieve Uzamere, "'Ghostbusters' Cast Mates at War—Why Did Kristen Wiig Start the Feud?," *Star*, January 20, 2016, https://starmagazine.com/photos/ghostbusters-drama-on-set-kristen-wiig-fighting-cast-mates.

24. Author interview with J. J. Dalton, April 6, 2020.

25. Author interview with Mark Hawker, April 7, 2019.

26. Author interview with Mark Hawker, April 7, 2019.

27. "Call Me," *Dayton Daily News*, July 2, 2016, SPD 6.

28. Author interview with Brent White, January 25, 2021.

29. "Melissa McCarthy Found 'Ghostbuster' Experience Creepy," IANS English, July 13, 2016.
30. Author interview with Jefferson Sage, June 4, 2019.
31. Matt Giles, "Ghostbusters' Proton Packs Get a Makeover," *Popular Science* 288, no. 4 (July/August 2016), 90; Tamara Dietrich, "Physicist Answers 'Ghostbusters' Call: Jefferson Lab Employee Served as a Technical Adviser on Upcoming Movie," *Newport News*, July 3, 2016, A1.
32. Sugandha Rawal, "Chris Hemsworth Blew Female 'Ghostbusters' Away: Melissa McCarthy," IANS English, July 4, 2016.
33. Lindsey Bahr, "Q&A: Laughing Along with the Wickedly Funny 'Ghostbusters,'" *New York*, July 13, 2016.
34. Mottram, "Chris Hemsworth Says."
35. Peter Caranicas, "'Bridesmaids' Caught Improv on Film," *Variety*, May 17, 2011, https://variety.com/2011/film/columns/bridesmaids-caught-improv-on-film-1118037164.
36. Mottram, "Chris Hemsworth Says."
37. Author interview with J. J. Dalton, April 6, 2020.
38. Author interview with J. J. Dalton, April 6, 2020.
39. Author interview with Andrew DeCristofaro, July 30, 2020.
40. Ben Child, "Bill Murray Confirmed for New Ghostbusters Movie," *The Guardian*, August 10, 2015, https://www.theguardian.com/film/2015/aug/10/bill-murray-confirmed-for-new-ghostbusters-movie; Jamie Sharpe, "Bill Murray on Why He Agreed to Make a *Ghostbusters 3* Cameo," Vulture, August 31, 2015, https://www.vulture.com/2015/08/bill-murray-on-why-he-did-ghostbusters-cameo.html.
41. Ben Child, "Who Ya Gonna Call Back? Sigourney Weaver Set for Ghostbusters Reboot," *The Guardian*, September 25, 2015, https://www.theguardian.com/film/2015/sep/25/sigourney-weaver-to-return-for-ghostbusters-remake.
42. Ryan Parker, "Rick Moranis Reveals Why He Turned Down 'Ghostbusters' Reboot: 'It Makes No Sense to Me,'" *Hollywood Reporter*, October 7, 2015, https://www.hollywoodreporter.com/movies/movie-features/rick-moranis-reveals-why-he-829779.
43. Author interview with Brent White, January 25, 2021; author interview with Saul Saladow, March 25, 2019.
44. Bryan Bishop, "Analyzing the Ghostbusters Trailer with Director Paul Feig and Writer Katie Dippold," The Verge, March 3, 2016, https://www.theverge.com/2016/3/3/11150960/ghostbusters-interview-paul-feig-katie-dippold-trailer.
45. Jon Blistein, "Melissa McCarthy Explains 'Very Confusing' 'Ghostbusters' Trailer," *Rolling Stone*, May 3, 2016, https://www.rollingstone.com/movies/movie-news/melissa-mccarthy-explains-very-confusing-ghostbusters-trailer-65176.
46. Clarisse Loughrey, "Ghostbusters Trailer: Anger Over 'Add-On' Black Female Character in Movie Reboot," *The Independent*, March 3, 2016, https://www.independent.co.uk/arts-entertainment/films/news/ghostbusters-leslie-jones-character-criticised-for-a6909681.html; Leslie Jones, "Why can't a regular person . . .," Twitter, March 4, 2016, https://twitter.com/Lesdoggg/status/705636446162460673.
47. Elizabeth Day, "Haunted by Expectation but Defiantly Undaunted," *The Australian*, July 6, 2016, 15.
48. "Ghostbusters Trailer 'Most Disliked' on YouTube," BBC News, May 3, 2016, https://www.bbc.com/news/entertainment-arts-36191146#; Natalie Stone, "'Ghostbusters' Is the Most Disliked Movie Trailer in YouTube History," *Hollywood Reporter*, April 30, 2016, https://www.hollywoodreporter.com/news/general-news/ghostbusters-is-disliked-movie-trailer-889114.
49. Bryan Alexander, "Will Internet Slime Stick to the New 'Ghostbusters'?," *Argus Leader*, July 10, 2016, U2.
50. Author interview with Jefferson Sage, June 4, 2019.

51. "It's a Ghoul Thing," *New Zealand Herald*, July 7, 2016, C5.

52. Nick Miller, "Ghostbusters: Melissa McCarthy and Kristen Wiig Pity the 'Bizarre' Haters," *Sydney Morning Herald*, July 6, 2016, https://www.smh.com.au/entertainment/movies/melissa-mccarthy-and-kristen-wiig-feel-sorry-for-the-bizarre--ghostbusters-haters-20160705-gpyup2.html.

53. Dave Itzkoff, "Afraid? Of Them?," *New York Times*, June 26, 2016, AR1.

54. Melissa Anderson, "Busted Flat: All-Too-Normal Activity Dominates the 'Ghostbusters' Remake," *Village Voice*, July 10, 2016, https://www.villagevoice.com/2016/07/10/busted-flat-all-too-normal-activity-dominates-the-ghostbusters-remake.

55. Stephanie Zacharek, "Review: The New *Ghostbusters*, Modern and Vital, Goes for the Gusto," *Time*, July 10, 2016, https://time.com/4399395/review-the-new-ghostbusters.

56. Jen Yamato, "'Ghostbusters' Review: Kate McKinnon's Probably-Gay Gearhead Steals the Show," The Daily Beast, July 10, 2016, https://www.thedailybeast.com/ghostbusters-review-kate-mckinnons-probably-gay-gearhead-steals-the-show.

57. Peter Travers, "Ghostbusters," *Rolling Stone*, July 12, 2016, https://www.rollingstone.com/movies/movie-reviews/ghostbusters-97719.

58. Richard Lawson, "*Ghostbusters* Is a Flat, Occasionally Charming Disappointment," *Vanity Fair*, July 10, 2016, https://www.vanityfair.com/hollywood/2016/07/ghostbusters-review.

59. Yamato, "'Ghostbusters' Review"; Manohla Dargis, "Our 'Ghostbusters' Review: Girls Rule. Women Are Funny. Get Over It," *New York Times*, July 10, 2016, https://www.nytimes.com/2016/07/15/movies/ghostbusters-review-melissa-mccarthy-kristen-wiig.html; Jake Wilson, "Sassy Reboot Slays Cynical Naysayers," *The Age*, July 14, 2016, 26.

60. Bridget Kies, "Ghostbusters," *Queer Studies in Media & Pop Culture* 2, no. 2 (2017), 265–69.

61. Jake Coyle, "'Ghostbusters' Holds Its Own, but 'Life of Pets' Still No. 1," Associated Press News Service, July 17, 2016; Pamela McClintock, "'Ghostbusters' Heading for $70M-Plus Loss, Sequel Unlikely," *Hollywood Reporter*, August 10, 2016, https://www.hollywoodreporter.com/news/general-news/ghostbusters-box-office-loss-sequel-unlikely-918515.

62. Author interview with Audra Avery, March 9, 2021.

63. Author interview with Anthony Lamberti, August 2, 2020.

64. Author interview with Jefferson Sage, June 4, 2019.

65. Kate Conger, "Harassment of Ghostbusters' Leslie Jones Shows Twitter Needs to Change," TechCrunch, July 19, 2016, https://techcrunch.com/2016/07/19/leslie-jones-twitter-harassment.

66. Alex Abad-Santos, "Rio 2016: Leslie Jones's Olympics Play-by-Play Is a Gift from the Greek Gods," Vox, August 8, 2016, https://www.vox.com/2016/8/8/12401368/leslie-jones-olympic-commentary-live-tweet.

67. Germain Lussier, "Nope, *Ghostbusters* Did Not Suddenly Get a New Title," Gizmodo, September 1, 2016, https://gizmodo.com/nope-ghostbusters-has-not-suddenly-gotten-a-new-title-1786062339.

68. Dade Hayes, "Dan Aykroyd Blames Director Paul Feig for 'Ghostbusters' Reboot: 'It Cost Too Much,'" Deadline, June 4, 2017, https://deadline.com/2017/06/aykroyd-blasts-paul-feig-in-tv-interview-1202107198; Gregg Kilday, "Dan Aykroyd Blasts 'Ghostbusters' Director Paul Feig: 'He Will Not Be Back on the Sony Lot Anytime Soon,'" *Hollywood Reporter*, June 4, 2017, https://www.hollywoodreporter.com/movies/movie-features/dan-aykroyd-blasts-ghostbusters-director-paul-feig-he-will-not-be-back-sony-lot-anytime-soon-1010055.

69. Taylor Ferber, "Paul Feig Regrets That His *Ghostbusters* Remake Turned Into a 'Cause,'" Vulture, November 20, 2017, https://www.vulture.com/2017/11/paul-feig-regrets-that-ghostbusters-remake-became-a-cause.html.

70. Katharine Trendacosta, "The Extended *Ghostbusters* Cut Fixed the Film's Biggest Plot Hole," Gizmodo, September 29, 2016, https://gizmodo.com/the-extended-ghostbusters-cut-fixes-some-of-the-films-b-1787212329.

71. Author interview with Brent White, March 12, 2022.

72. David Mack, "This 'Ghostbusters' Premiere Photo Shows Why Representation Matters," BuzzFeed News, July 14, 2016, https://www.buzzfeednews.com/article/davidmack/kristen-wiig-ghostbusters.

CHAPTER 12: HAVE YOU MISSED US?

1. "Dan Aykroyd," *The Big Interview with Dan Rather*, 2018, https://www.axs.tv/channel/the-big-interview-with-dan-rather-season-6/the-big-interview-with-dan-rather-season-6/video/dan-aykroyd; "The Big Interview with Dan Rather: Dan Aykroyd," IMDb, accessed February 22, 2022, https://www.imdb.com/title/tt9272732.

2. "'Ghostbusters' Animated Feature in Development at Sony," The Tracking Board, October 1, 2015, https://www.tracking-board.com/exclusive-ghostbusters-animated-feature-in-development-at-sony; "Ivan Reitman Talks About Ghostbusters Future at #SDCC," YouTube, posted by Matt Jarbo on July 21, 2017, https://www.youtube.com/watch?v=DqVzKiYOlQw; Brent Lang, "Sony Plans Animated 'Ghostbusters' TV Show," *Variety*, June 20, 2016, https://variety.com/2016/film/news/sony-plans-animated-ghostbusters-tv-show-1201799530; John Nugent, "Empire Podcast #272: Comic-Con Special with Ivan Reitman, Jeph Loeb, Scott Buck, Roel Reiné," *Empire*, July 23, 2017, https://www.empireonline.com/movies/news/empire-podcast-272-comic-con-special-ivan-reitman-jeph-loeb-roel-rein-scott-buck.

3. "Dan Aykroyd," *Big Interview with Dan Rather*; "Big Interview with Dan Rather: Dan Aykroyd," IMDb.

4. "Ivan Reitman Talks," YouTube; Jada Yuan, "Ivan Reitman on Bill Murray, Internet Trolls, and Why He Fought for the *Ghostbusters* Reboot," Vulture, July 14, 2016. https://www.vulture.com/2016/07/ivan-reitman-ghostbusters-bill-murray-qa.html.

5. Anthony Breznican, "*Ghostbusters* Resurrected: Jason Reitman Will Direct a New Film Set in the Original Universe," *Entertainment Weekly*, January 15, 2019, https://ew.com/movies/2019/01/15/new-ghostbusters-movie-jason-reitman; Anthony Breznican, "Watch the First Teaser for Jason Reitman's Secret *Ghostbusters* Movie," *Entertainment Weekly*, January 16, 2019, https://ew.com/trailers/2019/01/16/jason-reitman-ghostbusters-movie-teaser.

6. Catherine Shoard, "Jason Reitman: 'Growing Up Sucks, Doesn't It?,'" *The Guardian*, January 19, 2012, https://www.theguardian.com/film/2012/jan/19/jason-reitman-young-adult.

7. Sharon Waxman, "The Son Also Directs," *New York Times*, September 10, 2005, B9; Anthony Breznican, "For Reitmans, Films Are the Family Business," *Greenville News*, February 23, 2010, Pg 2C; "Review: Jason Reitman's One-Joke Short Film Consent (2004)," *Black Is White*, February 7, 2014, https://blackiswhiteblog.wordpress.com/2014/02/07/review-jason-reitmans-one-joke-short-film-consent-2004; "Kids in the Hall: Geralds," YouTube, posted by SketchiT on February 14, 2020, https://www.youtube.com/watch?v=mGSyNG2ZbJs.

8. Waxman, "Son Also Directs"; Shoard, "Jason Reitman."

9. Matt Hoey, "Sunshine & Smoke," *Los Angeles* 11, no. 2 (February 2007), 45; Waxman, "Son Also Directs."

10. Roger Ebert, "Death For Sale," RogerEbert.com, March 23, 2006, https://www.rogerebert.com/reviews/thank-you-for-smoking-2006.

11. Peter Travers, "Thank You for Smoking," *Rolling Stone*, no. 996 (March 23, 2006), 75.

12. Hoey, "Sunshine & Smoke," 44–45; Bill Winter, "Jason Reitman—Libertarian," Advocates for Self-Government, archived at https://web.archive.org/web/20070202033411/http://www.theadvocates.org/celebrities/jason-reitman.html.

13. Joe Pompeo, "*Juno* Crosses the $100 Million Mark, Becomes 'Too Cool,'" *New York Observer*, January 31, 2008, archived at https://web.archive.org/web/20080404143558/http://www.observer.com/2008/i-juno-i-crosses-100-million-mark-becomes-too-cool; David Germain, Associated Press, "Academy Awards Nominations: List of Nominees," *Star-Gazette*, January 23, 2008, 3D; "The 80th Academy Awards—2008," Academy of Motion Picture Arts and Sciences, accessed February 22, 2022, https://www.oscars.org/oscars/ceremonies/2008; Christine Spines, "'Juno': Inside Oscar's 100 Million Dollar Baby," *Entertainment Weekly*, December 5, 2007, archived at https://web.archive.org/web/20080203033215/https://www.ew.com/ew/article/0,,20007870_20164475_20175163,00.html.

14. Jim DeRogatis, "Why 'Juno' Is Anti-Rock," *Chicago Sun-Times*, January 8, 2008, archived at https://web.archive.org/web/20100821083920/http://blogs.suntimes.com/music/2008/01/why_juno_is_antirock.html.

15. Larry Carroll, "Jason Reitman Doesn't Want to Cross Streams with His 'Ghostbusters' Dad," MTV News, December 19, 2007, https://www.mtv.com/news/2429515/jason-reitman-doesnt-want-to-cross-streams-with-his-ghostbusters-dad.

16. Hoey, "Sunshine & Smoke," 44–45.

17. Kenneth Turan, "'Up in the Air,'" *Los Angeles Times*, December 4, 2009, archived at https://web.archive.org/web/20091208104356/http://www.calendarlive.com/movies/reviews/cl-et-up-in-air4-2009dec04%2C0%2C471447.story; Claudia Puig, "Timely 'Up in the Air' Rises to Challenge with Humor, Heart," *USA Today*, December 4, 2009, https://usatoday30.usatoday.com/life/movies/reviews/2009-12-04-upintheair04_ST_N.htm; Jonathan Romney, "Up in the Air, Jason Reitman, 109 Mins, (15)," *The Independent*, January 17, 2010, https://www.independent.co.uk/arts-entertainment/films/reviews/up-in-the-air-jason-reitman-109-mins-15-1870029.html; David Germain, Associated Press, "With 10 Nominees, Oscar Outlook Is Up in the Air," *Post-Crescent*, January 12, 2010, B3.

18. A. O. Scott, "Once a Prom Queen, Still a Spoiled Princess," *New York Times*, December 9, 2011, C6.

19. Jason Guerrasio, "'Ghostbusters: Afterlife' Director Jason Reitman Used His 'Complicated' Relationship with His Father to Take on the Franchise He's Avoided His Whole Life," Insider, November 19, 2021, https://www.insider.com/ghostbusters-afterliife-jason-reitman-interview-2021-10; Jay A. Fernandez, "Michael Bay Reveals James Cameron's Secret Role in the Making of 'Transformers,'" *Hollywood Reporter*, May 25, 2011, https://www.hollywoodreporter.com/news/general-news/michael-bay-reveals-james-camerons-191774; Pamela McClintock, "'Transformers: Dark of the Moon' Crosses $1 Billion Mark," *Hollywood Reporter*, August 2, 2011, https://www.hollywoodreporter.com/news/general-news/transformers-dark-moon-crosses-1-218339.

20. Breznican, "*Ghostbusters* Resurrected."

21. Breznican, "For Reitmans."

22. Guerrasio, "'Ghostbusters: Afterlife' Director."

23. Dana Stevens, "Labor Day," Slate, January 31, 2014, https://slate.com/culture/2014/01/jason-reitmans-labor-day-kate-winslet-and-josh-brolin-make-pie-and-whoopie.html; Claudia Puig, "'Labor Day Is Reitman's Melodramatic Misfire," *USA Today*, January 30, 2014, https://www.usatoday.com/story/life/

movies/2014/01/30/labor-day-review/3584709; Rafer Guzmán, "'Men, Women & Children' Review: Tired Morality Tale Draped in Tech," *Newsday*, October 17, 2014, https://www.newsday.com/entertainment/movies/men-women-children-review-tired-morality-tale-draped-in-tech-1.9508191; Wesley Morris, "Small(er) Movie Roundup, 'Gone Girl'-Free Edition," Grantland, October 8, 2014, http://grantland.com/hollywood-prospectus/pride-men-women-children-annabelle-two-faces-january; Helen O'hara, "Men, Women & Children Review," Empire, October 21, 2014, archived at https://web.archive.org/web/20180324172919/https://www.empireonline.com/movies/men-women-children/review.

24. David Sims, "Where Jason Reitman Went Wrong," *The Atlantic*, October 13, 2014, https://www.theatlantic.com/entertainment/archive/2014/10/the-fall-of-jason-reitman/381044.

25. Mike Ryan, "Jason Reitman on 'Men, Women & Children,' Adam Sandler and What He Learned from the Failure of 'Labor Day,'" ScreenCrush, October 1, 2014. https://screencrush.com/jason-reitman-men-women-children-tiff-2014.

26. Emma Brown, "Jason Reitman and the Next Generation," *Interview*, October 20, 2014, https://www.interviewmagazine.com/film/jason-reitman-men-women-and-children.

27. Michael Nordine, "Leslie Jones Calls Jason Reitman's 'Ghostbusters' Sequel 'Something Trump Would Do,'" Indiewire, January 21, 2019, https://www.indiewire.com/2019/01/leslie-jones-ghostbusters-jason-reitman-trump-1202036977.

28. Clarisse Loughrey and Jack Shepherd, "Ghostbusters Director Paul Feig Offers Support to Leslie Jones Over New Sequel Reaction," *Independent*, January 22, 2019, https://www.independent.co.uk/arts-entertainment/films/news/ghostbusters-3-paul-feig-leslie-jones-twitter-jason-reitman-remake-sequel-reaction-a8738136.html.

29. Chloe Melas, "Jason Reitman Attempts to Clarify Controversial 'Ghostbusters' Comments," CNN, February 21, 2019, https://www.cnn.com/2019/02/21/entertainment/jason-reitman-ghostbusters-controversy/index.html; Kevin Burwick, "Ghostbusters 3 Director Calls It Love Letter to Fans, Sparks Immediate Controversy," Movieweb, February 20, 2019, https://movieweb.com/ghostbusters-3-director-sexist-comments-fan-controversy.

30. Jason Reitman, *Ghostbusters: Afterlife*, Sony Pictures, 2021.

31. "Monday Morning Podcast 2-18-19," *Bill's Monday Morning Podcast*, February 18, 2019, https://billburr.com/monday-morning-podcast-2-18-19.

32. Borys Kit, "'Captain Marvel' Actress McKenna Grace Nabs Starring Role in Jason Reitman's 'Ghostbusters,'" *Hollywood Reporter*, March 29, 2019, https://www.hollywoodreporter.com/movies/movie-news/mckenna-grace-star-jason-reitmans-ghostbusters-1198214; "Grace McKenna," IMDb, accessed January 23, 2022, https://www.imdb.com/name/nm5085683.

33. Xandra Harbet, "Ghostbusters: Afterlife Actress McKenna Grace Dishes on the OG Cast, Paul Rudd, and the Reitmans," Looper, November 22, 2021, https://www.looper.com/666055/ghostbusters-afterlife-actress-mckenna-grace-dishes-on-working-with-the-og-cast-paul-rudd-and-the-reitmans-exclusive-interview; Steffanee Wang, "'Ghostbusters' Star McKenna Grace on the Reboot & Her Debut Song 'Haunted House,'" Nylon, November 19, 2021, https://www.nylon.com/entertainment/mckenna-grace-ghostbusters-afterlife-actress-haunted-house; Dave Schilling, "Ghostbusters: Afterlife Director Jason Reitman Crosses the Streams of Reality and Sequel Lore," Polygon, November 21, 2021, https://www.polygon.com/interviews/22792218/ghostbusters-afterlife-casting-story-interview-jason-reitman.

34. Brian Davids, "Finn Wolfhard on 'Stranger Things,' 'Ghostbusters 2020' and Hanging Out with 'It' Co-Star Bill Hader," *Hollywood Reporter*, July

12, 2019, https://www.hollywoodreporter.com/movies/movie-news/finn-wolfhard-stranger-things-mike-will-fight-ghostbusters-1223941.

35. MTV News, "From #CinemaCon . . .," Twitter, April 2, 2019, https://twitter.com/MTVNEWS/status/1113235870298124288?ref_src=twsrc%5Etfw; Ash Crossan, "Celeste O'Connor & Logan Kim Interview: Ghostbusters Afterlife," ScreenRant, November 12, 2021, https://screenrant.com/ghostbusters-afterlife-celeste-oconnor-logan-kim-interview.

36. Schilling, "Ghostbusters: Afterlife Director."

37. Dirk Libbey, "Why Ghostbusters: Afterlife's Carrie Coon Was Initially Hesitant to Join the Film," Cinema Blend, September 15, 2020, https://www.cinemablend.com/news/2554744/why-ghostbusters-afterlifes-carrie-coon-was-initially-hesitant-to-join-the-film.

38. Marah Eakin, "We Asked Will Ferrell to Pick His Favorite Paul Rudd Movie," AV Club, November 10, 2021, https://www.avclub.com/we-asked-will-ferrell-to-pick-his-favorite-paul-rudd-mo-1848026423; Eric Ditzian, "Original 'Ghostbusters' Cast Onboard for Reboot, Says Harold Ramis," MTV News, March 27, 2009, http://www.mtv.com/news/1607995/original-ghostbusters-cast-onboard-for-reboot-harold-ramis-says; Crossan, "Paul Rudd & Carrie Coon."

39. Monica Sisavat, "Celeste O'Connor's Love Advice Is Simple but So Necessary," Popsugar, November 15, 2021, https://www.popsugar.com/celebrity/celeste-oconnor-popsugar-crush-interview-48580400.

40. Rick Marshall, "How Ghostbusters: Afterlife Used VFX to Bring Everyone Back," Digital Trends, January 17, 2022, https://www.digitaltrends.com/movies/ghostbusters-afterlife-visual-effects-interview-vfx.

41. Sean Wilson, "Rob Simonsen on Answering the Call to Score Ghostbusters: Afterlife," Spitfire Audio: Composer, https://composer.spitfireaudio.com/en/articles/rob-simonsen-on-answering-the-call-to-score-ghostbusters-afterlife. Accessed March 3, 2022.

42. Marshall, "How Ghostbusters: Afterlife Used VFX."

43. Ian Failes, "Shotmakers: The Making of That Muncher Moment in 'Ghostbusters: Afterlife,'" Befores & Afters, December 7, 2021, https://beforesandafters.com/2021/12/07/shotmakers-the-making-of-that-muncher-moment-in-ghostbusters-afterlife.

44. Marshall, "How Ghostbusters: Afterlife Used VFX"; Hannah Shaw-Williams, "Frozen Star Josh Gad is the Voice of Muncher in Ghostbusters: Afterlife," SlashFilm, November 14, 2021, https://www.slashfilm.com/660680/frozen-star-josh-gad-is-the-voice-of-muncher-in-ghostbusters-afterlife.

45. Lexi Stewart, "The Phantasmic Makeup & Creature FX of Ghostbusters: Afterlife," Stan Winston School of Character Arts, January 11, 2022, https://www.stanwinstonschool.com/blog/ghostbusters-afterlife-behind-the-scenes-practical-makeup-effects-live-action-creature-fx-designer-arjen-interview.

46. "Ghostbusters: Afterlife," MPC Film, accessed February 2, 2022, https://www.mpcfilm.com/film/ghostbusters-afterlife; Jazz Tangcay, "How VFX Contenders Crafted Key Sequences in 'Ghostbusters,' 'Shang-Chi' and 'Army of the Dead,'" *Variety*, January 14, 2022, https://variety.com/2022/artisans/awards/vfx-contenders-ghostbusters-shang-chi-1235154578.

47. Scott Mendelson, "'Ghostbusters: Afterlife': Sony Signs New Deal with Jason Reitman and Gil Kenan," *Forbes*, November 29, 2021, https://www.forbes.com/sites/scottmendelson/2021/11/29/ghostbusters-afterlife-sony-signs-new-deal-with-jason-reitman-and-gil-kenan; Brian Lloyd, "The Marvel Cinematic Universe in Numbers," Entertainment.ie, https://entertainment.ie/movies/movie-news/the-marvel-cinematic-universe-in-numbers-227156/#. Accessed March 3, 2022.

48. Keegan Prosser, "Ghostbusters: Afterlife Stars Gush Over the Film's Practical Effects," CBR, October 12, 2021, https://www.cbr.com/ghostbusters-afterlife-stars-on-practical-effects.

49. Daniel Strohl, "The Ecto-1 Hearse in the New Ghostbusters Flick Is Actually the Once-Neglected Ecto-1A," Hemmings, December 13, 2019, https://www.hemmings.com/stories/2019/12/13/the-ecto-1-hearse-in-the-new-ghostbusters-flick-is-actually-the-once-neglected-ecto-1a; Summer Rogers, "30 Years After Its Big-Screen Appearance, 'Ghostbusters' Car Is Looking Good," *Orange County Register*, March 6, 2014, https://www.ocregister.com/2014/03/06/30-years-after-its-big-screen-appearance-ghostbusters-car-is-looking-good.

50. "Session 3: Ghostbusters Afterlife Gunners Seat & Sentry Proton Packs," *The Black Firehouse Podcast*, January 25, 2022, https://open.spotify.com/episode/1Nq9oBsvBb5RmFEYZS6PJf.

51. Kaylee Gundling, "Ghostbusters: Afterlife's Proton Packs Feature a Major Hidden Upgrade," CBR, October 26, 2021, https://www.cbr.com/ghostbusters-afterlife-proton-pack-switches.

52. Wilson, "Rob Simonsen on Answering the Call."

53. Marshall, "How Ghostbusters: Afterlife Used VFX."

54. Catherine Shoard, "Peter Cushing Is Dead; Rogue One's Resurrection Is a Digital Indignity," *The Guardian*, December 21, 2016, https://www.theguardian.com/commentisfree/2016/dec/21/peter-cushing-rogue-one-resurrection-cgi; Kelly Lawler, "How the 'Rogue One' Ending Went Wrong," *USA Today*, December 19, 2016, https://www.usatoday.com/story/life/entertainthis/2016/12/19/how-rogue-one-ending-went-wrong/95519816.

55. Marshall, "How Ghostbusters: Afterlife Used VFX"; Jason Fitzsimmons, "Original Ghostbusters Director Stood in as *Spoiler Character* in Afterlife," Ghostbusters News, November 25, 2021, https://ghostbustersnews.com/2021/11/25/original-ghostbusters-director-stood-in-as-egon-spengler-in-afterlife.

56. Ryan Parker, "Harold Ramis' Daughter Reflects on 'Ghostbusters: Afterlife' and Her Beloved, Iconic Father," *Hollywood Reporter*, November 22, 2021, https://www.hollywoodreporter.com/movies/movie-features/ghostbusters-afterlife-harold-ramis-daughter-violet-movie-1235044849.

57. Guerrasio, "'Ghostbusters: Afterlife' Director."

58. Ash Crossan, "Ivan & Jason Reitman Interview: Ghostbusters Afterlife," ScreenRant, November 11, 2021, https://screenrant.com/ghostbusters-afterlife-ivan-reitman-jason-reitman-interview.

59. Anthony Breznican, "Hanging with Bill Murray on the Set of *Ghostbusters: Afterlife*," *Vanity Fair*, January 23, 2020, https://www.vanityfair.com/hollywood/2020/01/hanging-with-bill-murray-on-the-set-of-ghostbusters-afterlife.

60. "Guest Dan Aykroyd Joins the Show Discussing His Long Movie Career and His Most Iconic Scenes from Saturday Night Live," *The Greg Hill Show*, November 8, 2019, https://omny.fm/shows/the-greg-hill-show/ghs-guest-dan-aykroyd-joins-the-show-discussing-hi.

61. Anthony Breznican, "The Day Bill Murray, Dan Aykroyd, and Ernie Hudson Became Ghostbusters Again," *Vanity Fair*, November 22, 2021, https://www.vanityfair.com/hollywood/2021/11/ghostbusters-afterlife-ending.

62. Breznican, "Hanging with Bill Murray."

63. Ryan Parker, "Ernie Hudson Calls Making 'Ghostbusters: Afterlife' an 'Almost Spiritual' Experience," *Hollywood Reporter*, November 19, 2021, https://www.hollywoodreporter.com/movies/movie-features/ernie-hudson-ghostbusters-afterlife-almost-spiritual-experience-1235048845.

64. Breznican, "Day Bill Murray, Dan Aykroyd."

65. "Ghostbusters: Afterlife's Gozer The Gozerian Was Played By Three Actresses." *Ghostbusters News*. December 31, 2021. https://ghostbustersnews.com/2021/12/31/ghostbusters-afterlifes-gozer-the-gozerian-was-played-by-three-actresses/

66. Jo Craig, "Where Was Ghostbusters: Afterlife Filmed? Is Summerville a Real Place?," HITC, November 18, 2021, https://www.hitc.com/en-gb/2021/11/18/where-was-ghostbusters-afterlife-filmed-is-summerville-a-real-place; Ghostbusters: Afterlife—Official Trailer (HD)," YouTube, posted by Sony Pictures Entertainment on December 9, 2019, https://www.youtube.com/watch?v=ahZFCF--uRY; Patrick Hipes, "Jason Reitman's 'Ghostbusters' Movie Gets a Title and a Poster," Deadline, December 6, 2019, https://deadline.com/2019/12/ghostbusters-movie-ghostbusters-afterlife-release-date-poster-jason-reitman-1202802534.

67. Kate Kelland, "Italy Sewage Study Suggests COVID-19 Was There in December 2019," Reuters, June 19, 2020, https://www.reuters.com/article/us-health-coronavirus-italy-sewage/italy-sewage-study-suggests-covid-19-was-there-in-december-2019-idUSKBN23Q1J9; James T. Areddy, "China Rules Out Animal Market and Lab as Coronavirus Origin," *Wall Street Journal*, May 26, 2020, https://www.wsj.com/articles/china-rules-out-animal-market-and-lab-as-coronavirus-origin-11590517508; Amy Maxmen, "Wuhan Market Was Epicentre of Pandemic's Start, Studies Suggest," *Nature*, February 27, 2022, https://www.nature.com/articles/d41586-022-00584-8; Yuan Li, "China's Rifts Laid Bare by Outbreak," *New York Times*, January 29, 2020, B1.

68. "Coronavirus Disease 2019 (COVID-19) Situation Report—51," World Health Organization, March 11, 2020, https://www.who.int/docs/default-source/coronaviruse/situation-reports/20200311-sitrep-51-covid-19.pdf.

69. Taylor Telford and Abha Bhattarai, "Long Lines, Low Supplies: Coronavirus Chaos Sends Shoppers Into Panic-Buying Mode," *Washington Post*, March 2, 2020, https://www.washingtonpost.com/business/2020/03/02/grocery-stores-coronavirus-panic-buying.

70. "Coronavirus Updates from March 16, 2020," CBS News, March 17, 2020, https://www.cbsnews.com/live-updates/coronavirus-updates-cases-fears-deaths-us-latest-2020-03-16.

71. Ryan Faughnder, "AMC and Regal Close All U.S. Theaters Amid Coronavirus Crisis," *Los Angeles Times*, March 16, 2020, https://www.latimes.com/entertainment-arts/business/story/2020-03-16/as-l-a-theaters-close-due-to-coronavirus-amc-reduces-capacity-to-50.

72. "Here Are All the Movies Delayed Because of the Coronavirus—With Some New Release Dates," Vulture, updated April 9, 2021, https://www.vulture.com/2021/04/here-are-all-the-movies-and-tv-shows-affected-by-coronavirus.html; Mia Galuppo and Pamela McClintock, "Sony Delays Release of 'Morbius,' 'Ghostbusters,' More Films Due to Coronavirus," *Hollywood Reporter*, March 30, 2020, https://www.hollywoodreporter.com/movies/movie-news/sony-delays-release-morbius-ghostbusters-due-coronavirus-1285759.

73. Jeremy Furster, "Universal to Release 'Trolls World Tour' for Digital Rental on Same Day as Theatrical Release," The Wrap, March 16, 2020, https://www.thewrap.com/universal-to-release-trolls-world-tour-for-digital-rental-on-same-day-as-theatrical-release.

74. Pamela McClintock, "AMC Theatres Refuses to Play Universal Films in Wake of 'Trolls: World Tour,'" *Hollywood Reporter*, April 28, 2020, https://www.hollywoodreporter.com/movies/movie-news/amc-theatres-refuses-play-universal-films-wake-trolls-world-tour-1292327.

75. Anthony D'Alessandro, "Universal & AMC Theatres Make Peace, Will Crunch Theatrical Window to 17 Days with Option for PVOD After," Deadline, July 28,

2020, https://deadline.com/2020/07/universal-amc-theatres-theatrical-window-crush-pvod-agreement-1202997573.

76. Anthony D'Alessandro, "AMC Theatres Shifts Reopening Date to July 30 after 'Tenet' & 'Mulan' Delay," Deadline, June 29, 2020, https://deadline.com/2020/06/amc-theatres-reopening-new-date-tenet-mulan-1202972756; Alaa Elassar, "This Is Where Each State Is During Its Phased Reopening," CNN, updated May 27, 2020; https://www.cnn.com/interactive/2020/us/states-reopen-coronavirus-trnd; Ryan Lizza and Daniel Lippman, "Wearing a Mask Is for Smug Liberals; Refusal to Is for Reckless Republicans," Politico, May 1, 2020, https://www.politico.com/news/2020/05/01/masks-politics-coronavirus-227765; "Coronavirus: New Covid-19 Cases Rising Rapidly," BBC, October 19, 2020, https://www.bbc.com/news/election-us-2020-54603158.

77. Rebecca Rubin, "'Ghostbusters' Sequel Moves to Summer 2021," *Variety*, October 21, 2020, https://variety.com/2020/film/news/ghostbusters-afterlife-release-date-summer-1234812430.

78. "Here Are All the Movies Delayed," Vulture.

79. Megan Scudellari, "How the Pandemic Might Play Out in 2021 and Beyond," *Nature*, August 5, 2020, https://www.nature.com/articles/d41586-020-02278-5.

80. Adam Chitwood, "'Ghostbusters: Afterlife' Release Date Delayed as Fall 2021 Becomes the Blockbuster Event of 2020," Collider, January 22, 2021, https://collider.com/ghostbusters-afterlife-release-date-delayed-november-2021.

81. Frank Pallotta, "Scarlett Johansson Is Suing Disney Over 'Black Widow' Disney+ Release," CNN, July 30, 2021, https://www.cnn.com/2021/07/29/media/scarlett-johansson-disney-lawsuit/index.html; Gene Maddaus, "Scarlett Johansson and Disney Settle 'Black Widow' Pay Lawsuit," *Variety*, September 30, 2021, https://variety.com/2021/film/news/scarlett-johansson-disney-lawsuit-settled-1235078355.

82. Brent Lang and Matt Donnelly, "Eddie Murphy's 'Coming 2 America' Moves from Paramount to Amazon Studios," *Variety*, October 13, 2020. https://variety.com/2020/film/news/eddie-murphys-coming-2-america-moves-from-paramount-to-amazon-studios-1234799523.

83. Pamela McClintock, "Box Office: 'Tenet' Races to $53 M-Plus Internationally," *Hollywood Reporter*, August 30, 2020, https://www.hollywoodreporter.com/movies/movie-news/box-office-tenet-races-to-53m-plus-internationally-4052446.

84. Anthony D'Alessandro and Nancy Tartaglione, "Sony Surprises at CinemaCon with 'Ghostbusters: Afterlife' Screening," Deadline, August 23, 2021, https://deadline.com/2021/08/ghostbusters-afterlife-surprise-cinemacon-screening-1234820582.

85. "Ghostbusters; Afterlife—Official Trailer (2021) Paul Rudd, McKenna Grace, Finn Wolfhard," YouTube, posted by IGN on July 27, 2021, https://www.youtube.com/watch?v=xaG_5ZZ2PyM.

86. Rebecca Rubin, "'Ghostbusters: Afterlife' Release Date Delayed a Week," *Variety*, September 1, 2021, https://variety.com/2021/film/news/ghostbusters-afterlife-delayed-1235054013.

87. "Brynn Metheney (Concept Artist, Ghostbusters: Afterlife) Interview!," YouTube, posted by The Containment Unit on January 26, 2022, https://www.youtube.com/watch?v=iD2ukZHAZz8.

88. Gracie Lowes, "McKenna Grace Talks 'Ghostbusters: Afterlife,' Her Debut Song 'Haunted House' and Upcoming Projects," Celeb Secrets, December 29, 2021, https://www.celebsecrets.com/mckenna-grace-talks-ghostbusters-afterlife-her-debut-song-haunted-house-and-upcoming-projects-exclusive.

89. Wang, "'Ghostbusters' Star McKenna Grace."

90. Anthony D'Alessandro, "'Ghostbusters: Afterlife': Jason & Ivan Reitman Throw a Surprise Screening," Deadline, October 8, 2021, https://deadline.com/2021/10/ghostbusters-afterlife-nycc-surprise-screening-1234853086.

91. Kirsten Acuna, "Fans Were Surprised with a Very Early Screening of the Next 'Ghostbusters' Movie at New York Comic Con and It Was a Clear Hit," Insider, October 8, 2021, https://www.insider.com/ghostbusters-afterlife-comic-con-screening-2021-10; "Finn Wolfhard & McKenna Grace Bring a Surprise Screening of 'Ghostbusters: Afterlife' to NYCC!," Just Jared, October 9, 2021, https://www.justjaredjr.com/2021/10/09/finn-wolfhard-mckenna-grace-bring-a-surprise-screening-of-ghostbusters-afterlife-to-nycc.

92. Johnny Oleksinski, "'Ghostbusters: Afterlife' Review: Finally, a Watchable Sequel," *New York Post*, October 9, 2021, https://nypost.com/2021/10/09/ghostbusters-afterlife-review-finally-a-watchable-sequel.

93. Christian Holub, "*Ghostbusters: Afterlife* Review: A Gloomy Nostalgia Trip Through the Ruins of American Culture," *Entertainment Weekly*, October 9, 2021, https:// ew.com/movies/movie-reviews/ghostbusters-afterlife-review.

94. Jesse Hassenger, "*Ghostbusters: Afterlife* Is a Dispiriting Nostalgia Exercise," AV Club, October 9, 2021, https://www.avclub.com/ghostbusters-afterlife-is-a-dispiriting-nostalgia-exer-1847831687.

95. Charles Bramesco, "Ghostbusters: Afterlife Review—A Slimy, Stinking Corpse of a Sequel," *The Guardian*, October 11, 2021, https://www.theguardian.com/film/2021/oct/11/ghostbusters-afterlife-jason-reitman-paul-rudd-review.

96. Manohla Dargis, "I Ain't Afraid of No Franchise," *New York Times*, November 19, 2021, C13.

97. Tom Brueggemann, "'Ghostbusters: Afterlife' $44 Million Opening Box Office Sets Up Sony to End the Year as a Star," Indiewire, November 21, 2021, https://www.indiewire.com/2021/11/ghostbusters-afterlife-box-office-sony-king-richard-1234680717; Rebecca Rubin, "Does 'Ghostbusters: Afterlife' Box Office Debut Signal a Revival of a Fading Franchise?," *Variety*, November 22, 2021, https://variety.com/2021/film/box-office/ghostbusters-afterlife-box-office-franchise-future-1235116871.

98. Pamela McClintock, "Box Office: 'Spider-Man: No Way Home' Soars to Record $260M U.S. Opening, $600,8M Globally," *Hollywood Reporter*, December 20, 2021, https://www.hollywoodreporter.com/movies/movie-news/spider-man-no-way-home-box-office-opening-1235065128.

99. "Coronavirus in the U.S.: Latest Map and Case Count," *New York Times*, updated March 1, 2022, https://www.nytimes.com/interactive/2021/us/covid-cases.html; "The Possibility of COVID-19 After Vaccination: Breakthrough Infections," Center for Disease Control and Prevention, December 17, 2021, https://www.cdc.gov/coronavirus/2019-ncov/vaccines/effectiveness/why-measure-effectiveness/breakthrough-cases.html#; Dennis Wagner, "The COVID Culture War: At What Point Should Personal Freedom Yield to the Common Good?," *USA Today*, August 2, 2021, https://www.usatoday.com/story/news/nation/2021/08/02/covid-culture-war-masks-vaccine-pits-liberty-against-common-good/5432614001; Jack Guy, Melissa Mahtani, Melissa Macaya, Meg Wagner, and Aditi Sangal, "The Omicron Variant Is Now Dominant in the U.S.," CNN, December 21, 2021, https://www.cnn.com/world/live-news/omicron-variant-coronavirus-news-12-20-21-intl/index.html; Becky Upham, "Can Vaccination Protect You from Long COVID?," Everyday Health, December 22, 2021, https://www.everydayhealth.com/coronavirus/can-covid-19-vaccines-protect-you-from-long-covid; Ewen Callaway, "Omicron Likely to Weaken COVID Vaccine Protection," *Nature*, December 8, 2021, https://www.nature.com/articles/d41586-021-03672-3; Roshan Abraham and Aparupa Mazumder, "U.S. COVID-19 Deaths Reach 800,000 as Delta Ravaged in 2021," Reuters, December 12, 2021, https://www.reuters.com/business/healthcare-pharmaceuticals/us-covid-19-deaths-approach-800000-delta-ravaged-2021-2021-12-12.

100. Etan Vlessing, "Jason Reitman, Gil Kenan Ink Sony Pictures Overall Deal," *Hollywood Reporter*, November 29, 2021, https://www.hollywoodreporter.com/business/business-news/jason-reitman-gil-kenan-sony-pictures-deal-1235054047.

101. Dave Schilling, "Ghostbusters: Afterlife Director Jason Reitman Crossed the Streams of Reality and Sequel Lore," Polygon, November 21, 2021, https://www.polygon.com/interviews/22792218/ghostbusters-afterlife-casting-story-interview-jason-reitman.

102. Roger Ebert, "Nostalgia for the Feel of Early Spielberg," RogerEbert.com, June 8, 2011, https://www.rogerebert.com/reviews/super-8-2011.

103. Steve Weintraub, "J. J. Abrams on What He Collects, Favorite Video Game Systems, Supreme Leader Snoke and Pokemon Go," Collider, July 20, 2016, https://collider.com/jj-abrams-star-trek-beyond-star-wars-interview.

104. Leah Asmelash, "Mid-Budget Movies as We Knew Them Are in Decline. What Does That Mean for Cinema?," CNN, February 26, 2022, cnn.com/2022/02/26/entertainment/mid-budget-movie-decline-cec/index.html; Jason Guerrasio, "I def asked . . .," Twitter, November 8, 2021, https://twitter.com/JasonGuerrasio/status/1457795070921351168.

105. Guerrasio, "'Ghostbusters: Afterlife' Director."

106. Jack King, "Deepfake Luke Skywalker is Another Step Down a Ghoulish CGI Path." *GQ.* February 10, 2022, https://www.gq-magazine.co.uk/culture/article/boba-fett-luke-skywalker.

107. Hadley Freeman, "Ivan Reitman: 'Sigourney Weaver Got on All Fours and Started Howling Like a Dog on My Coffee Table," *The Guardian*, October 6, 2014, https://www.theguardian.com/film/2014/oct/06/ivan-reitman-draft-day-ghostbusters-sigourney-weaver.

108. Lindsey Bahr, "Ivan Reitman, Producer, 'Ghostbusters' Director, Dies at 75," AP News, February 13, 2022, https://apnews.com/article/ivan-reitman-dead-d67947aa895371cd9f5840e6e9339440.

109. Ryan Lattanzio, "Jason Reitman Hints at 'Ghostbusters: Afterlife' Sequel Possibilities: 'We Have Ideas Moving Forward,'" Indiewire, November 21, 2021, https://www.indiewire.com/2021/11/ghostbusters-afterlife-sequel-jason-reitman-follow-up-1234680754.

110. Anthony D'Alessandro, "Sony Calling Up Another 'Ghostbusters' Movie—CinemaCon." *Deadline.* April 25, 2022. https://deadline.com/2022/04/ghostbusters-5-new-movie-1235009684.

111. "It's Official! A New Ghostbusters Film Was Just Announced at CinemaCon!" *Ghostbusters News.* April 25, 2022. https://ghostbustersnews.com/2022/04/25/its-official-a-new-ghostbusters-film-was-just-announced-at-cinemacon.

112. Hadley Freeman, "Who Ya Gonna Call? Ivan and Jason Reitman on Resurrecting Ghostbusters Together," *The Guardian*, November 19, 2021, https://www.theguardian.com/film/2021/nov/19/who-ya-gonna-call-ivan-jason-reitman-ghostbusters-hadley-freeman-film.

Index

Index

About the Author

James Greene, Jr., has previously written *This Music Leaves Stains: The Complete Story of The Misfits* (which is not so complete anymore since their big reunion concerts) and *Brave Punk World: The International Rock Underground From Alerta Roja to Z-Off*. As a freelance writer, he has contributed to such publications as *Crawdaddy!*, *New York Press*, *Orlando Weekly*, *Hopes and Fears*, and *Hard Noise*. He has never been to Wichita, and his favorite Stooge is Iggy.